Prison Religion

Prison Religion

FAITH-BASED REFORM AND THE CONSTITUTION

Winnifred Fallers Sullivan

PRINCETON UNIVERSITY PRESS
PRINCETON AND OXFORD

Published by Princeton University Press, 41 William Street,
Princeton, New Jersey 08540
In the United Kingdom: Princeton University Press, 6 Oxford Street,
Woodstock, Oxfordshire OX20 1TW

Library of Congress Cataloging-in-Publication Data

Sullivan, Winnifred Fallers, 1950–
Prison religion : faith-based reform and the constitution / Winnifred Fallers Sullivan.
p. cm.
Includes bibliographical references and index.
ISBN 978-0-691-13359-1 (hardcover : alk. paper) 1. Americans United for Separation of Church and State—Trials, litigation, etc. 2. InnerChange Freedom Initiative—Trials, litigation, etc. 3. Prison Fellowship—Trials, litigation, etc. 4. Religious work with prisoners—Law and legislation—United States—Cases. 5. Church and state—United States—Cases. 6. Criminal—Rehabilitation—Iowa. 7. Iowa—Trials, litigation, etc. I. Title.
KF228.A653 .S85 2009
344.7303'566—dc22 2008027764

British Library Cataloging-in-Publication Data is available

This book has been composed in Sabon

Printed on acid-free paper. ∞

press.princeton.edu

Printed in the United States of America

10 9 8 7 6 5 4 3 2 1

FOR BARRY

Labore est orare

Contents

Acknowledgments ix

Introduction 1

CHAPTER 1
The God Pod 19

CHAPTER 2
A Prison Like No Other 64

CHAPTER 3
Biblical Justice 94

CHAPTER 4
The Way We Live Now 140

CHAPTER 5
Beyond Church and State 180

Conclusion 227

Notes 237

Bibliography 273

Index 293

Acknowledgments

In researching and writing this book I have had the generous support of many institutions and individuals. Co-extensive fellowships at the American Bar Foundation and the Martin Marty Center at the University of Chicago Divinity School gave me the time and space, and collegial companionship, to make a wonderful start on the ideas for this book. Moving back and forth between these two exceptional communities kept me honest as a student of both law and religion. I am particularly grateful to Bob Nelson and Wendy Doniger, directors of these two research centers for that year. A year following at the National Humanities Center, with the support of the Lilly Foundation, enabled the bulk of the writing. The National Humanities Center (NHC) has created the perfect space for academic writing; the understated attention to detail and the quiet collegiality of its Fellows Program, under the gentle and intelligent leadership of Kent Mulliken and Geoffrey Harpham, is unmatched. I am also grateful to Dean Nils Olsen, who enthusiastically gave me the ability to accept the NHC fellowship in my first year on the faculty of the University at Buffalo Law School.

I had the opportunity over the last year to test these ideas at three faculty workshops: the Legal Theory Workshop at Columbia Law School, the Religion in America Seminar at Columbia University, and the Book Manuscript Workshop at the Baldy Center for Law and Social Policy. All three were occasions that significantly helped me to see how my argument was being heard and thus to improve its presentation. John Bartkowski and Philip Hamburger, as formal respondents at the Baldy workshop, were particularly generous and helpful in their critiques of the manuscript.

The friendship and support of many friends, family, and colleagues who willingly read drafts, talked about the book endlessly, cheered me on, or perhaps just unwittingly gave me courage, was indispensable. I thank Dan Arnold, Dianne Avery, Celia Brickman, Alexandra Brown, Mary Anne Case, John Comaroff, David Engel, Margaret Fallers, Clark Gilpin, Sarah Barringer Gordon, Terry Hallisey, Philip Hamburger, Sally Hughes, Julie Ingersoll, Rebecca Janowitz, Stanley Katz, Fred Konefsky, Beth Lamanna, Cynthia Lindner, Tomoko Masuzawa, Lynn Mather, Elizabeth Mensch, Elizabeth Mertz, Helen Newlin, John Parry, Martin Riesebrodt, Connie Rosati, Heather Miller Rubens, John Schlegel, Susan Schreiner, J. Z. Smith, Brin Stevens, George Sullivan, Lloyd Sullivan,

Mateo Taussig, Rachel Weil, and Robert Yelle. Their care and generosity is without peer. Aparnaa Bhatt, Allison Mull, and Heather Miller Rubens served ably as research assistants.

But, most important, I thank—again—my friend, colleague, and teacher, Frank Reynolds. I feel most fortunate to be his student.

I also benefited greatly from the careful and thoughtful responses of the anonymous reviewers for Princeton University Press and the encouragement of Fred Appel, religion editor for the Press.

Note about Sources

This book is based on my reading of the public record in the trial. I had no private access to the trial witnesses.

Note about Biblical Translation

The evangelical Christians who are the subject of this study orient their lives around readings of the Bible in a distinctive way. Although there is an elite evangelical tradition of reading scripture in the original languages, for the purposes of lay religious practice, the Bibles read by American evangelicals are in English. No single translation is used by all conservative American Christians or is considered uniquely authoritative. I have sometimes provided alternative versions of certain verses from widely used translations in order to call attention to the role played by modern American English versions in the formation of contemporary Christianity. I do not evaluate the relative merits of these translations from a theological or linguistic standpoint. From a scholarly point of view, what is termed "The Bible" in a devotional context is not a unitary text but rather a complex collection of texts, edited over millennia, possessing no single, authoritative interpretation in all times and places. The easily available online translations of the biblical texts today make it possible for anyone with Internet access to view those texts in the ancient languages in which they were written and compare translations of those texts.

Prison Religion

INTRODUCTION

What is the faith in "faith-based"? After ten years of public policy promoting the greater integration of faith-based organizations into the ranks of government funded social service providers, the nature and role of faith in this effort remains elusive. This book takes a close look at a recent trial concerning one such faith-based provider with a view to understanding better what faith-based reform is about and why so many Americans think it makes sense.

In December 2006, in Des Moines, Iowa, a U.S. District Court judge found unconstitutional a faith-based, in-prison rehabilitation program operating in the Newton Facility of the Iowa Department of Corrections, a program known as InnerChange Freedom Initiative (IFI).[1] The lawsuit, brought by Americans United for Separation of Church and State (AU), had complained that the contract governing the rehabilitation program—an agreement between the State of Iowa and Prison Fellowship Ministries (PFM)—constituted "a law respecting an establishment of religion," and was, thus, in violation of the First Amendment to the United States Constitution as applied to the states through the Fourteenth Amendment. After the decision, pending appeals, IFI continued to operate in the Iowa prison without state cash reimbursement—the state discontinued funding in June 2007—although it continued to receive in-kind aid. Approximately a year after the District Court's decision, the U.S. Court of Appeals for the Eighth Circuit found Prison Fellowship Ministries at the Iowa prison to be acting "under color of state law" in a program of conversion and discrimination.[2] The Iowa Department of Corrections finally terminated its contract with InnerChange on March 10, 2008. (IFI programs are currently present in the prisons of five other states: Arkansas, Kansas, Minnesota, Missouri, and Texas. Private faith-based prison programs managed by other religious groups also exist in many states. Some states, including Florida, have initiated their own state-run, in-prison, faith-based programs. Because of variations in contracting arrangements, the effect of the Iowa court's decision on these other programs remains unclear.)

AU v. PFM is acknowledged to be one of the most significant recent court cases considering the application of the establishment clause of the First Amendment to the U.S. Constitution to the new "faith-based" social services. A legal and social climate substantially more hospitable to government/religion partnership than in the recent past has made possible an increase in the number of government contracts with private, "faith-based" social service providers, particularly those operating in prisons. Through a close reading of the background and events of the trial in *AU v. PFM*, this book considers the ongoing reintegration and "naturalizing" of religion in the United States and its intersection with evolving understandings of the meaning of "disestablishment." By "naturalizing" I refer to a legal and social process by which religion and spirituality are increasingly seen in the U.S. to be a natural, and largely benign—if varied—aspect of the human condition, one that is to be accommodated rather than segregated by government. Notwithstanding the actual decision in the case, set in the larger context of religion in the United States, the trial testimony reveals a religious culture in which the sacred and the secular can be seen to be sinuously and ambiguously intertwined and support for religious authority more thoroughly located in the individual rather than in traditional institutions.

In the prison context, this religious culture, which is at once an establishment and a disestablishment, is shaped by the convergence of two ways in which the United States is distinctive in comparison to other advanced industrial societies, differences that, arguably, have become more pronounced in recent decades. Americans are unusual compared to the citizens of these other societies in the extent to which they profess attachment to religion and in the high rate at which they incarcerate their fellows. By most measures—including surveys concerning frequency of prayer and regularity of worship, reports of church membership, and charitable giving to religious organizations, as well as ethnographic research—the U.S. is a place where religion proudly and independently flourishes. The U.S. is also a place where a higher percentage of the population is incarcerated than in any other country in the world. Both of these distinctions have become more marked in the last thirty-five years.[3]

An examination of the convergence and mutual dependence of these two distinctions, as exemplified in the new faith-based prison programs, will be used in this book to display the peculiar relationship of religion and law in the United States, one that makes disestablishment virtually impossible. Paradoxically, perhaps, disestablished religion depends on government for enforcement of moral norms. In a populist democracy, these norms are defined by majoritarian religious prejudices. Whereas countervailing checks exist to the worst excesses of this partnership—including internal religious practices of prophecy and dissent, and enforcement of the provisions of the Bill of Rights—popular religion and popular justice can reinforce each other in ways, sometimes difficult to detect and almost impossible to eliminate, that can be traced throughout U.S. history—from the Puritans to the so-called "values voters" of the early twenty-first century.

As with all such claims to exceptionalism, this one invites counterexamples. Conventionally the United States is compared to what are regarded as the more secularized countries of Europe, including the United Kingdom and the countries of the former British Commonwealth, but countries to which the U.S. ought to be compared depends on the purpose of the comparison. Religious, social, and political conditions are rapidly changing in Europe and other parts of the world. Virtually every country contains multiple religious minorities and boasts of legal protection for religious freedom. Rates of incarceration are also rising in many countries. Perhaps the comparison group should include countries such as India, which is a pluralist democracy that shares a legal tradition with the United States and has religious and political cultural formations that are parallel in interesting ways to the U.S.[4] It is also important to note that Europe—particularly an expanded Europe—is arguably more religious than generally acknowledged. Nonetheless, I believe it is still useful to regard the United States, as a result of its unusual history and demography, as distinctive with respect to what are called church-state issues.

Among relevant American distinctions are the absence of any history of the comprehensive legal and cultural privileging of a single religious tradition; the religious and ethnic diversity produced by conquest, slavery, and immigration; the pervasiveness of egalitarian and capitalist ideologies; the competitive style of American religion; and the highly mobile nature of the population.[5] As Grace Davie explains with respect to the vaunted secularism of Europe,

> The crucial point to grasp is that Europeans, by and large, regard their churches as public utilities rather than as competing firms. . . . Most Europeans look at their churches with benign benevolence—they are useful social institutions, which the great majority of the population are likely to need at one time or another in their lives . . . this attitude of mind, . . . rather than the absence of a market accounts for a great deal of the data.[6]

The persistence of established religious institutions in Europe does not mean that institutional religious authority in Europe has not declined, but it does mean that the decline is less likely to have been accompanied by a rise in entrepreneurial religion, as in the United States. Instead, Davie argues, self-appointed guardians of traditional religious institutions conserve memory on behalf of the community.[7] Davie's observation would be relevant in many countries.

Importantly, religious and Enlightenment influences have not been mutually exclusive in the United States. The Puritans believed in reason. Reasonable Christianity, a theological tradition emerging out of seventeenth- and eighteenth-century philosophical inquiry, has a strong legacy in the

United States. Evangelicalism and immigration deeply changed the contours of this American Christianity over the next two centuries, but confidence in the rationality and effectiveness of religion persisted. Religious revival and law-and-order populism are not unique to the United States, but the U.S. stands out in both respects. The two are connected, historically and sociologically, and the story of either one cannot be fully told without implicating the other.

The religion discussed in this book happens in a prison. Prisons are a post-Enlightenment invention. Before the nineteenth century, punishment in Europe, its colonies, and most of the rest of the world, for ordinary criminal offenses, was usually corporal: whipping, branding, public shaming, exile, or hanging. Confinement had been used before the nineteenth century mostly for pretrial detainment or, occasionally, for distraining debtors, but not usually for punishment. Prisons, as we know them, were invented in the late eighteenth century in England by Christians.

In the United States, prisons were promoted in the early Republic as a more humane form of punishment, a more Christian alternative to what was perceived to be the casual brutality of corporal punishment as practiced in Europe.[8] Early prototypes of the enlightened prison were the Auburn State Prison in New York and the Eastern Penitentiary in Pennsylvania. Famous U.S. visitors such as Alexis de Tocqueville and Gustave Beaumont traveled to see these newly created American prisons where solitude, work, silence, and religious instruction and exhortation were intended to lead to penitence and reform.[9] They were often viewed as the place, par excellence, for the formation of the democratic subject, also understood as a religious project.[10] The subsequent history of prisons in the United States is often characterized as exhibiting a cyclical pattern of alternating periods of corruption and overcrowding followed by well-meaning reforms. The history of U.S. prisons is also intimately bound up with the history of slavery, particularly in the southern states where a harsh post-emancipation system of leasing prisoners to private contractors was common into the twentieth century.[11]

Prisons are a persistent trope in the imagining of modernity. Scholars and writers have repeatedly turned to prisons in the hopes of finding clues to understanding the modern condition. This, David Rothman suggests, is partly because prisons, although they now seem an entirely natural part of the landscape, when viewed in the context of the longer history of punishment, are a strange invention. "Why invent a system of incarceration?" Rothman asks, and then continues:

> Why substitute confinement in segregated spaces and invent a system of bell-ringing punctuality and steady labor? Why channel the impulse

> to do good into creating something as strange as prisons and mental hospitals—a system that more than 150 years later can still prompt an inmate to want to meet the man who dreamed it all up, convinced that he must have been born on Mars?[12]

Rothman and other historians of the prison have found the answers to these questions in a troubling mix of genuine benevolence, a disciplinary dark side to liberal governance, the growth of scientific knowledge about human behavior, and a coming together of fear and self-interest, all of which are evident from the earliest projects of religiously as well as secularly motivated prison reform.[13]

Norval Morris and David Rothman, in their introductory essay to *The Oxford History of the Prison,* discuss what they describe as "the basic dysfunction of the prison itself." Notwithstanding that imprisonment has become the punishment of choice in many places, the authors write, "most students of the prison have increasingly come to the conclusion that imprisonment should be used as the sanction of last resort, to be imposed only when other measures of controlling the criminal have failed or in situations in which those other measures are clearly inadequate." To be sure, they add, "the usual public response to such a proposition is that it could be made only by someone who cared not at all, or certainly too little, for citizens' safety. . . . [T]he public has always overwhelmingly supported whatever punishments were inflicted as a means of either reducing or preventing an increase in crime." However, they conclude, "research into the use of imprisonment over time and in different countries has failed to demonstrate any positive correlation between increasing the rate of imprisonment and reducing the rate of crime."[14]

Prisons do not work, Morris and Rothman conclude, yet new ones are being built every day. In many depressed areas in the United States they are seen simply as opportunities for private industry and job creation.[15] Law professor Melvin Gutterman states it starkly:

> Today, as at the beginning, the most serious social consequence of the prison system is the disintegration of the human personality of those committed to its confines. The prisoners suffer from what may be called a loss of autonomy as they are constantly "subjected to a vast body of rules . . . which are designed to control their behavior in minute detail." The deprivation of autonomy represents a serious threat to their self-image as adults. . . . While attempting to "re-impose the subservience of youth," the convicts are told to take their medicine like adults. As the normative form of punishment, imprisonment may not be much of an improvement over corporal punishment. Even public flogging did not contribute to the degradation and disintegration of the human personality as much as conditions do in our prisons today.[16]

Gutterman insists that, "a prisoner, to be prepared for a life of freedom, must be trained in some sort of social environment, which, as to his liberty and responsibility, has a fair resemblance to the society he will re-enter."[17]

Punishment is usually understood to be a core function of the modern state; it is what distinguishes the modern state from premodern societies, where punishment was a private prerogative for settling scores or obtaining compensation.[18] The power of the state might be understood to be concentrated in the prisoner's situation and in the shadow the prisoner casts across the landscape.[19] But prisons are perhaps ironically, places where one cannot get away from the state's relationship to religion.[20] The modern state is also perhaps at its most religious when it exerts total control over its citizens and attempts to coercively remake them into new human beings. Religious and political authority and sovereignty in prison are homologous with each other in several ways: state/church, judge/god, crime/sin, prisoner/penitent. Even when explicitly religious language is absent, the sacred haunts the prison and all who work there.[21]

Indeed, both the prison and religion, as distinct institutions, emerge with the modern state. The gradual articulation of secular power distinct from church power, the separation of national citizenship from religious identity, and the contemporaneous discovery of "other" religions made possible the invention of "religion" as we know it—as a universal and *sui generis* institution within human societies,[22] an articulation that is simultaneous with the sacralization of state power.[23] Although all religion in modern states occurs within spaces determined by the rule of law, the modern state's comprehensive authority over prisoners makes possible a particular intimacy in the way in which such spaces are created. U.S. courts have, in the last quarter of the twentieth century, found in the Constitution an obligation on the part of the state to affirmatively provide religious opportunities to prisoners, but that obligation is understood to be seriously limited by judicial deference to the demands of prison governance, domestic security, and national defense. Religion in prisons and prison religions are distinctive products of the modern state and its ongoing interest in producing certain kinds of subjects.

Notwithstanding the common acceptance of the prison as the preferred form of punishment in the modern West, lingering questions remain: "Why imprison?" Does prison work? Under what circumstances should a modern democratic state restrict the freedom of one of its citizens or of any person under its control? The existence of the U.S. detention center at Guantanamo Bay is a daily reminder of the unsettled nature of this issue. But the millions of Americans who are confined in state and federal prisons throughout the United States are no less a matter of concern. A commonplace among scholars of criminology is that little or no data or theory of human behavior or society exists to support reliance on the prison as *the* answer to crime. No theory of justice, and no theory of how best to prepare prisoners for return to society, can justify the many lengthy sentences meted out by U.S. courts. Furthermore, given the meager resources dedicated to the rehabilitation of prisoners in the United States, there is little hope for addressing the needs of those prisoners; 90 percent of them suffer from substance abuse and 50 percent from mental health problems and a substantial number are nonliterate.[24] Under these conditions, what can imprisonment hope to accomplish other than the temporary removal of some of society's members and emotional satisfaction for those who fear them?

These persistent issues with respect to prisons are a subset of a larger set of questions about law in late modernity In the last century the claim that law is a carrier of the best of modern liberalism has been substantially undermined by nationalist abuses of legalism, by various schools of legal realism, as well as by postmodern critiques.[25] David Luban, in his book *Legal Modernism*, quotes the legal philosopher Roberto Unger describing " 'a basic, common experience in modern society' " as that of having " 'the sense of being surrounded by injustice without knowing where justice lies.' "[26] Luban himself understands the modernist crisis in law as created partly by an over-reliance on scientific models, forsaking the critical need for narrative.[27] Richard Sherwin sees law undermined through its fusion with popular culture.[28] Countless articles and books have considered the legal conditions of early-twenty-first-century man as those of a person who has undertaken the responsibility of perpetual self-reflection and criticism in a situation of unstable foundations. Great hopes are pinned on the global possibilities of the rule of law, a rule that continues to carry with it the dark figure of the prisoner.

Although not often noted by legal scholars, religion is a part of this modern legal story, and not just in prisons. Some see religion as the cause of law's problems,[29] whereas others see it as the solution.[30] A growing number see law and religion as intimately related. Rejecting an ideologically driven separatist worldview, many historians are reexamining the interesting and perduring connections between law and religion. The legal secular, as Vincent Pecora and others have noted, emerges in relationship to a constant imagining of the religious "other."[31] In other words, the secular, in its critique of religion, necessarily preserves religion but at the same time takes on some of the tasks of the religious.

Modernity has, among other effects, resulted in the continuing elaboration of two domains, the religious and the secular. Until quite recently, the relationship between the two has been understood to be primarily embodied in the formal bureaucratic division of labor between church and the state. That understanding is continuously challenged and undermined, however, by local forms of non-Christian religion, by antinomian popular religion, and by romantic elaborations of the value of individual subjectivity.[32] Over time, the secularization of law has played a central role in enabling both the separation and the ongoing cooperation between church and state.[33]

Imprisonment is extremely seductive as a metaphor for life. It is as if the prison is not only where the state is most state-like and most church-like but perversely where the individual is most human. We use the narrative of the prison experience for our own purposes, turning it into an opportunity to ponder life in general—sometimes, in the process, effacing the squalid, inherently violent, and humiliating particularities of imprisonment itself. To be human in the United States today is to be free to make rational choices. We expect our free modern selves to choose everything, including religion. How might one live as oneself in prison? It would be easy to see the recurrent eruption of the religious in the prison, indeed in law generally, as a symptom of this unfinished business.

I am acutely aware of my own privileged position in relation to the experiences of prisoners. I am not a specialist in the criminal justice system, and I do not pretend to speak for all U.S. prisoners, or even for any of the individuals whose testimony is retold in this book. I take their public action of filing a lawsuit and their public testimony in that action as an intervention in a public debate about an issue that is of moment today in the United States and elsewhere: how to think about the relation of religion and religious differences to law in our pluralistic, egalitarian society in which religious authority has been formally disavowed as an explicit partner of the state.

Massive incarceration and religious revitalization are converging today in prisons around the world, challenging us to think carefully about what we mean by religion, religious freedom, and the separation of church and state. This book concerns one religiously based—now commonly known in the United States as "faith-based"—rehabilitation program in an Iowa prison that a U.S. District Judge, in 2006, declared an unconstitutional establishment of religion. I focus on the way that lawyers, witnesses, and judges used various religious discourses in that trial, suggesting that we need to rethink the validity of the theoretical structure underlying disestablishment. Although there are reasons to find the Iowa arrangement inappropriate, it is not possible to locate those reasons in the isolation and separation of the "religious" for the purposes of public law and policy.

This book forms a pair with my previous one, *The Impossibility of Religious Freedom*,[34] where I considered the impossibility of isolating religion for the purposes of protecting its free exercise. Here I examine the implications of that impossibility in relation to disestablishment. In each case, the privileging of religion in an egalitarian context of radical diversity and deregulation in the religious field, one in which religious authority has shifted to the individual, leads to discrimination and legal incoherence. In the correctional context, in what one might call a parody of theories of the modern self, prisoners participating in the InnerChange Freedom Initiative are asked to reinvent themselves as free moral subjects by using the tools of a populist and punitive theory of justice combined with various forms of vernacular Christianity, all the while disadvantaged by addiction, illiteracy, racism, and childhood abuse.

Echoes of larger political issues about the nature of the state and its relation to the individual can be seen at every step in the evolving institution of the prison in the United States and the evolving cultural politics of religion. The limits and constraints of secularization as a basis from which to describe and theorize the modern are under active reconsideration today from various disciplinary and political perspectives. While set in the context of the interpretation of the religion clauses of the First Amendment to the U.S. Constitution, particularly the establishment clause, this study is inspired by the current debate on secularization, particularly by Talal Asad and his proposal to reconsider the secular and its varying relationships to the sacred, as a formation of the modern, and by José Casanova's widely read challenge to rethink the ongoing presence of public religions in the modern world.[35]

The public discussion of religion, law, and politics in the United States today is highly polarized, with the language itself so stale from excessive use as to discourage anyone who would seek a sane conversation. Stanley Fish, in his essay "How the Right Hijacked the Magic Words," described this linguistic stalemate.[36] In his inimitable style, Fish explained how "the Right" uses such words as equality, rights, and freedom to mean the very opposite of what "the Left" means by them. So, he points out, affirmative action, it turns out, is a denial of, rather than a means to, the realization of equality—and Christians turn out to be a minority with rights just as African Americans are. While explaining how this "sleight of hand," as he calls it, is performed rhetorically, largely by focusing on the motivations and intentions of particular individuals rather than on large-scale structures and effects, Fish mocks the Left for standing by with their mouths open while the language is stolen from them. He concludes his essay—and the book in which it appears—with the words: "and before we know it all the plovers will be gone and all the subcontractors will be white."[37] And, many liberals would add, the United States will be a theocracy.

The culture wars, as played out in the U.S. legal-political context, have been described as a struggle over control of the language. Specifically, who decides what the words mean? Although in the American political context this struggle is often seen as the result of a deliberate, carefully planned, and subversive campaign by conservatives, something larger and more complex is at work here. The "linguistic turn" in law is beyond the scope of this book; however, the need to pay attention to the meaning of words as a way to understand the culture is certainly evident in debates over constitutional interpretations and the purported universalism of the language of international legal instruments. The need to attend to the meanings of words has many explanations, but in the U.S. context, it is heightened by the extraordinary biblicism of U.S. religious culture, sometimes derisively termed "bibliolatry."[38]

Is what Fish regards as a hijacking of words by the Right simply a cynical rhetorical trick to disarm and distract the Left so that conservatives can reverse the course of history? Worse yet, is it a trick authorized and legitimized by religion? Is this effort, one the Right might prefer to describe as an attempt to repossess rather than hijack the words—part of a concerted effort to reject the Enlightenment and return us to a premodern world of divine authority and hierarchy, a world without equality, rights, *or* freedom? Is the religion of conservatives, indeed, any religion, the antithesis of all that is most cherished about free, liberal, and open societies, societies that are governed by the rule of law? That is a view widely held in U.S. legal circles.

A source of genuine amazement (often accompanied by fear) to most liberals is that religious conservatives wish to participate in the common political culture. Particularly puzzling to the Left is that the so-called Religious Right goes further and boldly lays claim to the universal, a realm liberals regard as their own. Religion is supposed to know its place, and its place, at most, is as a minority party. Most liberals in the United States seem most comfortable with religion that is "sectarian," sociologically speaking, religion that stands apart from the larger culture.[39] As long as entry and exit from sectarian religious communities are understood to be voluntary, then consenting adults wishing to live in these religious societies are to be tolerated, even occasionally admired and respected for their discipline, whether they are Amish, Orthodox Jews, Buddhists, or members of any number of religions. Liberals also seem to be comfortable with religious rhetoric and culture in the service of what they understand to be political liberation agendas such as the prophetic language that is conventionally understood to have propelled the civil rights movement.[40] The problem the Left has with religion emerges when people who are perceived as religious or who use religious language are not content simply to live in their own worlds or provide freedom songs or cultural color, but instead want to challenge common politics and culture, to "hijack" *our* words and, worse, *our* politics, indeed our very definition of what it means to be human.

The only version of public political religion that many liberals can imagine is what is often derisively called theocracy—either of the premodern European Christian type or, now more commonly, that of the imagined return of the Islamic caliphate. Liberals assume that the Religious Right secretly wants a religious state.[41] What is universal is modern and is understood to be secular. Universalist anthropologies, cosmologies, and values are to be secularly derived and expressed. Religion is particular, a vestige of the premodern. The particular is to be controlled and governed by the modern and universal, that is, by the rule of law. These prejudices among liberals not only make it difficult for them to hear what religious conservatives are saying; they make it extremely difficult for liberals to achieve their proclaimed goals.

Religious conservatives in the United States, for their part, are divided within themselves. Like most liberals, most of these conservatives believe strongly in the separation of church and state, and in voluntary religious affiliation. Protestants, by and large, are the group that rejected state authority in religious matters. It was mostly Protestants who rejected ritual and other outward forms of observance in favor of an interior and subjective religious experience. Many Protestant conservatives today, however, also want to participate in creating the values of a pluralistic society. In sociological terms, they want to be both a church and a sect.[42] American religious conservatives do not want a theocracy; they do not desire rule by priests, for they believe in universal priesthood. They do want to rid the world of what they understand to be the pernicious human-centered pessimism of moral relativism and secular humanism. They want to convert the world to an anthropology of values that are transcendental and eternal, and founded in biblical truth. To do that, they must find ways to translate their religiously derived values into universal ones, and to use state authority to impose those values on all.[43]

Fish would say that the problem is the liberals' failure to see the particularism of their version of the universal. The Left should simply admit that their realm is not universal and simply be willing to defend it as "better."[44] Pecora and others would argue that we have now come to a point at which it is clear that both are right, and the practical political task of learning to reinvent the universal together becomes more urgent by the day.

In this book I explore the lack of understanding and communication across the cultural divide in the United States by examining the notion of the legal and religious self implicit in faith-based social service programs. The current argument in the United States about the role of religion is between groups that have largely shared a modern legacy concerning the nature of human beings[45] and are ambivalent as to whether social-scientific approaches are a viable basis for law, social policy, and practices that can reform individuals. Much has been written recently by philosophers and social scientists about the "self"—about subjectivity, consciousness, and the social imaginary—in an effort to describe what is peculiar to the anthropology, epistemology, and sociology of the modern.[46] Several aspects of the models of the self are implied in the lawsuit, models that exemplify the convergences, and divergences, that I see between liberal and conservative social imaginaries, and the selves they imply. When we consider these questions in the context of faith-based social services for prisoners, we can see the practical consequences of losing faith in freedom, equality, rights, and reason.

I will describe PFM and IFI as evangelical, notwithstanding its contested meaning today both in the scholarly community and among evangelicals themselves."Evangelical" in its narrowest etymological sense can be used to modify any Christian activity that derives from the writings of the Evangelists, that is, the writers of the four canonical gospels. The word has been used throughout Christian history in many languages and cultural contexts, but I am most concerned here with describing and understanding certain aspects of the evangelical Christianity that has flourished and evolved in the United States since the American Revolution. That modern U.S. form of Christianity is, of course, related to a larger, religious event that traces its roots to early modern Europe and has since spread around the globe, but it takes a particular form in the United States, in part because of the legal structuring of religion in U.S. life. I discuss American evangelical Christianity at greater length in chapter 2.

American evangelicals and their liberal critics share much of the modern social imaginary, as well as practices of self-discipline, born in the early modern period. What the Right, and the Left, in the United States want, for the most part, are disciplined and productive citizens. Both understand authority and the capacity to change to reside in the individual.[47] Troubling evidence suggests, however, that self-discipline, even self-discipline with God's help, cannot adequately cope with current emerging and pressing issues on that individual: the pathos of the divided self, globalization, and radical epistemological and normative pluralism, religious *and* secular.[48]

One of the most visible areas in which the politics of religion in the United States is being reinvented has resulted from the deliberate effort to involve new religious groups in the delivery of social services. Government contracting with private agencies (both profit and nonprofit) to provide social services has greatly expanded in the United States in recent years.[49] Coinciding, to a certain extent, with this privatization of government has been a concerted effort, at the local, state, and federal levels, particularly since the election of George W. Bush, to extend such contracts to what are called "faith-based" providers.[50] "Charitable choice," as that effort is often known, is based on an asserted right to equal opportunity for certain new religious providers as well as on the assertion that neither the government nor the traditional, large, religiously affiliated providers, such as Catholic Charities, are adequately delivering social services. Equal opportunity is said to be necessary to "level the playing field," giving small-scale (that is congregational) and evangelical religious groups, allegedly previously discriminated against by the government, an opportunity to compete for government funds on a par with large established §501(c)(3) religious social service providers. Lew Daly argues convincingly that the most serious shortcoming of the new faith-based initiatives is that they are intended to, and, in fact, do, benefit religious groups rather than the poor.[51] But it is also claimed by those who advocate on behalf of faith-based initiatives that local churches and para-church organizations that use "faith" in their service plans can do the work better because they treat clients holistically. Faith is understood to be both more effective and more efficient for delivering certain social services.[52] The need is great, they say, and there are armies of compassion just waiting to be tapped.

After more than ten years of experience with faith-based initiatives, many questions remain. When we speak about "faith-based" groups, whose faith and whose right to equal opportunity is being invoked—the provider's or the client's? Is faith the motivation for the service or a component of the service? How do we evaluate these efforts? And to what extent is the expression "faith-based" not substantive but merely rhetorical and strategic, just code words concealing partisan constituencies and agendas? Religion scholars would argue that "faith" is not the defining characteristic of many religious traditions outside Protestant Christianity.[53] To translate religion as faith from this perspective is itself to discriminate against the religious practices of those other religious communities. Although welfare has certainly been transformed in the last ten to fifteen years, and religion itself adapts in protean ways to the new legal and social environment, currently there is little hard evidence that the much-vaunted faith-based component of the new social services accomplishes the grand goals claimed for it.[54] Little rigorously peer-reviewed quantitative data are available concerning the effectiveness of faith-based social services, partly because there has not been enough time for long-term longitudinal studies. Specifically regarding prisoner rehabilitation, claims concerning the greater efficacy of faith-based programs are largely anecdotal or self-promoting. It is also difficult to compare private and public programs in all areas of social services, as private agencies have greater discretion in who they admit to their programs and when clients can be expelled.

A comprehensive study of the effectiveness of faith-based interventions in crime was commissioned by the Department of Justice in 2004. The final report, prepared by Caliber Associates, contains a description of studies of the relationship between religiosity and crime over the last half century, a discussion of sociological research concerning the relationship of religiosity to delinquent behavior, and a list of exemplary faith-based organizations in this field, including PFM and IFI.[55] Asserting that "religion is a broad and complex theoretical construct" and emphasizing the inconclusive results of current research, the study reviewed various intervention theories, including hellfire theory, social control theory, social bond theory, and social learning theory, and concluded that, in a general way, "faith does work" for crime prevention and that further research is needed along with partnering with faith-based organizations to address crime prevention.[56]

In the end, though, bids for government contracts have been fewer than expected from faith-based organizations. Many smaller religious organizations lack the infrastructure necessary for government contracting, and some are simply not interested in the work. There has been no increase in dedicated government funds for such purposes, although there is evidence that a higher percentage of available funds has gone to faith-based providers in the last several years.[57] Meanwhile, while there is enormous variety among the states, most states lack the resources to monitor contract compliance (as to efficacy, fiscal responsibility or constitutionality).[58] Private studies are few and their results inconclusive. Some real gains do seem to exist, although the evidence is mostly anecdotal and ambitions remain high—nowhere more so than in the case of prisoner rehabilitation.

I do not review comprehensively the recent proliferation of faith-based prison rehabilitation programs in the United States; many religiously based projects exist in both state and federal prisons.[59] Instead, I focus on one evangelical Christian rehabilitation program implemented in one Iowa prison. An enormous variety of religion is everywhere in U.S. prisons, religion facilitated by prison chaplains, various external organizations, and groups attached to the large conglomerates of world religious traditions, as well as every form of small-scale and new religious movement. Prisoners themselves also initiate investigations into religion through mail-order courses, reading projects, bodily practices, renewal of family religious traditions, explorations of ethnic and racial identities, meetings with fellow prisoners, and negotiations with prison authorities. For the most part, prison authorities welcome such interest and activity by prisoners unless it appears to be clearly aimed at undermining prison authority.

What is new in the last decade, however, is the effort to design and implement extended and holistic *residential* prison reform efforts based on explicitly religious cosmologies and anthropologies. Echoing the projects of early-nineteenth-century Christian prison reformers, these programs require the prisoners' full immersion in a Christian environment of penitence and reform. This book will use the record in the trial, *AU v. PFM*, to reflect on contemporary discourses about religion and the models for the creation of selves that are used by philosophers, social scientists, lawyers, and religious reformers. Should the projects of evangelical faith-based prison rehabilitation programs be understood as attempts to *re-sacralize*, in a traditional sense, society and the modern self? The version of the self that these programs evince is firmly rooted in modern refashionings of the self that were first imagined by Protestant reformers and liberal political thinkers, both religious and secular, in the seventeenth century. But these refashionings continue, albeit in new and transformed ways, to partake of the dominant modern understanding of the self that undergirds projects of self-discipline worldwide in the twenty-first century, both religious and secular, an understanding influenced as much by global capitalism, deracination, and the mass media as by religion.

One more caveat. In the landscape of faith-based social services, it is important to distinguish between the types of social services provided. Although constitutional issues have been raised across the board—for example, regarding discrimination in hiring—it is particularly those social services that are designed to effect personal transformation that most acutely focus attention on *religious* "technologies of the self."[60] Faith-based soup kitchens, homeless shelters, and medical clinics, as well as child care, after school, and job training programs, while catering to vulnerable populations and arguably requiring a heightened attention to constitutional standards of care, are less directly concerned with personal transformation in a comprehensive sense. Family counseling, substance-abuse programs,[61] and prison rehabilitation, on the other hand, are explicitly directed at the creation of new selves. What new selves do Americans want to create? How is that to be done? Where are these questions to be debated? And what does the U.S. Constitution and the rule of law permit when these selves are prisoners of the state?

The faith-based rehabilitation program at issue in the trial, InnerChange Freedom Initiative (IFI), is a subsidiary of Prison Fellowship Ministries (PFM). Unlike previous PFM prison programs, IFI was designed to be a comprehensive pre-release program, preparing prisoners over the course of eighteen months for life on the outside. It is described in its own literature and on its Web site as an eighteen-month, 24/7, "Christ-centered," "Bible-based" course designed to reduce recidivism through personal transformation. As administered by IFI in Iowa, the program was run by paid counselors and volunteers, and included an "aftercare" mentorship to assist prisoners in returning to the world. The description here of IFI's Iowa program is based on the trial transcript and findings of the district court, as well as on publicly available information from PFM and IFI. Self-descriptions of PFM and its in-prison program, InnerChange Freedom Initiative, can be found at www.pfm.org and www.ifi.org.[62] As of June 2, 2006, approximately $1.7 million (35–40 percent of the total cost of the program) in direct payments had been made to IFI for its program in Iowa, the money largely coming from the Healthy Iowans Tobacco Trust and the Inmate Telephone Rebate Fund.[63]

Nine Iowa prisoners and their families, supported by Americans United for Separation of Church and State,[64] brought the action challenging the constitutionality of Iowa's contract with PFM. It was tried before Judge Pratt[65] over a three-week period in the fall of 2006. The plaintiffs were represented during the trial by two staff lawyers for Americans United, Alex Luchenitser and Heather Weaver, as well as by a Des Moines attorney, Dean Stowers. The defendants, PFM and IFI, were represented by the Richmond, Virginia, office of the national law firm Troutman, Sanders, L.L.P. The lead trial attorney for the defendants was Anthony Troy. The State of Iowa was represented at trial by Gordon Allen, Deputy Attorney General, and Lorraine Wallace, Assistant Attorney General. I was an unpaid expert witness in this trial, and I will briefly describe my testimony. My role is not the focus of this book. (My evidence is discussed in chapter 5.)

Trials are complex events, and many different stories can be told about any one trial. An entire literature has explored what happens in the courtroom. Particularly helpful to me in writing this book were Robert P. Burns's *A Theory of the Trial* and Dominic LaCapra's *"Madame Bovary" on Trial.*[66] Burns argues that, contrary to the received wisdom—that the trial "is the institutional device for the actualization of the rule of law"—the trial is, in fact, a complex performance of practical morality that, at best, provides knowledge of the practical truth about a situation. In trials, Burns says, decisions about the truth of what happened are always connected to judgments about what should be done about it. The collective performance of a trial, he observes, is to "think the concrete," to give "consistent attention to the thing itself," and "to achieve a truth beyond storytelling."[67] Ideally, he says, the trial aims to achieve "moral realism," in the sense explored by Iris Murdoch.[68] Although Burns concedes that not every trial completely succeeds as an act of moral realism, his detailed reconstruction of what goes into the making of a trial "force[s] the mind downward toward the concrete, intensif[ies] the competition over the meaning of the events being tried, and cultivate[s] the suspension of judgment until all aspects of the situation are explored."[69]

As an accomplished trial lawyer and philosopher of law, Burns is primarily interested in defending the justice of what happens in the courtroom. His performative reading makes another claim, however, a descriptive one. Like anthropologists of the law, Burns treats law as a social and cultural form that incorporates the assumptions underlying the wider cultures in which it is embedded. Along with Lawrence Rosen and others,[70] Burns insists on the particular as necessary to understanding and making real the general. Dominick LaCapra's account of the trial of Gustave Flaubert's *Madame Bovary* for immorality adds to these the peculiar intertextuality that results when a cultural artifact is put on trial. Misreadings of the novel by both prosecutor and defense reinforced the instability of the text itself and the difficulty of identifying the moral. "Secularization," LaCapra comments, "itself furthered the tendency of a desire for transcendence to merge unsettlingly with the possibility of transgression."[71]

Trial witnesses are not ethnographic informants in the usual sense. Their words are shaped in a special way by the legal context. The prisoners in this case were not there to represent their religious communities but were selected through the logic of constitutional advocacy litigation. But all texts and all speakers are shaped by their circumstances and speak to multiple audiences out of multiple histories. Trial transcripts are texts that can be read using the tools of textual analysis, informed by an understanding of the peculiar demands of the law and of the moral realism of which Burns speaks. Words matter in the courtroom in a special way. That they have such a purpose does not diminish their value as resources for cultural understanding. This is true particularly of words about religion in the United States, words that have historically been shaped by law.

This book offers an ethnographic reading of the trial transcript and other texts relevant to the civil lawsuit *AU v. PFM*. I contend that by paying close attention to the language and arguments of the witnesses, the judge, and the lawyers, and to the circumstances surrounding trials that center on the twin religion clauses of the First Amendment, we may better understand what counts as religion today, and how it might be fairly regulated in a democratic pluralist society? Should religion be specially protected—or specially restricted—by law, or should law treat equally those who call themselves religious and those who do not? Does law have a choice?

Religion, as conveyed by the traditional word "church," particularly in the way it is related to the European state, is rapidly disappearing. Religion in various forms appears to be a persistent aspect of human (and perhaps nonhuman) life, but it has taken different forms in different places. New forms of religion require new forms of law. I believe that "religion" is not a useful term for U.S. law today, because there is no longer any generally accepted referent that is relevant for defensible political reasons. I think it is valuable to use the word "religion" outside of legal contexts. In wishing to use religion-neutral language in the law, I am not claiming that religion does not exist or that neutrality is achievable in a comprehensive way.

The first chapter presents the Iowa program as the prisoners described it at the trial. The second chapter looks at the purpose and theology of PFM, setting that purpose and theology within the longer historical context of American evangelical Christianity. Chapter 3 examines religious and secular theories of crime and punishment, and the ambiguities of their interrelationship as exemplified in IFI. Chapter 4 considers the nature of religion today in the United States and in contemporary life generally, and chapter 5 reconsiders disestablishment in the U.S. in light of this trial and its contexts. The conclusion discusses the trial in the light of the category of the secular.

CHAPTER 1

The God Pod

THE IOWA DEPARTMENT OF CORRECTIONS (DOC) was established in 1983. Its purpose was to centralize and modernize county correctional agencies and to begin to address overcrowding in prisons.[1] Iowa had had a history of penal progressivism, but, like most of the rest of the United States, it was dealing in the early eighties with what, in retrospect, was just the beginning of the trend toward massive incarceration. The total inmate count for Iowa on October 1, when the DOC was created, was 2,650, housed in seven prisons. By 2006, at the time of the *AU v. PFM* trial, the inmate count had tripled, reaching more than 8,500.[2] Yet no significant change had occurred in the overall population of the state in the intervening years. Iowa prisoners are now housed in nine prisons located in mostly rural areas around the state. The Newton Correctional Facility, a 750-bed, medium-security prison for men in which InnerChange Freedom Initiative's Iowa program operated from 1999 to 2008, is located in the town of Newton, thirty-five miles east of Des Moines. The Newton facility was built in 1997 on the site of a former prison farm constructed in the early 1960s.

Iowa's correctional expansion parallels national trends. Over the course of the last thirty-plus years, a huge increase in the state and federal prison populations across the United States has resulted from years of "law and order" politics. Law and order politics led to the criminalization of an increased range of behaviors, including drug-related offenses, and a larger number of persons, including more juveniles, not to mention an increase in sentence length and the imposition of mandatory sentencing policies. Although for many years little public attention was paid to the intractable social problems created by criminalizing and imprisoning such a comparatively large number of people, today there is increasing political and academic notice of these issues. The political will to tackle them, however, remains distressingly weak.

The State of Iowa, in 2007, commissioned a professional assessment of its correctional facilities. The resulting report, *State of Iowa Systematic Study for the State Correctional System,* produced by the Durrant Group, a Des Moines–based engineering and planning firm, recommended substantial changes to the Iowa DOC, particularly with respect to mental and medical health treatment.[3] The Durrant report revealed that 90 percent of

Iowa prisoners suffer from substance abuse problems, and 30 percent suffer from mental health problems. Treatment capacity is only 1,894 places in substance-abuse treatment programs in any year for a prison population of 8,877. Mental health services are not meeting current professional standards and are grossly underfunded and understaffed. Prisoners are serving longer terms because of the lack of availability of places in mandated treatment programs. The Durrant report is sobering in its assessment of the facilities and services of the Iowa Department, noting outdated and inadequate facilities for treating an aging prison population, those with medical and mental illnesses as well as those with the special needs. A recent national study of safety in U.S. prisons confirms the Iowa findings.[4]

With respect to InnerChange Freedom Initiative, the Durrant report mentions its presence in the Newton facility and the ongoing lawsuit, simply noting that there is no evidence as to its effectiveness. The Durant study also mentions that thought is being given to transforming Unit E, the part of the prison used by IFI, into a residential substance abuse facility, apparently without a faith-based ideology.[5] Both the Department's own planning documents and the Durrant report stress the Iowa Department's dedication to treating the prison population with dignity and its conviction that most prisoners can successfully reenter the world at large.

At this time there seem to be two dominant models in the United States for incorporating religion into the urgent project of comprehensive prison reform. The older model saw religion as an accessory to secular rehabilitation programs provided through prison chaplaincies and through the incorporation of religious communities and volunteers in reentry programs administered by the state. Under this model, the overall responsibility for insuring safety, decent medical and mental health care, job training, and increased educational opportunities for prisoners belongs to the state. The new model creates comprehensively faith-based prisons, or wings of prisons. In this model, religion infuses every aspect of the prisoner's in-prison experience. Treatment, education, and job training take place in an environment that is explicitly religious. Still unresolved is whether these new projects are effective or can be designed in such a way as to be constitutional. Staffing them is also hugely challenging, as they are labor-intensive and require instructors with specialized knowledge. The Iowa Department has used both models.

This chapter offers a picture of Iowa's InnerChange Freedom Initiative in-prison, faith-based rehabilitation program using primarily the words of prisoners who testified at the trial. In later chapters I look at the understanding that Prison Fellowship Ministries and InnerChange Freedom Initiative have of what they are doing and where PFM and IFI fit in the context of American religious and correctional history, as well as current constitutional law regarding religion.

Building a Faith-Based Prison Unit

When the new correctional facility at Newton was being built in 1997, a shortage of funds meant that very little programming for prisoners was planned for the new facility. Indeed, the new prison was "value-engineered" to cut costs. "Value engineering" is a euphemism for lowering building standards to meet budget shortfalls. In this case, the result was, among other things, that one wing, Unit E, was built with wooden doors for cells, rather than metal ones, and with common bathrooms rather than in-cell toilets. Overall space for programming was also reduced because of financial constraints. In the several years before IFI was established at Newton, Unit E was used as an honor dorm to reward prisoners with good disciplinary records. With the advent of IFI and its takeover of Unit E in 1999, however, Unit E, now housing exclusively IFI prisoners, would come to be known by other prisoners at Newton as the "God Pod."[6]

The director of the Iowa DOC from 1997 to 2000, Walter Kautzky, began his tenure as director as a veteran corrections professional. His first prison job had been in Florida in 1966, and he had subsequently worked in the state prisons of Washington, North Carolina, and Colorado, as well as in U.S. military prisons. Kautzky is now executive director of the Tony Lamberti Foundation, a Des Moines–based foundation that funds a number of social service programs for ex-offenders, including the Fund for Faith-Based Re-entry and Bridges for Iowa.[7]

Director Kautzky testified at his pretrial deposition in *AU v. PFM* that as he anticipated the Newton facility being completed and coming on line he began to look for programming possibilities for the new prison: "We were so short of both money and resources to deal with the 750 people that we were loading into a brand new facility at Newton where we had literally cut out most of the . . . program space."[8] He explained:

> We were, as a practical matter, looking for anybody that might help us put these offenders into some sort of productive activities. We were looking for a way, a very low-cost way, to utilize and put some activities in place within a very, very large, and very, very new prison where there were literally no activities. There was no space for education. There was a small library with a law library squashed into it, and there were

> a couple of very small rooms, and beyond that, there was almost nothing for these 750 folks to do.[9]

Lacking productive activity for the prisoners in his new facility, Kautzky put the prisoners to work finishing the prison:

> We even had the inmates put up the perimeter security fence, believe it or not, just in order to find something for them to do. We had them put in all the concrete for the basketball courts and volleyball courts and whatnot. But beyond that, when we ran out of that, there was no continuing basis for activities within the institution and clearly no money that was in contemplation from the Republican governor at the time to support programming. That simply wasn't in the cards."[10]

Urgently needing programming, and persuaded that what he had heard about a new faith-based prison rehabilitation program in Texas might be effective, Kautzky said that he began to look into the possibility of introducing into the Newton prison what he called at trial "values-based" programming (pp. 1674, 1703, 1764, 1816–17).

Kautzky testified that he was particularly interested in the then relatively new in-prison, faith-based initiative at the Jester II facility in Sugarland, Texas (now known as the Carol S. Vance unit), a program created in 1997 and administered by Prison Fellowship Ministries.[11] Kautzky and others who testified at the trial denied that "values-based" is a code word for faith-based, although there was considerable ambiguity in the testimony. "Values-based" is apparently, however, not a widely used term in corrections outside the faith-based context. Current professional corrections theory describes itself as being "evidence-based."

PFM is an international prison ministry founded in 1976 by Charles Colson, former adviser to President Richard Nixon, after his release from the federal prison where he had served his sentence following conviction for his part in the Watergate break-in scandal. Colson had pleaded guilty to obstruction of justice related to the burglary of the office of Daniel Ellsberg's psychiatrist. After serving six months of a two-year sentence he was granted early release because of his son's arrest on a drug charge.[12] Colson reported at the time of his release that his conversion to Christianity, just shortly before his incarceration, had saved him from a prideful life dedicated to the exploitation of power and that he would henceforth work to bring the same conversion experience to other prisoners. He has spent his subsequent thirty-plus-year career ministering to prisoners, and he is widely admired for his dedication to improving the lot of prisoners through personal visits with prisoners, consulting with corrections departments, establishing specialized ministries, and lobbying for legislation. PFM is well funded and professionally staffed; in the fiscal year 2006–2007, its annual income was listed on a respected charity watchdog site at approximately $50 million.[13] PFM's ministry is conducted through short-term Bible study programs as well as in other more comprehensive and elaborate programs, such as IFI, that are operated as para-church[14] organizations. (PFM and IFI are described in greater detail in the next chapter).

Kautzky testified at the trial that, by the time he began working in Iowa, he had had a long professional association with Colson, whom he first met in 1979 when Kautzky was director of the North Carolina prison system. He testified about their friendship and of Colson's willingness to step in to troubled situations in prisons:

> I've known Mr. Colson for a long time, 20 years, and I don't consider our relationship to be, you know, to be one that is personal, but at a business level. I have worked with him in Washington State, I have worked with him in Colorado—not with him personally sometimes, but at his request with the Prison Fellowship strategies that he had in mind, and I have been with him personally at the Walla Walla State Penitentiary in Washington State where we in fact went cell to cell. I was with him as we visited with prisoners on death row, and in other parts of a very troubled institution. And he was kind enough to come help try—help us sort out an almost impossible situation in Washington. And, again, his objective was to, you know, to leave a foundation of—a connection between the church community and those offenders who literally had very little going for them inside the institution. We did work through those issues in those respective states. (p. 938–39)

Kautzky summarized their relationship: "I consider him, you know, a professional friend in terms of his help to prisoners throughout the various states that I've been in. And in his role as Prison Fellowship he's reached out to me, and I've tried to help Prison Fellowship along the way" (p. 939). While resented by some for his competition with existing chaplaincies, Colson is respected among many correctional professionals for his long-standing willingness to work personally and directly with prisoners and prison administrators in difficult contexts.

Having admired Colson's work in the prisons and having met with representatives of PFM in Iowa, as well as with then Iowa Parole Board member Chuck Hurley and several Iowa state legislators who were interested in bringing faith-based prison programs to Iowa, Kautzky decided to send some of his staff to visit the IFI program then newly under way in Houston. At least one of the Iowa team, Kenneth Burger, then Iowa director of offender services, testified that he understood the purpose of the visit to be to determine whether Iowa should try to replicate the Texas program, but in a secular version. The other Iowa staffers knew, however, that financial considerations prohibited such an innovation. Indeed, one attraction of IFI for Kautzky and others was that it was largely privately funded and volunteer-staffed.

The Texas visit impressed all the Iowans with IFI's potential effectiveness in changing prison atmosphere and reducing recidivism. Asked by the lawyer for the defendants about his reaction to the visit, Kenneth Burger commented: "The thing that impressed me was the behavior of the inmates in the program. And then the warden also talked about the recidivism rate being much lower for the population that had completed the IFI program as compared to the folks in the general Texas system down there. And those were the things that impressed me the most" (p. 1587). In August 1998 Iowa issued an official request for proposals for an in-prison values-based program, closely modeled on the Request for Proposal (RFP) that had been used in Texas in 1997 when IFI was initiated there.

The Iowa RFP clearly announced to potential bidders that no state funding would be available. IFI's subsequent 1999 bid to Iowa, which was made following visits by IFI personnel to the Newton facility, was the only bid that was found to meet state specifications.[15] In its negotiation with Iowa prior to finalizing the contract, IFI specifically requested that the program be allowed to use Unit E, the value-engineered wing of the Newton facility which was then being used by the prison as an honor dorm. After further negotiation, including IFI's successful appeal for state reimbursement for certain "nonsectarian" costs, IFI was awarded the contract, at an annual cost to Iowa taxpayers of approximately $300,000.[16]

The contract between Prison Fellowship and the Iowa Department of Corrections was renewed each subsequent year until 2007. Although the program was substantially the same over the course of the contract, the payment scheme was adjusted to more nearly approximate what IFI and Iowa state lawyers apparently took to be the requirements of a voucher-like system, as had been approved by the U.S. Supreme Court for public funding of religious schools in Cleveland. Under this new scheme, beginning in the 2004–2005 contract year, the State of Iowa was charged for the IFI program on a per prisoner, per diem basis.[17]

IFI commenced its work at Newton in December 1999. Iowa corrections officials testified that what appealed to them most about IFI was that it offered a comprehensive residential pre-release and post-release program, and it did so for considerably less money than the state could afford on its own. IFI prisoner participants would be living in an enveloping environment exclusively with other IFI prisoners as they received treatment, counseling, post-release mentoring, and other services as a total package. In contrast, other Iowa state prisoners had to apply for individual treatment programs, such as for substance abuse and anger management, which were then scheduled by state officials as room became available and depending on a prisoner's release date and the need to transfer prisoners to facilities that offered particular treatment and training programs. In 1999, when IFI started its work in Iowa, the Iowa Department was in desperate need of programming for their prisoners, particularly at Newton. Judge Robert W. Pratt commented at the conclusion of the trial that "On July 12, 2002, [more than two years] after the implementation of InnerChange, Kautzky reported to the Iowa Board of Corrections that 400 offenders, department-wide, were still serving sentences longer than necessary because of the lack of substance abuse programming."[18] Iowa officials testified at trial that they estimated that the cost of replicating the program would have been at least two to three times what they would pay to IFI (p. 2680).

"The words of the thirty-fourth Psalm coursed through my mind as we celebrated the opening of the InnerChange Freedom Initiative unit," Thomas Pratt, then president of PFM, wrote to Director Kautzky after Pratt had attended the opening of the IFI program in Iowa. He described the opening and the people who attended and had been instrumental in bringing IFI to Iowa, and he delineated the hand of God in every step of the process that led to the selection of IFI for Newton:

> There was Mr. and Mrs. Stewart who had felt the leading of the Lord to pray that the Lord would use the place on which the present IFI unit sits for His glory. . . . [T]here was Chuck Hurley, the ex-state legislator and parole board member who . . . was unaware of their prayer. Yet he was impressed several times with the sense that the place where IFI sets was holy ground, a place set apart for the Lord's purposes. He was the same person who . . . contacted Jerry Wilger and inquired about bringing IFI to Iowa. . . . He is the same man who went to the Governor about IFI and within a week obtained his agreement. Next he went to the Secretary of Corrections who also agreed in short order. And who was the secretary? None other than Mr. Kip Kautzky. He was the very same man who had facilitated Chuck [Colson]'s visits to Walla Walla, Washington. . . . And under Kip was Warden John Mathes, a believer and a man of integrity and compassion. In the face of all of this who could help but praise the Lord at all times.[19]

In Thomas Pratt's view, a web of prayer and like-minded individuals had combined to produce the Newton IFI program, which set aside a portion of a state prison as, he said, "holy ground, a place set apart for the Lord's purposes."

Although some details of life on Unit E changed over the years after initiation of the IFI program at Newton in December 1999,[20] the stated rationale, theology, religious culture, and basic structure of the program remained the same. On the eve of its Newton opening, Larry Lipscomb, the Iowa DOC corrections officer who had volunteered to manage Unit E, sent a memo concerning the upcoming new program to the entire Newton staff, describing its objectives and outlining which prisoners would be eligible to participate. Volunteers who would not object to the faith-based nature of the program were explicitly sought from among Newton corrections officers (p. 1640). In the memo, Lipscomb described the program as "Christ-centered, biblically based," "providing opportunities for spiritual growth," one "in which the offender works to restore himself, the community, the victims, his family, and God . . . using Biblical teachings":

> First and foremost the offender must volunteer for the program being fully aware of the requirements and the Christ-centered, biblically based curriculum. The objectives of Inner-Change are to create and maintain a corrections environment in which productive work, human dignity, self-worth, responsibility, and accountability are among the key values taught to inmates; to provide training and work-skill related programs relevant to the current and future needs of inmates, including continuity of services after release; to address the holistic needs of inmates, by providing opportunities for spiritual growth and character development; and to involve volunteers and community resources in this program.
>
> The program emphasizes restorative justice in which the offender works to restore himself, the community, the victims, his family, and God. Features of this program include: teaching values-based life skills using Biblical teachings, family counseling, intensive community service work, a strong aftercare program, extensive use of volunteers, both in the programmatic phases and the aftercare portion.[21]

The memo's blended use of religious and secular language to describe IFI is typical of that used by IFI staff and employees about the program in their printed materials and at the trial.

Over the time that the decision to institute the IFI program at Newton was being made by the DOC, IFI was also recruiting inmates for their new unit at Newton by making presentations at Iowa's prisons. Rumors about the new program circulated among prisoners throughout the Iowa prison system. IFI recruiters were explicit about what they called the Christian "perspective" of the program, but they also insisted that no religious test was required for participation. Everyone was welcome. IFI staff members testified that what they were looking for were prisoners "with the motivation to change" (p. 2428). Prisoners testified about their experience of the recruiting process, about the incentives IFI offered them, and about their individual reasons for wanting to be in the program. (The prisoners were not present in the courtroom during the trial; they all testified through a video feed—a practice that distanced the prisoners from the proceedings, created problems of communication, and made the showing of documents to the prisoner witnesses awkward.)[22]

Prisoner John Hammers was the first witness. He spoke about the IFI recruitment pitch given during the introductory program he had attended at Fort Dodge Correctional Facility in Fort Dodge, Iowa. Asked by the plaintiffs' lawyer about any promises that were made by IFI, he responded:

> That we would . . . go to the honor dorm; that there was a trailer where there would be computers and you can learn music, and stuff like that. . . . That when you completed the IFI program, all your treatment would be done except SOTP [sex offenders' training program] and batterer's education. . . . They said that it would look favorable on you because all the treatments that would normally be recommended, you volunteered to take ahead of time, and—The Parole Board would look favorably on you because all your treatment was done. (pp. 32–34)

Hammers did apply to the IFI program and was accepted to transfer to Newton. He spoke at length at trial about his appreciation of the conditions on Unit E. Hammers successfully completed the in-prison portion of the IFI program and was returned to general population in Newton Unit C to complete his sentence.

Bryan Chandler, another prisoner witness at the trial, responding to questions from one of the plaintiffs' lawyers, also described what happened during IFI's recruiting efforts. He was one of the plaintiffs in the lawsuit against PFM and the State of Iowa. At the time of the trial, he had been imprisoned in the Newton facility since 1997. Chandler said that he was attracted by the warmth of the recruiters and the efficiency of the integrated program. Concerning his first encounter with the IFI recruiters, he said:

> They came to all the cell houses on a little tour . . . letting us know what was happening on Friday, when they had a revival. At the time I was living in E Unit, so they stopped there as well as part of the tour . . . *and they was not afraid to come up to any of us and shake hands* and let us know what was going to happen. . . . Basically that they was going to bring a religious program into the institution, and *make each of us a little bit better of a person*, and that he actually said that by joining the program, *you could walk—you could walk the path of the sidewalks here in the prison and hold your head up higher as being part*

> *of this program* because of the intensity of it and how they could help one more than, let's say, if you wasn't to join the program to when you head outside for mentors and stuff like that . . . *everything would be wrapped up into one*, going through the program. The treatment that the State of Iowa requires us to get while we're here as part of your treatment to—before you come out on the streets, that it was all going to be taken into one. (emphasis added) (p. 679–81)

IFI promised a dignified environment, but they also promised more contact with the prisoner's family, help with the parole board, and continued attention after release. Chandler recalled at the trial that he had heard the IFI recruiters say that IFI prisoners would have

> more visits with your family, more of a relationship with them, because *they was going to have your family come in and be part of a study program* as well to keep your family involved in the program as well . . . *how going through the program would allow you to get out quicker* to become—with the mentors' help out on the streets, because they would have a certain amount of pull, if you would allow me to use that, on the parole board of getting out quicker. (emphasis added) (pp. 682–83)

The longing Chandler expresses here was common in the prisoners' testimony. Chandler had been living on Unit E as an honor inmate before IFI came to Newton, and he testified that he had wanted to stay on Unit E so he decided to go through the six-week IFI orientation program as a means to that end. In the end, however, he said, "I decided not to join the program because I thought it would conflict with my upbringing of being a Catholic" (p. 692). As soon as he made that decision he was transferred out of Unit E into general population.

Prisoner John Lyons also spoke at the trial about the seductive approach of the IFI recruiters:

> At that particular time of my incarceration I was spending a lot of time doing artwork. . . . Mr. Paulus [an IFI staff member] saw me sitting there in the recreation area and approached me. He at first would just inquire about my artwork and talk a little bit, and eventually he began to tell me the benefits of getting into a program such as IFI, spoke a little bit of many things. . . . He brought a guitar, and he was singing some Christian music, and he was just in his roundabout way witnessing. He was a very flamboyant, charismatic man. (p. 563–64)

They talked about the advantages of joining IFI:

> He told me many different benefits to coming to a program such as IFI, and I asked him one thing, "And what's this going to do for me?" And

> he says, "Well, if you take what you learn at IFI and you apply it into your life, that *not only will you get out of prison but you'll stay out of prison." . . . [T]here were benefits of a spiritual nature, where you would grow closer to God.* There were benefits in just—in a behavioral nature, where if you were devoted to God, that you would—your behavior would change. *You would be doing things more compliant with society, and which to me is—was what I was keyed in on.* They also had some material benefits, such as living environment . . . And a lot of things they had hoped to do in the program they were unable to do, like the thing with the Vermeer [jobs program for released prisoners] and the industry that we would work at Vermeer, just different things. But there was like material things offered, just that *you would be in a more comfortable living environment, you know.* I could go on. I mean *we talked about comfortable carpeting and seating and plants and pictures on the wall and all these things they happened to create this environment.* (emphasis added) (pp. 564–65)

IFI seemed to promise both material and spiritual improvement. Lyons concluded: "We'd have a kind of a—I don't want to call it a utopian society, where we would separate ourselves from the run of the mill general population, and we would be in a spirit-filled environment" (p. 564).

For some prisoners, like Russell Milligan, the attraction of the opportunity to transfer to Newton for the IFI program was very practical. Milligan had been serving his twenty-five-year sentence on a drug charge in North Central Correctional Facility in Rockwell City, Iowa. He explained his decision to join IFI in 2003: "I wanted to change my life, for one thing. That was a big factor. Also, it was a lot closer to my family, make life a little easier on them visiting me. I could be closer to them" (p. 222). The Newton facility was much closer to where many of the prisoners' families lived, in the Des Moines area.

Michael Bauer, another of the prisoners who testified, was asked at his deposition about why he decided to apply to be in the IFI program. Like many others, he said that he believed that IFI had influence with the parole board:

> I guess it could have been a culmination of things . . . guys that I knew and had known and worked with in the Department of Corrections for some years were joining and felt that it was going to be a good thing and a way to, you know, show that they have changed their lives and are looking to, you know, get on with life outside corrections. . . . The Department of Corrections, the parole board, you know, the governor, who else, you know, whoever had any say-so in their leaving, getting out on some type of release. . . . It would go as far as to say at times that *when you go up for parole, we will be in the room with you, we*

> *will be there with your counselor before, you know, when you have your pre-parole hearing, before you even see the parole board.* And then like I said again, *we'll be there with you when you see the parole board to support you and to field any questions that the parole board may have about the individual pertaining to his time in the program or what the individual may be doing when he does reach the streets, you know, for involvement with the program after they get out, with the aftercare and things such as that.*[23] (emphasis added)

And, again, at the trial, Bauer testified about his hopes for the effect that being in IFI would have on his life:

> Well, there was a couple different reasons. No. 1, it looked like it was going to be something different, *something that could give a little more meaning, a little more success to my life. Some of the people that were becoming involved with it looked like people that I would like to surround myself with. . . .* Another reason was I thought that *it would probably look good in front of the Department of Corrections and the parole board* and maybe I could get myself a parole. (emphasis added) (p. 399)

Bauer joined IFI but left after twelve months.

Timothy Green, another prisoner, previously incarcerated at Clarinda Correctional Facility, also testified about his decision to apply for admission to the IFI program. He answered questions by the plaintiffs' lawyer:

> *Q.* Can you just briefly tell the Court your reasons for deciding to join IFI?
> *A.* I was looking for a change in my life, and I thought that any treatment I would receive would be accomplished at IFI. I thought it would help my chance for release from the prison system, and that I was mainly looking not to reoffend.
> *Q.* And are there any other reasons that you wanted to join IFI?
> *A.* Well, initially I think my own reasons were personal. The Newton facility I thought would be a better prison environment. Again, I expected that completing an intense program such as IFI would enhance my chances for release.
> *Q.* Why did you think that the Newton facility would be a better prison environment than Clarinda?
> *A.* Well, it's an open environment. It's controlled movement in Clarinda. You have more freedom of movement here in Newton. (pp. 2015–16)

Green was in IFI from May 2003 until December 2004, when he was asked to leave the program.

Prisoner plaintiff Joel McKeag was also living on Newton's Unit E when IFI arrived at Newton. He, too, testified about the recruiting efforts: "After work each day we would meet in the gym where we would have a session, a religious session of a little teaching, some songs, and then we would break off into smaller groups where we would discuss open topics. And then, after that was done, then we finished up doing some workbooks in small rooms after that" (p. 1974). And the amenities that were promised:

> When they got going they were going to have charcoal grills and jamboree-type sessions, and that they would have a music room, and that they would have computers and a library, and some other privileges that IFI would have . . . he did mention that they would have the training all under one roof, as in substance abuse, and anger management, and those type of classes. He did state that it would show favoritism towards—when we came for parole. (pp. 1975–76)

Again one hears the yearning. Many of the prisoners seem to have hoped that IFI was going to supply everything that was then lacking in the Iowa prisons, as well as in their lives. But, best of all, they hoped it would help them get out. "Get out and stay out," as IFI literature promised. McKeag, like Chandler, decided not to join IFI and was immediately transferred out of Unit E.

Prisoners testified that various benefits were promised as inducements to join the program: a better prison environment, proximity to family members, consolidation of treatment, help in improving their capacity for law-abiding living, and the hope of early release. The prisoners responded to the enthusiasm of IFI recruiting staff with their own hope that IFI would help provide them with a new beginning, but they were also alert to the possibility of learning something, of bettering the conditions of their life in prison in concrete ways, and of a possible chance of early release.

Iowa prisons were overcrowded and prisoners were underserved when the Newton facility came on line. The location of the Newton prison is desirable to many prisoners because it is closer to Des Moines where many of the prisoners' families live. It is also a newer facility and more attractive to some for that reason. Prisoners at other Iowa facilities had heard that the new IFI program would take place in a special wing with a more congenial environment and with access to computer training, athletic facilities, musical instruments, and more library privileges. They had also heard that all required treatment programs would be consolidated into their eighteen months in IFI, rather than strung out as available. IFI told prisoners, as it had told its benefactors and volunteers, that IFI could help prisoners "get out and stay out," through influence with the parole board as well as post-release mentoring, or "aftercare." IFI, prisoners hoped, would provide that elusive context in which they could change their lives, gain dignity, and find "meaning" and "success."

While prisoners were being recruited for the program, IFI was soliciting in local Iowa churches for financial contributions and for the hundreds of volunteers who would make the program administratively and economically viable. Charles Colson wrote personally to local Iowa pastors in April 1999, soliciting contributions:

> I have wonderful news. On July 1, Prison Fellowship will open in Newton, Iowa, the second site for the most remarkable Christian prison program in the country—The InnerChange Freedom Initiative™.
>
> As you may remember, this is the bold, 24-hour-a-day Christian program we launched two years ago in Houston, Texas. Because of the generous support of friends like you, *we were able to take over a large section of a state prison and run it according to biblical principles.* . . .
>
> It's almost unimaginable—with all the resistance to Christian truth—that we should be running a prison that is, by the grace of God, *turning hardened criminals into disciples of Christ.*[24] (emphasis added)

PFM produced brochures urging volunteers to give their time and money. In one brochure, IFI was described as "a 24-hour-a-day Christ-centered, biblically based program that promotes personal transformation of prisoners through the power of the gospel . . . a joint effort between Prison Fellowship and the state . . . confronting prisoners with the choice of embracing new life in Christ and personal transformation or remaining in the grip of crime and despair."[25] A second fund-raising brochure, titled "Invest in a Real Crime Stopper," described IFI as follows:

> IFI is a faith-based transformational program developed by Prison Fellowship, the nation's largest Christian ministry to prisoners. It is based on the belief that *real and lasting change happens from the inside out as a person repents of his sin*, receives forgiveness and salvation through Christ and draws upon His mighty power day by day. Prisoner participants live in the community—and are *steeped in biblical values 24 hours a day.*[26] (emphasis added)

Contributors were promised that their contributions would be used to make new Christians.

Promotional videos were also produced. One of the prisoners, in response to the plaintiffs' lawyer's question about the continual production of videotapes to help in the fund-raising and recruitment of volunteers, made this comment:

> Q. And were these activities, the community meeting, the Sunday service, and the Friday night revivals, videotaped, to your knowledge?

A. All of the Friday night revivals are videotaped, and I believe that the—actually, yes, the Sunday morning services are videotaped as well.

Q. Were you aware that these videotapes were being used by the IFI program to promote the program in church groups, and things, and to raise funds for the IFI program?

A. Yes. That's pretty much common knowledge for most people in IFI. (p. 1921)

Ongoing fund-raising and reliance on church volunteers makes it possible for PFM to offer IFI to financially strapped state departments of corrections at a greatly reduced cost. In some of the states where IFI operates, the program has been offered entirely free of direct payment, although IFI receives many in-kind benefits in all the states where it operates.[27]

In December 1999, on the eve of the new millennium and of the opening of IFI in Iowa, Charles Colson wrote in the Prison Fellowship newsletter of his hopes for IFI: "Now as the calendars of Christendom momentously turn, I see God's hand similarly placing Prison Fellowship Ministries at a threshold of unparalleled opportunity. Even the secular world sees that the great utopian visions of the past century—fascism, socialism, humanism—lie in ruins. Individual autonomy touted as the great good of modern life has led to moral chaos."[28] While the prisoners hoped for a better life, Colson envisioned IFI as forming a piece of PFM's ongoing effort to convince "the secular world" of the inadequacy of its impoverished and ruinous visions.

InnerChange Freedom Initiative

Once IFI and the Iowa DOC conditionally approved prisoners for the program, those who were not then resident at Newton were transferred to Unit E at Newton. IFI prisoners from other units at Newton were also transferred to Unit E, which was emptied of its previous residents. (Several of the plaintiff prisoners had been moved out of Unit E to make room for IFI and were motivated to complain about IFI in part for that reason.)[29] These new IFI recruits were then given a six-week orientation. After these six weeks, IFI staff invited those in the orientation who they thought would be successful to join the program. In considering IFI's claims of success in reducing recidivism, it is important to remember IFI's careful selectivity in recruiting participants, and its ability to eliminate anyone who was not succeeding according to their lights. Although at various times, because of low levels of recruitment, IFI admissions standards were relaxed to include prisoners with worse records and longer sentences, for the most part IFI concentrated on prisoners who seemed promising candidates for rehabilitation and who were close to their release dates.

Orientation gave prisoners a taste of the intensive program. Responding to the plaintiffs' lawyer's question, prisoner Chandler described his experiences in the six-week IFI orientation:

A. Orientation started out with a prayer, maybe a song or two in the gymnasium. And after that it would break down into five, six, ten different groups, depending upon who showed up, how many inmates, meaning who showed up, and we would get broke down into smaller groups, leave with one of the IFI staff into certain areas of the gym, and other areas of H Building here, like smaller other classrooms; and we'd hold a Bible study there of the handbook that they gave us at the beginning of orientation that required us to do homework, look in the Bible type verses in there, look in the Bible for the answers. The next day we would have studies on them answers and questions in the study group.

Q. And what did you do in the orientation program on Friday nights?

A. Had a revival on Friday nights. They gathered at the gym, sung, listened to some prayers, sermons, if you would, of God, Jesus, stuff like that, and they would bring in a band to sing rock-and-roll, Jesus rock-and-roll songs.

Q. And at the revivals was there anything that you were required to do?

A. Other than pray with the rest of the people. Sing if you wanted to sing. And during the six weeks orientation, at the revivals was a way for them to also mingle and try to get the people that was at the revival interested in joining the program. (687–88)

Although prisoners had been told of the Christian identity of IFI in the introductory programs, the orientation proved something of a revelation to Chandler because his own Catholicism differed from IFI's evangelical-style Christianity. The plaintiffs' lawyer asked him about this difference and how he felt about it:

A. I wasn't even actually thinking about what type of religion it was going to be at the time. But as I was in one of these study groups, I have my own Catholic Bible, and that's the Bible I was using for this handbook . . . and I wrote down answers which I thought were the correct ones out of my Bible, and I was referred to by not just Bruce [one of the IFI recruiters] at one time but one of the other volunteers that had our study group, that I might use their Bible

because it would have a more—it would have more meaning to their workbook than what mine is. It might not be so confusing to me.
Q. And how did you feel when you were asked to do this?
A. Basically what I was taught wasn't worthy of what they was trying to teach . . . We was told that it was a nondenominational program, and that was the first sign that it wasn't, to me. (688–89)

Having learned about the difference, Chandler questioned IFI staff about how his Catholic training would be accommodated if he were to join IFI. One of his goals, he said, was to learn to be a better Catholic. He continued:

> After the incident with my Bible and their Bible, I had waited until I met up with Bruce. I don't know if it was that day, a couple of days later, but I wanted to bring that point up to him, and that was the question I did ask, the purpose of me—if I was going to join a program such as that, is probably like no other, to get all my treatments done, to try to get out of prison quicker. That's why most people use the program. But it was to maybe learn more about Catholicism, and I felt that I could—it would help me be closer to my dad because that's, like I said, how I was raised; and *I had brought it to Bruce, the whole Bible thing, and that I would like to learn more about Catholicism, and he had told me at that time that that's not what they was going to be teaching, and that their program consisted of a seven-day, 24-hour a day type religion, still not letting me know exactly what kind of religion they was going to be teaching, but was letting me know, basically, mine was taking a second seat to what they was going to teach.* (emphasis added) (p. 689–90)

It was not just the Bible: "The prayers—Catholics as you know, they get on their knees and pray. The prayers were different, and of course they had no confessions or nothing like that. Their services are different than a Catholic service" (p. 690).

Chandler and other Catholic prisoners asked IFI to accommodate the program to their Catholic practices. They specifically asked whether a Catholic priest could be invited to come in and offer mass. Chandler described the response to their effort:

> I and many others had asked the same question, and the answer was, no, not on their time. You can do what you wanted and study what you wanted on your time. But let me remind you, he was pretty strict on saying that their program was intense, seven days a week, 24 hours a day; and I felt that that was the key telling me that, no, I would not have no time for such things as a Catholic priest coming in or any possible services that I could go to that. (pp. 690–91)

Having confirmed to his satisfaction that IFI would not accommodate his Catholic practice, Chandler decided not to apply. He explained his decision in answering questions from the plaintiffs' lawyer at the trial:

A. I believe that I would have to change to—if a person joins the program for the proper reason, and to get more—to get a religion out of it, it would be to change my religion.
Q. And did you finish the orientation program?
A. Yes, sir, I did. I got a certificate—a certificate saying that I completed this six-week course of orientation for IFI.
Q. And at that point did you have a decision to make as to whether to proceed with the rest of the program?
A. Yes. There was a handful of us that took it down to the very last week of not deciding to leave the unit or join the program and be able to stay there longer. I thought about it, but the minute—the minute that I decided, I had let my unit manager know, and he moved me to C unit.
Q. And why did you decide not to continue the program?
A. *I decided not to join the program because I thought it would conflict with my upbringing of being a Catholic.* (emphasis added) (pp. 691–92)

For some prisoners, living on Unit E, previously known as the "honor dorm," was incentive enough itself to join the program. Among its other benefits, the prisoners emphasized two of the most basic physical attributes of Unit E, the toilets and the cell doors. John Lyons, for example, compared living on Unit E to his previous cell on Unit C, beginning with the toilets. Lyons testified:

A. In Unit C you got the sink right above the toilet that you defecate in, where you wash your face and brush your teeth, and generally wash your hands. There's really no way to keep yourself away from your toilet while you're doing all that stuff. Plus it is about a foot away from somebody's bed when you're flushing the toilet or going to the bathroom and they have to sleep on their sheets and blankets and stuff which is right next to the toilet; whereas, opposed to Unit E, you don't have to worry about that stuff because it's in a whole separate place on the unit.
Q. In terms of physical comfort, can you tell me which toilets are more comfortable, the Unit E or the Unit C ones?
A. Unit C ones are steel, and they've got cold water running through their system, so they're just freezing, especially in the winter. On Unit E they're porcelain and you don't have to worry about none of that because they're warmer and not as—they're set up as a

normal toilet, whereas the other ones don't have seats, or anything like that.

Q. Just to clarify, the Unit E toilets do have seats?

A. Yes, they do, ones that you can raise and lower.

Q. And the Unit C toilets, what do the inmates sit on?

A. Just the metal of the toilet. (pp. 52–53)

As a faith-based prisoner at Newton, you got porcelain toilets and toilet seats, toilets that were located outside your cell.

Lyons also testified that there was greater privacy and security in Unit E, in contrast to general population Unit C, because the IFI prisoners were issued keys to their cells:

Q. And you also mentioned keys, keys to cells. Do inmates in Unit C have keys to cells?

A. No. It's a lockdown unit. You can't open anything. You're not even issued or supposed to have a drawing of a key in the other units, anything that resembles a key.

Q. How are the doors in Unit C opened and closed?

A. By the guard on the control post through a computer.

Q. And how does it work in Unit E?

A. The inmates are all issued a key for their particular room that they're assigned to, and they have locking mechanisms to where you, the guard, and your roommate, or roommates, are the only ones that can get in that cell.

Q. And I believe you mentioned that the keys provide better security; is that correct?

A. On C Unit it's impractical to lock your door every time you leave it because the guard just would be spending his whole day opening and closing—or opening doors for the inmates for the 90-odd cells that are in the unit, whereas on E you can actually close it and lock it and nobody else can get to your stuff. But on C the cells are left open.

Q. Psychologically how did having your own key in Unit E make you feel?

A. Well, it makes you feel better, it gives you a sense of responsibility that you've earned some trust back, so to speak, that you can be trusted with a key and security of your own door, when you want it opened and closed, say, to use the rest room at night, or you just got your commissary and you can lock your door; whereas in C it's all metal and all white. It's a different color. The wooden doors are brown, which you don't see much of, and you just can lock your stuff up properly. (pp. 53–55)

Wooden doors were preferred to metal ones, even because of their color, because they gave prisoners a sense of responsibility.

At the trial prisoner John Hammers also emphasized the fact that the doors on Unit E were made of wood rather than metal, and the importance of that difference to him. He was asked: "Why did it matter to you what the doors were made of?" and he answered,

> Because the wooden doors with the keys give you more of a sense of security that your stuff is secure, and responsibility that you've actually been good enough for them to trust you with a key to your own door . . . I mean, you always feel better about yourself, that you're doing good, and about your environment when you have a little bit of control over your environment, whether it be as small as the door to your cell that the guards can get in at any time, or whether it's somebody not flushing a toilet a foot away from your bed, it just makes you feel good inside. You ain't as prone to be aggressive. You tend to let things slide because being on E means that you're responsible enough—or somebody thinks you're responsible enough to be there. (p. 56)

Being on Unit E gave prisoners a sense of dignity, a sense of being trusted.

John Lyons was asked to compare the two units overall and asked which he preferred. He was eloquent about the difference it made to live on Unit E:

> By far Unit E is better. I mean the rooms are *more spacious* because they're absent a toilet and sink. So there's more storage and there's a little *more comfortable* environment. It's *much nicer* to have a wooden door with a window on it versus a metal door that locks behind you when you go in. You know, it's so much nicer to have that—you know, if you could see the different units, Unit E is a clean—when you walk into that unit, it's just nice. You know, this is Unit E, this is the honor dorm with the wooden doors, and they take a lot of pride making it nice. They did prior to IFI being there, and they still do now that IFI is there. It is the unit to get to. You are good in the general population but while living on Unit C and living on Unit D, you are—your behavior, you make sure you're doing good, you're not disobeying the rules or doing the wrong things so you can earn that status. *You know, to carry that key in your pocket gives you this—it's a different kind of freedom. Even though you have a fence around you, if you can still go in and out of your house—"house" meaning cell—in and out of your cell as you want to, you know, I mean it's—you know, it's kind of a psychological thing to look at a room with a wooden door and look at a room with a steel door.* (emphasis added) (pp. 589–90)

IFI offered a "more spacious," "more comfortable," and "much nicer" environment: "*it's a different kind of freedom. Even though you have a fence around you.*"

The contract with the state provided that IFI could, involuntarily and unilaterally, return prisoners to the general population who, in its judgment, were not progressing satisfactorily. Prisoners who were dismissed from Unit E were returned first for a period of time to Unit B in Newton, a lockdown unit.

Although the IFI prisoner's daily routine on Unit E was in some ways less restricted than that of the general population, in other ways it was more restricted and regimented. Much discussion during the trial concerned whether the physical amenities in the IFI wing, along with the increased freedom of movement and greater privacy, when balanced against the stricter behavioral expectations, constituted a discriminatory incentive to prisoners to volunteer for IFI or, as emphasized by IFI lawyers, they were a disincentive when contrasted to conditions in the general population. While the atmosphere is calmer and there is more freedom of movement and more privacy on Unit E, personal televisions, pornography, and profane language are forbidden. The IFI prisoner's day is also highly structured. Prisoners in the general population may, unlike the IFI prisoners, choose not to engage in jobs and treatment programs. Overall, Judge Pratt found that "InnerChange inmates enjoy a less restrictive security environment, largely the result of living in a former honor unit."[30]

The IFI prisoner in Iowa woke at 5:00 A.M. for 5:30 A.M. devotions, which are half-hour meetings of small groups of prisoners who take turns offering prayers and reflections. "Everybody was required to attend," prisoner John Hammers recalled, "Everybody would sit at four to a table and either pray or read scripture. And somebody would be up front, would read a devotional or read some scripture out loud, and then they would pray and you'd go to breakfast" (p. 37).Guards awaken IFI prisoners, if necessary, for devotions. As the IFI staff explained, IFI was considered "treatment," according to prison regulations, and prisoners are required to attend treatment in which they are enrolled. Judge Pratt found that,

> Inmates are required to attend all components of the InnerChange program in order to remain in InnerChange. Each component—classes, devotionals, community meetings, group sessions, worship services—are treated like any other Dept. of Corrections secular treatment program component. In fact, just as in any other full-time treatment program, inmates are financially compensated for the time spent in the InnerChange program. Also, just as in any other treatment program,

> an absence from any InnerChange component is grounds for official reporting and discipline under both InnerChange and Dept. of Corrections behavioral rules.[31]

Not attending devotions could be grounds for dismissal from the program.

Each weekday afternoon at 3:00 P.M. on the IFI unit there was a community meeting which several prisoners described. In the words of Prisoner Russell Milligan: "We would start off with a short prayer, then we would typically sing three worship songs. I believe that was followed up by another prayer from an inmate. Another inmate would get up and give a talk, I guess you would say, or a testimony. Then after that we would have information passed on to us about what was going on in the community" (p. 231). A "testimony," or what IFI participants sometimes called a "witness," is an account of what the speaker understands to be evidence of God working in his life. It is the recounting of an incident in one's life as read through the evangelical biblical worldview. Learning to give such accounts is central to the training of evangelical Christians.

Prisoner Michael Bauer also testified about the opening of the community meeting: "It was usually opened up with a little kind of ditty called, 'This is my Bible,' and somebody would get up and say that, and then the whole group would say it. If I remember right, it went like, 'This is my Bible, a lamp to my feet, light to my path, it's words that I will hold in my heart so that I may not sin against God' " (p. 417). The "ditty" to which Bauer refers is taken from Psalm 119. Bauer continued:

> There was singing. I wasn't required to sing. I'm not a very good singer so a lot of times I didn't sing. . . . Somebody would usually do their little devotion almost the same as like in the morning. And then staff would get up, whether it be DOC staff, or IFI staff, and, you know, give us information about things going on in the community, about upcoming dates with things that we needed to be aware of, or people coming in, or what have you. It was just an informational community meeting where everybody got together. (p. 417)

Typical of IFI teachings, biblical training and devotion were fused with practical concerns.

Each day during the week, morning and evening, over the eighteen months of the program, the IFI prisoner had classes and work assignments. Classes taught by IFI paid staff included Old and New Testament Survey, Spiritual Freedom, Experiencing God, Battlefield of the Mind, Substance Abuse / Anger Management, Victim Impact, Financial Management, and Criminal Thinking. These courses were taught using the Bible as well as texts drawn from the evangelical biblical counseling literature, books that are widely available to the public in shopping malls, on the Web and through Christian bookstores. Many are best sellers. Chris Geil, the program manager for IFI, testified at the trial that all the books listed in the IFI printed curriculum produced at the trial were actually used in various classes. The prisoners' trial testimony also confirmed that these same texts were used in the classes.

The required books for IFI prisoners for these courses include Neil Anderson, *Victory Over the Darkness: Realizing the Power of your Identity in Christ,* and *The Bondage Breaker,* as well as the study book developed for groups using these books, titled *Breaking Through to Spiritual Maturity: Overcoming the Personal and Spiritual Strongholds That Can Keep You from Experiencing True Freedom in Christ*; Neil Anderson, Pete Vander Hook, and Sue Vander Hook, *Spiritual Protection for Your Children: Helping Your Children and Family Find Their Identity, Freedom, and Security in Christ*; Neil Anderson and Rich Miller, *Getting Anger under Control*; and Neil Anderson, Mike Quarles, and Julia Quarles, *Freedom from Addiction: Breaking the Bondage of Addiction and Finding Freedom in Christ*; Henry T. Blackaby and Claude V. King, *Experiencing God: How to Live the Full Adventure of Knowing and Doing the Will of God,* as well as *Experiencing God: Knowing and Doing the Will of God, Hearing God's Voice,* and *The Man God Uses*; Orrin Root, *Training for Service: A Survey of the Bible*; Joyce Meyers, *Battlefield of the Mind*; Henry Cloud, *Changes That Heal: How to Understand Your Past to Ensure a Healthier Future,* and *Boundaries: When to Say YES; When to Say NO; To Take Charge of your Life*; David and Debbie Bragonier, with Kimn S. Gollnick, *Getting Your Financial House in Order: A Floorplan for Managing Your Money*; and Dave Ramsey, *Total Money Makeover.* These books combine practical advice for living with religious teaching. Success in life is tied to obedience to God.

Some of the flavor of these works can be seen in the following excerpts. With biblical quotations on every page, *Getting Your Financial House in Order* teaches the reader about good financial management, using the rooms of the house as metaphors for various aspects of this project. In the chapter titled "The Master Bedroom," the couple is taught to view their marriage as covenantal, a marriage in which wives are to be submissive to their husbands. The book is promoted on the cover as follows: "Those who apply the principles in this book will discover God's true blessings and have a floor plan for getting their financial house in order." Henry Cloud's intention in *Changes That Heal,* in his words, is "to show you that there are biblical solutions for your struggles with depression, anxiety, panic, addictions, and guilt."[32] Cloud's *Boundaries* is a guide to healthy Christian relationships. Dave Ramsey writes, in *Total Money Makeover,* that "if you are a good person, it is your spiritual duty to possess riches for the good of mankind. If you are a Christian like me, it is your spiritual duty to possess riches so that you can do with them things that bring glory to God."[33] Andersen and the Vander Hooks introduce their *Spiritual Protection for Your Children* with these words:

> You are about to read a remarkable story of one family's victory over the powers of darkness. . . . Pete is a mainline evangelical pastor in middle America. He and his wife, Sue, are morally righteous parents whose children have not only attended Christian school but also home school. As a family they have courageously taken a stand for the sanctity of life. Pete and Sue Vander Hook are biblically uncompromising Christians who found themselves in a spiritual battle for their family. Their struggle to help their children led to their own freedom in Christ and ministry to others.

Classes taught by IFI volunteers are the Old and New Testament Survey, Community Bible Study, Family Series, Computer Training, Principles of Business and Industry, and Mentoring. The Bible courses use materials developed and produced by the Discipleship Training Department of the Sunday School Board of the Southern Baptist Convention, and include Thomas Lea and Thomas Hudson, *Step by Step through the New Testament* and Waylon Bailey and Todd Hudson, *Step by Step through the Old Testament*. The other courses are taught using Christian counseling and apologetic literature, including Ray Vander Laan, *Faith Lesson Video Series*; Henry Brandt, *Heart of the Problem*; Henry Blackaby and Tom Blackaby, *The Man God Uses* (a seven-week daily study guide training the reader in Christian living); Henry T. Blackaby and Melvin D. Blackaby, *Experiencing God Together: God's Plan to Touch Your World* (a sequel to *Experiencing God Together,* this book teaches how to develop the local church into a Christian community); T. W. Hunt and Claude King, *In God's Presence: Your Daily Guide to a Meaningful Prayer Life* (a six-week program to teach the reader how to pray); Robert McGee, *The Search for Significance* (teaches that self-esteem comes not from worldly success but from understanding that one is loved by Christ); Willow Creek Community Church, *Walking with God* series; Charles Colson and Ellen Vaughn, *Being the Body*; John Bevere, *Undercover: The Promise of Protection under His Authority*; and John Eldridge, *Wild at Heart: Discovering the Secret of a Man's Soul*. Eldredge writes that, rather than being told to be sensitive, "men need something else. They need a deeper understanding of why they long for adventures and battles and a Beauty—and why God made them *just like that*. And they need a deeper understanding of why women long to be fought for, to be swept up into adventure, and to *be* the Beauty. For that is how God made them as well."[34]

These classes and the teaching materials they used are not exclusive to IFI. Much of the content is common to other evangelical Christian parachurch programs. The publications used are produced by major evangelical publishers. Many of the authors are enormously successful within the evangelical subculture and have extensive other media outlets and ministries. But religious publications have a privileged status in prisons, being more often permitted to prisoners than secular publications. Much of the religious reading material available in the prisons is Christian, particularly charismatic and evangelical. The chapel libraries often consist entirely of donated books, and, furthermore, Christian authors themselves often donate books. Frequently given are the five-volume graphic novel version of the *Left Behind* series and *Chicken Soup for the Prisoner's Soul.* Joyce Meyer's books are also distributed without charge in many prisons. As a victim of domestic abuse who has become a successful entrepreneur, Meyer is a great favorite, particularly among women prisoners.[35]

Prisoner Allyn Gilbert testified about the teaching in the class Praise and Worship: "[The instructor] went through and showed different verses in the Bible that basically showed us how we should worship as far as raising of the hands, or singing, or dancing, or shouting to the Lord, for instance" (pp. 1918–19). In response to a question from one of the plaintiffs' lawyers, he also described his experience attending the class Training for Service:

> *A.* Training for service helped us to make an outline or a time line, basically, of the Bible. It was designed to help us to do a better Bible study, more meticulous Bible study, and understand the sequence of events that took place in the Bible as well.
> *Q.* And the name of the course was training for service. Service to who?
> *A.* Well, to God because the Bible was involved. (p. 1917)

Training for Service: A Survey of the Bible was first published in 1907 (rev. ed., 1983) as a text for training Sunday School teachers. In short chapters with maps, charts, and helpful memorization aids, followed by study questions, the author takes the student through the history and geography of the books of the Protestant Bible.

The class Experiencing God was mentioned as a particular favorite by the two prisoners who testified on behalf of IFI. For example, Robert Robinson was asked about the class by the IFI lawyer:

> *Q.* You mentioned that you got a lot of understanding from a class called Experiencing God; correct?
> *A.* Yes. That was my favorite class.
> *Q.* What did that class consist of, and what—tell the Court what you achieved or learned from that class.

A. That class, we go through a booklet that—called Experiencing God, and it's mainly about getting in touch with your innerself and who you really are, and help you get goals, set goals and visions and get a plan of life. It really touched home because I was able to think about my daughter, my son, I mean, the abuse, the things I've done, and be able to write it on paper, but also to sit and listen to other men that was in my class with me talk about their life experiences and their testimonies and be able to talk with each other and overcome those, that anger and hate that was inside of us. (p. 2911)

IFI's lawyer followed up:

Q. Did that course—I mean by the title, Experiencing God, suggest that it really was teaching only how to have God as your savior?

A. No, it wasn't. It had a lot of biblical standpoints in that Bible—in that book, it had a lot of different things you can read in your Bible, and a quote to help you to overcome. It had a lot of different things in it. It wasn't a book that send you to Christ, though. (pp. 2911–12)

The distinction made here by the lawyer and by Robinson between religion as a means of salvation and religion as a guide to practical living was a constant theme of the IFI defense, as discussed below. Another prisoner who testified for IFI, Jesse Wiese, was also asked by the IFI lawyer about what he learned in the same class. He replied:

> Experiencing God teaches—it teaches how to be—teaches us about relationships or fellowships, how to be in a relationship with God in order to be in a relationship with man. It teaches integrity, how to be honest in your daily life. Let's see. I mean, simply biblical principles. I mean we taught out of the Book of Mark, so the teachings of Jesus which are full of moral teachings. (p. 2795)

The implication was that state-funded religious teaching in the service of practical morality is constitutional. Not constitutional is the teaching IFI's lawyer referred to as "teaching only how to have God as your savior."

The class Experiencing God uses the text *Experiencing God: How to Live the Full Adventure of Knowing and Doing the Will of God* by Henry Blackaby and Claude King, two well-known evangelists. Students are trained by Blackaby and King to move back and forth between the biblical text and events in their own lives so as to "experience" God in those events. So, for example, the first biblical narrative recounted in *Experiencing God* is the story of Abraham and Isaac. Blackaby and King conclude their account of the binding of Isaac with these words: "When God saw

Abraham's faith and obedience, He stopped Abraham from sacrificing Isaac and provided a ram instead. Abraham named that place after the God he had just come to know by experience. He named the place 'The Lord-Will-Provide.' "[36] Blackaby and King then tell a story from Blackaby's life that illustrates his own experience of the Lord "providing" for him just as he had for Abraham.

Blackaby writes about hiring an assistant pastor for the new church where he was working as senior pastor at the time. As Blackaby recalls:

> We had no money for moving expenses and no money for a salary. Jack [the new assistant pastor] had three children in school, so we felt we had to pay him at least $850 a month. We began to pray that God would provide for his move and his needs . . . I began to ask myself "How in the world will God make this provision?" Then it dawned on me that as long as God knew where I was, He could cause anybody in the world to know where I was. As long as he knew my need, He could place that need on the heart of anybody He chose. . . . I then received a letter from First Baptist Church, Fayetteville, Arkansas. They said, "God has laid it on our heart to send one percent of our mission giving . . . to use however you choose."[37]

Just as with Abraham, Blackaby tells the reader, God had provided, in this case by causing a donor to make a needed contribution at that moment. *Experiencing God* guides the reader to make the same kind of identification of his life with the life of biblical characters who God takes care of. Everyday needs are to be prayed for with the expectation that they will be granted. This is a religion that operates very close to the ground and in which all causation is attributed immediately and specifically to God.

Every Friday evening, the IFI prisoner was required to attend a revival meeting led by a volunteer local congregation. In his trial testimony, John Lyons described the Friday night revival:

> Friday night revival, you would walk into the gym, and you'd have greeters at the door that would shake your hand and welcome you in. You'd find a seat, music would be playing. And we're not talking about a record player. We had the full band, the guitars, the drums, the big PV amps and a lot of praise and worship. Beautiful music playing. The guys would stand in the aisles and stand and listen to the music, clap their hands, and as the praise and worship ensued, they would raise their hands and start—as they would say, the spirit of God would start to flow, and everybody would get kind of giddy, you know, and then we'd all sit down and listen to the message that was provided by whatever volunteer had come. And there would always be an altar call, for the majority of the revivals, where you would go and be offered to turn

> your life over and accept Christ as your savior. You could go up front and be prayed for or throw out prayer requests for others. It was a lot going on. I mean we had all different kinds of denominations coming in, but, you know, it would be more excitable if the Pentecostal or charismatic Church of God movement would come in. It would be kind of mundane if they brought in any of the other outfits. But Southern Baptist, there was one gal that came in and she was—she got to touching people and praying for them, and they were falling down on the floor, and—I mean, I'm sure you've seen these things on—I've seen it on TV. I actually witnessed it there in the gym at Newton Correctional Facility. (pp. 570–71)

Lyons was describing a certain style of Christian worship that is characteristic of segments of the evangelical community, one that might be described as Pentecostal or charismatic. Lyons, brought up in the Lutheran church, said that he was not sure it was right for him:

> Folks would get to praying and get to talking into tongues there, and it was actually kind of a neat thing but a little scary for some of us that are more—more—I don't know, I'm from a Lutheran background, so a lot of it was extremely out there. Had I jumped up in my Lutheran church and said "Praise God," I'd probably got kicked out. So it was nice, you know, but it wasn't really for me. I did find myself—I forced myself to kind of get into it. You know, I kind of clapped my hands and stand up and enjoy the music but again it was almost too much for me. That doesn't mean that somebody else couldn't get something out of it. (p. 571)

The Lutherans he knows do not speak in tongues or engage in praise worship.

Most Friday night IFI revivals at the Newton Facility, Lyons testified, featured an altar call. Asked by the judge to explain what an altar call is, Lyons obliged. "An altar call," he said,

> is where you would go up to the front of the assembly and kneel down and pray with one of the volunteers that came to provide the praise and worship, and they would lead you through the sinner's prayer, which would be understanding that you're a sinner, that confessing that sin to God, accepting Christ as your Lord and savior and, you know, and they would pray for you, being new in Christ. And it could be—Even if you had accepted Christ, it could just be a reiteration of that confessing of Christ. You know, a lot of people like to recommit themselves. You know, maybe they've had some sinful behavior in their life that they are ashamed of and they want to go just let it out, and that was the opportunity to do so. The altar call, there really was no altar.

> It was just the front of the gymnasium where you could kneel down and before God and the body of Christ—and the body of Christ meaning the body of believers, the people that were all there in agreement, would all be witnesses that you are committing yourself. (pp. 572–73)

Altar calls were very popular with some inmates. Lyons commented:

> There were inmates that went to the altar call every time they had one. I can't deceive you and say that everybody had the same reason for going, you know. I mean for some people it was just a big show. Other people were extremely genuine and they had prayer issues. But, you know, I mean pretty much the volunteers that came in and provided the praise and worship for Friday night revival were from different area churches from all over, including the Christian colleges. They all pretty much offered an altar call, which would happen mid to late service, and, again, there was some people that would wait until maybe six months into the program before they ever jumped in there, and there were other people that from Day 1 to Day 365 they were still doing it. Every time they could do an altar call, they would jump on it. (pp. 571–72)

Like most of the other prisoners who testified, Lyons was curious but rarely openly critical of the religious practices of other inmates.

Every Sunday the IFI prisoner was also required to attend church services offered by IFI staff members. Indeed, after IFI came to Newton, IFI took over the administration of all the Protestant Sunday church services from the Newton chaplain Perry Stevens. Stevens testified that, before IFI, Sunday services were provided by various volunteer Protestant churches with varying worship traditions, "evangelical" and "liturgical" (pp. 649–50) (The categories "evangelical" and "liturgical" are conventional categories used in the allocation of positions in U.S. government chaplaincies, such as in the military, to insure the availability of a range of Protestant religious services for clients.)[38]

IFI also provided a state-licensed substance abuse program. The instructional literature for the IFI substance abuse program states that "only JC [Jesus Christ] is a cure for addiction."[39] The IFI substance abuse program was granted a two-year extension of its license on March 25, 2007, although it was in noncompliance in some categories. In the letter granting the extension, non-compliant categories were listed, including the following: "Staff Development and Training was in non-compliance because new staff members had not been oriented to the medical aspects of substance abuse." The letter also noted the non-implementation of a Quality Improvement Plan, as had been directed.[40] John Lyons testified at the trial about the substance abuse class he took while in IFI:

Q. Mr. Lyons, what did IFI teach as to what you needed to do to get off drugs and stay off drugs?
A. Drug addiction was recognized as a sin. And all we had to do was seek—confess that sin, repent of that sin, and just start doing things differently from that point forward.
Q. And what did IFI teach the cure for substance abuse problem was?
A. Well, I would say it was—again, if you've confessed your sin and you have—you were forgiven, then you were no longer bound by that sin, so therefore you could go ahead and move on. You were freed from that addiction. You were released from that addiction. (p. 596)

Through the study of biblical narratives, prisoners in the IFI substance abuse program were taught that "Scripture is our standard and is regarded as truth," and that one should put one's faith in God's order, rather than in the natural order.[41]

The text for the substance abuse course was *Freedom from Addiction* by Neil T. Anderson and Mike and Julia Quarles. (Anderson is a pastor and prolific author of Christian self-help books. Mike Quarles is one of Anderson's parishioners who overcame substance abuse with Anderson's help.) Step 1 in *Freedom from Addiction* instructs the reader/disciple in renouncing what it refers to as "satanically-inspired" occult practices and false religions. A "Non-Christian Spiritual Experience Inventory," a list included in most of Anderson's books, allows readers or disciples to check themselves for sixty-five different non-Christian spiritual experiences that must be renounced, including Dungeons and Dragons, fortune-telling, New Age medicine, fetishism, Christian Science, Mormonism, Unitarianism, Buddhism, Hinduism, and Islam. All of Anderson's books, both his own and those he co-authored, begin with a renouncing of counterfeit religion.[42]

The IFI substance abuse course adopts a doctrinal affirmation in Anderson's book, which, at some point, prisoners are expected to affirm:

I recognize that there is only one true and living God (Exodus 20:2, 3), who exists as the Father, son and Holy Spirit, and that He is worthy of all honor, praise and worship as the Creator, Sustainer, and Beginning and End of all things (Rev. 4:11; 5:6, 9, 10; Isaiah 43: 1, 7, 21).

I recognize Jesus Christ as the Messiah, the Word who became flesh and dwelt among us (John 1:1, 14). I believe that He came to destroy the works of Satan (I John 3:8), that He disarmed the rulers and authorities and made a public display of them, having triumphed over them (Colossians 2:15).

I believe that God has proven His love for me, because when I was still a sinner Christ died for me (Romans 5:8). I believe that He delivered me from the domain of darkness and transferred me to His kingdom and in Him I have redemption, the forgiveness of sins (Colossians 1:13,14).

I believe that I am now a child of God (I John 3:1–3), and that I am seated with Christ in the heavenlies (Ephesians 2:6). I believe that I was saved by the grace of God through faith, that it was a gift and not the result of any works by my part (Ephesians 2:8).

I choose to be strong in the Lord and in the strength of His might (Eph 6:10). I put no confidence in the flesh (Phil. 3:3), for the weapons of my warfare are not of the flesh (2Cor 10:4). I put on the whole armor of God (Eph 6:10–17), and I resolve to stand firm in my faith and resist the evil one.

I believe that Jesus has all authority on heaven and earth (Matt 28:18), and that He is the head (I John 3:1–3) over all rule and authority (Col 2:10). I believe that Satan and his demons are subject to me in Christ because I am a member of Christ's body (Eph 1:19–223). I therefore obey the command to resist the devil (James 4:7) and I command him in the name of Christ to leave my presence.

I believe that apart from Christ I can do nothing (John 15:5), so I declare my dependence on Him. I choose to abide in Christ in order to bear much fruit and glorify the Lord (John 15:8). I announce to Satan that Jesus is my Lord (I Cor 12:3) and I reject any counterfeit gifts or works of Satan in my life.

I believe that the truth will set me free (John 8:32), and that walking in the light is the only path of fellowship (I John 1:7). Therefore, I stand against Satan's deception by taking every thought captive in obedience to Christ (2 Cor. 10:5). I declare that the Bible is the only authoritative standard (2Tim. 3:15–17). I choose to speak the truth in love (Eph 4:15).

I choose to present my body as an instrument of righteousness, a living and holy sacrifice, and I renew my mind by the living Word of God in order that I may prove that the will of God is good, acceptable and perfect (Romans 6:13, 12:1,2).,ep>I ask my Heavenly Father to fill me with His Holy Spirit (Eph. 5:18), to lead me into all truth (John 16:13), and to empower my life so that I may live above sin and not carry out the desires of the flesh (Gal. 5:16). I crucify the flesh (Gal. 5:24) and choose to walk by the Spirit.

I renounce all selfish goals and choose the ultimate goal of love (I Tim. 1:5). I choose to obey the greatest commandment, to love the Lord

> my God with all my heart, soul and mind and to love my neighbor as myself (Matt. 22:37–39).[43]

Prisoners in the substance abuse program were urged to use this creed legitimized by the interlacing of fragments of Bible verses into its propositions—verses from often quite disparate biblical contexts—to structure their response to the biblical teaching of the program.

IFI also included a Bible study program for the families of prisoners. One incentive some prisoners mentioned for joining IFI was that they might be allowed more frequent family visits, albeit the visits would be in the context of family-oriented Bible studies. The family Bible study was described during the trial by Chris Geil, IFI program manager:

> In the family series, it's when anyone from—one of the inmate's visiting list who is 16 or older can come in and they can study with either their family member or their friend. It is facilitated by volunteers. And that curriculum . . . basically I think it's called What You Need to Know About Jesus, or something like that, is the name of it. . . . It is a short introduction for the family members to know the kind of thing that their loved ones and their friends and their relatives have learned while they're in. That's to give them a reference point when they get out, some of the things that they have—that they've learned. (p. 1187)

The family program is also known as the "Alpha" program, a fifteen-week course of Christian evangelizing developed in the United Kingdom in the early 1990s. The Alpha course, designed to teach Christian basics to non-Christians, has since spread worldwide.[44]

Several prisoners testified at the trial about the family series. John Hammers was asked by the plaintiffs' lawyer to describe it:

> *Q.* Mr. Hammers, can you tell me what Alpha Series or Family Series was?
>
> *A.* That is a class that took place in the visiting room with a volunteer and any inmate's family that was able to come up on Wednesday or Thursday nights to discuss, like, Christian curriculum, general curriculum from IFI.
>
> *Q.* So what actually was it that the inmates were supposed to be doing during these Alpha Series sessions?
>
> *A.* They were supposed to be going over an Alpha Series curriculum at the time.
>
> *Q.* What was it that usually actually happened?
>
> *A.* What would happen is that the people—the inmates that didn't have family members come up would talk about the curriculum, or whatnot, with the volunteer, and kind of just leave the other inmate that had the family member there be, because they're talking about

> other things. They're visiting. It's like another visit while they were there. (p. 65)

Russell Milligan also described family nights:

> *Q*. And would these family visits that you would receive be in addition to or taken out of visits that you had already been allowed under Newton visiting policies?
> *A*. They were in addition to.
> *Q*. And you've talked about some packets that you received.
> *A*. Yes.
> *Q*. Were there different packets for each session?
> *A*. For each session, yes. . . .
> *Q*. Can you give the Court an idea of what these packets would consist of?
> *A*. One of the packets was "Who is Jesus." It was basically about Christianity and the basics of Christianity, I believe.
> *Q*. Can you give the Court an idea of some of the other subjects that you recall in these packets?
> *A*. Some of them were comparing other faiths to Christianity.
> *Q*. Any others that you can recall?
> *A*. Not that I can recall.
> *Q*. Were any of the packets that were distributed for you to discuss with your family on these family nights of a non-religious nature that you can recall?
> *A*. No. (pp. 234–35)

The additional family time allowed to IFI prisoners was an opportunity for IFI to evangelize the prisoner's family.

The grandmother of Jesse Wiese, one of the prisoners who testified on behalf of IFI, participated in the Family Series. The IFI lawyer asked Wiese about it:

> *Q*. What was the curriculum? What were you learning?
> *A*. The curriculum was Alpha Series, hence the name. Since then we've changed the name to Family Series for the simple fact we use different curriculum. The curriculum is basically the same as what I discussed earlier, as far as teaching moral values. Basically what it was was a study that you and your family could go through teaching them about just the basic tenets of Christianity, what it means, things of that nature.
> *Q*. Did you participate in this Alpha Series with a family member?
> *A*. Yes, I did. My grandmother came.
> *Q*. Where does she live?

A. She lives in Keystone, Iowa, which is about 30 miles east of Cedar Rapids.
Q. How far away is that from Newton?
A. It's about an hour, an hour-and-a-half.
Q. Did she show up every Tuesday and Thursday while you were in the class?
A. You had class Tuesday or Thursday, and I had class on Tuesday, so she showed up every Tuesday.
Q. How did this Alpha class that you took with your grandmother differ from a normal visitation with your grandmother?
A. Well, it was not a visit in the sense that—I saw my grandmother, yes, but we were not able to discuss things like what's going on with the family, how are you doing, what's going on, we couldn't get to the vending machines, which is a high priority, as far as visits are concerned in prison. She came with her lesson prepared, we had a volunteer there who's ready to go. So when time was gone, we were going through this lesson, when it was over, she left. That was the extent of it. (pp. 2799–2800)

On redirect examination by the defendants' lawyer, Wiese was also asked about the Family Series:

Q. What was the main—from your knowledge, what was the main purpose of the Family Series?
A. The main purpose is obviously reconciliation, which is the key tenet, I believe, to the InnerChange program, reconciliation with God and reconciliation with your family, and mankind in general. Yes, reconciliation was a huge portion of it. Many persons in prison burnt bridges with their families from just being in prison alone. Just to have that environment there and to go through something together helps build those bridges back. (p. 2825)

According to *The Alpha Enterprise,* a sociological analysis of the Alpha course, "there are allegedly nearly 20,000 courses running world-wide in approximately 130 countries."[45]

Through the required devotions, classes, meetings, revivals, and worship services, the IFI prisoner at Newton was immersed in a world of Bible verses and Bible stories. He was trained to interpret his own experience of the world and to change his behavior by memorizing Bible verses and studying lessons drawn from Bible stories. At the trial, Lyons described the intense effect all this Bible instruction had on him. He first discussed the homework and tests:

> Well, I mean I could sum it up with two words, memory verses, you know, memorize, memorize. You'd have some—say we were going

> through the book of John, and we were following Christ's message throughout the book of John per the gospel of John, and we would learn about the different parables, what the parables meant. And throughout the Bible the instructor would find key verses. And there are several ways to do that, but he would find key verses in the Bible that would solidify your salvation—I don't want to say solidify; just encourage your salvation or endorse maybe is the word I'm looking for. But I mean it was good stuff. All positive stuff. Stuff if you memorized it, you know, you constantly drilled it in your head, I mean pretty soon that's—you're a walking, talking Bible. And that's really what they kind of want you to do is just kind of take all the junk that's in your head and kind of get rid of it and fill it full of good stuff. The more good stuff they can pack into your head, you know, the better. (pp. 573–74)

Prisoners were regularly tested on their knowledge of the events, characters, places, and words of the Bible. The tests asked for details of names and places mentioned in the biblical text, answers to basic doctrinal principles, and personal responses to such questions as "What does Jesus mean to you?" and "What has changed now that you have become a Christian?"[46]

Lyons characterized the program as a whole as centered on the Bible and Christ:

> Basically everything was centered on Christ. You take a biblical perception of anything—you know, the moral fiber of the Bible is still in every area of life, whether it be relationships, jobs, money, treatment issues, addictions, everything, all the answers were in the Bible, and we did have a curriculum that led us through those things. It was a—it was not an easy thing at times to swallow, meaning that some of the stuff was kind of tough, and you had to do some research so you not only had to go through the Bible, but you might also have to pursue a Bible dictionary so you could understand what the Bible was saying or maybe some form of commentary. But, you know, they kind of went with the fruits of the spirit. If you were expecting love, joy, peace, patience, kindness, goodness, or temperance, then you were starting to live what was taught in the Bible. And as they saw those things in your life change—They would kind of tell you if those things weren't changing, then you weren't putting those things in the application. I mean they encouraged you to quit smoking. They encouraged you to quit, you know, using anything that was, you know, bad for you. Which is all good stuff. There's nothing bad there. It wasn't a demand. It was an encouragement. They encouraged interaction with other inmates. And once, if you had confessed Christ as your savior, your mission as a Christian

> was then to go out and witness to others the salvation of Christ. And teaching Christ was crucified meant that you had to maybe have a good knowledge and be able to back it up with scripture, and they would teach you to do that with every aspect of your life. . . . I taught an art class. I tried to do the best I could to find scripture that backed encouraging God's creative spirit through each of his—I don't know how to say it, the people that followed God, and I mean I was teaching art and some people considered that a spiritual thing, other people don't. (pp. 567–68, 569)

The language of scripture served as the amniotic fluid of the highly ordered womb in which IFI members lived.[47]

Periodic evaluation of a prisoner's progress in the IFI program was performed in individual counseling sessions. When IFI was first initiated at the Newton facility, these sessions were structured through the use of a form called "Fruit of the Spirit Evaluation Log." On a scale of 1 to 5, prisoners were graded on whether they were evincing a particular "fruit of the spirit," referring to a theological elaboration of Paul's instructions to "walk in the spirit in his Letter to the Galatians (5:13–26)." A focus on the fruits of the spirit as a way to measure one's spiritual progress is particularly strong within Pentecostal churches. Evidence that one is doing so is said to be that one exhibits the fruits of the spirit, the Holy Spirit, which is understood to be a continual force in the lives of Christians, a force that is evidenced in an observable increase in "love, joy, peace, patience, kindness, goodness, faithfulness, gentleness and self-control." Although Pentecostal churches are the ones within the evangelical movement that particularly emphasize the works of the spirit, spirit theology, or pneumatology, is an aspect of the religious teaching of all Christian churches. The Catechism of the Catholic Church also speaks of the fruits of the spirit. A composite 1–5 grade for each experienced fruit of the spirit summed up a prisoner's progress. (On May 10, 2005, Norman Cox, vice-president of PFM, e-mailed a law student writing about the program that "inmates are not evaluated on their beliefs, but are evaluated on how their actions comply with the 'fruits of the spirit.' ")[48] Newer evaluation forms used by IFI were stripped of explicit biblical references and focused on the measurement of what they called "pro-social behavior."

On cross-examination, the plaintiffs' lawyers asked Wiese questions about the various IFI documents that were used to monitor a prisoner's progress:

> *Q*. It looks like these are case notes documenting your regular meetings with Mr. Kingery [one of the IFI staff]; is that right?
>
> *A*. Yes, I believe so. . . .

Q. And it says . . . "Jesse doing excellent, real open to info, and also a lot of questions. Very sincere. *Doing good in his walk, working on praying and praying in public.*" Do you remember discussing those topics with Mr. Kingery at your meetings?
A. I don't remember discussing it with him, but I remember when I was going through this in my life.
Q. I'm sorry. You remember what?
A. I remember when I was personally going through this. I don't remember discussing it with Mr. Kingery, but I'm sure I did. (emphasis added) (pp. 2849–50)

The lawyer focused first on the comment on prayer:

Q. That's true, you were working on praying, and praying in public?
A. Yes. I remember because it was a real struggle for me to pray because I was a very shy person.
Q. That made you uncomfortable, to have to pray in public?
A. Excuse me?
Q. It made you uncomfortable to have to pray in public?
A. It means that *I was having some dissonance in the fact that I wanted to pray in public, but I didn't think I had the ability to.*
Q. What do you mean "in public"? Is that a revival or a community meeting? Does that qualify as public?
A. Yeah, things of that nature.
Q. Okay. So Mr. Kingery was helping you work on your praying in public?
A. I wouldn't say helping me. I would say he encouraged me.
Q. I'm sorry. He was what?
A. He encouraged me. (emphasis added) (p. 2850)

Next, the lawyer asked Wiese about the meaning of a person's "walk," and "spiritual progress":

Q. When it says "Doing good in his walk," what is your walk? Can you explain what that is?
A. I think when Mr. Kingery wrote this, I would think—this would be conjecture, but this would be concerning my Christian walk.
Q. Your walk with God, right? You talk about that a lot in the program, walking with God; is that right? . . .
A. Yes, I chose to talk about it a lot, yes. If it was taught about—obviously it was a Christian program going in. . . .
Q. Okay. Now, Mr. Kingery on here seems to make note of the fact that you're progressing spiritually. Do you see that?
A. Yes.

Q. Did you feel that was true?
A. I believed it to be true, yes, I still do.
Q. I'm sorry?
A. Yes, I believe it to be true, yes.
Q. *And you talked about your spiritual progress with Mr. Kingery in these meetings, correct?*
A. Yes, I'm sure I did. (emphasis added) (pp. 2850–52)

And, finally:

Q. Let's look at one more fruit of the spirit. I'm going to put it on the screen. . . . Here Mr. Kingery writes—can you see his comments, "Additional comments from staff"?
A. Yes.
Q. He writes that *"Jesse is doing very well in the program, God's hand is evident in his life through his words and actions. Jesse is at the head of his class and his openness to God's leading is an encouragement to me."* Do you see that?
A. Yes.
Q. And he conveyed those sentiments to you at the meeting, correct?
A. Yes.
Q. That was encouraging to you as well, right?
A. Yes, it was encouraging to me. (emphasis added) (p. 2855)

IFI staff were shown in these documents, hundreds of which were produced during the discovery phase of the trial, to be engaging with the prisoners in what is called in a church setting "spiritual formation"—the intimate individual education of a Christian that is accomplished through pastoral counseling.

On cross-examination by the plaintiffs' lawyers about the evaluation of his progress in the program, Wiese testified about his upbringing in the Local Church Movement:

Q. You mentioned that you were—you mentioned The Local Church Movement that you were a part of growing up.
A. Yes.
Q. And can you explain, is that a Christian religion?
A. Yes, it's Christian.
Q. Is it any particular sect? Is it Lutheran? Is it Jew?
A. No.
Q. It's own brand of Christianity? . . .
A. I don't know if I would use the term brand. It's its own view on Christianity, yes. You could classify them as nondenominational, in a sense.

Q. And The Local Church, my understanding is that it's a very conservative form of Christianity; isn't that correct?
A. Yes, I would say that.
Q. And, in fact, it's more conservative in terms of a religion, in terms of Christianity, than the Christian model used for IFI. Would you agree with that?
A. I would agree with that.
Q. So they're not the same?
A. Right.
Q. And, in fact, The Local Church Movement members in some respects have different beliefs than the IFI program teaches?
A. I would agree with that. (pp. 2865–66)

The Local Church movement is a Christian church that moved from China to the United States in the 1960s. It is centered on what it calls the Recovery Version of the Bible.[49] Wiese seems to have been preoccupied with whether he should regard the movement as a cult, and therefore heterodox:

Q. Well, in your meetings that you had with Mr. Kingery each month, do you recall discussing your membership in The Local Church?
A. Yeah. At that time in my life I was going through—I was questioning a lot of things, what was true, what was not true. I wanted to know—I was reading a lot on The Local Church on my own, trying to figure out if it is indeed a cult. If it isn't a cult, where does it stand, how does it measure up, and those type of discussions I would have with Mr. Kingery. He'd be a sounding board.
Q. You testified earlier that you actually came to the conclusion that the movement—Local Movement is not a cult?
A. Yeah. To this day, where I am right now, I went through a long process and my mind has changed. My stance has changed considerably a number of times, but now I do not believe it is a cult. (pp. 2867–68)

The IFI lawyer then showed Wiese an internal IFI document with notes on his progress commenting, "So if you look at the second sentence in that it says—these are your case notes from your meetings with Mr. Kingery. It says, 'Recognizes that past affiliations with "Local Church" Movement was not good' " (p. 2869). Wiese answered: "Yes. I recognized that myself, yes" (p. 2870).

In describing the way that prisoner progress was measured in IFI, Judge Pratt found that "evidence presented at trial shows that, invariably, dismissals from the program were the result of minor infractions and attitudinal deficiencies"; he then explained:

One prisoner was told that, though his conduct was excellent, his demanding and manipulative ways meant that he simply was "not displaying the growth needed to remain in the program. Your focus is not on God and His Son to Change you." Another inmate was dismissed for having an "unteachable spirit," being spiritually arrogant, lacking in humility, and having a "Messiah Complex." As to the Messiah Complex, the inmate was warned about his effect on the InnerChange "congregation":

> There was only one sinless person that was Christ Jesus. The cults are filled with those that think they are sinless. . . . In conclusion you have a sincere position of your "sinless perfection" and you are and will be a strong influence on immature people or Christians to stumble and struggle. With these attitudes and qualities you would be destructive to a congregation and take advantage of others upon your release.[50] (citations to record omitted)

The language used to measure prisoners' success moved back and forth between that of Bible-believing Christians and that of the corrections community as if they measured the same thing.

Jesse Wiese remained at Newton and became an IFI "elder" after his graduation from the program because he had not yet completed his prison term. Many Protestant churches recognize members of their communities as elders, understood to have been an office in the early Christian community and therefore warranted by the New Testament. As an elder, Wiese continued to live on the unit and to mentor other prisoners. Wiese was asked by the defendants' lawyer about his role on the unit:

> *Q.* Mr. Wiese, did you agree to any conditions to stay on Unit E?
> *A.* Yes. I agreed that I would maintain a peer mentor relationship, that I would be an example to the men, that I would not participate in any activities that would take away from their progress in the program, and I would be available for any kind of space where they needed me, as far as leading small groups if they didn't have enough volunteers, or anything of that nature.
> *Q.* Okay. Did you in fact lead any small groups, for example?
> *A.* Yes, I did.
> *Q.* Were you viewed by other inmates as an elder?
> *A.* Yes, I was.
> *Q.* What does that mean?
> *A.* Basically it means that there was a couple guys, there were four to five men that were there that had been there for a while and that were considered to be elders by the men in the program in the sense that if they had an issue or had a problem, they could come to us

> and we would talk to and discuss with them about it. We kind of acted as intermediaries between the InnerChange staff and the men. (p. 2807)

Wiese testified at the trial on IFI's behalf. He also mentioned that he was then doing a correspondence course with Moody Bible Institute (p. 2777).

Upon release from prison, an IFI prisoner was placed in aftercare, during which time a volunteer mentor took him to church each Sunday and helped him to find work. This element of the IFI program is one of the most widely admired and most difficult to reproduce, dependent as it is on local churches and business connections that IFI cultivates. Judge Pratt found that "No other Dept. of Corrections therapeutic community treatment program comes close to offering the focused, extended aftercare programming available to inmates in InnerChange."[51]

Also testifying for IFI, Prisoner Robert Robinson responded to questions from one of the IFI lawyers by enthusiastically describing his positive experience in aftercare:

> *A.* I went to Newton, Newton, Iowa, when I was released to a Freedom House. And the aftercare was there to follow me. They really stuck beside me.
> *Q.* "They" being who?
> *A.* Meaning IFI with the support, make sure I had a job, a mentor of my choice, a church of my choice, and transportation. Any problem that I had, it was there.
> *Q.* All right. Now, did you eventually, when you were released from prison, become employed?
> *A.* I was employed when I left prison at Rock Communications. . . . I worked there for ten months while I was in prison, and six months when I got released.
> *Q.* All right. And there came a time when you changed employment?
> *A.* Yeah, I changed employment. I went to Vermeer Manufacturing in Pella. (pp. 2917–18)

Robinson was particularly eloquent about the help he received from IFI in finding employment:

> *Q.* How did you get that job?
> *A.* Well, it was a long story. Rod Brouwer [Iowa IFI aftercare manager] talked to Terry Butler, and I had an interview with Terry Butler at Pella—at Vermeer . . . and I talked to him . . . about me, about my life change, about what I've been through, my success since I've been out of prison. And so he got me an interview, and I got hired, but they called me back two days later and took the job back because they seen my PSI. I had a violent charge when I was 18, which

> I went to prison when I was 19 on. They got a strict policy there [at Vermeer] they want no violent—you can't have no violent offenses and work there. . . . So I lost that position. Rod kept on them. I ended up getting an interview with the owners of the company about six weeks later, Bob Vermeer. . . . In the meeting I gave a testimonial about my life and what I've been through and my vision and my goals. And I had a lot of guys that recommended me there through the IFI, and my success. And, you know, really I just asked for a chance to be a part of that company even though I know what the screen said about me, I knew I had a violent offense, and I knew what I did in my past, but *I was just asking for a second chance, an opportunity to show them that I'm different, I'm not the same person, that my life has been dramatically changed.*
>
> *Q.* What equipped you to be able to have a conversation with individuals who own a very substantial company like that?
>
> *A.* Going through the program, the tools, the discipline, the fellowship, I mean—the discipleship. I mean, all that in the program equipped me for who I am now, and a part of society. It just gave me a whole different view of life, and they're respectful people, and the love for people, and the opportunity to be able to show myself approval. (emphasis added) (pp. 2918–20)

This is what IFI boasts of: its preparation of prisoners for life as workers, family members, and churchgoers.

Robinson testified that IFI even helped him to find transportation and to work on his marriage:

> *Q.* How do you get to work?
>
> *A.* At first I didn't have no ride to work. Rod Brouwer helped me get a ride through another guy. And I rode with him for about a few weeks, and then him and his wife decided to buy this truck and they gave it to me so I could get back and forth to work. . . . He said it was laying on his heart to give it to me, so he did. I was shocked. I didn't know what to say . . . it's just unbelievable, you know, what people will do that you never thought would ever reach out for you.
>
> I had a big thing—I still had that kind of I'm going to this community, I'm black, nobody really want to step out and give me a chance, it's going to be too hard for me. . . . Today I'm living in Newton, I'm working at Vermeer, my wife works in Des Moines. *IFI has been there every step of the way. Even problems with my marriage they were there, someone to talk to, they were there, thoughts come in my head they were there. IFI, they go with you, if you decide to stay with them in the aftercare. Things I've accomplished since I've been out it's been a miracle.* (emphasis added) (pp. 2920–23)

Finally, Robinson summarized his IFI experience:

> It taught me how to live my life different than what I used to. I learned how to be a better husband, a better son, a father. . . . IFI, the treatments and the classes I went to helped me to get to the root of my problem, why I acted the way I acted, why I was so angry, a lot of the things that happened in my childhood, as I was growing up in my family with the abuse, sexual abuse, physical and mental abuse, and addictions. *They sit down and they say, "Listen, even though we know"—we all know it's got a biblical aspect, we've got the world view of life, and it's my decision what I want to do now. And they help you to choose that right decision so you won't convert back to what you used to do, and who you used to be* . . . in IFI, counselors in IFI, they give you the opportunity to tell you what's wrong with you, and they sit down and they work with you on that. And you have other men that you get to listening to that went through the same thing, and you all get to talk about how you can overcome the addiction, how you can overcome the anger, how you can overcome the bitterness, and know that you can be a different person in regard to who you used to be, and what people will see you as and view you as, because when you're in prison you're just nothing, you're the lowest of all. And that's just what the world thinks of you when you're in prison. Don't nobody want to stick their hand out and help you because nobody trust you. In IFI they trust you off the top. They give you that chance you always wanted. *They heard that cry for every man in prison that want to be different, that cry of hope to change. That's what IFI give us, the opportunity to get that.* . . . Many days I wanted to leave that program. . . . I didn't want to change, I didn't want to give up who I used to be. I wanted to continue to cuss, I wanted to continue to be angry at people and be mad at people. But in that environment there was so much love and lot of the men had given that up and changed their life. And, you know, the things I did in the past affected my children, affected my wife, I hurt so many people, I tore down so many bridges, now it's time to rebuild all that, that gives you the inspiration and the hope. . . . I didn't go to the program to get more religion or get religion, or anything like that. It happened. It just something I agreed on, something I accepted . . . *They're not there to try to force nobody to be a Christian, or force nobody to believe a certain way. They're there to help men to change their lives and live their lives a different way.* (emphasis added) (pp. 2904–13)

PFM's Web site and printed materials are full of such stories. Some of the prisoners who testified at the trial clearly believed that they had been helped by the IFI program.

Catholic prisoner Michael Bauer, notwithstanding his decision to leave the program because of what he believed to be discrimination, also had positive comments to make about the beneficial effects of the IFI program. At his deposition he testified:

> I am a proponent of IFI. I feel strongly that a program such as IFI can work in the Department of Corrections. I believe in anything that will help men become men, to become responsible adults, to stop crime, to stop the victimization of others, and basically, the betterment of life for all because of my beliefs and my strong feelings for others. If it only helps one man, well, so be it. That's one man that's going to go out there and is going to share his ideals and his beliefs with a society that seems to be going down the tubes. And I can say that because I was part of that society, and I was a man who simply took and took and took, and to this day I don't know why I ended up like that, but I do know why I ended up like I am today, and that's because I got tired of the taking. You know, that's not—that's not in me anymore. So I favor anything such as that. I favor programs such as the Sexual Offenders Treatment Program. I favor Alcoholics Anonymous and NA and helping with men's children while they're in here. You know, *any program that the DOC can put together that will better man for the simple fact of bettering the man, the inmate I should say, I'm for.*[52] (emphasis added)

Like many of the prisoners, Bauer saw IFI as beneficial, though, only if it were one among many programs. It was IFI's privileged benefits for Protestant evangelicals that concerned them.

John Lyons, one of the IFI prisoners who had graduated and been released but had then re-offended and been reincarcerated, testified at trial that he was heartbroken not to be readmitted to the program:

> I failed. I had every opportunity, and I failed. I went out and I tried and I failed. . . . [T]here's things I miss so badly about the program and there are things I don't miss. I mean if they had the politics all worked out and all that done, yeah, there's a lot to learn there. I mean *I felt better about myself while I was in that program than I ever felt ever.* I learned things about myself that I didn't even know. And I can't find that. I can't find it. I seek it and I can't find it. I keep using the word utopian feeling, you know, that I felt there. It was kind of this environment that is just hard to recreate anywhere. And, yeah, I want to feel good about myself again like that. I'm trying to find that here. I'm trying to find that amongst these walls, and it's not as easy. . . . I've not found that environment anywhere else at all. I've gone to churches that were

> similar in beliefs, but, yet, it just—*to live in that communal way, you know, all those like-believers together, I mean I don't know where you go to find something like that.* (emphasis added) (pp. 606–7)

IFI clearly found success with some prisoners. The God Pod gave them a home. Other prisoners, however, were profoundly disappointed with their experience in IFI. Some were dismissed from the program for reasons they felt were unfair. Others experienced discrimination based on religion or sexual orientation. These prisoners saw IFI as serving a particular religious community and would have liked a comparable secular program that was genuinely multireligious or multiple programs organized for various religious communities. Some saw IFI as a violation of the Constitution.

CHAPTER 2

A Prison Like No Other

THE IOWA VERSION of InnerChange Freedom Initiative was described in the previous chapter primarily from the perspective of the prisoners who testified at the trial. A few had graduated. Others had decided not to apply, had withdrawn, or were dismissed from the program. Some of the prisoners testified on behalf of the plaintiffs and some for the defendants. Many other stories about IFI could be told. This chapter describes IFI's own presentation of its purpose and practices in the context of the complex and contested history and practice of U.S. evangelical Christianity, as it is broadly understood, a context notoriously resistant to easy classification. My intent here is phenomenological, rather than theological, that is, to understand and describe PFM and IFI as forms of American religious culture rather than to offer a normative valuation of their theology. Prison Fellowship is the product of two American Protestant religious styles: an often dualistic and dogmatic neo-Calvinist revival, now being fostered by some evangelical intellectual leaders, and a more loosely textured pietist and pragmatic American lay evangelicalism as old as the country. These two forms are not always obvious and comfortable bedfellows.

Spokespersons for IFI are quick to characterize IFI's program as presenting a strong, transformative, and effective contrast to *secular* "therapeutic" prison rehabilitation programs. IFI emphasizes repentance and reconciliation but is careful to avoid what it considers to be an obvious or explicit reference to the doctrines of particular Christian denominations. IFI's ideology is often denominated simply as "Christian" or "biblical," in a strategic, unmarked gesture of ecumenism. Although described as strongly Christian in contrast to secular programs, its Christianity is presented as an entirely natural form of Christianity, one that is nonthreatening, nonsectarian, and nondenominational, a form that everyone, including non-Christians, should welcome and be able to embrace unproblematically.

In their testimony at trial, and in their publicity about the case and arguments on appeal (discussed in chapter 5), IFI's leadership and lawyers angrily resisted the characterization of IFI as being properly legally denominated "evangelical." To use evangelical in a legal context results, they say, in an unconstitutional fixing of religious boundaries, an effective "establishment" of religion by government. IFI staff members repeatedly described IFI's Christian theology at trial as "mainstream," "core," or "basic," meaning, apparently, Christianity with no sectarian peculiarities, a universal, "naturalized" Christianity that can be recognized and understood by an American court without expert assistance. Indeed, IFI charged that Judge Pratt unconstitutionally declared IFI to be legally evangelical, when, relying on my testimony, he characterized PFM and IFI as "evangelical in nature."[1]

This deliberately ambiguous discursive practice, claiming an exclusive Christian identity in some contexts and blurring that identity in others, is not uncommon for groups that must appeal to both their own constituencies and a larger public in a pluralistic society, and it has a respectable theological history and justification. Like many other Christian groups, IFI lays claim to a universalist Christianity that transcends denominations. Such a universalist Christianity has offered itself as a source of morality, as a civilizing presence, since the early days of the republic, a source and presence thought to be necessary in the new classless and religiously disestablished democratic society that is America. Viewed historically and sociologically, however, in the context of a multitude of "Christian" phenomena, the Christianity of IFI appears a distinctive and specific form of Christianity.

Evangelical Christianity today combines elements of confessional Protestantisms (Calvinist and Lutheran); pietism of the continental, holiness, and Wesleyan varieties; Pentecostalism; charismatic Christianity; and fundamentalism. This is an eclectic, sometimes oddly inclusive and often opportunistic amalgam of historically disparate theological traditions and religious practices. Each has made distinctive bargains with modernity and is often expressed within contemporary evangelical culture in a highly contemporary and streamlined corporatist and consumerist mode. Driven by a demanding and increasingly well-informed lay constituency, evangelical Christianity is a lively and rapidly changing form of religion. To regard the evangelicalism of PFM and IFI as "fundamentalist," in a premodern or even anti-modern mode, is misleading and inacurrate, as many have noted.[2]

IFI's claim to universality, and its appropriation and accommodation of contemporary culture, can also be understood as a kind of secularism, a "formation of the secular," in Talal Asad's words,[3] particularly given IFI's resistance to being denominated as "religious." It is secular in the way that we are all secular in the modern period, living as we do in a pluralistic world governed by the rule of law. In chapter 4 I consider IFI's universality as part of a wider discussion of the phenomenology of religion and the secular today. In this chapter I discuss Prison Fellowship within the context of contemporary U.S. evangelical culture.

Prison Fellowship Ministries

Prison Fellowship Ministries, InnerChange Freedom Initiative, and other PFM corporate names and slogans are now registered trademarks. PFM and IFI are also incorporated as §501(c)(3) organizations under the provisions of the Internal Revenue Code. Prison Fellowship Ministries started simply, however.[4] It began with a series of seminars held in Washington, D.C., during 1975, seminars designed "to train Christian inmates in living the Christian life."[5] As described in *Life Sentence*, Colson's emotional account of his gradual discovery of his religious calling and of the founding of PFM, selected prisoners were initially brought to Washington, D.C., in groups for an experimental, intensive, week-long program of evangelization. The first seminars were made possible through the intervention of Senator Harold Hughes, Democrat of Iowa, and Norman Carlson, then director of the Federal Bureau of Prisons. The seminars were modeled on a form of Christian living then practiced by a group of American business and political leaders in Washington known as The Fellowship.

Colson tells of being haunted after his release by his memories of prison and of the men he met there—some with whom he had engaged in prayer and Bible study and others who were uninterested in such pursuits—and of his first intuitions about how he might help these men:

> It began like any Saturday morning. . . . Then suddenly startled, I stared back at my reflection. A series of pictures flashed across my mind. Men in prison gray moving about. Classes. Discussions. Prayers.
>
> "Of course, of course," I whispered as if in response to obvious commands. "Take the prisoners out, teach them, return them to prisons to build Christian fellowships. Spread these fellowships through every penitentiary in America.". . .
>
> Then I realized something else: I had never thought of anything like this before. It was not my idea, but something I was reacting to . . .
>
> Was it of God?[6]

Was it "of God"? Colson called his friend and prayer partner, Senator Harold Hughes. "'It's of God, no doubt about it,' [Hughes] declared."[7] Hughes was then retired from the Senate. He was active in Alcoholics Anonymous and other addiction programs. Like Colson, he understood his own life history in evangelical Christian terms. A former Democratic senator, Hughes was a pacifist and a bitter critic of the Vietnam War. He was also a recovering alcoholic and was very active in Christian circles in Washington when he met Colson.[8] Several weeks later, after considering with Colson various ways of implementing his vision, Hughes arranged an appointment for the two of them with Norman Carlson.

Colson described the meeting and Carlson's reaction to their plan in *Life Sentence.* " 'Mr. Carlson,' " Colson concluded his presentation to the director, " 'the prisons—your prisons—aren't helping these men. Everybody there, even the best of your staff, are looked upon as cops. But one Person can make a difference: Jesus Christ. His love and power to remake lives is the answer. He will heal and reconcile. I know it. I saw it happen. Give us a chance to prove it.' "[9] He then described Carlson's response:

> Carlson's face remained enigmatic. "Let me ask you a question. A few weeks ago my wife and I were at Terminal Island Prison in Southern California. On Sunday we went to chapel. At one point in the service the chaplain asked the inmates to join in with spontaneous prayers. In the back . . . a man prayed for my wife and me. I was surprised that he did that." . . .
>
> "Well, Mr. Carlson, he's a Christian," I finally said. "We're taught to pray for those in authority. I did for the warden at Maxwell."
>
> "I know that," Carlson replied, his eyes bright with emotion. . . . "But I'm the one keeping him in prison."
>
> It was an electric moment. "Mr. Carlson," I said, "that man prayed for you because he loves you."[10]

Colson's faith in Christian love conveyed from individual to individual, as an antidote to a life of crime, is evident throughout his writings and in the work of Prison Fellowship. Also evident is his confidence in established authorities.

Colson is not atypical of American evangelical Christians in his approach to social problems. In a book concerning persistent divisions between black and white evangelicals, sociologists Michael Emerson and Christian Smith summarize their interviews with lay evangelicals about social problems and their solutions. Emerson and Smith contrast structural analyses by social scientists with the evangelical language of conversion:

> Given that issues of inequality, systematic injustice and group conflict are not part of their assessment, we did not expect to hear these addressed as a part of the solution. And we rarely did. What we did hear from many was what others have called the "miracle motif." The miracle motif is the theologically rooted idea that as more individuals become Christians, social and personal problems will be solved automatically. What is the solution to violent crime? Convert people to Christianity because Christians do not commit violent crimes. . . . Derived in part from the cultural tools of freewill accountable individualism and relationalism, the miracle motif holds . . . that society is im-

proved by improving individuals.[11]

Emerson and Smith characterize the evangelical approach to social problems, black and white,[12] as an approach that focuses on God's intervention in individual lives rather than as based on systemic analysis of issues, whether the issues are related to crime or to the results of racial inequality. Likewise, Colson and Prison Fellowship see change as happening through individual changes of heart.

After his meeting with Colson and Hughes, Carlson issued an order to the federal prison management; Colson and Hughes were to be allowed to select prisoners to take to Washington for "training in Christian living." Notably, given that thirty years later this embryonic program was to take control of an entire wing of an Iowa prison, Normal Carlson grew up in Iowa. Iowa was also Harold Hughes's home state, where he had been governor from 1963 to 1968. These early personal connections were significant twenty-five years later when IFI came to Iowa.

Colson and his supporters were pleased with the success of the first seminars in Washington. Once officially established, Prison Fellowship's initial mission was to extend and more firmly institutionalize these experimental sessions through the development of regular, short-term Bible-study classes for prisoners and ex-offenders to be offered on a voluntary basis to various prisons around the country. In 1977, at Carlson's request, a program was added to supply PFM-trained chaplains to federal prisons.[13] Over the ensuing thirty years, Prison Fellowship has expanded and diversified, adding other programs for prisoners and their families, developing a system of regional directors, and internationalizing its operations.[14] Colson himself has also engaged in much personal advocacy and intervention on behalf of prisoners. Until 1997, though, notwithstanding PFM's influence and access in both state and federal correctional operations, its programs were mostly formally external to the actual operation of prisons.

Beginning in 1997, however, and inspired in part by a religiously based prison program in a Brazilian prison,[15] PFM undertook, at the then governor George W. Bush's invitation, to develop for the first time in a modern U.S. prison an extended, residential, comprehensive faith-based in-prison pre-release prison rehabilitation program, InnerChange Freedom Initiative. This program would address and integrate the lives of a segregated select group of prisoners within a separate Bible-based, Christ-centered curriculum—24/7, as they like to say. During the opening ceremony of the Texas unit, Governor Bush was photographed singing "Amazing Grace" with the prisoners.[16] That new program, IFI, was first implemented at the Texas state prison in Houston but has subsequently been adopted by several other states,[17] including Iowa.

Over the last thirty years Charles Colson and PFM have also, partly through the opportunity offered by the administration of a highly successful enterprise, increasingly addressed an audience beyond the prison. In its 2006–2007 *Annual Report*, Prison Fellowship unveiled a new vision and a new name, a vision expressing its mission beyond the prison and a name that it compared explicitly to a commercial brand. In the report's "Letter from the President," the second president of Prison Fellowship and Colson's successor, Mark Earley,[18] outlines this vision and name change. "Where you have usually seen the words Prison Fellowship, you will now see PFM." Earley explains:

> As Chuck Colson moved into his seventies, we had to think more strategically about our post-founder stage of ministry. . . . [O]ver the years, two distinct but entwined threads had developed in Prison Fellowship. The first, of course, was our outreach to prisoners. . . . The second was our worldview teaching ministry, initiated when Chuck realized that Christian truth must be brought not only into the prisons but also into our culture, helping transform the distorted messages and values of a spreading self-centered relativism. . . . We have chosen PFM as the "umbrella" over our two areas of ministry. . . . Kentucky Fried Chicken became KFC as its menu grew. The American Association of Retired People officially changed its name to AARP. . . . [W]hat we have always been about . . . is the *transformation of lives* through Jesus Christ. Whether we are talking about the transformation of prisoners into law-abiding, committed disciples of Christ . . . or the transformation of believers into powerful defenders of God's truth in their spheres of influence.[19] (emphasis in original)

What began as a project to transform prisoners has become a mission to transform everyone. The story is one of almost continuous growth. Like the multinational corporations it aims to emulate, PFM's vision is catholic as to product and therefore its name is opaque as to content.

PFM comes by this passion for presenting an ambiguous identity honestly. When Prison Fellowship began its work in 1976, it was under the protection of a quiet, highly disciplined, and powerful organization in Washington variously known as The Fellowship or The Family, a then forty-year-old association of Christian politicians and businessmen with a distinctive extra-church vision of Christian political influence. The Family was founded in Seattle in 1935 by Abraham Vereide, a Norwegian-born Methodist preacher and inventor of the prayer breakfast.[20] Believing that the economic depression in the United States was the result of moral and spiritual decline at the top, Vereide made it his mission to reach out to the rich and powerful. As his biographer, Norman Grubb, put it: "Concern for the 'down and out' is fairly common. Their need is obvious.

Concern for the 'up and out' is more rare. . . . True leadership demands true men. True men are God's men."[21]

Vereide first sought to rid Oregon politics of materialism and socialism, and then, with his move to Washington in the early 1940s, he sought to do the same for national politics, and finally to cleanse the world of communism. All through the convening of powerful men at prayer breakfasts. Once in Washington, Vereide established a retreat house as headquarters for these efforts. Then known as International Christian Leadership (ICL), during the 1950s Vereide and the ICL played a role in the U.S. government's anticommunist activities.[22] Vereide's first national prayer breakfast, held in January 1942 and patterned on the many prayer breakfasts Vereide had organized for business executives and leading politicians across the country, was on February 5, 1953, in the Mayflower Hotel. President Dwight D. Eisenhower, recently inaugurated, was present. Now known as The Fellowship, the organization's most visible activity today is its sponsorship of the ongoing annual National Prayer Breakfast.

But today's relatively inclusive National Prayer Breakfast is often described as the Fellowship's most modest and ecumenical activity. Its longer-term, more religiously sectarian goal is to bring the world to conformity with Christ, as Vereide had outlined in 1946. Vereide described his vision:

> One world in active cooperation in commerce, science, labor and education should be one world in spiritual unity and moral convictions. *There is only one Book for the whole world—the Bible.* There is one Personality for all ages, all races and all people, the only One in whose life there is no discrepancy, in whose character there is no flaw, demanding universal obedience because of who he is. . . . He is Jesus, the Christ.[23] (emphasis added)

Vereide's vision continues to guide the work of The Fellowship, now based in their retreat houses in the Washington, D.C., area, and the organization continues to boast substantial national and international influence. (There is much fevered recent journalism about this group, describing its allegedly obsessive secrecy and imperialist politics.)[24]

As Colson has repeatedly described in his numerous publications, it was through The Fellowship that he became a Christian.[25] Colson recounts in his first book, *Born Again*,[26] that he experienced a religious conversion during the investigation into the Watergate scandal as the result of reading C. S. Lewis's apologetic work *Mere Christianity*,[27] given to him by his client Tom Phillips, a member of The Fellowship and then president of international defense contractor Raytheon Industries.[28] After his conviction, disbarment, and six-month imprisonment, Colson announced that he had seen through the hollowness of his previous life and decided to spend his life ministering to the inmates of U.S. prisons.[29]

Colson is now a much-fêted evangelist, and PFM is the world's largest Christian prison ministry. Among many awards and honorary doctorates, Colson was the 1993 recipient of the Templeton Prize for Progress Toward Research or Discoveries about Spiritual Realities, a prize then worth $1 million. (The 2007 recipient of the award was the philosopher Charles Taylor.)[30] Colson donated the money to Prison Fellowship. The success and current public profile of PFM offers a glimpse into a little understood and curiously amorphous, but influential, U.S. subculture. The names of the men who nurtured and taught Colson during his evangelical Christian conversion read, for those in the know, like a who's who of the most powerful figures in a certain segment of U.S. evangelical Christianity. These individuals—mostly men and a few women—have always had considerable access to politicians and diplomats, and they are well financed. They do not, of course, speak for all evangelicals, even all evangelicals who work for PFM. No one does.[31]

In 1975, Raytheon president Tom Phillips sent Colson to Douglas Coe,[32] then spiritual leader of The Fellowship. Douglas Coe had come to the group from The Navigators, a successful international evangelical college ministry. Coe introduced Colson to Senators Mark Hatfield, Frank Carlson, and Harold Hughes, and Congressman Albert Quie, and many others, all members of The Fellowship and self-described "brothers in Christ."[33] Colson writes, "There was, I discovered to my astonishment, a veritable underground of Christ's men all through the government."[34] Colson was also tutored by evangelical giants Billy Graham, Francis Schaeffer, Carl Henry, and James Dobson.[35] These men and their predecessors have formed a network of business leaders, politicians, pastors, and seminary professors since the 1930s, when The Family, along with other evangelical organizations, was founded to fight socialism. Although PFM has grown and diversified over the years, it has lived very much under the patronage of The Fellowship, as its name indicates, and the religious rhetoric of its programs in many ways reflects the religious politics of that leadership.

The Fellowship is not exclusively conservative, in U.S. political terms. Reflecting the often unexpected conjunction of Christianity and politics in the United States, Democrats as well as Republicans, liberals as well as conservatives, are active in The Fellowship.[36] (Hillary Clinton, for example, is reportedly a frequent participant in their prayer breakfasts.[37]) Harold Hughes, governor and senator from Iowa,[38] a liberal Democrat of almost saintly reputation who quit politics in 1975 to devote his life to Christian good works, was a stalwart of The Fellowship. Hughes, a lay

Methodist reader, was a member of the small prayer group that Colson was invited to join. In his autobiography, *The Man from Ida Grove*,[39] Hughes describes Vereide's vision for The Fellowship:

> Vereide had come to the United States from Norway as a young minister, settled in Seattle in 1935 where he worked for the poor and helped start Goodwill Industries. Seeing the need for a genuine religious revival throughout the nation, he began encouraging local Seattle businessmen to gather together for prayer. . . . [T]he prayer breakfasts began in Washington after Congress convened in January 1942 following Pearl Harbor.[40]

Hughes also describes his own prayer group: "Doug Coe; Al Quie, Republican congressman from Minnesota, a six-foot-two outdoorsman who wore western boots; Graham Purcell, a tall, silver-haired former Democratic congressman from Texas; and me. When we'd first met, we'd politely shake hands. After we came to know and trust each other, the handshakes became bear hugs." Hughes concludes: "If I had known that this fellowship would lead to my embracing one of the most ruthless, hateful men on Capitol Hill, I would have become physically sick."[41] That man was Charles Colson.

Like Colson's books, Hughes's account of his life is laced with references to the Bible and to his training in reading the work of God in his life. Toward the end of the book, he describes his reluctant first meeting with Colson, emphasizing his dislike of Phillips: "Colson himself seemed hale and hearty, which somehow bothered me. The man who supposedly had led him to Christ was Tom Phillips, president of the Raytheon Corporation in Massachusetts. Raytheon was one of the largest manufacturers of weapons in international warfare." Hughes was a pacifist. "Yet *I knew that I had to respect a man's relationship with God, whether or not we agreed on worldly problems*. It was up to God, not me, to choose his disciples. . . . 'Chuck,' I said, leaning forward, 'tell me about your encounter with Jesus Christ' "[42] (emphasis added). Having heard Colson tell his account of his conversion, Hughes commented in his memoir:

> I sat there feeling the presence of the Holy Spirit in the room. My God, I thought, it really happened. I didn't have to ask the hard questions. It didn't make any difference anymore. I knew in my heart he had been forgiven through the blood of Jesus Christ and the Holy Spirit, just as I had been forgiven. . . . Brother, I said, my voice choking, "obviously you've had a confrontation with Jesus Christ and the Holy Spirit and *I for one will stand with you, walk with you and be with you wherever God takes us for the rest of our lives*."[43] (emphasis added)

Hughes, with the rest of the prayer group which Colson was invited to join, later offered to go to jail for him. Colson writes often of his overwhelming gratitude for the friendship of these men.[44]

Notwithstanding the enormous gulf separating the politics of Charles Colson from those of Harold Hughes, Hughes's account of his life and his commitments reflect similar understandings of what it means to be a Christian and the nature of Christian public life. The last chapter of Hughes's book tells of a meeting arranged by The Fellowship with a group of UN ambassadors in the early 1970s, including Soviet ambassador Yakov Malik: "We met Dick Hightower there. In a corner of the room, the four of us got on our knees. 'It's your luncheon Lord, not ours.' "[45] Hughes then tells of a conversation between himself and Malik. Malik asked him why he had retired from the Senate. The conversation continued:

> "Well, Mr. Ambassador," I began. "I'm glad to answer that question. But I must tell you that it causes me to testify to my faith in Jesus Christ and my trust in God Almighty."
>
> "Well, Senator," he demurred, his eyes crinkling in Slavic humor, "you know I don't believe those Hebrew myths."
>
> "Mr. Ambassador, perhaps you don't believe the Bible is inspired by God, but I do. And I believe that its truth will eventually bring about the brotherhood of man if we learn to live by it."

Malik answered Hughes: "You know, Senator, I'm a Marxist-Leninist. I believe that Communism will bring about the brotherhood of man."[46] Concluding his account of their Cold War interchange, Hughes quotes his own witnessing to Malik concerning his Christian calling:

> I want to tell you to Whom I'm giving my life. It's to Jesus Christ and I want to make a clear distinction between him and Christianity. I found out long ago that the term "Christian" turns off more people in the world that it turns on . . . My belief in Christ has led me to reject war as an answer to problems. I don't believe peace on earth will come by negotiation or treaties, alliances or balances of power. I think that peace will come when Christ enters the hearts of men so they can love one another.[47]

And yet, despite his many opportunities for Christian political leadership, Hughes withdrew from public life to devote himself privately to helping those with addictions—to the immense regret of his many admirers who hoped he would run for president.[48]

Colson told the story of his own conversion in his first book, *Born Again*, and one sees there the themes that continue to govern his writings and the programs that his vision has engendered: his continual reminders to his readers of his alliance with powerful men, a dream of Christian hegemony, a highly dualistic view of a world threatened by modern, secular, relativistic humanism, an identification of himself with the country, a compressed and revisionist approach to history, and a personal approach to the religious life. Reflecting on his experience of the Watergate scandal, and echoing the classic jeremiad of American Protestantism, Colson writes in *Born Again* of the country's crisis during Watergate and of his sense of his own Christian mission:

> Could there be a purpose to all that had happened to me? . . . The nation was in darkness; there was anger, bitterness, and disillusionment across the land. While my inclination was to think in terms of grandiose reforms, God seemed to be saying that *the renewal of the national spirit can begin with each person*—with the renewal of the individual spirit.[49]
>
> How magnificently has God honored the covenant of our forefathers. *How richly has He blessed our nation.* So deep are our religious roots, but so far we have strayed . . . Watergate has raised so many questions. Can humanism ever be the answer for our society? There is an almost sanctified notion that man can do anything if he puts his will to it. . . . And my most sincere and humble prayer now in this time of judgment is for a revival of the flagging national spirit. It can come in only one way—as each of us bows in submission to Him and as the Almighty leads us from darkness into light—so that once again we might stand together, truly *one nation under God.*[50] (emphasis added)

The United States, and the world, are to be rescued from darkness, from secular humanism, by individual changes of heart, accomplished through a reaching out from man to man in Christian love.

Colson saw meaning in his own suffering and in the unflagging support of his new "brothers" in The Fellowship, and in *Born Again* he repeatedly speaks of his own sense of mission: "In the days that followed, men whom I hardly knew did not hesitate to ally themselves with me, each with the same message spoken in a dozen ways: 'As brothers in Christ we stand together.' "[51] And of his opposition to the "unbelievers": "Doug Coe once explained that Satan doesn't waste time on those unbelievers who follow the world's ways; in time they drift into his fold without much persuasion. But those who choose Jesus Christ are Satan's chief enemy."[52] Colson wrote that, at the time of his sentencing, the support of his prayer group convinced him that Christ's love was real:

> Doug Coe sent me a handwritten note. All the brothers [the powerful members of his Bible study support group] would volunteer to serve my sentence. . . . It was almost more than I imagined possible, this

> love of one man for another. Christ's love. . . . It was that night in the quiet of my room that I made the total surrender. . . . "Lord, if this is what it is all about," I said, "then I thank You. *I praise You for leaving me in prison, for letting them take away my license to practice law—even for my son being arrested.* I praise You for giving me your love through these men, for being God, for just letting me walk with Jesus."[53] (emphasis added)

Colson saw his own vicissitudes—even his son's suffering—as a felicitous part of God's plan for his own redemption. As Colson's writings demonstrate, the effort to regenerate the world from the top down is accomplished by reaching out from person to person at key moments, and reading those moments as God's action in the world. It is also how the apologetic is accomplished—not through a philosophical argument for the rationality of belief—but through a demonstration of the accumulated evidence of such stories.

A significant factor in understanding PFM and its mission today is that there continues to be a close fit between the political theology and anthropology of The Fellowship and PFM. IFI's pedagogical program is a recognizable product of The Fellowship's religious culture, which continues to view the present as a time of crisis, although the war on terror and the clash of civilizations have succeeded communism and Watergate as the focus of the crisis. Christianity is understood to be a highly personal movement of like-minded individuals, mostly men, and its ultimate goal is the submission of the world to Christ. The mission is to be accomplished through quiet work in the corridors of power, and elsewhere, work denominated as God's work. The enemies are humanism, secularism, and moral relativism—all characterized as the works of "Satan".[54] Representatives of the U.S. government are understood to be key domestic and international players in this transformation.

Neither The Fellowship nor PFM represent all evangelical Christians, but both organizations and their leaders are influential within the larger evangelical culture. There is resistance among evangelicals, as there is among most Americans, to viewing prison work as a priority. Law-and-order populism is not a partisan phenomenon. The ambivalence, or worse, of many Christian conservatives *and* liberals about acknowledging the humanity of those arrested for crimes sets Colson's commitment apart and causes many who would otherwise differ with him to honor it. But Colson's approach to prison work is very much like the rest of The Fellowship's other work: highly personal. Training for the various missions is accomplished one person at a time, man to man, through calling for an admission of sin and the acceptance of Jesus, and then living one's life in conformity to biblical standards. Individual evangelists and their teachings are held up as exemplars for Christian living.

The IFI Web site explicitly uses Colson's own life and extensive writings as the pattern for Christian living. Even Colson's reading of the Bible is offered as authoritative. For example, in 2006 the Web site read:

> A key concept in Chuck Colson's writings is that you must be born again. As inmates are transformed by the power of God, they learn to turn from a sinful past, recognizing that "*sin is not simply the wrong we do our neighbor when we cheat him, or the wrong we do ourselves when we abuse our bodies, Sin, all sin, is a root rebellion and offense against God.*"[55] Admitting our sinfulness and asking God's forgiveness is the first step. "*We have the capacity to change anything about our lives . . . but we cannot change our own sinful nature*" (p. 144). Repentance is a change of mind and heart away from sin and toward God.
>
> Focus on the Bible is essential in this step. Colson learned this process while he was in prison. "*For it was the Bible that caused me to hunger for righteousness and seek holiness; and it is the Bible that continues to challenge my life today. That is radical stuff. It is irresistibly convicting. It is the power of God's Word and it is, all by itself, life-changing*" (p. 39).
>
> "*Christianity must evoke from the believer the same response it drew from the first disciples: a passionate desire to obey God, a willingly entered-into discipline. That is the beginning of true discipleship. That is the beginning of loving God*" (p. 38).
>
> Repentance and reconciliation are an ongoing state of mind and do not simply exist in one moment of time. IFI emphasizes this realization, and fosters humility and a teachable attitude that, in turn, creates opportunities for prisoners to break free from old habits. They learn new life skills, rooted in Biblical principles and God turns their lives around. "*Repentance is an inescapable consequence of regeneration, an indispensable part of the conversion process that takes place under the convicting power of the Holy Spirit. But repentance is also a continuing state of mind. We are warned, for example, to repent before partaking of communion. Also, believers prove their repentance by their deeds. Without a continuing repentant attitude—a persistent desire to turn from our own nature and seek God's nature—Christian growth is impossible. Loving God is impossible*" (p. 109).[56] (emphasis in original)

Support for the desire to be born again is gained through Bible study, Christian fellowship, and following the example of successful men. Evidence of God's work is sought and revealed in the highly personal, careful, and carefully edited recounting of individual acts that confirm God's interest in our lives—in spite of our status as sinners—and our capacity to understand that interest.

Colson's writings form a part of a larger and longer context, however, beyond that of prison ministry and Washington Christian fellowship, as PFM president Mark Earley advertised in his letter announcing the previously noted name change. In 1999 Colson, with co-author Nancy Pearcey, published a lengthy comprehensive guide to contemporary life titled *How Now Shall We Live?*—a book that diagnoses the ills of contemporary society and proposes a cure.[57] According to the dust jacket testimonials,

> [The book is] a radical challenge to the church and to all Christians to go beyond salvation—to understand biblical faith as an entire worldview, a perspective on all life. . . . In *How Now Shall We Live?* Chuck Colson and Nancy Pearcey show that the great spiritual battle today is a cosmic struggle between competing worldviews. . . . [T]hey demonstrate:
>
> - How to expose the false views and values of modern culture
> - How to live a more fulfilling and satisfying life in line with the way god created us to live
> - How to be more effective in evangelism by understanding how nonbelievers think
> - How to contend for the faith in a winsome way in every walk of life
> - How to build a society that reflects biblical principles

How Now Shall We Live? is densely sprinkled with personal anecdotes illustrating the correct way to understand the evidence of God's working in the world, identifying the culprits from Emerson to Stalin, and prescribing the solution.

Significantly, the title of Colson and Pearcey's book is a direct reference to an influential apologetic work published in 1976 by Francis A. Schaeffer, a popular mid-century American evangelist who established a Swiss retreat house to minister to the modern world.[58] Schaeffer's own book, *How Should We Then Live?*[59] is subtitled *The Rise and Decline of Western Thought and Culture* and was accompanied by the release of a video series with the same title.[60] Written during the Cold War, Schaeffer's book and video series are whirlwind tours through Western philosophy and history,[61] delineating where things went wrong. Humanism, or the autonomy of man, is understood to be the result of a corruption of biblical thinking and the direct effect of Thomas Aquinas's division between nature and grace.[62] The central problem for Schaeffer in the 1960s, and for Colson and Pearcey at the beginning of the twenty-first century, is said by them to be the secular denial of absolute truth. The Bible offers absolute truth about everything. (Pearcey was a disciple of Schaeffer's and now works for a number of Colson's media outlets.) Like Schaeffer, Colson and Pearcey aim to change individual minds—believing that is how best to change the world.[63]

One of IFI's fund-raising brochures, "A Prison Like No Other," exhorts churchgoers, in Colson's words, that, "The InnerChange Freedom Initiative(TM) is our chance to demonstrate, in a way secular people will never be able to doubt, that Christ changes lives, and that changing prisoners from the inside out is the *only* crime-prevention program that really works." The brochure continues: "These men have tried things their way. Now they're willing to try *God's* way. We are calling upon the Church to assist us in this effort. Please prayerfully consider how you might become involved in this redeeming ministry."[64] Convincing "secular people" is the challenge. The proof of the work Christ does is to be found in tackling one of the most difficult social problems facing Americans. *Then*, Colson insists, "they" will have to believe the Christians.

PFM, Colson, and Pearcey are purveying what they call a "worldview." (The term is also used as an adjective, as in a "worldview ministry.") Secular people are spoken of as lacking a worldview. A major segment of PFM's Web site in 2007 was titled "Worldview: A Christian Perspective on Today's News and Culture."[65] One of the PFM ministries listed in this section was BreakPoint, described as follows:

> BreakPoint is the worldview ministry of PFM. Our mission is to seek the transformation of believers as they apply biblical thinking to all of life, enabling them to transform their communities through the grace and truth of Jesus Christ. BreakPoint provides a Christian perspective on today's news and trends via radio, interactive media, and print.
>
> Chuck Colson's daily BreakPoint commentary airs each weekday on more than one thousand outlets with an estimated listening audience of one million people. The BreakPoint website and *BreakPoint WorldView Magazine* feature Colson's commentaries as well as feature articles by other established and up-and-coming writers to equip readers with a biblical perspective on a variety of issues and topics.
>
> Teaching products such as *Rewired* and *Wide Angle* assist believers in teaching others to understand and apply the truths of Scripture in everyday life. The Centurions Program is an intensive biblical studies program that equips Christians to engage their church, community and culture with biblical truth.[66]

To have a worldview implies that one's personality is oriented toward the Bible.[67]

"Worldview" may seem, in common parlance, to be a fuzzy, if benign, catch-all category, like the popular words "paradigm" or "culture." In this sense, worldview suggests a relative multiplicity and tolerant multiculturalism. It suggests that everyone has one and that all worldviews should be respected as being mostly of equal value or at least as deserving of a certain minimal respect.[68] "Worldview" was promoted by comparative religionist Ninian Smart, for example, in his widely used world religions textbooks, as a useful cross-cultural category for comparing religions. For Smart, "worldview analysis" is a way of studying religion, cross-culturally and non-confessionally. Smart believed that all cultures, all people, have a worldview.[69]

"Worldview," for evangelical Christians, is employed in a polemical manner to set themselves apart from those who live without the unity and integrity that only Christianity can provide. To have a worldview is to claim a unified, integrated explanation for human existence. In this sense, it is to some extent continuous with other politically conservative organic notions, including nationalism, intégrisme, tradition, and so on, although it is on the individualist and cognitive end of this spectrum, implying that the unity is provided by the viewer rather than inhering in the hermeneutical object itself. The capacity to view life as a whole is deemed to be characteristic of religious people generally, but particularly of Christians. It is a capacity that stabilizes morality.

The intellectual genealogy of "worldview," in contemporary English usage, is complex and sometimes murky. Its etymology suggests a lineage beginning in an English translation of *Weltanschauung*, a term used in German idealist thought and variously employed by post-Kantian philosophers. Sigmund Freud understood the desire for possession of such a unified worldview as the product of a wish for security, a dangerous wish characteristically connected to religion.[70] U.S. evangelical historians today trace what they call "worldview thinking" most immediately from twentieth-century Scottish Presbyterian and Dutch Reformed theologians who sought to establish Christianity as a comprehensive cognitive reality opposed to what they understood to be dangerous forms of European secularism.[71] Colson and Pearcey are updating Dutch Calvinist, early-twentieth-century-European concerns and Schaeffer's Cold War critique for the twenty-first-century American. Without Christ, humankind's only choice is nihilism and despair.

Although the analysis is accomplished by neo-Calvinist leaders through a reading of philosophy, preventing nihilism and despair is understood to be very practical and down to earth. The achievement of a new unity—an integrated life founded in a Christian worldview—is a daily task at the level of the individual. Both Schaeffer and Colson reject any separation of the religious from daily life, and any privatization of religion. Whereas some evangelicals are moving toward the inclusion of other kinds of Christians, as well as non-Christians, in their projects of humanitarian outreach, Colson leads a community that formally rejects the possibility that any other religious tradition truly represents God's will, and he believes that salvation is impossible outside of the born-again experience.[72]

The authority of evangelical leaders is always being undermined by their received theology, which teaches ordinary evangelicals to be suspicious of institutionalized religious authority, and instead to respect their own reading of the Bible and their own experience of God, including their experience of religious difference. That experience in the United States includes a more general belief among Americans, finding its source in a reading of the Constitution, among other places, in the cardinal importance of voluntarism and individual choice in religious matters. One can see the influence of both the discipline of the Schaefferian/Colsonian integrated worldview and the tolerance of evangelical Christian pragmatism, sometimes in tandem and sometimes in tension, in IFI's self-explanation and in its daily operation.

U.S. Evangelicalism

Much evidence today indicates that most evangelicals in the United States, like most Americans, tolerate far more contradiction in their lives than the expressed theology of their leaders would suggest; they simultaneously hold a belief in the exclusiveness of the Christian message as well as a wide tolerance and even admiration for other religious and nonreligious ways of life. The sociologist Christian Smith reports, based on survey data of conservative Christians, that "most evangelicals do not . . . want Christianity to be America's established religion—much less want America to be a formal Christian state. They fully believe in the American system of liberal representative democracy."[73] Speaking for his team of investigators, Smith adds that, comparing self-described conservative Christians with other Americans, "we find no evidence suggesting that conservative Protestants feel significantly greater distance from or prejudice against people of other religions or races."[74]

How does the version of Christianity embodied in the ministries of PFM and IFI, as defined and articulated by a resurgent neo-Calvinism and by rank-and-file conservative Christians, fit into a broader history of American Protestantism? IFI repeatedly claims to teach a generic, mainstream form of Christianity that is truly universal. But religious historians would describe what they teach and how they teach it, as I testified at the trial, as exhibiting the characteristics of a specific variety of Christianity that is typically American but that does not encompass all forms of American Christianity. Indeed, a recurrent issue in American legal history is whether PFM, IFI, and other American evangelical Christian formations are in some sense generically Christian, or even at their most expansive, simply generically nonsecular, or whether they, like other Christian formations of the past two millennia, should be understood to be, in the words of the Supreme Court, a "sectarian" form of Christianity.

These three possibilities have structured the development of First Amendment interpretation. In other words, the nature of American evangelical Christianity was an issue during the Iowa trial partly because of the language of Supreme Court opinions interpreting the religion clauses of the First Amendment, language that both forms and is formed by American religious culture, as well as by the background history of the jurisprudence of the First Amendment.[75] Those decisions, and the evidentiary challenges that they raise, are discussed in chapter 5. Here I consider how one might describe the particularities of U.S. evangelical Christianity.

The 1997 move for PFM from the administration of short-term Bible studies and various supplemental programs—including the Sycamore Tree Project, a restorative justice program, and a Christmas gift mission to prisoners' kids called Angel Tree—to the establishment of an ambitious and comprehensive holistic Christian in-prison community within, and in cooperation with, a government institution, cannot help but seem a very significant step, particularly in retrospect. PFM was, by then, a well-respected and established Christian ministry to prisoners, but such a move was fraught with historic resonances for American Protestant churches. Bible studies and other religiously based programs that outside volunteers conduct, apart from the prison's administration and programs, exemplify the outreach work of a church that is classically separatist in its relationship to the state; IFI, however, has been substantially funded and assisted by government and has aspired to work within, and to discipline—even to replace—the entire prison culture. In its most expansive mode, PFM and other evangelical para-church organizations today sometimes appear determined to change the entire world culture in explicit partnership with the state. This close cooperation can look like classic establishment, and in today's politics it echoes other projects for the resacralization of government.

There is a long history to the question of whether Christians should see themselves as small communities of believers living exemplary lives apart from the world, or as insiders actively engaged in, and inevitably compromised by, the wider culture, or somewhere in-between. The two polarized modes of church-state relations were defined by Max Weber and Ernst Troeltsch as the sect and the church—a church discontinuous with a particularly political community and a church continuous with such a community. Each model reflects and implies its own theo-political solution to religious pluralism and has its roots in the long history of religion and politics in Europe. In the United States those models were modified through first, the reinvention of European models of church-state arrangements, beginning with the settlement of the first European colonies, and then, through the particular form that legal disestablishment and democracy have taken in the United States. Religious *and* political authority reside in the people, and jealously so.

How to be at once a Christian or moral society—the two have mostly been seen as synonymous—while at the same time not abridge religious freedom or have the state co-opt religion has been a perennial issue for Americans ever since the nation's inception. Periods of religious quiescence have alternated with periods of public awakening in response to social instability, wars, immigration, and foreign ideologies. This four-century-old American Christian story has been complicated by the increasing—or perhaps only increasingly acknowledged—diversity in the U.S. religious community.

U.S. religious historians debate how to characterize the religious multiplicity of the colonial and early republican periods, before the substantial Catholic, Jewish, and Asian immigration in the nineteenth century. Arguably Native and African-American religious practices and the remarkable diversity of Protestant churches made a national religious homogeneity impossible even before later immigration, however desirable homogeneity might have been to some—and fixed the practical limitations of national consensus in religious matters, narrowly understood. Diversity has almost always been accompanied, however, by the assumption that all shared in a common religious morality, "religious" here being broadly understood. Since the 1970s, a new tension has emerged in U.S. evangelical Christian culture with respect to this common culture, a tension reflected in the IFI program and how it is described by prisoners and by its own literature, as well as by the staff that testified at the trial.[76]

The initial impetus for conservative Christians' new public activism in the 1970s—sometimes labeled the "rise of the Religious Right"—is variously explained. Conflict between religious and secular cultures was largely absent from public life for fifty years after the Scopes trial, but some would say it was touched off again by decisions of the U.S. Supreme Court in the 1960s and 1970s. Often *Roe v. Wade*[77] or the school prayer decisions are mentioned as decisively awakening conservative Christians to the dangerous amorality and secularism of national culture. The historian Sarah Gordon argues that the school prayer decisions in the 1960s initially galvanized many conservative Christians, and that evidence for this can be found in the history of the activist organizations formed in the wake of those decisions.[78] But the salience of religion is not limited to what is denominated the Right. The Court's decision in the peyote case, *Employment Division v. Smith*,[79] provided an opportunity for the coalescence of a broadened pro-religion constituency, also arguably with longer roots. In the early 1990s, concern about secularization made new sense among the public beyond the traditional conservative religious base.

Other historians of Christian conservatism, wary of attributing too much to the popular reception of particular decisions of the Supreme Court, find broader social causes for the increased public presence of religion in the 1970s.[80] Mark Noll identifies three waves of evangelical political awakening beginning in the 1970s: first, a group responding to the abortion and school prayer decisions, led by Jerry Falwell and James Dobson, among others; second, increased public activism of the Pentecostal and charismatic wings of conservative Christianity, led by Pat Robertson and crystallized around his bid for the presidency; and, third, grass-roots mobilization through such groups as the Christian Coalition.[81]

A fourth wave may well be under way. The political scientist Michael Lienesch reviews various earlier Christian campaigns and describes the current resurgence. "In the 1980s," Lienesch recounts, "coinciding with the resurgent conservatism represented by Ronald Reagan, religious conservatives carried on a campaign that combined anticommunism, support for economic reforms, and a platform of social politics that included opposition to abortion, homosexuality, and pornography, along with support for school prayer." [82] Lienesch concludes with a description of the failure of the "moral majority" in the collapse of Pat Robertson's presidential campaign. However, the fifteen years since Lienesch's work in the early 1990s further reinforce the accuracy of the larger cyclical context of which Lienesch speaks. He describes a conservative Christian community divided within itself but also committed to the long-term development of a grass-roots base that would support significant social change. Lienesch foretold a further boost for contemporary conservative Christians that would come with the presidency of George W. Bush.

The American religious historian Joel Carpenter, citing Martin Marty in the conclusion to his history of American revivalism, speaks of evangelicalism's extraordinary adaptability:

> As Martin Marty once put it, "there has been a symbiosis between unfolding modernity and developing Evangelicalism." Indeed, Marty asserted, "Evangelicalism is the characteristic Protestant way of relating to modernity." . . . Evangelicals have responded readily to modernity's compartmentalization of life because theirs is an intensely personal religious experience. Modern society is often structured to favor voluntarism and choice-making . . . and evangelicals have responded with ag-

> gressive recruiting and creative institution-making while more established faiths have tended to take the church's place in life for granted. Because the modern temper is intense, impatient, and egalitarian . . . modern people commonly expect to have quick and personal access to knowledge and experience. *By offering authoritative religious knowledge and intense religious experience to "whosoever will" rather than reserving them for scholars and mystics, evangelicals have provided an accessible faith for millions of modern people, including at least a quarter of today's American adult population.*[83] (emphasis added)

All these characteristics—its intensely personal nature, its voluntarism, impatience, aggressiveness, creativity, and egalitarianism—make evangelicalism a formidable opponent for traditional separationists, secular and religious. They also make evangelicalism attractive to a wide variety of religiously identified people, not just those within the traditional conservative churches. One might say that separating evangelical Christianity from American politics is impossible as they are two of the engines of U.S. history and, in a sense, creatures of each other. PFM is a recognizable product of this religio-political culture, and it has evolved in response to changes in that culture.

"Evangelical," in the U.S. context today, is a term that scholars use to group together American Protestant groups with roots on the conservative side of the historic split in the American Protestant churches in the second half of the nineteenth century. Contemporary evangelicalism includes holiness, Pentecostal, pietist, and fundamentalist Christians. According to some scholars, for many years these groups had little more in common than the person and ministry of the well-known evangelist Billy Graham.[84] Today, however, unity is also provided by the huge expansion of an intentionally produced Christian subculture that bridges the differences between them. Christian pop music, Christian bookstores, Christian colleges and law schools, and Christian businesses together have reproduced something like the Roman Catholic ghetto of the nineteenth and early twentieth centuries in the United States, a ghetto that permits its constituents to live in a safe subculture. And, notwithstanding a range of ecclesiologies and theologies, certain key ideas and practices are held in common, including an encompassing biblicism, a low Christology, commitment to the significance of the born-again experience, and a persistent moralism.

The ongoing invention of a Christian subculture today exacerbates an inherent tension for evangelical Christians—whether or not to participate in the larger political and cultural orders. Some conservative evangelicals look to the creation of a complete alternative political and cultural order. Lienesch describes this politics:

> Arguing that the authority of existing public institutions will continue to be weakened by their own incompetence and overwhelmed by social crises, [the conservative theologian Gary North] makes the case for constructing private agencies to take their place. . . . Describing what he calls "a new theology of dominion," he calls for the creation of "alternative schools, orphanages, poorhouses, half-way homes, drug rehabilitation centers, and all the other institutions that bring the gospel of salvation and the message of healing through adherence to God's law." [85]

This alternative vision is maintained by a sometimes paranoid defensiveness that casts Christians as under attack and victims of a hostile secularism. Randall Balmer calls this tendency "the rhetoric of marginality."[86] Christian Smith reports of his survey of American evangelicals, "Most of the evangelicals we interviewed maintained that American Christians face widespread opposition and prejudice from the secular world. And, in our telephone survey, 92 percent of self-identified evangelicals agreed that 'Christian values are under serious attack in the United States today.' " [87] Concern about the decline of Christian values leads others to engage the wider culture.

For the purposes of this book, I will speak collectively about evangelicals, while understanding that different kinds of Christians are associated with PFM. They share some beliefs but also have significant differences. Legal disestablishment of religion in America means, among other things, that religious leaders and institutions do not speak authoritatively for individual Christians. Nor do academic scholars of religion. Notwithstanding the pervasive apologetic rhetoric, it is not at all clear that evangelical Christianity actually functions as an organic worldview that organizes all of life for most evangelicals. American Christians of all kinds are free, both legally and, to a large extent, theologically, to interpret their own traditions as they see fit and to voluntarily associate with institutional representations of those traditions. This may seem self-evident, but the form this freedom takes in the United States is quite radical. One reason often given for the continued flourishing of American Christianity, in contrast to European Christianity, for example, is the competition and capacity for reinvention that is made possible by disestablishment. The churches are not a take-it-or-leave-it product. The product can always be redesigned to fit one's taste. The entrepreneurial inventiveness of evangelical Christianity has a long history in the United States, as mentioned. New ideas and institutions were needed, because the established churches of Europe were not imported wholesale with the immigrants. European churches were tied to European political and social institutions that did not exist in the United States.[88]

Mark Noll, a leading evangelical historian of American evangelicalism, has described the creation of the U.S. "evangelical mind" over the course of the nineteenth century.[89] That mind was significantly affected, he says, beginning as early as the seventeenth and eighteenth centuries, by the fact that the intellectual settlement that American Protestants made with modernity was by way of the didactic Scottish Enlightenment, rather than by way of the skeptical or revolutionary enlightenments.[90] Noll argues that, after the Puritan break with the Church of England, the 1776 Revolution, and the effective separation of church and state in the fledgling country,

> the intuitive philosophy provided by the Scots offered an intellectually respectable way to establish public virtue in a society that was busily repudiating the props on which virtue had traditionally rested . . . For early nineteenth century evangelicals who wanted to preserve traditional forms of Christianity without appeal to traditional [*established*] religious authorities, the common sense reasoning of the Scottish enlightenment (as least as that philosophy took on a life of its own in North America), was the answer. . . . Explicit in the lectures and textbooks of the nation's Protestant leaders was the Enlightenment belief that *Americans could find within themselves* resources, compatible with Christianity, to bring social order out of the rootlessness and confusion of the new nation.[91] (emphasis added)

The goal then, as it is now, was moral reform of a society that could not depend on established religious and political institutions.

Reviewing the long-term intellectual influences on the later American evangelical thinkers of the nineteenth and twentieth centuries, Noll enumerates (and laments) what he sees as the characteristics of the resulting "Baconian" intellectual habit of mind: a habit that he sees as having been shaped by a paradoxical devotion to both the inerrancy of the Bible and to a certain understanding of objective, or scientific, truth. The evangelical mind was characterized, Noll points out, by an "overwhelming trust in the capacities of an objective, disinterested, unbiased, and neutral science."[92] "Fundamentalist naïveté concerning science," he explains, "was matched by several other nineteenth century traits":

> a weakness for treating the verses of the Bible as pieces in a jigsaw puzzle that needed only to be sorted and then fit together to possess a finished picture of divine truth; an overwhelming tendency to "essentialism," or the conviction that a specific formula could capture for all times and places the essence of biblical truth for any specific issue concerning God, the human condition, or the fate of the world; a corresponding neglect of forces in history that shape perceptions and help

> define the issues that loom as most important to any particular age; and a self-confidence, bordering on hubris, manifested by an extreme anti-traditionalism that casually discounted the possibility of wisdom from earlier generations.[93]

American "supernatural rationalism," as Noll terms it, can sometimes seem like an anti-intellectual parody of positivist empirical scientific enquiry, but one can also argue that it has been an extremely successful form of individual, American-style reasoning. The marriage of common-sense philosophy and faith in intuitive moral reasoning and liberal market theory combined with a naïve biblicism to produce a new style of Christian public intellectual engagement in the new world, a style that was ideal for a new country with no established religious authority. From the beginning it was also extraordinarily patriotic, identifying the United States, often uncritically, as a "Christian commonwealth."[94] Noll writes as an avowed and concerned evangelical Christian about his own community. Much of what he laments, however, is applicable to American habits of mind more generally, those of self-consciously religiously committed persons, and others.

In the second half of the nineteenth century the American Protestant community divided and crystallized in its encounter with modern post-Enlightenment historical and scientific thought.[95] The conservative wing of the evangelical Christian alliance, which Noll terms fundamentalist and anti-intellectual, rejected the new physical and social sciences, as well as the new political ideologies and embraced biblical dispensationalism, a form of biblical interpretation involving an encoded correlation between human and biblical history.[96] These conservatives also largely withdrew from public life. In the last half of the twentieth century, post-fundamentalist evangelicals reengaged with the culture, bringing with them the supernatural rationalism they had inherited and that had served them well.

A new form of American evangelical church has emerged, sometimes called the new paradigm churches. There are many continuities; they are Bible-believing churches that emphasize conversion, but their worship style and menu of ministries are contemporary and flexible, tailored to their members' needs. The sociologist Don Miller sees a parallel with the democratization of Christianity that Nathan Hatch described in the new republic of the early nineteenth century.[97] Miller calls it a modern primitivism, "a certain exhaustion with reason."[98] But it is not mystical. "The faith of new paradigm Christians is empirically based. The Bible seems to assume authority for these individuals as they practice what it says and have prayers answered, see people healed, watch people being transformed morally, and experience the "leading" of the Holy Spirit in their own lives."[99] At the same time, many new paradigm church members actively participate in an advanced market economy that demands an unwavering commitment to reason of a highly instrumental character. Although it is dangerous to generalize about the present character of the many and diverse religious communities that can be grouped together as the descendants of nineteenth-century fundamentalists, IFI's epistemology and social philosophy can be broadly understood as having been shaped in important ways by the intellectual and social history that Noll and others have described. It is a belief that, perhaps paradoxically, both holds the Bible to be literally true and yet is committed to a positivist epistemology.

Many antebellum American Protestants rejected traditional church authority for theological and practical reasons. In the spirit of the Revolution, they took to heart with a vengeance the Reformers' demand that individual Christians could and should read and interpret the Bible for themselves, without the mediating role of the churches. The need to evangelize a population that largely belonged to no church also led to the adoption of revivalist techniques that simplified theologies and emphasized individual experience. The new preachers of the antebellum period were no longer the product of elite institutions of higher learning, but they taught from the heart and from their own, often untutored, reading of the Bible.[100]

All of life was approached by the frontier evangelists with the Bible in one hand and the teaching of common sense in the other: "The Bible is to the theologian," stated the nineteenth-century theologian Charles Hodges, "what nature is to the man of science. It is his store-house of facts; and his method of ascertaining what the Bible teaches, it is the same as that which the natural philosopher adopts to understand what nature teaches."[101] The method was positivist[102] and scientist, short-circuiting both academic scientific inquiry and critical study of Scripture. The birth of this method in the early republic, when the American churches in a newly deregulated field were in stiff competition, further led, as Noll explains, to a seamless overlap between nationalism, free market economics, and evangelical anthropology.[103]

Being Countercultural

IFI leaders, like the evangelical Christians of the nineteenth century, rely on a special combination of populist, common sense, moral reasoning, confidence in market economics and faith in American democracy, and appeal to the Bible as the sole source of truth in order to interpret contemporary social issues and to manage their individual lives. In addressing the problem of recidivism, IFI seeks to create persons who will be responsible, self-controlled, and productive members of society—"civilized" persons with what IFI understands to be universal values. IFI sees the model for such individuals in the biblical narratives, just as most of our early-nineteenth-century ancestors did. But IFI is also deeply influenced by evangelical Christian developments in the twentieth century.

Noll himself looks with hope to a more critical evangelical position, seeing certain shifts in the second half of the twentieth century as promising:

> Four developments in the 1930s and 1940s prepared the way for distinct improvement in evangelical thinking. . . . Against the heritage of intuition appeared somewhat more self-criticism, against simple Biblicism a growing awareness of the complexities of Scripture, against populism an increased longing for advanced higher education, and alongside activism the beginnings of respect for study.[104]

Noll welcomes this reengagement with the larger academic culture for the sake of both the evangelicals and their new interlocutors. Noll quotes Michael Novak to the effect that "better than the philosophers, Jesus Christ is the teacher of many lessons indispensable for the working of a free society," and then he continues,

> One of the most bracing encouragements to think and act like Christians in the political sphere has been to hear contemporary neo-Calvinists of various sorts . . . quote the spine-tingling tocsin that Kuyper first declaimed 115 years ago at he opening of the Free University of Amsterdam. "There is not an inch," he roared, "not an inch in the entire domain of our human life of which Christ, who is sovereign of all, does not proclaim 'mine.' "[105]

These words of Kuyper's are also quoted in PFM's 2006–2007 *Annual Report*.[106] Noll seems to hear Kuyper's words as a clarion call to evangelicals to get involved. Others may hear it as a declaration of imperial and intolerant ambition, an ambition whose natural conclusion would be something they would call theocracy.

Abraham Kuyper was a Dutch Calvinist minister and prime minister of the Netherlands from 1901 to 1905. Kuyper, opposed to the individualism and secularism he believed to be the heritage of the French Revolution, espoused a political policy called "sphere sovereignty," which would shift government power to families and churches—to the private sphere where it belonged. As Lew Daly argued in his account of the history of the faith-based movement, the political justification of the movement has explicit Calvinist roots as Kuyper's ideas were cited as an explicit source by the architects of President Bush's faith-based politics. Daly himself decries conservative Christians who would combine free-market capitalism with disestablishment, arguing that they misread Kuyper, who was far more radical in his ambitions for the income redistribution that he believed biblical teaching demanded.[107] What all of Kuyper's American disciples take from him is the insistence on the continued relevance of religious authority in matters of values and his universalist vision of Christianity.

Evangelicals are indeed ambitious for their vision, but their ambition is not for theocracy, as liberals charge. Theocracy is rule by clerics. The authority of the church as a visible hierarchical human institution is deeply distrusted by many conservative evangelicals. Theocracy is understood by them to be a feature of the medieval corruption of biblical Christianity and of wayward forms of Protestant establishment in Europe. To be "religious" is likewise a negative attribute for evangelicals. The Iowa prisoners were often instructed that "religiosity is a bad thing" (p. 1232). "The second time I spoke with [the IFI director]," Allyn Gilbert, one of the Catholic prisoners, said, "was to be brought in and told that I was a religious person and not a faithful person, and then he handed me a book . . . and told me that I needed to write a book report on it" (p. 1921). To be religious is to put one's faith in outward things, in ritual and hierarchy.

For Colson, and for many other evangelicals, the story of the church as an institution is a long story of decline. What is needed in its place is Bible-believing Christians throughout both government and private institutions. Colson explains in his book about the founding of Prison Fellowship that he understood this more fully when he visited Europe for the first time as a Christian:

> Haenssler [a German friend of Colson's] helped me see how dead the church is when it becomes a national institution as it is throughout Europe. In 312 A.D under Emperor Constantine the process began that a few decades later would make Christianity the official state religion of the empire. The church along with the state then declined in vitality, its influence first co-opted, then corrupted . . . The church's corruption became complete as biblical doctrines were distorted, the church defying and then denying scriptural authority. The lessening moral influence of the church opened the door to renaissance humanism.[108]

U.S. Christianity, in contrast, has had an opportunity to cure this long-entrenched European corruption.

The rejection of traditional European-style church authority led, in part, to a relocation of authority in the individual Christian. Colson explains, using the work of Martin Luther:

> Luther, without question, overcame servitude through devotion but only by substituting servitude through conviction. He shattered the faith in authority by restoring the authority of faith. He transformed the priests into laymen by turning laymen into priests. He liberated man from external religiosity by making religiosity the innermost essence of man. He liberated the body from its chains because he fettered the heart with chains.[109]

Colson observes that he learned from Luther that to be a Christian is to have one's heart, rather than one's body, in chains. But unlike Luther, for whom, as Colson neglects to mention, Christian liberty existed only in the context of state-sponsored religious conformity, the goal for American evangelical Protestants is not theocracy, or even religious establishment, but the conversion of humanity, one by one, and thereby the conversion of society.

The way to this envisioned re-Christianization of culture is highly intentional and strategic. It relies on the mobilization of resources both human and material, but the way is not through the establishment of a national church. The apologetic goal is made, in part, through the strategic and consistent public use of a disciplined language that rejects Christian denominational or ecclesiological specificity, thus masking what is, in many ways, an exclusivist Christian worldview. In contrast to the insider language of Christian exclusivity, this public language, with its apparently bland lack of religious specificity, allows everything else to be assimilated to this worldview. Unlike the prisoners quoted in the first chapter, who spoke in religious terms about their IFI experience, IFI employees at the trial carefully avoided religious language. The employees tended to translate theology into the language of pop psychology and behavioral science, distancing themselves from specifically Christian claims and categories, which they discussed only in a functional and reductionist manner. The language of religious commitment is reserved for insiders and one-on-one evangelism.

In the end, this approach backfired as a legal strategy, as their insistence on speaking of their own religious commitments in an oblique manner appeared to greatly frustrate the judge who was, I believe, prepared to be sympathetic to a straightforward assertion of a Christian mission for a good cause. He was less sympathetic to the claim that Prison Fellowship is not really an evangelizing organization but is something more like a secular social service provider that happens to have gotten it right.

PFM's claim is that it has responded to the huge increase in incarceration in this country, and the accompanying crisis of recidivism, by creating a professionally developed and administered program of personal transformation that is uniquely successful in addressing the manifestly secular, governmental purpose of reducing recidivism. But PFM seems undecided about whether it wants to claim that it is uniquely successful *because* it is faith-based. Opponents of faith-based programs see them simply as thinly disguised, even disingenuous, efforts at the unconstitutional religious proselytizing of a vulnerable population. This notwithstanding IFI's ociferous and often expressed claim that people of all religious commitments, or those with no commitment at all, are welcome to enter the program and that conversion to Christianity is not a requirement of successful completion.

A continuing source of misunderstanding at the trial was the apparent secularism of the cultural discourse and practices of many PFM insiders. It is a challenge to represent this subculture to other U.S. subcultures, as it does not present itself as exotic, and so appears to be something other than what it seems. The form of Christianity to which PFM and IFI belong, has, like all forms of Christianity, a distinct history and character, but one of its most interesting aspects is that is uses almost invisible linguistic marking conventions that promote its intimate role in the formation of a modern American consciousness.[111] When PFM and IFI staff use the word "Christian," they do not refer neutrally, as a historian would, to all the extraordinarily diverse mix of ideas, institutions, and persons that can be identified in some sense with the first communities that formed around the disciples of a first-century person known as Jesus; instead, they are referring to a specific, contemporary reading of those ideas, institutions, and persons. "Christian" means true or evangelical Christian, as each of them defines that community at any moment in time. This language is usefully ambiguous—a frequent characteristic of apologetic language—in that it holds out the hope for a possible identity with a much larger constituency, one that might sometimes include other Protestants, even Catholics, Orthodox Christians, and Jews, or even all religious persons. ("Church," "churches," and "the church" were likewise used in an ambiguous manner to allow PFM and IFI to move between different conceptions of Christianity.)

Randall Balmer, professor of American religious history at Columbia University, reads evangelical language as highly coded. When the code is broken, it appears intentionally deceptive, revealing a kind of stealth religion. This linguistic practice has both passive and intentional aspects. Its very blurriness licenses a set of cultural and political practices that can work to confuse and co-opt the naive. But it can also be genuinely open to influence from other sources. Sorting out when the language is closed and when it is open is difficult.

In this respect, PFM has some significant affinities to another evangelical effort to engage the larger male culture: the Promise Keepers. The sociologist John Bartkowski comments in his new book about the Promise

Keepers that PK typifies the evangelical subculture in its capacity to build bridges while at the same time maintain boundaries, what Bartkowski calls "an approach-avoidance dance" of "selective borrowing" from the secular mainstream. On the one hand, "the evangelical emphasis on personal conversion and the formation of grassroots religious networks resonate quite well with the American values of individualism, choice and populism." But Bartkowski says, "Evangelicals keep the cultural mainstream at arm's length by continuing to defend the infallibility of the Bible in the face of scientific rationality and the higher criticism of scripture that emerged in the wake of the enlightenment." And, pertinent to such projects as IFI, Bartkowsi emphasizes that evangelicals share a particular understanding of human nature: "In contrast to benign or 'tabula rasa' views of human nature, evangelicals underscore their subcultural distinctiveness by contending that human beings are inherently sinful. The evangelical counterbalance to human depravity is equally distinctive; salvation in this subculture is only possible through one's acceptance of Jesus Christ as one's "personal Lord and Savior."[112] Like the Promise Keepers, PFM keeps its critics off-balance by alternatively drawing lines in the sand and making common cause.[113] PFM prisoners are told they are different because they have rejected Satan, but they are also told that they can be the same as other people because being a Christian simply means being a responsible member of society. The contradictions in these positions are left unexplored and unresolved.

In other words, in many important ways evangelicals are just not that different from other Americans. To read Noll and other evangelical historians is to encounter an understanding of the human being in society that is deeply rooted in a common American experience, an understanding that, arguably, is shared in broad outline by IFI *and* many of its critics. Notwithstanding their different politics and theologies, IFI and their critics share very American assumptions about the nature of people. Personalities are not determined by received cultural or biological situations in life. Personalities can change and improve; indeed, people have a positive obligation to improve, and they can do that through a combination of self-help and magical thinking. This view of human beings was, historically, largely influenced by a blend of eighteenth-century Enlightenment philosophy and Protestant theologies, while socially it was formed in the democratic crucible of the early republic. And it is not limited to Christians. John Lardas Modern describes mid-nineteenth-century prison reformers using phrenology and spiritualism as vehicles for reform projects that echoed and blended with that of Evangelicals.[114]

CHAPTER 3

Biblical Justice

"I KNOW ABOUT MY WRONGS. I can't forget my sin. You are the one I have sinned against. I have done what you say is wrong. So you are right when I speak. You are fair when you judge me."[1] Thus speaks King David to God, translated into contemporary English, in *The Sycamore Tree Project*, PFM's curriculum to foster offender-victim reconciliation. The project, the instructor's manual declares, "deals with sin and its consequences, with offenders and victims, offering a biblical model of transformation." The offender and the victim are invited to understand themselves and their relationship to each other, as the psalmist understands the relationship of King David to his God. Through the translation, King David becomes a convicted and imprisoned American; sin is defined by U.S. law, and the victim (a proxy for the criminal justice system) stands in for God.

Biblical warrant for what IFI presents as the biblical practice of reconciliation is also found in the story of Zacchaeus as told in the New Testament's Gospel of Luke.[2] According to the IFI lesson plan for class 1, Zacchaeus was a crooked tax collector who was so short of stature that he climbed a sycamore tree to get a glimpse of Jesus passing through Jericho. The IFI account says that "he became very rich by stealing from his own Jewish neighbors." Jesus saw Zacchaeus in the tree and called out to him, saying that he would come to Zacchaeus's house that evening for dinner. Zacchaeus climbed down to speak to Jesus and, later in the chapter, he is reported to have repented of his sins. The IFI lesson describes Zacchaeus as "an offender" who repents of having profited from his position and promises thereafter to give to the poor and restore any amounts he has unjustly gained.

This first lesson of *The Sycamore Tree Project* teaches the prisoner to identify with Zacchaeus as a sinner/offender and to seek reconciliation with God and his victims, as Zacchaeus reportedly did. The difficulty with this reading of the story of Zacchaeus is that in the biblical text Zacchaeus is not portrayed as having committed any offense against Roman law. Zacchaeus was not a criminal. As the IFI lesson plan itself later strangely acknowledges, Zacchaeus's practices were not merely legal under Roman law; Jewish tax collectors were compensated for their work by the surcharge they received, not by the Roman government. Without the label of criminal, Zacchaeus's faults might be seen as more generally attributable to his being human, and not to his being a lawbreaker; and his subsequent promise to reconcile himself with anyone he might have harmed a response to the general demands of Christian charity and not his reconciliation with the victim of a crime. On this more common reading, Zacchaeus is everyman, every sinner, one of the many ordinary sinners with whom Jesus consorts. We are all supposed to identify with Zacchaeus, not to identify him as a member of a criminal class. Indeed, Zacchaeus is a favorite of many Sunday School students because he is represented as short, and thus inconsequential, as the children may feel themselves to be. In *The Sycamore Tree Project*, Zacchaeus is reinvented as an "offender" in order to give biblical legitimacy to IFI's purposes.

IFI uses King David's hymn to a merciful God, and the story Luke tells of Jesus consorting with ordinary people like Zacchaeus, to underwrite the program's message that "crime is sin. . . . The Bible tells us that crime is *sin*" (emphasis in original).[3] Throughout PFM's materials, this equivalence, crime = sin, is used to confer legitimacy on both the U.S. criminal justice system and PFM's role in it, in a kind of mutual reinforcement. The IFI prisoner's "sin" is defined by the statutes of the State of Iowa. The criminal justice system is just because it punishes sinners, and PFM is godly because it reforms criminals and brings them to reconciliation with their victims.

In this chapter I briefly describe the theories of punishment of the U.S. criminal justice system and that of Prison Fellowship, and then discuss the ways in which IFI might be seen to bridge these two worlds.

Mass Imprisonment

In the United States today more than 7 million people, or 3.2 percent of the population, are incarcerated or on parole or probation, the highest per capita rate in the world.[4] Russia is second.[5] According to the sociologist David Garland, a leading scholar of crime and punishment, writing in 2001, "This is an unprecedented event in the history of the USA and, more generally, in the history of liberal democracy. . . . The rate is five times as large as it was in 1972. Compared to European and Scandinavian countries, the American rate is six to 10 times higher."[6] In 1972 the incarceration rate in the United States was approximately 110 per 100,000 and had been for most of the twentieth century. In 2007 the rate was 737 per 100,000. Recidivism is a serious problem, as high as 70–80 percent in some places in the United States.[7] Costs have increased dramatically, while funding has increased at a lower rate, resulting in substantially strapped state and federal correctional systems. Federal and state systems have cut back on in-prison courses and rehabilitation programs. Meanwhile, there is tremendous ambivalence about prison reform, and law-and-order populism continues, largely unabated.

Garland, in *The Culture of Control*, a historical summary of recent penal policy in the United States, bemoans the equanimity with which the U.S. public has accepted the recent steep increase in incarceration:

> In the USA the public now seems quite accustomed to living in a nation that holds two million of its citizens in confinement on any given day, and puts criminal offenders to death at a rate of two or more per week . . . mandatory sentences, victims' rights, community notification laws, private policing, "law and order" politics, and an emphatic belief that "prison works," have become commonplace points in the crime control landscape and cause no one any surprise.[8]

If anything, the phenomenon he describes has become more acute since he wrote those words in 2000. A 2006 National Commission to study American prisons, co-chaired by John J. Gibbons and Nicholas de B. Katzenbach, concludes:

> We incarcerate more people and at a higher rate than any other country in the world. This reliance bleeds correctional systems of the resources that could be used to rehabilitate rather than merely to punish and incapacitate; it crowds whole systems and sometimes individual facilities to the breaking point; and it exacerbates racial and ethnic tensions in America through its disproportionate impact on African-Americans and Latinos.[9]

The Commission's report condemns the system's indifference to violence both by prisoners and their guards, the lack of educational opportunities, and the medical and mental health neglect of prisoners. It recommends major changes, challenging both legislatures and the public to take responsibility for the lifelong pain and shame caused to prisoners and their families and communities by massive incarceration.

Notably, as Garland insists, "as recently as thirty years ago . . . these phenomena would have seemed highly improbable, even to the best-informed and most up-to-date observer."[10] In *The Culture of Control*, Garland analyzes the changes in penal policy that are associated with broader social changes over the past thirty years or so in the United States and the United Kingdom,[11] particularly the development of what is called "massive incarceration."[12] The "culture of control," or what is sometimes called "governing through crime,"[13] is widely understood to characterize current penal policy in the U.S.

Compressing a large body of research, his own and that of others, Garland lists twelve signs of the dramatic transformation in American penal culture over the past few decades:

- The decline of the rehabilitative ideal as the result of critiques from the right and the left that have demolished the optimism of the "penal-welfare" framework.
- The re-emergence of punitive sanctions and expressive justice, the reappearance of "just deserts" language and an authorizing of discourse.
- Changes in the emotional tone of crime policy resulting in a new focus on fear.
- The return of the victim such that the victim is no longer an unfortunate citizen but is now a representative member of a class.
- The primacy given to the protection of a population that is increasingly risk-averse.
- The politicization of crime and populist politics evident in such policies as three strikes you're out laws and zero-tolerance.
- The reinvention of the prison as a place of incapacitation and punishment rather than rehabilitation.
- The transformation of criminological thought from treatment to control.
- The expanding infrastructure of crime prevention and community, including community policing.
- The commercialization of crime control through the privatization of security.
- New management styles and working practices characterized by managerialism.
- A perpetual sense of crisis in which expertise is discredited and disregarded in favor of lay solutions.[14]

All of these transformations, which Garland links to wider social changes, are echoed in the conclusions and recommendations of the National Commission Report.

Garland explains these developments as originating in the changing fortunes of three competing sets of cultural discourses and social practices about crime and punishment that he terms premodern, modernist, and late-modern.[15] The pre-1970s "rehabilitative ideal," which included the widespread use of indeterminate sentencing and gave wide latitude to judges, was far from perfectly implemented in practice but, as characterized by Garland, was classically modernist in its individualism, progressivism, and confidence in the perfectibility of man. This rehabilitative model was attacked in the 1970s from both the Left and the Right. The Left saw it as paternalistic, hypocritical, overly discretionary, and inappropriately modeled on white middle-class life as normative. The Right regarded the rehabilitative ideal as a failure in practice because of rising crime rates.

Although the crime waves of the sixties were already declining by the time law-and-order politics went into high gear, the collapse of confidence on the Left and criticism from the Right resulted, Garland suggests, in a perduring demonization of the criminal as "other" and a near universal call for "just deserts." The modernist ideal was replaced, Garland argues, with a combination of what he calls a premodern insistence on retribution and expressive punishment and a late-modern capitalist model of managerialism that normalizes crime and relies on rational choice theory. In late-modern society, crime, he says, is no longer commonly regarded as a social pathology but instead is treated as a natural part of the social order, like poverty—something to be managed through the use of gated communities and car alarms, not ameliorated through improvements in education and good mental health care.

Rather than seeking alternatives to incarceration, given the devastating criticism of penal policy and the near-universal conclusion in the 1970s that prisons "don't work,"[16] more and longer prison sentences were given, existing prisons were expanded, and new prisons were built. The new penal ideal, to Garland's evident distress, is epitomized by the prison that does not pretend to "work" as far as rehabilitation is concerned. Rather, it "punishes *and* protects." It "condemns *and* controls." The social costs of these transformations have been a hardening of social and racial divisions, reinforcement of conditions leading to crime, reduction of civic tolerance, and a tendency toward authoritarianism. Public reliance on the new faith-based prison programs likewise evinces a lack of confidence in modernist reform.[17]

Garland describes similar trends in the United States and the United Kingdom. Other sociologists argue that the differences between the two are significant, leaving the U.S. in a uniquely punitive mode. The sociologist Marie Gottschalk, for example, sees the distinctiveness of the recent U.S. situation as founded in the peculiarly American forms that the politicizing of crime took in America in the last thirty-five years, particularly the successful activism of victims' groups after the failure of the prisoner rights movement.[18]

The legal historian James Q. Whitman also sees the United States as distinctive in its penal policy, but he sees that distinction as already evident in colonial times. In *Harsh Justice*, Whitman argues that the "widening divide" between the United States and Europe with respect to cultural practices of criminal punishment can be traced to divergent paths that the U.S. and Europe took in the post-Enlightenment reforms of the then existing class-based differences in punishment on both sides of the Atlantic. The United States, Whitman says, eliminated elite privileges in favor of lowest-common-denominator and degrading forms of punishment, whereas European systems eventually aspired to grant everyone the respect formerly due only to aristocrats and "gentlemen." (Picture Voltaire in the Bastille entertaining his friends in comfort.) The U.S., in effect, takes its commitment to not "respecting persons" to an extreme as a result of our strong insistence on formal equality. And, Whitman concludes, "when formal equality in sentencing is married to the electoral equality of mass politics, the results are explosive."[19]

As one small but significant example of European penal culture, Whitman points out that prisoners in French and German prisons are addressed with courtesy titles, Mr. or Ms. But the differences, he says, can be seen throughout the prison. "American high-security prisons," Whitman notes, "are characterized by a number of practices that have waned or entirely vanished in Europe":

> First is the practice of keeping inmates in cells with barred doors and the like through which they are not just observed (as they would be through peepholes) but thoroughly exposed—inmates having, as the Supreme Court has held, "no reasonable expectation of privacy."
>
> Second is the obligation to wear prison uniforms, a practice with especially interesting psychological consequences. Along with uniforms, there are prison regulations on personal grooming, regulating hair length, facial hair, and the like. Transvestites in particular (unlike their European counterparts) have been denied the right to wear female clothes and cosmetics. These are all measures through which American inmates are denied all control over their "presentation of self," to borrow a famous phrase of Irving Goffman.
>
> Also important are a range of restrictions on visitation, including in some cases the practice of separating inmates from their visitors behind a glass partition; and a spirit of regimentation represented notably by the practice of common dining in a common mess hall where prisoners may have no choice of foods and may be hustled out after as short a time as twelve minutes.[20] (footnotes in original omitted)

"All of these are practices," Whitman emphasizes, "that Europeans have, in one measure or another, condemned as incompatible with inmate 'dignity.'" [21] And one could list many other indignities in U.S. prisons—loss of the right to vote, the prevalence of violence, public use of toilets, body cavity searches, little educational opportunity, and poor health care.

Whitman's historical argument is complex. Critical to the difference in the United States, he believes, is the presence of a weaker state. Criminology and rehabilitation are far less subject to electoral politics in France and Germany, as legal and bureaucratic elites are insulated from, and therefore more able to resist, social pressure to be punitive. A stronger European state has also, perhaps paradoxically, resulted in a tradition around political prisoners that led to the elevated dignity of all prisoners.[22]

Also important, however, is the religious culture. As Whitman says, "Part of what makes [the U.S.] harsher than continental Europeans is the presence of some distinctively fierce American Christian beliefs."[23] Whitman, and others, see the American commitment to the death penalty as being rooted in religion.[24]

Together, the weaker state and the stronger religious culture in the United States arguably provide a space for greater punitiveness across the board and for the acceptability of the equivalence of crime and sin. In the U.S. more acts are understood to be *mala in se* (evil in themselves) rather than *mala prohibita* (merely prohibited); individual crimes are graded higher, on average (i.e., more acts are graded as felonies); more types of individuals are criminalized (e.g., juveniles are increasingly tried as adults); sentences are more often mandatory (with little concern for the traditional legal doctrine of proportionality); and sentences are much longer (sometimes as much as ten times longer).[25] Pardoning power is rarely used in the United States, whereas the stronger European state carries a tradition of the possibility of mercy. In all these areas, a vastly disproportionate effect is felt by minority populations, particularly African Americans.[26] Whitman summarizes:

> Because the [European] state is sovereign . . . [b]ecause they are able to defer to state power, they are able to treat some offenses as merely forbidden, rather than as evil—as *mala prohibita* rather than *mala in se*. The contrast with the United States is strong; our liberal, antistatist tradition leads us to conclude that nothing may be forbidden by the state unless it is evil; otherwise the state would have no right to forbid us to do it. Indeed, we still have much of the quasi-Christian attitude that David Rothman identified in describing the pre-Revolutionary American world: "The identification of disorder with sin," he writes, "makes it difficult for legislators and ministers to distinguish carefully between minor and major infractions."[27]

Recent rhetoric in the United States identifying immigrants as criminals reflects these attitudes.

These studies of crime and punishment synthesize vast amounts of data across a diverse American penal landscape, a landscape that in Iowa and elsewhere continues to include dedicated professionals working to help prisoners prepare for a better life on the outside. In broad strokes these studies create a well-known picture of the sorry state of American prisons, one that is reflected in the story told by the Iowa case. The testimony given by senior corrections officials confirms that in Iowa government resources for rehabilitation have been drastically reduced over the last thirty years. Iowa correctional statistics and the testimony of the prisoners at trial confirm that many prisoners are serving dramatically longer sentences for an increased number of drug-related offenses, mandatory minimum sentences are common, and key prison services are being contracted out to private firms that have an expressive and managerial approach to corrections and tend to reject progressive penal programs and processes.

Crime Equals Sin

During roughly the same thirty-five-year period of which Garland speaks, scholars note a transformation of American religion that is parallel in significant ways to the ascendancy of an increasingly punitive penal system. During that period, there was a significant abandonment of a liberal "modernist" religion that desires to engage rationally and optimistically with modernity. Replacing that modernist religion are religious ways of life that are, in Garland's terms, late-modern (consumerist and managerial) and premodern (pietist, moralistic, expressive, and superstitious), and possibly postmodern (as I discuss in chapter 4). In this relatively new penal context "faith-based" prison rehabilitation programs have made their bid, promising to reduce recidivism dramatically through personal transformation. As with so many other former government services, charitable organizations are being asked to take up the slack for reductions in government spending. The next chapter focuses on the nature of American religion generally today in the context of a global religious revival. At this point, however, I will consider contemporary evangelical theories of punishment and the desire to institute what Charles Colson and IFI call "biblical justice." Whether one can conclude that dominant contemporary Christian theologies of punishment actually contributed directly to the increased punitive nature of U.S. society, there is no question that the two are culturally congruent and mutually recognizable.

PFM's response to the statistics of massive incarceration is expressed in its 2006–2007 *Annual Report*. The *Report* gives the current statistics, and then continues:

> That is why the ministry of Prison Fellowship in partnership with the local church is more necessary than ever before. Through the gospel of Jesus Christ the Church can help accomplish what the government alone can never do—change prisoners' lives from the *inside out*, reconciling them to God, to their families, and to their communities as Transformed people. What's more, the Church can help revamp the criminal justice system itself, by working for legislation and policies that reflect biblical standards of justice and the dignity of all people.[28] (emphasis in original)

PFM is an acknowledged early leader in the faith-based prison rehabilitation movement, but it is certainly not the only player.

Many religious organizations of many varieties are present in the many federal and state prisons in the United States. The Nation of Islam has been a significant leader in ministering to prisoners for decades, including post-release care, often in the face of considerable resistance from prison authorities. Black Muslims first entered prisons in large numbers during World War II because of their conscientious objection to military service.[29] Malcolm X called public attention to their prison ministry in his autobiography.[30] That ministry continues today. The increase in the number of Muslim prisoners, and the diversity of their religious beliefs and practices, has resulted in the increased presence of various forms of Islam in U.S. prisons.[31] But programs sponsored by Buddhists, neo-pagans, Quakers, Roman Catholics, Native Americans, and many others, from across the entire religious spectrum, are also reaching out to prisoners. Although all U.S. prisons have formal chaplaincies, much of the religious work done in prisons is done by volunteers. Because most Americans are Christians, most of these programs are Christian.

Moving beyond chaplaincies and volunteer ministries to prisoners, some states are looking to institutionalize the new faith-based rehabilitation concept. Florida has, in the last several years, built several entire prisons designated as "faith-based." The first such prison was described in an article on the Web site of the *Florida Baptist Witness*, inviting financial donations: "Prison officials are appealing to individuals and churches for help in guiding the spiritual lives of almost 800 prisoners who have chosen to be housed at Lawtey." The article goes on to explain that "Southern Baptist churches and individuals are sponsoring two dorms . . . The sponsor provides the dorm with a dorm chaplain, mentors, educators and volunteers; and provides funding for the dorm. Start-up cost per dorm is about $10,000 for the first year." Quoting the Mission Statement of the prison to the effect that, "the mission of the Lawtey Faith Based Institution is to provide the Florida Department of Corrections with a prototype correctional institution that incorporates personal faith as a catalyst to effect inner transformation of inmates," the article warns that "volunteers must be screened by the Department of Corrections, attend a 2-hour DOC training course and a 2-hour training session about the distinct differences of a faith-based prison." "'We know that we are being watched by separatists groups, and we are careful to not force faith on anyone. We walk a tightrope,' Smith said. 'We are respectful and we do not proselytize. However, we do want those of other faiths to see the Christians' walk and know Who is the true God.'"[32] Prisons have become a "giving opportunity." In Florida, according to the Florida Department of Corrections, "currently, there are three Faith-and Character-Based Institutions (FCBIs) and seven facilities with Faith-Based/Self-Improvement Dorms (FB/SIDs). Combined, these two programs total 3,564 beds."[33]

PFM is a part of this correctional trend. One result of the increased visibility and volubility of evangelical Christians is that there is also now an elaborated Christian (meaning evangelical Christian) point of view on many topics. Christian schooling has developed a Christian curriculum for all levels from nursery through graduate and professional school, and biblical counseling has spawned a set of institutions parallel to those of secular psychotherapeutic theories. Institutions promoting "biblical justice" take their place next to those teaching secular criminologies.

In the development of a contemporary Christian theology of punishment, a key text for evangelicals is C. S. Lewis's 1949 essay, "The Humanitarian Theory of Punishment," published in an Australian journal, in which Lewis contrasts what he calls the "Humanitarian Theory" with what he terms the "Retributive Theory." "According to the Humanitarian Theory," he says,

> to punish a man because he deserves it, and as much as he deserves, is mere revenge, and, therefore, barbarous and immoral. It is maintained that the only legitimate motives for punishing are the desire to deter others by example or to mend the criminal. When this theory is combined, as frequently happens, with the belief that all crime is more or less pathological, the idea of mending tails off into that of healing or curing and punishment becomes therapeutic. Thus it appears at first sight that we have passed from the harsh and self-righteous notion of giving the wicked their deserts to the charitable and enlightened one of tending the psychologically sick. What could be more amiable?[34]

But, he insists,

> One little point which is taken for granted in this theory needs to be made explicit. The things done to the criminal, even if they are called cures, will be just as compulsory as they were in the old days when we called them punishments . . . My contention is that this doctrine, merciful though it appears, really means that each one of us, from the moment he breaks the law, is deprived of the rights of a human being.[35]

Lewis argues that to punish for the purpose of deterring others or mending the criminal is unjust and inhumane, because either approach treats prisoners like objects, whereas punishing prisoners because they deserve it is just and humane, as such punishment treats the prisoner like a responsible human being.

Justice is understood to be accomplished, according to Lewis, under the Retributive Theory—when justice *is* done—as he goes on to explain, not only because the defendant is understood to have exercised free will in choosing to commit the crime but also because the judge is understood to fix the sentence with "guidance from the Law of Nature, and from Scripture."[36] In contrast, Lewis continues, the Humanitarian Theory "removes sentences from the hands of jurists whom the public conscience is entitled to criticize and places them in the hands of technical experts whose special sciences do not even employ such categories as Rights or Justice." He sums up indignantly:

> To be taken without consent from my home and friends; to lose my liberty; to undergo all those assaults on my personality which modern psychotherapy knows how to deliver; to be remade after some pattern of "normality" hatched in a Viennese laboratory to which I never professed allegiance; to know that this process will never end until either my captors have succeeded or I have grown wise enough to cheat them with apparent success—who care whether this is called punishment or not?[37]

The Humanitarian Theory, according to Lewis, removes punishment from the jurists whom "the public conscience" is entitled to criticize and gives the condemned to the care of specialists in human psychology who know no democratic control. Having condemned the offspring of the "Viennese laboratory," Lewis then argues that deterrence is an even more dangerous goal, because it can be used to justify the punishment of an innocent man in the name of the greater good.

In a number of columns and essays citing Lewis, Charles Colson has also addressed the justifications for punishment. Apparently finding common cause with Lewis's scorn for the dangerous and inhumane expertise of the social sciences, Colson writes: "To justify punishment by whether it 'deters or cures' is the triumph of sociology over justice."[38] Colson, too, promotes retribution as more just—and more biblical. Justice for Lewis, however, under the Retributive Theory, critically depends on a judge's professional training and his responsiveness to the conscience of the community he serves, a conscience signified in Lewis's essay by a judge's "guidance from the Law of Nature and Scripture," as well on the legitimacy of the democratic regime "to which [the prisoner] professed allegiance." Justice, for Lewis, is not inherent in the state. For Colson, mercy and rehabilitative assistance are denied because the authorities wield the God-given power to punish moral evil.

In an online essay on capital punishment, Colson goes further: "I am coming to see," he writes, "that mercy extended to offenders whose guilt is certain yet simply ignored creates a moral travesty which, over time, helps pave the way for collapse of the entire social order."[39] Colson finds in Paul's Letter to the Romans the argument that the civil magistrate should properly be understood as wielding God's authority:

> This is essentially the argument of Romans 13. Romans 12 concludes with an apostolic proscription of personal retribution, yet St. Paul immediately follows this with a divinely instituted prescription for punishing moral evil. It is for eminently social reasons that "the authorities" are to wield the sword, the *ius gladii*: due to human depravity and the need for moral-social order the civil magistrate punishes criminal behavior. The implication of Romans 13 is that by not punishing moral evil the authorities are not performing their God-appointed responsibility in society.[40]

For Colson, punishment, or what he calls "just deserts," is justified not through an appeal to the professionally formed conscience of the judge responding to and honoring the independence of the freely taken action of another human being, or to the legitimizing authority of democratic governance, but to the absolute authority of the state that is understood to be divinely established. The state's failure to exact retribution is, in Colson's view, the first step to "collapse of the entire social order."

C. S. Lewis was, I believe, far less sanguine than Colson about the godliness of the magistrate's authority. Indeed, in discussing the danger of the deterrence argument Lewis, writing in the shadow of World War II, notes that, "every modern State has powers which make it easy to fake a trial."[41] In his essay, Lewis points to the dangers of harsh punishment, and he relies on jury nullification or the moral outrage of the community to control such excesses. But at least in this essay he is most concerned about the dignity of the individual prisoner, not the collapse of the moral order. The possibility of individuals being used as objects is what worries him about the social scientific and the utilitarian approaches, approaches he calls "those humane pretensions which have served to usher in every cruelty of the revolutionary period in which we live."[42]

Lewis, best known in the United States as the author of the *Narnia* children's book series, was a noted Cambridge University scholar of Renaissance literature and a Christian apologist.[43] His fantasy fiction and apologetic works are read across the contemporary Christian churches, but he is an authority of particular reverence in the evangelical community. According to the evangelical historian Roger Olson, "Lewis is probably quoted more often than any other single person after Jesus Christ and the writers of Scripture," because "he presented an example of an intellectual engaged in the life of a major secular university holding high his Christian identity and vigorously criticizing the excesses of secular culture."[44] Olson adds that "it is doubtful that Lewis himself [an orthodox Anglican] ever understood his passionate embrace by North American postfundamentalists"—or, one might add, that those postfundamentalist fans of Lewis, such as Colson, really understand Lewis, who was a regular commicant throughout his life in the Church of England.

Two faculty members at Asbury Theological Seminary, Scott Burson and Jerry Walls, have recently written a book comparing the apologetic theologies of the American Francis Schaeffer and the Englishman C. S. Lewis. Conceding that neither was a professional theologian, the two authors see much in common between Schaeffer and Lewis in their vigorous mid-century defense of orthodox Christianity. A revealing difference between the two is relevant to their common reappropriation by American evangelicals today. In a section of their book, titled "The Fate of the Unevangelized: Tough Love or Tough Luck?" Schaeffer's predestinarian Calvinism condemning the unevangelized to hell is compared to Lewis's Anglican Arminianism that allows the salvation of all who live good lives, Christian and otherwise. The differences between their theologies, Burson and Walls note, is in their understanding of God as judge. For Schaeffer, God is just, and non-Christians are justly condemned because all are equally judged according to the degree of revelation they have received; Lewis also sees God as just, but non-Christians are not automatically damned because the equality of men means that the accident of birth should not condemn a person.[45]

Although Schaeffer and Lewis, and Colson, emphasize the objective truth of Christian revelation and the hollowness of secular philosophies, Schaeffer and Lewis and their continued popularity preserve a tension in evangelical Christianity, a tension between more and less "established" ecclesiologies. Lewis believed that respect for prisoners demanded that punishment be defined as a penalty for a voluntary, wrongful act, but he did not accept that the state stood in for God. Consistent with Church of England ecclesiology, Lewis's theology separates ecclesiastical and secular jurisdictions, a separation, according to Lewis, that is enabled by the establishment principle.

Notwithstanding Colson's strong affirmation of the importance of punishment, IFI, at least in its Iowa program, is a curious hybrid. IFI constantly states that crime equals sin, and rejects secular theories of humanity, yet IFI's program also uses social psychological theory to promote exactly the kind of "treatment" that both Colson and Lewis deplore. Compassionate fundamentalism, one might call it, embraces contemporary behaviorism. Colson and his lieutenants, for all their talk of sin and judgment, do not, in fact, reinvent prisons merely for punishment but as places where persons are saved through Christian love. Ironically, though, that love is transmuted through the professional training of IFI staff and the colonization of Christian self-help literature by the language of professional psychology and sociology. IFI prisoners do indeed, in Lewis's words, "undergo all those assaults on [their personalities] which modern psychotherapy knows how to deliver"—and personalities are "remade after some pattern of 'normality' hatched in a Viennese laboratory to which [they] never professed allegiance"—and all in God's name. Tough love is expressed, in IFI, through the language of Christian psycho-social science. Prisoners are assumed to need help, not punishment.[46] This is the supernatural rationality of which Noll speaks, in action.

IFI and its like are a replay of the early-nineteenth-century church-state prison reform projects in the United States, projects that also mixed social-scientific theories of the human with religious discipline. David Rothman describes the avowed purposes of the Auburn, New York, and the Pennsylvania systems:

> The advocates of Pennsylvania and Auburn were both committed to the rehabilitative potential of the prison and were both convinced that the routines imposed on the inmate would transform him into a law-abiding citizen. Reform, not deterrence, was now the aim of incarceration. The shared assumption was that since the convict was not innately depraved but had failed to be trained to obedience by family, church, school or community, he could be redeemed by the well-ordered routine of the prison.[47]

Like Colson and his colleagues, the Jacksonian reformers also saw promise in the reform of prisons for reform of society generally. Rothman recounts: "The reformers hoped that the solutions that they devised would be relevant to the wider society. With no ironies intended, they talked about the penitentiary as serving as a model for the family and the school."[48] Dickens and Beaumont were doubtful, as Rothman recounts:

> Charles Dickens, on his 1842 tour of the United States, went to Philadelphia expressly to see the prison and found it "cruel and wrong." Its intentions, he conceded, were humane and reformatory. But its designers, he was convinced, did not know what they were doing. ". . . I hold this slow and daily tampering with the mysteries of the brain, to be immeasurably worse than any torture of the body." . . . Tocqueville and Beaumont were more measured in their summary judgments. "We have no doubt," they wrote, "but that the habits of order to which the prisoner is subjected for several years, influence very considerably his moral conduct and his return to society." . . . But these points notwithstanding, the prisons that they visited did not fit with the America that they saw. "While society in the United States gives the example of the most extended liberty, the prisons of the same country offer the spectacle of the most complete despotism. The citizens subject to the law are protected by it, they cease to be free when they become wicked."[49]

For Dickens, Tocqueville, and Beaumont, the American prison was a betrayal of basic principles.[50]

The expressed rationale for the specific details of the IFI program as a program of state-sponsored personal transformation comes from a movement known as biblical counseling, a product of the new conservative, evangelical activism and institution building originating in the 1970s.[51] Biblical counseling is a large and active network of publishing, training, degree-granting, certifying, and delivery institutions. Biblical counselors now serve throughout the faith-based social services world, in churches and in institutions of all kinds, providing parallel services to all forms of secular counseling, including marriage counseling. A White Paper, written by Henry Brandt and Kerry L. Skinner, two well-known biblical counselors for IFI and published on the IFI Web site,[52] describes "transformation," the behavioral theory underlying the program, contrasting it to what are termed "therapeutic" (that is, secular) models. The Paper includes a table comparing the two models:

Transformation	*Therapeutic*
• Transformed persons seek to appropriate God's ways as revealed through Biblical truth.	• Therapy seeks to manage according to human understanding.
• Criminal behavior is a manifestation of an alienation between the self and God	• Criminal behavior is a result of an alienation of self from society.
• Transformation enables prisoners to see the world and others as God sees them.	• Therapy seeks to help prisoners see how the world can meet their needs.
• Acceptance of God and Biblical principles results in cure through the power of the Holy Spirit.	• Relief of symptoms is dependent on the power of human love and commitment through support groups and community.
• Transformation emphasizes the change in behavior as a result of encountering Jesus Christ.	• Therapy emphasizes the management of behavior as it impacts on others.
• Insight into one's problems is gained from reading, understanding, and applying Biblical principles.	• Insight into one's problems is gained through group and individual interaction.

Transformation	*Therapeutic*
• All problems in life arise from a condition of sin.	• Problems in life arise from past inability to have one's needs met.
• Focuses on honesty with self and God first; honesty with others will follow.	• Focuses on honesty with self and others.
• Focuses on the power of the Creator. It holds up Christ as the source of that power and the work of the Holy Spirit as the way to true change.	• Focuses on the power of Creation. Therapy may or may not point to some higher power.
• The quality of our relationships to each other is conditioned by the quality of our relationship to Jesus Christ and his love as reflected in others.	• Mental health and healthy relationships are dependent on the expression and affirmation of our needs.
• Transformation happens through an instantaneous miracle; it then builds the prisoner up with familiarity of the Bible.	• Therapy seeks gradual change of self as one interacts with one's environment.

In the transformation model, all personal problems and social ills are attributed to sin.[53] The *single* cure is said to be a relationship with Jesus Christ mediated through an encounter with the Bible. The promise of transformation, once and for all in an instantaneous miracle, is held out in contrast to the limits of the therapeutic approach, which depends on gradual change through limited human understanding and human interaction.

A book by Brandt and Skinner, *Heart of the Problem*, summarizes their approach as biblical counselors and is listed as a text in the IFI curriculum. *Heart of the Problem* trains readers to interpret their lives and problems entirely with reference to the Bible. Brandt and Skinner divide all people between the mass of those who do not believe in God—whom Brandt and Skinner call "Goliath"—and a tiny group of believers they call "David." In the first chapter, "The Myth of Complexity," they summarize their creed:

> We agree with the Goliath crowd that these words accurately describe the dark side of human behavior (hostile, hateful, resentful, rebellious,

> frustrated, confused, angry, cruel, selfish, dishonest, destructive). At this point in the road, however, we come to a fork. We disagree that these words describing human behavior are socially and culturally caused. Our guidebook is the Bible. This book puts all those descriptive words under one heading. The heading is *sin*.[54]

The biblical counselor's work with the client pivots on this acknowledgment.

IFI's rhetoric, too, is built on this simple pivot. The White Paper summarizes IFI's model of healing, contrasting it to the "therapeutic model":

> Therapeutic communities seek to equip prisoners for life after prison by learning to manage behavior. Support groups and classes connect prisoners with a loving community of like-minded people who can encourage them and give affirmation. Healing one's relationship with others is the primary focus.
>
> The IFI model seeks to "cure" prisoners by identifying sin as the root of their problems. Inmates learn how God can heal them permanently, if they turn from their sinful past, are willing to see the world through God's eyes, and surrender themselves to God's will. IFI relies and directs members to God as the source of love and inner healing. Members then build on this new relationship to recast human relationships based on Biblical insights.[55]

IFI offers prisoners, once they have acknowledged their sin, a mix of education and salvation, to enable them to "recast" their human relationships.

Biblical counseling, which presents itself as an alternative to traditional psychotherapies, gives epistemological priority to "special revelation" (i.e., biblical revelation) over "general revelation." The biblical text is said always to be given preference over understanding God's purpose as it can be discerned by human reason and observations of the natural world. Special revelation restricts salvation to those who have accepted Jesus as Lord. The guiding principles of biblical counseling are defined in terms of oppositions between the secular and the religious. Advanced degrees in biblical counseling are now available at Christian colleges and universities.

As seen in the evidence offered by IFI counselors at the Iowa trial, however, biblical counselors now often combine the biblical idiom with the language of behavioral psychology. This hybrid practice is also seen in the evidence submitted in a recent lawsuit challenging the constitutionality of state funding provided to the Northwest Marriage Institute (NMI) in Tacoma, Washington.[56] The Institute is directed by Robert Whiddon, a biblical counselor with a Ph.D. in biblical counseling from Trinity Theological Seminary in Indiana, an online seminary which is accredited by the National Association of Private, Nontraditional Schools and Colleges, an organization with three accredited members. The Marriage Institute has received two federal Compassion Capital grants and one Healthy Marriage demonstration grant. After the suit was filed, Whiddon cleansed all his materials of biblical references, explaining at his deposition that "provable psychology and the Bible do not contradict one another." The NMI then successfully petitioned the court to dismiss the case on the grounds that state funds were not being used to fund a religious activity. For the court, religion inhered in the use of explicitly religious language.[57]

IFI at Newton

Biblical counselors contend that their treatment is effective because it brings about "transformation." Transformation is sold as a once-and-for-all event that encloses the convert in a world of biblical consistency and unity, where crime equals sin. Yet biblical counseling incorporates many of the gradualist techniques used by secular counselors. For example, during the trial, the corrections professionals who work for IFI often fell into speaking during the trial of the religious aspect of IFI as a functional component of the treatment they offered, rather than as an overarching horizon or worldview. Asked about the two counseling models described in the White Paper, PFM vice president Norman Cox, the highest-level officer of PFM to testify, explained: "Well, the two models are very similar in many ways . . . A therapeutic model uses some type of treatment effect to change behavior. The transformational model uses the purposeful introduction of religion as the change agent. It also focuses on teaching religious values." (p. 2132). He continued: "The purpose is to change the way people behave, to restore the family, to restore the individual to the community, not only as a crime-free citizen, but also as a person who gives back to the community, be a productive citizen. Recidivism is the way we measure the success of the program" (p. 2132).

However IFI might present itself on its Web site and in its literature, its culture, as presented at the trial, sometimes seemed to be more accurately described as therapeutic and pedagogical, based in behavioral psychology, rather than as transformational or salvational. The biblical narrative was often described only as supplying a subordinate motivating role. And the dominance of the behavioral therapy approach has only increased over the years. IFI staff, many of whom trained and had previous professional experience in corrections, constantly referred approvingly in their testimony to professional corrections theory and practice. And, as is clear from the language and practice of biblical counselors, secular therapeutic practices are incorporated into and translated into a biblical idiom at many points. At times IFI prisoners seem to have received a synthesis of behavioral therapy presented as God's punishment. At other times, the synthesis appears more benign, with a largely benevolent God basically blessing behavioral theory. In either case, in the gap created by an increased prison population and decreased funding, prisoners are being given an often amateur amalgan of Bible and behavioral modification that, literally, they cannot refuse.

What exactly is IFI, religiously speaking? IFI sometimes speaks of itself as a church, a claim legitimized by the use of biblical citation. So, for example, each prisoner who joins IFI is required to sign an Accountability Covenant, which explains that IFI is a church that is called upon to discipline its members, as in the early Christian community. When IFI was instituted in Iowa, the IFI covenant began, "the church, at times, must exercise discipline towards members who have sinned." It concluded with the words, "I, ———, agree to hold the members of InnerChange accountable and to have them hold me accountable as long as I am in the InnerChange Church."[58] In 2005 the form was rewritten as follows:

> I understand that the principles in Matthew 18:12-35 will be applied to my life within the IFI community. Those principles are
>
> 1. Error leads us to danger (vs. 12)
> 2. The heart of correction is to restore (vs. 13, 14)
> 3. It is the responsibility for those involved to reconcile on an interpersonal level (vs. 15)
> 4. Peer mediation is to be utilized if necessary (vs. 16)
> 5. Removal from the community is a last resort (vs. 17)
> 6. Conflict resolution builds a strong community (vs. 18-20)
> 7. Interpersonal forgiveness of others is a condition of personal forgiveness from God. (vs. 21–35)[59]

Here, the explicit identification of IFI as a church is removed and verses from the New Testament are translated into the language of contemporary social psychology—"community," "interpersonal," "peer mediation," and "conflict resolution"—with biblical verses providing a biblical seal of approval to IFI's own behavioral psychology and ecclesiology.[60]

Four key staff members of PFM and IFI testified at the Iowa trial: Norman Cox, vice president of PFM and national director of IFI since 2003, and three former local program administrators in Iowa, Sam Dye, Dale Kingery, and Chris Geil. Their collective testimony during the Iowa trial reflected a disciplined use of the neutral words that professional social service workers use to describe IFI's methods and objectives, apparently subordinating their Christian identities. The goal is always presented in secular terms: reduce recidivism. The success of IFI also was always measured in secular terms. This rhetorical strategy continues to be remarkably effective in cutting across and confusing the streamlined, separatist language of establishment clause jurisprudence, a language that relies on identifying and segregating religious and secular activities.

Cox had spent thirty years in various positions in the criminal justice system before he went to work for PFM. He holds a B.A. from Virginia Polytechnic Institute and State University and an M.A. in criminal justice from Auburn University. He was in the U.S. Army for four years, serving in Europe and Vietnam. After leaving military service, he worked for the Virginia Probation and Parole Board. He subsequently taught in the criminal justice program at the University of Texas in San Antonio, served as a jail administrator and then founded his own correctional consulting firm (pp. 2102–2119). At the trial, Cox said that he and his wife had been inspired to change their lives after reading evangelist Rick Warren's best-selling book, *The Purpose Driven Life*,[61] with a study group. The book has forty chapters designed to be read, one a day, to guide the reader in a forty-day spiritual journey in imitation of Jesus's forty days in the wilderness.[62] Warren teaches that life is meaningless without God. Laced with hundreds of biblical quotations, the reader is trained to see that God intends everything in life to be explained and guided by biblical revelation.

One of Warren's chapters explains the Great Commission, or what Warren calls "becoming a world-class Christian."[63] The Great Commission, as Jesus's instructions to his disciples concerning the obligation to proselytize are known, states: "Go ye into all the world and preach ye the gospel to every creature."[64] Warren teaches his reader that:

> God invites you to participate in the greatest, largest, most diverse, and most significant cause in history—his kingdom. History is *his story.* He's building his family for eternity. Nothing matters more, and nothing will last as long. From the book of Revelation we know that God's global mission will be accomplished. Someday the Great Commission will be the Great Completion. In heaven an enormous crowd of people from "every race, tribe, nation, and language" will one day stand before Jesus Christ to worship him.[65] (emphasis in original)

There is little room in Warren's apocalyptic vision for non-Christians. Only Christian conversion can make life meaningful. The only true change is from God, the God of the New Testament.

At the trial, Cox explained how he was affected by studying *The Purpose Driven Life*: "You study a chapter or two each session. And then at the end—it helps you reevaluate where you are in your Christian life. At the end there's a little test that you take and determine how well you're doing on evangelism, service and various aspects of your religious life.

My wife and I felt like we needed to expand our service. I started looking for opportunities to do so" (pp. 2120–21). Shortly after taking the test, Cox saw an advertisement for the position with Prison Fellowship; he applied and was quickly hired.

Yet at the trial Cox was careful when describing how IFI works to change prisoners and spoke of his own religious perspective as personal, as simply one perspective. The implication was that it was only one approach among many that might bring about change, But religion is also easy to fake and cannot be measured because it is internal: "We introduce religion," Cox said, "because we, as Christians, believe that the only true change and lasting change occurs through spiritual transformation, but we don't require it. We don't compel it. We don't track it. It would be foolish to try to do so [because] a person can verbally say yes, I have been transformed or I have been changed, but you have no way of measuring that or determining whether that's true, or not" (p. 2134). Cox explained:

> We teach values from a Christian perspective, which includes the spiritual side of the Christian religion, which includes the transformation through the spirit, and we also teach the values that you should live by as a Christian, and then we measure behavior. Because behavior is what reflects the change. Secular research tells you that one of the first signs of a changed individual has nothing to do with the source of the change, but one of the first signs of a changed behavior is respect for authority. They change the way they relate to authority. (p. 2134)

What Cox seems to be saying is that the only part of the process that should interest the law is how prisoners relate to authority. Change is measured by the behavioral standards of secular researchers. How and why change is accomplished is not the law's business. Law can have no legitimate interest in men's souls. Christians know that change is God's work and that all the law can know is behavior.

In his direct examination, the IFI lawyer asked Cox explicitly about the necessity of Christian conversion for success in the program:

> *Q*. Mr. Cox, with regard to the goals of IFI and using the transformational model to change criminal thinking, is it necessary in this transformational model that there be a conversion to Christianity?
> *A*. We, as Christians, believe that, but as far as the program goes, it does not.
> *Q*. Is a conversion to Christianity required for an IFI inmate for enrollment?
> *A*. No.
> *Q*. For progression through the program?

A. No.
Q. Or for graduation from the program?
A. No. (p. 2144)

The lawyer then shifted to what is required, that is, a behavioral change reflecting new values:

Q. Is there a necessity for enrollment progression or graduation, for an IFI inmate to demonstrate a conversion from antisocial behavior to pro-social behavior?
A. Yes. That's the way we measure success.
Q. And are these based on what the record has already indicated, the six core values of the IFI program; integrity, restoration, affirmation, productivity, reconciliation and fellowship?
A. Yes.
Q. Are these exclusive values, exclusively Christian values in your mind?
A. No, certainly not. We teach them in the context of Christian religion and it's Bible based. We go to the Scripture for examples of these values. There are many stories in the Bible that illustrate these Christian values, as we consider them, but they are not unique to Christians by any stretch of the imagination. (pp. 2144–45)

Religious conversion is not required. Conversion to pro-social behavior is the goal. Left open is who determines what constitutes pro-social behavior, how exactly the conversion is accomplished, and what work the Bible does, if any.

One way that PFM employees structure this careful separation of their religious ministry and the secular goals required by the law is through the corporate distinction they make between PFM and IFI. The court's only legitimate interest is in IFI, they say, the party that actually administers the program at Newton and has a separate corporate identity, and a separate product, from PFM. The judge asked Cox to explain the difference between the two: "Mr. Cox, I had a question based on your definitions this morning. You told me that PFM was a ministry while IFI is a Christ-centered values program" (p. 2225). He asked Cox to explain the difference. Cox first described PFM:

> Prison Fellowship's primary goal is to minister to those in prison, to establish the Gospel of Jesus Christ to them, to teach it to them, and to try to help them turn their lives around. That's their primary goal. Sometimes they work through the children, sometimes they work directly with the individuals, sometimes they work through the family. Their goal is to take the Gospel of Jesus Christ into the prison to those

> that are incarcerated there and whose lives have been ruined by whatever reason that put them there. (p. 2225)

Cox then turned to IFI, distinguishing between the motives and language of the staff and the secular goals of the program:

> Now, the IFI program, many volunteers come as a part of their Christian beliefs that they are supposed to go out and visit prisoners because the Bible does tell them that. They come to help that prisoner, to guide that prisoner through a process, to coach that prisoner through a process that results in a return to the community in a more positive environment than the one that put them in prison. We use a values-based approach. We do use Christian doctrine and Christian values. We do—we're true to the Gospel in the sense that we talk about the salvation that Jesus Christ offers. We don't dwell on it. We don't measure it. We don't keep records of conversions. We don't count conversions. That's not how we measure success. We don't count the hours in Bible study, PF does. We focus on those individuals in prison that are preparing for release. . . . Primarily our focus is on those persons returning to the community. We try to fill the gaps that we see in the system. It's a program, one of the very few programs in the United States, perhaps the only one in the United States, that starts 18 months prior to release and continues 12 months after focusing on the same individual, but making sure that preparation is there, that needs are met and the support is there and the community. (p. 2225–26)

The judge translated the distinction into establishment clause terms: "Okay. So one attempts to accomplish a secular purpose, the other attempts to accomplish conversion?" Cox responded, "Correct" (p. 2225). According to Cox, PFM is in the business of conversion. PFM measures its success by counting hours in Bible study and numbers of conversions. IFI, on the other hand, is in the business of teaching Christian values and Christian doctrine as a part of a process of coaching prisoners in their successful return to the community, success being measured in secular, not religious, terms. Separation of church and state is accomplished through the U.S. law of corporations.

The judge also asked Cox about the therapeutic and transformational models and why IFI fit the transformational model (Judge Pratt followed the creation of the transcript by the court reporter on his laptop in front of him, kept notes, and frequently asked questions of witnesses, in order to clarify points):

> THE COURT: Now, at the outset of your testimony you told Mr. Troy about the differences between the therapeutic model and the transformational model. Do you recall that?

THE WITNESS: Yes.

THE COURT: Okay. Why does the Christian program, in your view, best fit, the, quote, transformational model?

THE WITNESS: Because it focuses on transforming the individual's belief system and way of thinking. It offers a spiritual transformation to those who choose it. It offers a value system for those who choose to internalize those values, both of which result in transforming the individual from antisocial to prosocial. (p. 2227).

Cox said that IFI accomplishes its secular goal by "transforming the individual's belief system and way of thinking." "It offers," he told the judge, "a spiritual transformation." The judge then asked: "Mr. Cox, could you accomplish this through other religions?" "Yes." Cox said (p. 2227).

Knowing that the insistence on conversion as a goal—on actual evidence of the fruits of the spirit in the life of a particular prisoner—is likely to be viewed as unconstitutional, IFI, and other faith-based social service providers, have solved the legal problem by seeming to give up on their public claim to the absolute truth and objective efficacy of their religion. They can do that partly because their theology teaches them that conversion is the work of God—of grace—not of man. This theology permits, indeed demands, that they disclaim any necessary connection between IFI's teaching and conversion. But they can also do that because the religion clauses are part of their theology. Religious freedom and the separation of church and state is a part of their religious creed as well as their civic creed.[66]

By abandoning any explicit claim to be seeking religious conversion and simultaneously refusing psycho-social scientific explanations for behavior, IFI is, however, left with no public explanation for how IFI can work. IFI staff shifts from explanation to measuring behavior, leaving the reasons for any such changes unarticulated. IFI does what it does. Prisoners participate for whatever reason they wish. The prisoners who graduate succeed or not, but no public explanation can be given for the different outcomes. As in an absurdist play, causation is abandoned. IFI is claiming that it is doing what no one else will do. Criticism is met with the response: "We are doing what God tells us to do. We are loving our neighbors. What are *you* doing?"

Yet the probable explanation that gradually emerges for why the program might be successful—if and when it is—is consistent with secular corrections models. Objective observers might suggest that IFI works, to the extent that it does, not because of miracles or religious conversions, but as a result of the combination of selectivity in admissions, intense staff involvement with prisoners, residential community support, and close mentoring during and after the in-prison portion of the program. IFI might be understood to work because it supplies the human concern, community, and common sense that is lacking in many prisons today. As was evident from Iowa DOC staff's initial interest in the possibility of a secular version of IFI, the program does offer some of what secular planners believe is necessary for successful prisoner reentry, and at a lower cost because much is done with volunteers.

During his testimony, Cox described the "social learning" model as one contribution he had brought to the IFI program, a model he had come to trust based on his long professional experience in prison work:

> The community model of re-socialization was—has always been with us, but it was highlighted in the mid-nineties. And that basically is where you bring people that are experiencing a common problem together in a housing unit, for example, where they live together so that the learning process continues after class stops. If they spend three-and-a-half, four hours a day in class, they go back to the dorm, or back to the housing unit, or back to the day room and they sit there and talk about it, sometimes they argue about it, but they learn from it. That's the social learning model, social theory of learning. Many programs, whether it's substance abuse or whatever, rely on the community model as a part of the learning process. (p. 2140–41)

IFI is designed, Cox explained, with professional criminological processes in mind:

> One of the things that we do in every reentry program is we front load the services. In other words, that first six months they get a lot of attention, a lot of intensive service because we know that that's when they are at their greatest risk for re-offense. After three years it's only 67 percent. Almost half of that occurs in the first six months. That's what I mean about going to the secular literature and looking at the program and seeing what we're doing right and what we're doing wrong. That's what I focus on. That's what Sam [Dye][67] and other directors focus on because we want to make sure that we address these attributes. IFI does that. (p. 2141)

IFI does not simply preach the gospel and then wait for a miracle. IFI brings the best of what its staff knows of good correctional practice to bear on the program design.

Cox, on behalf of IFI, fuses criminological with Christian language, just as Noll's theory predicts. Cox explained, "We go directly to the criminal thinking issue. We go there with Christian principles and we teach them that they can live a different life, and that a life of service is better than egocentric thinking" (p. 2141). What Cox calls "social learning" could indeed be understood as a form of Christianity but in many ways it sounds like the Christianity of the social gospel, the Christianity of Hull House, rather than the Christianity of Colson's dualistic neo-Calvinism. IFI's challenge might be understood to be trying to combine Christian individualism, in the sense of honoring the worth, dignity, and responsibility of the individual, with collective approaches to social service delivery, rather than allowing Christian individualism to reinforce market liberalism. This is a challenge faced by much of contemporary Christianity, as well as other critics of individualism, secular and religious.

Sam Dye, after serving as the Iowa director of IFI from 2000 to 2004, became IFI's national director. His previous professional experience was in health care administration, a professional identity that was reflected in his testimony. Dye holds an undergraduate nursing degree from the Iowa Methodist School of Nursing and a master's degree in health administration from the University of Osteopathic Medicine and Health Sciences (p. 2231). He authored the IFI substance abuse program.[68] Dye's testimony was characterized by a stubborn insistence on the nonreligious nature of the program. He carefully avoided explicitly religious language, preferring the instrumental language of treatment rather than the language of punishment or religious transformation. (Although Dye testified on cross-examination that he sometimes attended the evening curriculum with his wife, who participated in the volunteer-run Bible study that met Wednesday evenings [p. 2330].)

After preliminary questions about his employment history, IFI's lawyer asked Dye about the nature of IFI. Dye responded that "IFI is a pre-release program with a community reintegration component, basically, in a nutshell." Like Cox, he explained by contrasting IFI to PFM:

> The objective of a religious program is usually under the auspices—for instance, Prison Fellowship volunteers come under the auspice of a chaplain. They would be there with the objective solely to share the Gospel and meet with inmates for that objective. A treatment program, we operate out of a contractual relationship with the State. We are—our objective is to meet the treatment needs of the inmate. And from a pre-release point of view, we're looking to help them out and keep them out of prison. (pp. 2236–37)

IFI is a treatment program not a religious program, Dye insisted. Dye explained his own theory of the effectiveness of IFI as a "values-based" program by analogy to child rearing:

> I think we, in our very educated culture, tend to think that if we can didactically teach something in a classroom, and transmit information

in a classroom, we accomplish something. I think values actually are caught more than taught. As you live in a community of people, particularly I think we see it less. Our children, as they are raised, really take on our values. We don't sit down and teach honesty 101 and give a lecture on honesty to our kids. As they grow up they learn honesty from the relationships that they have with us. In IFI, one of the key things in the IFI community, through the staff, through the volunteers, is that you see these values fleshed out, and you live in that milieu, and you take on those values and begin demonstrating them. (p. 2241)

Values are something, in Dye's words, that are more to be "caught" than "taught.

Although Dye contended that learning values is environmental, he complained when prisoners spoke of their own past criminal activities in environmental terms: "One of my pet peeves," he said, "is when . . . I hear an inmate say that they caught their case, like it's a virus and they are not—they don't have any responsibility, it just kind of popped on them. We'll back up and say, 'No, you didn't catch your case, you committed a crime. You decided to do something evil'" (p. 2243). The tension was tangible in the testimony at the trial between environmental and moral explanations for human action, a tension reflecting a larger social unease in America on the subject. Indeed, IFI itself seems undecided about whether environment or individual choice accounts for human behavior. In Dye's testimony, individual choice, sin, a deliberate turning away from God, accounts for the commission of the crime, but a pro-social environment is the cure. In comparing IFI's program to the secular state-run class in criminal thinking, Dye commented:

> I would say that in a typical criminal thinking class, a GP [General Population] inmate would go across the yard, they would be in the classroom for two hours, they would learn those principles. They walk back across the yard. They go into the GP dorm and there is no practice of those values. The didactic teaching and practice is separated. In our program, because we're a community, what you learn in the class is constantly supported and emphasized, modeled and evaluated within the community setting. (pp. 2246–47)

Although the IFI literature suggests that the cure is divinely bestowed, the testimony of the staff suggests that they understand their cure in very human terms, namely, as the result of applying the best corrections practice, one that uses what Cox calls a "social learning model."

Knowing that conversion cannot, constitutionally, be an object of IFI's efforts, and knowing from their professional training that rehabilitation is a social process, Dye and his colleagues strove constantly to separate the process from the explanation. The IFI lawyer asked Dye to explain the purpose of the religious element of the program, given their disclaimer regarding any effort to proselytize:

Q. [W]hy are IFI teachings Bible-based? Why are the principles discussed in the context of Jesus Christ?

A. I guess I would answer that by saying as a Christian that's my point of view, that's my point of reference. If someone would ask me an opinion on those I would give that opinion. Our primary objective is to keep guys out of prison. Whether or not there is a conversion is a side issue . . . if you would ask me the question do I want people to adopt the way I look at the world and my way of thinking, I guess I would answer yes, because I think most people would like people to come to their understanding and point of view. I would say that because I have that opinion doesn't necessarily mean that I force that opinion. . . . I don't force anybody to believe my Christian point of view. I don't force people not to believe my Christian point of view. I guess that's how I would make the analogy. (pp. 2248–50)

IFI criticism of secular programs is that they focus on behavioral and environmental explanations for crime rather than belief and values. But because they believe that the Constitution forbids them to talk openly about the nature and source of their value system, and because they speak the behavioral language of the social service professions, they imply that membership in a law-abiding society is based on behavior that is formed through one's participation in a community and not through conviction or miracle.

The IFI lawyer took him through the prisoner's day. Dye testified that each of the components of the IFI schedule are designed to teach the IFI values. Dye used virtually no religious language in this testimony:

A. Morning devotionals are a time when guys . . . decide what they want to do in the morning for 15 minutes. . . . IFI staff is not involved. It's totally up to the guys to get out of bed. There's a guy in the group that's assigned to take attendance. It really is a measure of *integrity*. Will a guy be where he's supposed to be and will the attendance taker hold him accountable or lie for him. It's a great test.

Q. What other values are being taught through the morning devotionals?

A. The values, again, *integrity, responsibility*, being where you're supposed to be. We're not there to see who is out of bed at 6 o'clock. It's totally up to the guys whether they get up. (emphasis added) (pp. 2287–88)

Classes, too, teach universal values, not Christianity. Dye was asked:

Q. What values are being taught through the classroom setting?
A. Some of the values, classroomwise is, again, the idea of *responsibility, being accountable* for your time, doing what is expected of you, *following through* on an activity. Particularly in classrooms, and, say, also in the community meeting. Sometimes we set aside time for what we call *affirmations*, where guys will get up and they will publicly affirm one of the other community members or something good that they are doing or they have seen them do. Specifically how they respond to conflict. How they respond to someone who isn't treating them well, to kind of praise them for demonstrating a new way of life . . . positive reinforcement is obviously good. It helps re-enforce behavior. It's good because typically within prison guys don't get involved in affirming each other for good stuff. (emphasis added) (p. 2289)

Work is required because:

> many guys who come to prison don't work. We have guys that have come to prison who have never worked. They have never held a job, all they have done is sold dope. For them to be given a task that is to be accomplished on a daily level is a whole new idea. One of the reasons we started our program at 6 o'clock in the morning is many guys come to prison, have their schedules reversed. They are up all night horsing around doing bad and sleeping all day. When they come to IFI we reverse that schedule. We get them up at 6 o'clock. They get up themselves. Once they are released, they are habitual, they are up, doing something positive, kind of thinking what their day is going to be, what they are going to accomplish. You teach an ethic of work. It's good to excel in something you do. Many of them have never learned that value of *responsibility* and excelling in something and doing something well. (emphasis added) (p. 2290)

He also described "Community Meeting":

A. [It] is a time where all of the inmates will be together. There is an inmate devotional, a thought. There is singing. Community is also a time that staff speaks. If there are issues that are public issues and they need to be dealt with publicly, we'll deal with them publicly. That is an occasion where we challenge inmates to be *honest*, particularly if things are going on that we think are dishonest. We talk about it and mix it up.
Q. What values are talked about through community?
A. I would say *fellowship*, building a *community*, taking *responsibility* to what you input in the community, will give an output, and you

can have some *pride* in the fact that you are contributing to something bigger than yourself.

Q. What are the inmates role in organizing helping to present community?

A. Well, the assignment to give devotions, if you want to call it that, is rotated among the inmates and they are all scheduled through that. If an inmate—we may have, from time to time, an inmate who is scared to death to speak publicly. He's terrified. We will give him a pass and do an alternative assignment.

Q. Why are inmates asked to give public speeches or devotionals?

A. Well, public speaking is important because it is a good skill to develop. One of the things that's interesting, a lot of media come and visit us. We have a lot of visitors, that type of thing. They are always struck by how well the guys stand up and speak. We don't coach guys on what they're going to say. They just stand up and speak. They do well because they practice it. They practice presenting information in public speaking. It's great *self-confidence* building. Public speaking is the No. 1 fear of people. (emphasis added) (pp. 2290–92)

Evening classes are also about community:

> Evening curriculum is a lot of different things. It is basically 6:30 to 8:30, and it's delivered by volunteers. All of the curriculum is delivered in the evening. The primary thing we want to accomplish is fostering relationships between the volunteers and guys. Obviously, building up that *community*. Making conditions that may lead to relationships when they're released, that type of thing. (emphasis added) (p. 2292)

No mention is made in this testimony that most of these activities are thoroughly religious in content.

Even the twice-weekly worship services are said by Dye to be about teaching universal values. He described revivals:

A. A revival is usually a church group that comes in from somewhere outside the state. They may bring musicians, they may not. They may bring a speaker, they may not. It's a way to get usually a larger group of community people in one spot with all the guys. One thing we want to do is connect guys, when they're released, with *prosocial* groups on the outside. Mainly we use churches. Again, they get a good dose of many people that come in. Chris [Geil, IFI's program manager,] doesn't allow people to come over more than twice a year. . . .

Q. What values are trying to be taught through revivals?

> *A.* Again, it's the *responsibility* of being somewhere. It is the value of *fellowship*, building your *community*, and continuing to build those relationships with *prosocial* people that you continue this relationship on the outside. (emphasis added) (pp. 2292–93)

Sunday church services are also explained in this light:

> *Q.* Inmates are expected to go to church on Sunday as well; right?
> *A.* They are expected to attend, yes.
> *Q.* Why is that?
> *A.* Because I think we want them to realize that there are *things bigger than them*. I think Norm [Cox] spoke about the egocentricity of inmates, which is a huge problem. They think only of them. One of the things I think fosters attending church on Sunday, or service on Sunday morning, is that there is *a community*, again, that's bigger than them. When they are on the outside there are things bigger than them that they need to plug in to. If not a church, then maybe a civic club or maybe another *prosocial* group of people. (emphasis added) (p. 2293)

Churches are about being prosocial. Worshiping God seems incidental.

No sociologist could be more functional in explaining religion than Sam Dye. IFI prisoners testified that devotions are a time for prayer and witnessing, classes a time for learning to be a Christian, community meetings a time for public witnessing and singing, and the evening curriculum an exclusively Bible-oriented study taught by church volunteers. In contrast, IFI staff described devotions, Bible study, revivals, and church attendance as useful tools for teaching the values of "getting up in the morning," "being where you are supposed to be," "being accountable," "following through," "doing what is expected," "doing something positive," recognizing something "bigger than themselves," "community," "integrity," "responsibility," "pro-social" behavior, "honesty," "pride," a good "work ethic," "self-confidence," and "fellowship." Apparently, for the staff, everything is being taught except that Jesus is the Lord and God has a purpose for one's life.

For Dye, it seems, the program's focus on the "daily activities of life" is the key to its success. The IFI lawyer asked Dye to explain how IFI teaches values. He responded, again, with an analogy to child rearing:

> I would say it's taught even more outside class. For instance, if you're going through the serving line and you're a big bruiser and you have got some skinny little new kid passing out chicken, will you make him give you double the chicken? That happens all the time in GP. Will you intimidate other people to give you more than your fair share. That's a

> measure of integrity. We talked about a guy here with jelly packets. You think, man, jelly packets, man you're being picky. That's theft. I always told my kids, "If I can trust you on the small things, I can trust you on the big things." I tell the guys that too, "If I can trust you in the little things like jelly packets, I can trust that you're not going to take my car keys and steal my car." A lot of those things are taught in the normal course of life, such as going through the dinner line, on the basketball court. How you conduct yourself in the weight yard. All of that stuff, you can see whether they are demonstrating any of those values. All of those are wrapped up in the daily activities of life. (p. 2294)

Teaching prisoners is like raising kids, he said. Most important is the behavior and example of the staff/parents, not the explanation.

Several times the IFI lawyer asked Dye explicitly about the importance of religion in IFI. Like Cox, Dye insisted that IFI was not about conversion to Christianity:

> *Q*. At any point along the way, phase one, two, three or four, are inmates graded or evaluated based on their religiosity or their Christianity?
> *A*. They are not. (p. 2298)
> *Q*. You mentioned that part of the aftercare component is setting them up with a church. Are they required to attend church?
> *A*. Yeah, they are required to attend church. We've never had anyone ask us to set them up, say, with a mosque, but we would do that.
> *Q*. They're not required to attend a Christian church?
> *A*. No.
> *Q*. Does IFI instruct inmates what churches they need to join as part of an aftercare program?
> *A*. They are not required to join a church, they are only required to attend. The intent of that is that you not necessarily have to join a church, the intent is that it's a large group of people that have a propensity to volunteer and to be prosocial. That's an easy network for us to plug people into. (pp. 2303–4)

The requirement to attend church is about networking, volunteering, and being pro-social, not about going to Heaven. A mosque would do that just as well.

On cross-examination, Dye did acknowledge another role for religion in IFI, namely, to provide an identity for IFI employees. The plaintiffs' lawyer asked him about an employee who was terminated for not adhering to the Statement of Faith:

> *Q*. In fact, isn't it correct, Mr. Dye, that there was an employee of the IFI program. . . . And he was terminated because after he signed

the statement of faith, and after he was an IFI employee, it was determined that he was in fact not a believer in all aspects of the statement of faith; is that true?

A. It was determined through my conversations with him that he didn't believe the statement of faith. So, therefore, he lied when he signed his name.

Q. What aspects of the statement of faith did he not believe in? . . .

A. I believe the issue was that he did not believe the Bible to be true.

Q. He didn't believe the Bible to be true?

A. Yes.

Q. Was there specific aspects of the Bible?

A. I believe the deposition reflected the first ten chapters of Genesis. He believed it to be myth. (pp. 2347–50)

During his re-cross the lawyer for the plaintiffs returned to the topic of this prisoner's termination and to the requirement to believe in biblical inerrancy:

Q. Now, you were asked about Mr. Boe and why he was terminated, and you said that because he didn't believe the Bible was true. Would you agree that different Christian faiths . . . think differently about the status of the Bible as a written document? Some people believe it is literally true, everything in there is literally true. Other people think that it is in some—it is something less than that. Would you agree with that?

A. I would see that there is probably varying opinions on that issue, yes.

Q. Some people think that the Bible is black and white, literally an historical document, that it's telling about real, actual things that happened in history. Would you agree with that?

A. Yes.

Q. And that's the IFI and the Prison Fellowship way of thinking about the Bible, isn't it, that it's a literally true document of historical factual events; isn't that true? (p. 2389)

Dye was argumentative:

A. I guess I couldn't answer for everyone if that's the spin they want to put on it, as you have described it.

Q. I didn't call it a spin. I'm just saying isn't that the IFI approach to teaching and educating about the Bible and the PFM approach as well?

A. I'm not sure I would agree with that, Mr. Stowers.

Q. Statement of faith requires the people that sign it to indicate that they believe the Bible is literally true?

A. If you want to show me a copy, I'll discuss it. I don't want to talk off the top of my head. (pp. 2389–90)

Then, returning to the employee who had been dismissed:

Q. Well, in any event, Mr. Boe is indicating that he didn't believe the Bible was in all respects literally an historically factually truthful document?
A. That is a piece of it, yes, sir.
Q. And I think Mr. Boe also had the view that the Bible, in some respects, may involve some characterizations of events that were more vivid than reality had them in actuality?
A. I would say that's true.
Q. But it was still a very important religious document to Mr. Boe, it just didn't have the status that you felt it should have?
A. It wasn't what I felt. It was the fact that through our conversation it became apparent that he did not believe the statement of faith, and that was admitted within our conversations, so that was the issue.
Q. And one of the issues was he didn't believe in creationism?
A. I'm not so sure that specific in a sense because many Christians have different views on how creation occurred, and we would accept differing views.
Q. Didn't believe in the Great Flood?
A. That was one of the issues. That was one of the things he said. (pp. 2390–91)

The issue was honesty, not faith. Dye insisted that IFI is not in the business of legislating Christian orthodoxy. In some sense, it did not really matter that Dye could not remember the precise wording of the Statement of Faith without looking at it, as it primarily served as a marker of identity and probity.

On cross-examination, the plaintiffs' lawyer also asked Dye about IFI's policy concerning homosexuality:

Q. Now, you indicated that the IFI program's open to those who consider themselves to be homosexuals?
A. Correct.
Q. One of the things, however, that happens with regard to persons of that sexual orientation is that they're encouraged to take on a different sexual orientation as part of the IFI program?
A. I would disagree with that.
Q. They're taught that it's a sin to be homosexual?

A. There is no class lecture that homosexuality is discussed and the class is told "It's a sin, and you better not be a homosexual." That's a mischaracterization, I believe, of what we do in class.
Q. There's no class that says that, but that's the teaching of the IFI program, whether it's taught as a part of a curriculum or not; isn't that true?
A. If you want to ask me if a gentleman asked me if I thought it was morally wrong, then I would answer yes, but I can't say that it's—in the way that you've stated it. (pp. 2353–54)

These markers of identity, the literal truthfulness of the Genesis account of creation and the immorality of homosexual behavior, for Dye, are simply opportunities for testing honesty and loyalty. In Dye's testimony, they are presented as extrinsic to the actual work of IFI in the Newton facility. The Statement of Faith is not intended to get in anyone's way. "The statement of faith," he insisted, "is a document that seeks to display sort of a core set of beliefs that, in my opinion, most people who identify themselves as Christians would agree to" (p. 2268).

One of the prisoners who testified in the trial, Clint Kirkpatrick, is a gay Catholic. When asked to leave the IFI program, he believed he had been discriminated against because of his sexual orientation. In response to questions from the plaintiffs' lawyer, Kirkpatrick testified as follows:

Q. Can you explain to the Court what your sexual orientation or sexual identity is?
A. Like I said, I was molested when I was younger, so growing up I didn't know, and at this point I mean I'm sexually attracted to the same sex; but there's also things I love about the other sex as well, so maybe that's something I'm still trying to figure out.
Q. Can you tell me what IFI's teachings about homosexuality were?
A. That it was wrong.
Q. And did IFI have any teachings on whether a homosexual can enter heaven?
A. It's—according to them, it's not possible.
Q. Did they have any teachings on whether there was any way it could be possible or what a homosexual would have to do to make it possible?
A. I'm not remembering anything right off on that.
Q. And what was your understanding of what IFI's teachings on homosexuality were based on?
A. Scripture out of the Bible.
Q. And what are your religious beliefs with respect to homosexuality?

> *A.* God, as I understand him, isn't judgmental. Two consenting adults should be allowed to do what they would want to do.[69] (pp. 489–90)

During his cross-examination, Kirkpatrick acknowledged that his views were contrary to the official teaching of the Catholic Church.

In his opinion, Judge Pratt summarized his findings with respect to IFI teaching on homosexuality:

> InnerChange also condemns the human experience of homosexuality, teaching that homosexuality is wrong and sinful. InnerChange's disapproval of homosexuality is based on Prison Fellowship's policy, which is based on Prison Fellowship's understanding of biblical principles. This is in contrast to the Dept. of Corrections official policy, which takes no official stand regarding homosexuality. The only related Dept. of Corrections policy commands that there be no physical contact between inmates or sexual displays, regardless of gender. . . . The testimony and evidence presented at trial clearly show that the InnerChange program, as practiced at the Newton Facility, indoctrinates inmates in the belief that homosexuality is morally wrong and profoundly sinful.[70]

IFI testimony reflected the belief that the "core" of Christianity excludes practices regarded as peripheral, such as a non-literal reading of the Bible or homosexuality. Certain devotional practices were also outside the core. IFI's lawyer asked Dye about how IFI accommodated Catholics and other nonevangelicals:

> *Q.* Are Catholics allowed to have a Catholic Bible or rosary?
> *A.* Yes.
> *Q.* Are inmates of other religions allowed to maintain some of the study materials and—
> *A.* Yes.
> *Q.* —tokens of their religion?
> *A.* Sure.
> *Q.* Are Catholics allowed to attend Mass or confession?
> *A.* Yes.
> *Q.* In the IFI program?
> *A.* Yes, they are. (pp. 2262–63)

"Tokens" of other religions are permitted, but you should "shoot for the core," as Dye explained:

> *Q.* Are they allowed to say the Hail Mary prayer in the group settings?
> *A.* That was the issue that I think started all this hullabaloo. Basically Augie Bauer [Michael Bauer] brought that to me, some people were

> upset because somebody said a Hail Mary prayer. The background is, when I talked with Augie, we tried, in group settings, not to inject any one church's method or doctrine or way of doing things. When I talked to Augie, he said, "Well, can we pray an Our Father prayer?" I'm not Catholic. I didn't know what the Our Father was. He prayed it, and he said, "That's *the same thing that any Protestant would pray.*" That's fine. It would be the same for the Pentecostal folks. We say you can't speak in tongues in large group settings because not everybody understands that. *We try to shoot toward the core* in large group settings. If you're in a small group of guys you can do your own thing, do what you want to do. It isn't an issue. If we're in a community setting, large group setting, we ask people to shoot toward the core. All of us can agree, 80, 85, 90 percent on what's there. (emphasis added) (pp. 2263–64)

Marian devotion and speaking in tongues are measured according to whether these practices are part of the "core," a core that is defined by contrast to the standard, the standard being "the same thing that any Protestant would pray."

At the end of the trial Dale Kingery, the then new IFI program director for Iowa, was recalled as a defense witness. The defense hoped to persuade the court that whatever mistakes had been made in the past, at the time when the program was first initiated, IFI had recently cleaned up its religious act. Defense attorneys first questioned Kingery about prisoner recruitment procedures, and he answered in wholly secular terms. Then he was asked:

> *Q.* Do you ask them about their religious beliefs?
> *A.* I do not.
> *Q.* Do you ask them whether they are homosexual or not?
> *A.* I don't.
> *Q.* Do you deal in biblical phrases or references in the introductory class, or introductory meetings?
> *A.* I don't only inasmuch to again emphasize to the applicants that *it is a religious program, it's a Christian focus, a Christ-centered Bible-based reentry program.* (emphasis added) (pp. 2404–5)

The implication here was that the IFI disclosure that "it is a religious program, it's a Christian focus, a Christ-centered Bible-based reentry program" was like a Miranda warning and was supposed to immunize IFI from criticism. The prisoner had consented to being a part of what followed and to have ceded to IFI control over the line between Christian and secular. This point was made often at the trial: because all the prisoners were completely informed in advance about the religious nature of the program, they had no basis on which to complain.

Like Dye, Kingery was also asked by the defense lawyer to characterize the purpose of the various required elements of the IFI program and their relation to the program's "core" moral values. For example, the IFI lawyer asked: "What is a morning devotional, and what values are you, the director of the IFI program, hoping are inculcated in the morning devotion?" Kingery answered, refocusing the question on results rather than intentions:

> [L]et me turn it around and ask for what I look for when a man is out. I look for a man when he is on the street to be able to conduct himself in a way that he manages his own behavior. He's where he's supposed to be when he says he'll be there, he gathers information and makes decisions, and that comes at his own motivation, he's able to do that on his own. He has the *integrity* to do what he says he will do. Now, these are fundamental values that I noticed early on, even working with very young offenders, that if you don't begin to develop in them a framework to function independently, even though they're in a community, they will not be a part of that community. Many of these offenders have not been engaged in a pro-social community at all. And so *I look through morning devotions for a man to show up on time, to participate, to think about the course of the day.* Rather than the day happening to him, for him to begin and plan and say, "What are my goals for the day, and what are my thoughts, or how will I approach this day?" That, to me, is a critical piece of that morning time. And what I noticed, when I talk to men on the street, I will ask them, "Do you still get up in the morning and spend some time ordering your day?" And the men who are successful, one after the other, will say, "I still get up in the morning, get my head straight, plan my day, and move on." (emphasis added) (pp. 2411–12)

Like Dye, Kingery emphasized that the goal is managing one's behavior, fostering the community and pro-social values. Devotions are about getting up in the morning and planning the day, not about prayer.

In his cross-examination, the plaintiffs' lawyer also asked Kingery about the process of recruiting inmates for IFI. Kingery, like Dye, was very cautious, even argumentative. In a frustrating series of exchanges, the plaintiffs' lawyer tried to pin him down about exactly what the prisoner was consenting to when he joined the program. The lawyer first asked whether the Christian nature of the program was something the prisoner had to "accept":

Q. When we talk about criteria for admission, the one criteria for admission I didn't hear you say . . . is that the inmates who are volunteering to join in this program of IFI, have to be willing to accept the Christian and biblically-based nature of the program. Is that true?
A. What would you mean by "accept"?
Q. Well, do they have to have some level of acceptance of it?
A. I still don't understand what your definition is.
Q. Do you know what the word "accept" means?
A. No, not as you're using it, I don't, sir.
Q. Do you understand that the inmates who have to join—or is there some understanding that the inmates who choose to join the IFI program have to be accepting of the Christian teachings of the program, as you explain them to the inmates prior to them joining?
A. *What I do in the introduction is I make it clear that they will encounter Christian teaching. I make no reference in them accepting it, and there is no requirement that they accept or agree with what's being taught. I want to make sure that they understand coming in what they are joining, and what they will be exposed to on a day-to-day basis.* (emphasis added) (pp. 2426–27)

By joining the program they consent to exposure and participation. But, as with Cox and Dye, Kingery was unable to clarify the purpose, if any, of the Christian content for the program if prisoners were not being asked to "accept" that content. Agreeing to describe the prisoner's implied mental attitude as one of "acceptance" apparently might imply requiring actual religious conversion.

The lawyer for the plaintiffs asked Kingery again about informing prisoners that the program is Christian:

Q. Why does it matter if they know that if they don't have to be accepting of it to some degree?
A. . . . [M]y experience is that if you do not provide a paradigm to reinforce a value that the value will not stand on its own. Most people will not accept a value with the answer of just because.
Q. So in order for them to be teachable within the program, they have to be willing to accept a Christian biblical paradigm; is that true?
A. No, sir. (p. 2427)

The two dueled on about the words, moving from "accept" to "participate" to "engage:"

Q. So they . . . could be objecting to the Christian teachings of the program and still be good participants in the program. Is that your testimony?

A. I think you would have to explore a couple of those issues more carefully. To participate means to engage, to discuss, to examine. That's what is looked for in any treatment setting, for the individual to come in and engage.

Q. You've used that word, and I don't know what that word means to you. I know what it means to me. What does the word "engage" mean as you use it?

A. Sure. My experience is that there is nothing gained by inducing someone to come into treatment, such as court-ordered substance abuse treatment. A person has to have a personal motivation, there has to be some intrinsic value to them. And so *I'm looking for a person that will come in with the motivation to change, and will give a look at what's being introduced, because it doesn't always mean agreeing. What it means is wrestling with what's being introduced and where they've been and how to apply things to their life for a different outcome.* (emphasis added) (pp. 2427–28)

What he is looking for in a prisoner, Kingery claimed, is an openness to change—"*wrestling with what's being introduced and where they've been and how to apply things to their life for a different outcome.*" First comes a motivation to change—and then actual change. The role of Christianity remains ambiguous.

The plaintiffs' lawyer continued to try to pin him down about what exactly change means to IFI:

Q. And the change you're looking for is this change in the heart. I think you talked about that in your earlier testimony a few weeks ago.

A. I give no value to what a person says at any given time. What I value and measure is what a person can consistently produce in their life. I want to see what a person can do day in and day out across a number of different settings. To me that inherently involves internalizing information, and then putting it into practice hopefully with an increasing degree of success.

Q. The internalization that you're talking about is in the person's heart, the transformational process that's described in all those materials?

A. I'm looking for a person to adopt prosocial values and display them on a consistent basis.

Q. But the change is a religious change, isn't it?

A. The change is a change in thinking and believing.

Q. In Jesus Christ?

A. In a value system.

Q. In the biblically-based Christ-centered value system taught by the InnerChange Freedom Initiative program, isn't that what you're talking about?

A. What I explained to you is that *values have to be presented in context. They need to be connected to something, to a philosophy or a paradigm that will not stand, in my opinion, on their own. So participants in the program are introduced to widely-accepted values from a Christian paradigm. . . .*

The change that I'm looking for is the change that I've looked for in any client that I've worked with. Are you able to conduct yourself in a manner consistent with community and societal expectations on a consistent basis across a number, a broad number of settings? What I mean by that is can you carry these habits to work? Can you display them in your family? Can you display them in your neighborhood and community? (emphasis added) (pp. 2428–32)

It is all about results—about values exemplified in pro-social conduct. The Christian paradigm is just one way to get there. It provides a "context."

Judge Pratt intervened here and asked: "Mr. Kingery, here's the way I'm construing his question. . . . He's saying does this transformation have to occur by an inmate developing a relationship with Jesus Christ?" Kingery responded, "Obviously not. Obviously many people in our communities conduct themselves in a pro-social manner that would not describe themselves as Christians" (p. 2432). So, one does not have to be a Christian to be pro-social but how do non-Christians achieve that? Questions lingered: How do the prisoners become pro-social? And how will the implementation of IFI accomplish that? What role does the pervasively biblical language of IFI's curriculum play?

Finally, the plaintiffs' lawyer returned to Kingery's secular description of what IFI calls "devotions," contrasting his description to the one offered by the prisoners who had testified in the plaintiffs' case. First, regarding Kingery's own understanding of the purpose of the devotional:

Q. Now, you talked about the morning devotionals, and . . . what I heard you say to the Court was that the morning devotionals are about inmates getting their days organized, as if that's the time that they get together in these small groups and go through a list of things to do, that they're going to do for the day. Is that what a morning devotional is, or am I misinterpreting what you're saying?

A. You may have misinterpreted what I said. My opinion on the importance of that morning time is—the observation over the course of my career is that many people react or see the world happening to them, rather than planfully thinking about what their values are, what their attitude is for the day, especially in prison. But even in life you can fall out of bed and encounter things quickly that will have great impact on your tone and your life if you have not pre-

> pared yourself, including setting your attitude or kind of your agenda for the day. (pp. 2436–37)

Then, as to the testimony of the prisoners:

> *Q.* Well, a number of inmates have testified about what happens at the morning devotionals, and you've sat through the testimony of those inmates, didn't you?
> *A.* I believe so. I don't know the names. . . .
> *Q.* Do you remember them talking about praying and reading biblical verses during morning devotionals?
> *A.* Yes.
> *Q.* Do you think that happens during the morning devotionals?
> *A.* Yes, it does. (p. 2437)

How does Kingery explain the difference?

> All I can answer to is my understanding and intent, the importance that I feel there is in that morning devotion, and that is getting up, being where you're supposed to be, taking part in a community event. And, again, evaluating what your values are, really, in effect, what your plans are for the day, getting your attitudes set for the day, what's important for me, what steers my life. (pp. 2437–38)

Devotions, Kingery insisted, are about planning your day.

The lawyer tried to be more direct, this time focusing on Kingery's own personal practice:

> *Q.* Do you know what a devotional is, sir?
> *A.* You have to define that.
> *Q.* Well—
> *A.* I told you what that time is used for.
> *Q.* Is it used to give devotion to God, to Jesus Christ? Isn't that what a devotional is all about?
> *A.* I could not speak to what every man individually does at each individual table. I can speak to you about broad generalities.
> *Q.* Well, is that what a devotional is?
> *A.* Sir, I can't answer that question.
> *Q.* So you don't know what a devotional is?
> *A.* I know personally what a devotional is.
> *Q.* Okay. What is it?
> *A.* It may be something different to you.
> *Q.* What is it personally to you?
> *A.* Devotional to me, or devotional time is what I told you, a time that I would set aside purposely to review important issues in my life,

guiding principles in my life that I don't want to have the day start without me thinking about.

Q. *And those principles would include giving devotion and thanks to Jesus Christ; is that not correct?*

A. *For me personally?*

Q. *Yes.*

A. *For me personally, it could, yes.*

Q. *Isn't that what the inmates are taught they're supposed to do in the morning devotional, sir?*

A. *No, sir.* (emphasis added) (pp. 2438–39)

It is as if they are speaking different languages. Kingery, like the other IFI witnesses, austerely refused to characterize the prisoner's religious experience, or even to standardize language usage. A devotion is whatever you want it to be. That is a part of the American creed and religion. While we expect you to plan your day and be where you are supposed to be, we don't tell you what your words mean.

Judge Pratt, a Roman Catholic, heard the IFI witnesses describing the practices—the bodily disciplines—that constitute a religious community. He concluded that "the programming, and the daily schedule, all combine to create a sort of modern, evangelical Christian monastic setting in which every waking hour is devoted to living out an intentional Christian experience."[71] The IFI witnesses were describing what they understood to be only outward signs, which, in their theology, can never be true religion. True religion is of the heart, accessible only to God. There was a close, almost seamless fit between IFI's theology, a highly individualized Protestant evangelical religion of the heart, and the secular ideology of individualism and behavior-based assessment. That fit permits IFI to claim that it is not establishing religion. Those practices necessary to make the religion of the heart possible, in Catholic terms, have been secularized.

Sin, too, is worked into this protestant/secular economy. Referring to a form used to evaluate prisoner progress, Chris Geil was asked by the plaintiffs' lawyers about the expression "admission of sin":

Q. Do any IFI counselors use the term "admission of sin"?

A. As I sit here, I can't recall a time that we have used that phrase, admission of sin.

Q. Do you have any understanding of what that term—

A. I do have, yes. I do have an understanding of what that is.

Q. What is that?

A. Well, *any time that you break the law, it's a sin.* And so you need to admit the times that you have broken the law, broken the rules. (emphasis added) (p. 1159)

Geil was asked to explain:

> *A.* You're asking me what it means to admit sin? You're asking me what that is?
>
> *Q.* Yeah. What that is.
>
> *A.* Okay. All these men are in prison because they have committed for the most part heinous crimes against people, against the state, and so they came to prison not falsely and not under any kind of duress. They earned their way there because *they have broken the laws of the state. We are very clear in telling men that the things that they did were not mistakes but choices, and they are choices that they made without regard to other people's feelings or without regard to other people's property, and without regard to the values of society. Those things are wrong, and we do label them as sins. Those are sins.* Those are wrong things. And now a great practice for men is to admit times in their heart and in their actions when they go out and do things that are wrong, they need to admit those things. "That's right, I got angry at that person. I yelled at that person. I had no right to yell at that person. I had no right to take two chickens when I was going through the line. I had no right to come out— That's against the law for me to come out from the tier early and get in line." And they need to admit when they do things wrong and they need to own up. That's one of the pillars that we talk about is *responsibility and honesty. Those are two of those great pillars in our program.* So they have to be honest, and they have to take responsibility. They have to be accountable. And so, *yeah, we talk about sin.* We say when you do things wrong that are against people and against society and against what's right, that's sin. And you need to admit that, and you need to come and say, "Hey, Chris, let me tell you something that I did," and you admit that, and then we talk about that. And that self-disclosure is good for their hearts, and it's just good for them. (emphasis added) (pp. 1160–61)

Admitting sin is understood to be good for the prisoner, whether it is taking two chicken entrees at a meal or stepping out of the cell early to get into the lunch line. Self-disclosure leads to responsibility and honesty and "regard for the values of society."

IFI's claim is that it seeks to address what almost everyone agrees is a legitimate and secular governmental purpose, the reduction of recidivism, and it does that by promoting personal responsibility. IFI seeks to accomplish this goal through a program of individual transformation taught from an avowedly Christian perspective that will cause its members to adopt universal values of civilized behavior. No religious conversion is necessary, as religion is merely the means, not the end, of IFI. Because religion is defined in this functional, universal way, and because IFI does not, in a narrow sense, have religious goals, the program does not understand itself as limiting prisoners' religious freedom. When asked by the plaintiffs' lawyer about the risk of violating prisoners' rights to religious freedom, Director Kautzky displayed a hostility toward the prisoners that rarely occurred during the trial:

> *Q.* Are you aware that part of the change that was being suggested would be a change in religious practices for some of the inmates who would participate?
>
> *A.* I'm not sure I understand the question. I mean—was I aware that that would require—*most inmates don't know how to spell religion much less have religious practices.* So I suspect to answer your question, yeah, there would be significant change for some of them to expect to go to Bible study and be expected to do some other things requiring some level of discipline in their lives. That would be a pretty significant difference for many of them."[72] (emphasis added)

Going to Bible study is about discipline, not religion. Religious preference seems to be a luxury for those on the outside, those who already have the discipline of "biblical" values.

Sam Dye was also asked about sin: "Does IFI teach that sin is the root of all problems?" He replied:

> *A.* I don't like the word sin. I think it's a religious word that carries a lot of baggage. I address it. I will speak for myself, sin comes from the archery word meaning to miss the mark. There is not a guy in prison that hasn't missed the mark. The way I address it is when you miss the mark, particularly when you're dealing with community standards of good and evil, you do damage to yourself, to your family and the community. In that sense you create a lot of havoc for other people.
>
> *Q. Have any inmates ever been removed from IFI because of their religious beliefs?*
>
> *A. No.* (emphasis added) (p. 2299)

Again, IFI is not about religion. Sin is secularized using a common evangelical reference to the word choice of sixteenth-century Bible translators.

Yet, whereas IFI staff consistently expressed a sole desire to foster the secular religion of responsibility through the use of biblical tools, Charles Colson spoke the language of an evangelist. In an opinion piece in the *Wall Street Journal* in 2004, Colson discussed the presence of Islam in U.S. prisons and summarized PFM's answer to that presence:

> The long term answer lies in what ministries like Prison Fellowship do: bringing the Gospel into the prisons and telling inmates about the love of Christ. I've gone into 600 prisons around the world; when the gospel is preached, and men embrace Christ, they eschew violence. The prisons we run prove it. In Texas, Kansas, Iowa and now Minnesota, *our prisons are filled with once-dangerous men who now love Jesus and live new lives.*[73] (emphasis added)

One of the most interesting recent sociological studies of prisons considers the reasons for the apparent widespread failure of state-run rehabilitation programs. Sociologist Ann Chih Lin studied rehabilitation programs in five prisons[74] and concluded that the problem is not the impossibility of rehabilitation but that rehabilitation is rarely seriously attempted. Successful programs require successful implementation. Adequate implementation is often defeated by institutional needs and values centered on maintaining order, needs and values that repeatedly undermine how schedules are maintained, how staffing is handled, and what resources are devoted to the daily administration of the program. Lin urges detailed attention to how programs work in local settings. Her conclusions suggest that IFI success, such as it is, arises from dedication, staffing, and resources, factors that could also enable other prison treatment programs to succeed.

The newest *Annual Report* from PFM lists the "six C's of Transformation," what they call "the best practices of discipleship": community, consistency, character, comprehensiveness, continuity and collaboration.[75] Like the six values of IFI, these are said to be both "universal" and "biblical" values.

CHAPTER 4

The Way We Live Now

A STRIKING AND SIGNIFICANT ASYMMETRY between the evidence offered by the plaintiffs and that offered by the defendants in the Iowa case was that the latter offered no expert testimony on religion, either religion in general or any specific religion, either to support their case or to rebut the expert testimony that the plaintiffs offered. The defendants relied on the testimony of IFI staff and prisoners to prove that their program was neither religious nor an establishment of religion within the meaning of the First Amendment. The implication of not offering expert testimony was that an American judge can evaluate evidence about the presence, or absence, of religion, without expert assistance. IFI's position was that religion is the kind of thing, unlike, for example, the practice of medicine, about which expert testimony is unnecessary.

Expert testimony in a U.S. court is different from testimony about the actual events at issue in a particular trial, and is governed by special rules. Rule 702 of the Federal Rules of Evidence governs the admissibility of such evidence:

> If scientific, technical, or other specialized knowledge will assist the trier of fact to understand the evidence or to determine a fact in issue, a witness qualified as an expert by knowledge, skill, experience, training, or education, may testify thereto in the form of an opinion or otherwise, if (1) the testimony is based upon sufficient facts or data, (2) the testimony is the product of reliable principles and methods, and (3) the witness has applied the principles and methods reliably to the facts of the case.

The Notes to the Rule explain:

> Whether the situation is a proper one for the use of expert testimony is to be determined on the basis of assisting the trier. "There is no more certain test for determining when experts may be used than the common sense inquiry *whether the untrained layman would be qualified to determine intelligently and to the best possible degree the particular issue without enlightenment from those having a specialized understanding of the subject* involved in the dispute." (emphasis added)

Under the federal rules, the appropriateness of admitting expert testimony depends on whether the subject of the dispute is one that "common sense" would suggest an "untrained layman" is qualified to determine" or whether "enlightenment from those having a specialized understanding of the subject" is advisable. Even when expert testimony is offered, however, the question remains as to how the trier-of-fact, whether judge or jury, will evaluate such testimony. Debates within academic communities about the subject matters testified to by experts present real challenges to judges and juries, whether such expertise concerns fingerprints or religion.

In the Iowa trial, the plaintiffs offered expert testimony that IFI was evangelical Christian in its character. The defendants presented no expert witnesses to rebut the plaintiffs' testimony. Proof was made, rather, through the presentation of laypersons' opinions of IFI's secular nature and intention, and of the nature of religion in general. And those "lay" opinions were evaluated by a "lay" judge. The use of the word "lay" in the law emphasizes the "clerical" nature of the role of the expert, historically. An expertise that is largely rejected by American Christians. To be sure, by not offering expert testimony on religion, IFI lawyers were, at one level, making a judgment about trial strategy: they believed that IFI witnesses would be convincingly sincere and universalist in their outlook; indeed, perhaps their non-expert dedication to an unpopular mission would be more persuasive without expert support. But the defendants' decision also says something about religion in the United States and about modern religion in general. In the proceedings on appeal, it became clearer that the defendants were contending that receipt of expert testimony about religion in a U.S. court is itself establishmentarian, as it defines religious doctrine according to an authority beyond the individual, thus violating the individual's right to the free exercise of religion. In short, American religion is a thoroughly lay affair.[1]

Further, IFI is saying not just that defining religion violates the establishment clause in a formal legal sense, but that, whether or not its argument on this point is valid, as a matter of law it is logically impossible for it to establish religion because evangelical Christianity is the antithesis of established religion. Evangelical Christians largely, but not exclusively, trace their descent from churches that emerged to oppose any established religion. The transformation of those churches in the United States has created a religious phenomenology that has ingeniously fitted itself to the culture so completely as to make separation impossible. In other words, Evangelical Christians understand their forbears to have invented both the freedom of religion and free religion. By definition, free religion cannot be established or expertly defined.

I was thus the only expert on religion to serve in the Iowa case. There was no "duel of the experts" as is common in U.S. trials. I wrote a report that was filed in the case; I was deposed by counsel for the defendants; and I testified during the trial. On each occasion I offered the academic opinion—based on my reading of the documents obtained from IFI concerning the IFI program and of depositions given by prisoner plaintiffs and others, as well as on my knowledge of American religious history—that American religion scholars would classify PFM and IFI as evangelical Christian para-church organizations. I endeavored to show why scholars would so characterize them given the distinctive history, theology, and religious practices of these organizations compared to other U.S. Christian groups. I also offered the opinion that, although evangelical Christianity is a broad and diverse category, commonalities exist that would support its use for scholarly purposes. I made clear that my opinion was not a legal opinion as to the constitutionality of the IFI contract but was the opinion of a scholar of the comparative study of religion, particularly that of the United States. I regarded this opinion as uncontroversial.[2]

Throughout the trial prisoners and IFI staff repeatedly said, "this is a Christian program" or "we teach Christian values," as if those were self-evident truths, truths that were entirely compatible with the commands of the establishment clause, truths needing no expert explanation or constitutional excuse. Beginning with the struggle in the Iowa courtroom for the terms in which IFI should be described, this chapter reviews the religious life of the God Pod in the wider context of contemporary disestablished, deregulated, diasporic, and globalized religion. Drawing on scholarship concerning the re-imagining of the secular and the comparative study of contemporary religious practice, the evangelical self will be looked at in the context of the modern religious self generally, as well as in the United States and globally. I consider the broader claim that the defendants were making at trial: that IFI is not religious but is universal. Contemporary evangelical Christianity will be shown to be one iteration of a broader religious style within twenty-first-century religion. The next chapter considers both the defendants' strategy in the light of current First Amendment doctrinal interpretation and how the complaints of Iowa prisoners suggest needed change in the regulation of religion in modern pluralistic societies.

Proving Establishment

The First Amendment provides that "Congress shall make no law respecting an establishment of religion." That prohibition, initially imposed only on Congress, was extended to the states in 1947 when the U.S. Supreme Court ruled that the religion clauses of the First Amendment had been incorporated into the Fourteenth Amendment at the time of its passage in 1865.[3] For a plaintiff to prove a violation of the "establishment clause," he must demonstrate that the state's actions in a particular case amounted to a law respecting an "establishment of religion." For the most part, generalized governmental invocations of a deity, in such phrases as "In God We Trust," and symbolic government gestures of a generalized Christian nature, such as the celebration of Christmas as a national holiday, are not considered to be "establishments of religion." Something more must be present. What that something is, is not at all clear.

What is an establishment of religion in a country that has no officially endorsed and administered religious institutions? What were the drafters of the clause concerned about, and what should we be concerned about today? These are questions addressed by historians and doctrinal theorists of the First Amendment.[4] I am interested here in how the presence, or absence, of religion is proved in a court of law. What counts as evidence, and whose authority is dispositive?

Lawyers for the plaintiffs initially requested that I testify that IFI is "pervasively sectarian." I assume they did this because the term "pervasively sectarian" has been used in some U.S. Supreme Court opinions to characterize those religious institutions that may not constitutionally receive government aid. I answered that "pervasively sectarian" are not words that would be used by scholars of religion to characterize a religious group. Use of the words "pervasively sectarian" constitute a legal judgment, and my use of those words would amount to giving a legal opinion. Academic experts cannot testify in U.S. courts concerning legal conclusions because it is the judge's prerogative to interpret the law—although I was also concerned because the use of the term in legal contexts has been discredited in recent years because of its association with anti-Catholic bias underlying opposition to public funding of parochial schools. In his opinion for the plurality in *Mitchell v. Helms*,[5] a school-funding case, Justice Clarence Thomas argued that this discriminatory history entirely invalidated use of the "pervasively sectarian" standard in establishment clause cases; that, absent anti-Catholicism, there is no reason why religious institutions should not receive government funding to engage in secular projects as long as there is no religious coercion. Absence of coercion is to be proved not by proving the non-religiousness of the school or the agency but by showing that schoolchildren and social service clients have meaningful choices between religious and nonreligious providers.[6]

According to prevailing Supreme Court establishment clause jurisprudence, Judge Pratt had to decide whether, notwithstanding that Iowa had a secular purpose for funding IFI—that is, to reduce recidivism[7]—the program still had the "primary *effect*" of advancing religion. Although the continued salience of the "pervasively sectarian" standard is under a cloud, for the reasons mentioned above, Judge Pratt used a hybrid test, concluding that the contract with IFI did have such a primary effect because it is "pervasively sectarian." He reasoned that, compared to institutions that courts had found not to be pervasively sectarian, such as religiously affiliated colleges, in the Iowa case state funds flowed "to an institution in which religion is so pervasive that a substantial portion of its functions are subsumed in its religious mission."[8] Judge Pratt used the words "pervasively sectarian" to mean that IFI was so thoroughly religious in its activities in what amounted to a pervasively coercive context that the government was, in effect, funding a religious project, not a secular one. As Pratt argued in his published opinion,

> There are many factors that drive the conclusion that the InnerChange program is pervasively sectarian. The program requires attendance at worship services, religious community meetings, and weekly revivals, and orders its participants to engage in daily religious devotional practice. Furthermore, participants are required to lead prayers and share, publicly, a personal devotional at the weekly community meeting. InnerChange instructors and employees must sign the Prison Fellowship Statement of Faith. The curriculum is restricted and does not stray from the religious beliefs stated in the Statement of Faith. InnerChange teachers and counselors are allowed to teach only a pre-set, imposed religious curriculum authorized by InnerChange and Prison Fellowship. *Though an inmate could, theoretically, graduate from InnerChange without converting to Christianity, the coercive nature of the program demands obedience to its dogmas and doctrines.*[9] (emphasis added)

Pratt went on to conclude that "the transformation model employed by InnerChange at the Newton facility makes it impossible to distinguish between the secular and sectarian aspects of its rehabilitation programming. . . . *The overtly religious atmosphere of the InnerChange program is not simply an overlay or a secondary effect of the program—it is the program*" (emphasis added).[10] Furthermore, Judge Pratt said, prisoners have no real choice of treatment programs because of the significant incentives to join the IFI program and the virtual absence of alternative programs.[11]

Attempting to distinguish IFI from the kind of cultural Christianity represented by nationalization of the Christmas holiday, AU lawyers emphasized that IFI represents a distinct form of Christianity. In response, the defendants' lawyers argued that any judicial appraisal of a party's religious beliefs was forbidden, citing free exercise cases that disqualify judges from deciding whether members of a religious group are following the orthodox tenets of the group to which they belong. The plaintiffs' lawyer responded that orthodoxy was not an issue in establishment clause cases:

> This is not a free exercise case. This is an establishment clause case. One issue under the establishment clause is how sectarian the nature

> of a practice or program is. The more sectarian it is, the higher the level of scrutiny and the less likely that the program would be upheld. . . . I think here we've shown that this is a highly sectarian program, and Dr. Sullivan's testimony shows that this is not just a generic kind of Christianity, this is a very specific sectarian type of Christianity that's being taught here. You don't need to decide whether those teachings are right or wrong, or how important specific beliefs are to InnerChange, or resolve any doctrinal conflicts, though we had issues that these are very specific sectarian beliefs that many other Christians disagree with, and you don't need to decide who is right. (pp. 2071–72)

The judge agreed.

But why, theoretically speaking, should state-sponsored indoctrination into a generalized form of Christianity be considered less illegal than indoctrination to a specific form of Christianity? Unless cultural Christianity is considered, in some sense, synonymous with civilization. The defendants argued consistently during the trial and on appeal that IFI's use of religious materials was insufficient to prove that its purpose was Christian indoctrination. A constitutional violation could not be found, they said, unless the plaintiffs showed that IFI staff used all the apparently religious aspects of IFI specifically to convert prisoners. "Transformation" to biblical values in the IFI sense is not the same as Christian conversion, they were saying. It was not enough to show that IFI is an evangelical Christian organization. Moreover, it should not be inferred from expert evidence that evangelical Christians place a high importance on the obligation to proselytize or that they were doing so in this case. In order to make the case for a constitutional violation, they said, the plaintiffs had to prove an actual intention by these IFI staff members to convert these prisoners to evangelical Christianity. The plaintiffs, they said, had to prove that IFI staff members were lying when they disclaimed any such intention.

Defendants attempted to prove a lack of any intention to convert prisoners also through evidence that nonevangelicals voluntarily participated in the IFI program, and even that some had graduated from the program. The defense lawyer, during his cross-examination of me, pressed me to agree that the free choice of a nonevangelical prisoner to be a part of IFI is evidence that IFI's values are universal. He asked me:

Q. And, in fact, you yourself can imagine, can you not, a Jew or other non-Christian choosing to go through the program despite conflicts?

A. There are lots of reasons why . . . a particular individual might make these choices.

Q. And a particular individual might make the choice because, in Exhibit 73, there are certain principles that they are told about; integrity, restoration, responsibility, fellowship, affirmation, productivity; correct?

A. They might. . . .

Q. But the concept of integrity, being honest with yourself and others, doing the right thing whether or not people are watching, that concept, you know from your studies, can be found in the Koran, can be found in the Talmud, can be found in numerous teachings of numerous religions?

A. Certainly integrity is a value in many communities. Most religious traditions, including, as I understand it, Evangelical Christianity, understands these terms very much in their own idium [*sic*] and in their own culture. Indeed, I understand Evangelical Christianity, for the most part, to reject a kind of secularized universalized set of values and instead to insist on a . . . biblical basis for human life.

Q. But you yourself can understand that a Jew or other non-Christian could choose to go through the program, wanting to understand integrity, and could graduate from the program despite any conflicts that you believe they might feel; correct?

A. I believe that a particular individual who might have a Jewish heritage, or not, might make the decision to go through this program. There are lots of reasons why prisoners might make a choice to do a program like this. I don't think in a country, in the United States where there's complete religious freedom, I don't make any kind of judgment about why or how an individual would reconcile the participation in this kind of program. In this country people participate all the time in religious events that are outside their tradition because of inner-marriage [*sic*] and various reasons. I wouldn't make a judgment about a particular individual. (pp. 374–77)

The defense lawyer pressed hard to turn my agreement that some non-evangelicals might willingly join IFI for any number of reasons into an admission that IFI was an inclusive program teaching universal values. He insisted that I would have to change my opinion regarding the evangelical nature of IFI if I acknowledged its openness to nonevangelical prisoners:

Q. And, in fact, if Native Americans were allowed to go and—were accommodated and participated in sweat lodges, that too would change your opinion; correct?

A. It would depend on which Native Americans, what tribal affiliation, what kind of religious practice they had. I couldn't possibly generalize about that.

Q. And if a Native American was allowed, in the IFI program, to lead a prayer in their own tongue praying to the creator rather than to Jesus Christ, and that was part of the teachings that's actually going on in the IFI program, then that too would change your opinion and you would modify your conclusions; correct?

A. That would, obviously, reflect an effort on the part of IFI to be more accommodating to people of other religious faiths. . . . [T]hat would not change my view of the way that the Bible is . . . taught in this program, and the goal of this program, which is transformation or conversion.

Q. Is the accommodations of letting people go to confession, letting them go to sweat lodge, letting them lead prayers in their native tongue, praying to the creator, isn't that accommodations that are in contradiction to a goal of trying to convert people to Christ?

A. No, I don't think so.

Q. So they can do both?

A. Well, yes. (pp. 382–83)

I insisted that nonevangelicals might reconcile any tension implied in participating in IFI in any number of ways but that IFI could continue to be viewed as evangelical, even if it made limited gestures to accommodate other religious practices.

The judge acknowledged IFI's concern at one point, summarizing the defendants' argument during the trial, and referring to my testimony: "[Professor Sullivan] said, 'Well, look, because some members of one religion hang around,' I'm paraphrasing, 'with somebody of another religion, doesn't mean anything'" (p. 2079). He was referring to my testimony in response to the question of whether one could infer that a prisoner's choice to participate in IFI meant that he had converted. My opinion was that this inference could not be made regarding particular individuals but that such an inference was not necessary in order to conclude that IFI is evangelical, from a scholarly viewpoint. One could not infer from knowledge of a person's participation in a particular religious community that that person did or did not believe what the authorities within that tradition taught. One could, however, infer from an analysis of IFI's materials that IFI intended to convert prisoners to a "biblical" outlook on themselves and the world.

IFI and its practices were variously described at trial as Bible-based, Christ-centered, evangelical, Christian, sectarian, and religious. From a religious historian's viewpoint, these words signify different epistemological registers and political contexts. "Bible-based" and "Christ-centered" are insider words signaling fidelity to certain kinds of worship practices within the evangelical community, and they mark the border between them and "liturgical Protestants," Catholic and Orthodox Christians, Mormons, and other Christian groups. "Christian" and "evangelical" can be either polemical or apologetic in their connotation, or simply descriptive, depending on the context. "Sectarian" carries a stigma in the U.S. legal context historically, signifying the danger that Catholics were said to pose to U.S. culture and politics. "Religious" is a highly contested word today, with a long and complex history.

In my trial testimony, in a role I conceived to be that of a teaching expert,[12] I tried to use historically located words, avoiding general categories with legal implications such as "religion" and "sectarian." I attempted to teach the judge about how the term "evangelical Christian" would be used by most scholars of American religion. I gave a brief history of the term "evangelical" Christianity, including its etymological derivation, emphasizing that it is now used as an umbrella term covering several streams of American Christianity, including fundamentalism, pietism, Pentecostalism, and neo-Calvinism. I then pointed to several aspects of IFI that are characteristic of evangelical Christianity: a thoroughgoing biblicism, the desirability of adult conversion, dualism, moralism, a nonliturgical worship style, and an emphasis on evangelism. The plaintiffs' lawyer then took me through illustrations of these characteristics in IFI's materials, including IFI's curriculum and statement of faith (pp. 325–66).

I knew in advance that the judge was Catholic so I took my comparative examples from Roman Catholic theology and practice in order to facilitate his understanding of the distinctiveness of evangelical theology and practice. Toward the conclusion of my testimony, the judge said:

> THE COURT: Let me interrupt you. The third item you mentioned about Evangelical Christianity is that it was anti-sacramental.
>
> THE WITNESS: Yes.
>
> THE COURT: Is that with respect to all sacraments? Do Evangelicals not have, quote, sacraments?
>
> THE WITNESS: That would be generally true, yes. . . . Protestants generally recognize only baptism and the Lord's Supper within the seven sacraments that are recognized by Catholics. . . . [T]here is some difference in the theology, but for most Evangelical Protestants they would be regarded as ordinances, or things that ought to be done and ordained by the Bible as opposed to sacraments.
>
> THE COURT: I shouldn't bring up my Baltimore Catechism, but sacrament in this context is an outward sign of God's love?
>
> THE WITNESS: That would be what the Baltimore Catechism, how the Baltimore Catechism defines sacraments, yes. (pp. 337–38)

Whereas IFI employees took evangelical Christianity as the baseline for Christianity in general, Judge Pratt took his American Catholic teaching as the baseline. American Catholic religious educators used the Baltimore Catechism to teach Christian doctrine to American schoolchildren from 1885 to 1963, when a new catechism was issued.

I regarded my academic opinion concerning IFI's evangelical nature as uncontroversial. How could anyone argue that PFM and IFI are not evangelical? I did not believe that PFM and IFI would seriously deny this point. To my mind, the ultimate issue for the court was not whether they were evangelical Christians but how to interpret legal precedents for the application of the establishment clause. The particular religious community was irrelevant to that analysis, which centers on the nature of the services provided and the involvement of the state. Religious charities of various kinds have been contracting with government to provide social services throughout our history. Some such arrangements are plainly understood to be constitutional, while others are not.

I misjudged the defendants' reaction to these points. The defendants considered my description of them as evangelical to be presumptuous for several reasons, I believe. They regard expert testimony on the subject of religion as inherently suspect, because religious authority is understood to be located in the individual believer. But they also regarded that description to imply that IFI was organized and oriented exclusively toward religious proselytization, in a constitutional sense. They thought that my testimony impugned their honesty and patriotism. The defendants' response to my testimony was, first, to move to exclude my testimony on the grounds that I was unqualified to testify as an expert because I had not done an in-prison study of the program, including actually observing the operations and interviewing staff and prisoners. Absent this study, I was in their view unqualified to testify as to whether IFI was trying to convert prisoners. Judge Pratt denied their motion.[13]

On cross-examination, I was not challenged regarding my academic competence, or other academic opinions. Instead, the defendants' lawyer asked me whether I thought that IFI was lying when its published documents disclaimed the necessity of conversion. He began by referring to the Field Guide:

Q. Okay. Now, some of the documents that you testified today about, for example, Plaintiffs' Exhibit 73, that's the Field Guide. . . . [T]hat document does say that the InnerChange Freedom Initiative has certain goals; one, to reduce the rate of reoffense and the resulting social costs, and, two, to provide a positive influence in the prison. You agree that that's the goal, do you not?
A. I agree that's what it says in this document.
Q. And you agree that's their goal, do you not?
A. I agree that they say that's their goal.
Q. Would you think that people should be judged on what they do, then, rather than what they say?

A. Well, I'm not here to judge them. Absolutely. I understand this program to have as a goal the rehabilitation of prisoners.
Q. And that document that you have in front of you also indicates, does it not, on page 9, that—I'm paraphrasing the last part, that individuals can participate in the InnerChange Freedom Initiative regardless of religion or no religion; correct?
A. Yes. Correct.
Q. That's what the document says?
A. That's what the document says.
Q. And you don't believe, do you, that IFI is lying, do you?
A. I have no reason to believe that they're lying. (pp. 368–69)

Proof that the defendants did not violate the Constitution was to consist entirely of their good faith.

To challenge IFI's assertion that the program was non-proselytizing in nature was interpreted by IFI as an accusation that it had lied. Just as with racial discrimination or environmental deterioration, liability is to be a question of individual intention and probity, not one of systemic bias or effect. To argue, whatever IFI staff say, and whatever the intention of individual staff members, that the IFI program is, from an objective historical and social scientific perspective, the very model of evangelical Protestant proselytization because it teaches that sin is at the root of all problems and that healing comes through a relationship with Jesus Christ—and because it uses classic forms of religious discipline and habituation to shape prisoners—is to speak of an entirely different understanding of what religion is—and of the capacity of individuals to shape and define their own lives. It is, in Stanley Fish's terms, to advocate for saving the plover and hiring black contractors. That is not a scientific assertion, as IFI understands it.

IFI is deeply suspicious of any claim of expertise about religion as a social and cultural phenomenon rather than as an individual's voluntary response to God's offer of grace—particularly any interpretive historical and social scientific expertise.[14] And yet, without viewing religion as a socio-cultural activity, how could one prove the religiousness of a government-funded program? Is it necessary to prove that recipients of government funds are physically forcing confessions and literally counting ecclesiastically sanctioned conversions in order to find an establishment of religion?[15]

IFI's strategy also raises a question concerning the continued salience of social-scientific evidence, at least with respect to religion. The new litigation challenging faith-based initiatives raises the question as to whether courts are equipped to decide the constitutionality of society-wide shifts in religious culture. In American legal terms, evidence offered in court that characterizes entire segments of the culture and implies an understanding of how the individual is shaped by that culture is paradigmatically known as a "Brandeis brief." The Brandeis brief is exemplified by the social scientific evidence that the plaintiffs used in *Brown v. Board of Education*[16] to prove the damage that racial segregation caused to schoolchildren. Social-scientific research, the plaintiff argued, showed that segregated education had an adverse effect on schoolchildren, black and white, whatever the intention of particular administrators and teachers and whatever the effect on particular individual schoolchildren. Social scientific evidence of various kinds, including economic evidence, is widely used in U.S. courts, and has often been determinative in particular cases, given the attention it sometimes receives in judges' opinions. The use of such evidence raises a persistent question as to the appropriate division of labor between the courts and the legislature under the U.S. Constitution: Should judges be able to issue rulings that are based on broad policy grounds—which might be described as social engineering or as a usurpation of the legislative function—rather than on the basis of the specific intentions of specific parties in a specific case?

Whether courts can achieve such change, even if such decisions are supported by good research, is also a matter of debate. In his book about the capacity of courts to produce social reform, Gerald Rosenberg examined the legal decisions in *Brown* and *Roe*, and concluded that in these cases the courts had little effect on the social landscape; changes that occurred were independent of the courts' decisions. Rosenberg's book and its conclusions serve as a cautionary tale for those who would reform U.S. social policy through litigation:

> American courts are vested with the power to declare invalid acts of democratically accountable political actors. . . . Social reformers, with limited options, forgo other options when they elect to litigate . . . in assuming that courts can overcome political obstacles, and produce political change without mobilization and participation, reformers both reified and removed courts from the political and economic system in which they operate. . . . American courts are not all-powerful institutions. . . . To ask them to produce significant social reform is to forget history and ignore their constraints. It is to cloud our vision with a naïve and romantic belief in the triumph of rights over politics.[17]

First Amendment religion cases, too, can be used to illustrate the problematic situation that arises when courts decide cases based on broad historical, social-scientific, and cultural assumptions about religion rather than the facts of a case. All cases necessarily involve both kinds of decision making, tacking back and forth between the refining of general principles and their application in a particular case. But courts have limited expertise and limited ability to effect overall change in the religio-political culture of the United States.

Mark Noll laments that evangelicals' refusal to engage with modern academic methodology has short-circuited their capacity to engage modern intellectual and political life. But in the ten years since Noll published *The Scandal of the Evangelical Mind*, his complaint sounds increasingly like a minority report. What Noll calls "supernatural rationality" resonates deeply with many Americans. The self-evident and natural quality of this discourse is a resilient and populist anthropology that is extraordinarily resistant to expertise, skepticism, and critical thought, partly because of the close identification between American Christianity and national identity. Faith-based initiatives are popular not just because evangelicals are in power but because all Americans believe in a combination of magic and common sense. That is the natural end point of disestablishment. It finds echoes outside the United States as it proves a fruitful way to engage others anxious about the erosion of personal responsibility and the existence of free will.

Secular liberals, according to IFI, explain crime by means of what they term "Creation," that is, the use of prideful human speculation about the natural world, without the aid of special revelation, that is, the biblical text. Liberals, in the conservatives' worldview, believe crime is caused by environmental factors such as childhood trauma, poverty, and racial discrimination; the real cure for crime for them, then, is beyond the power of the individual and requires social programs that address poverty, mental illness, domestic violence, and school reform. The cure for the individual, liberals say, lies in education and behavioral modification. Spokespersons for IFI do not believe that their transformation model is incompatible with universal values, civilized behavior, and religious freedom, which they regard as inherently religious principles. They contend that the personal transformation model is more effective as a civilizing technique than liberal ones, and that the way to the universal is through the intentional acts of particular individuals guided by a particular moral culture, one embedded in texts and community. Secular humanist and professional psychotherapeutic models of human beings, as a basis for the civilizing project, rooted as they are in a naturalistic understanding of the human person, are constitutionally relativized while being theologically allegorized by this technique. Credible evidence locating religion in particular cultural forms tends to dissolve through the application of this anthropology.

Christian Universalism

Throughout the Iowa trial there was an apparent ongoing contradiction between, on the one hand, PFM's and IFI's self-proclaimed identities as comprehensively "Bible-based" and "Christ-centered" organizations engaged in creating "a prison like no other," and, on the other, their simultaneous claims to be engaged in addressing an entirely secular goal—the reduction of recidivism through the teaching of "universal" values, an activity that was properly evaluated on an entirely secular basis. They did not appear to see these two claims as mutually exclusive. It could be done because they were doing it.

I take this dual claim seriously, not simply as a cynical, manipulative strategy to circumvent the commands of the First Amendment. Lawyers and judges have played a role in shaping both the larger public discourse and the specific evidence in this case. But the argument and the evidence in *AU v. PFM* also reflect IFI's attempt to articulate and defend its engagement with the larger religio-political culture. This engagement is one that rejects the anachronistic, separatist apparatus of the post-Enlightenment religion-clause jurisprudence that is presumed in much political and legal rhetoric to perfectly structure the miracle of American religious freedom. IFI is both formed by the American experiment and is engaged, with others, in reinventing it.

In a very real sense, this trial can be seen as revealing the unresolved tension evident in the relationship of the religious to the universal in the modern period. In the context of this trial, that tension is framed by debates over the meaning of the establishment clause of the First Amendment to the U.S. Constitution, but that somewhat parochial American debate is properly also located in a longer theological and political history. Christian churches have, since their beginnings, debated and negotiated their relationship to rulers and neighbors: Jewish religious and legal traditions, Greek philosophy and culture, the Roman imperial and legal systems, other religions and religion in general, and, eventually, to secular governments. Other religious traditions have also engaged and been shaped by these matters. Only recently has religion been understood to be a bounded object properly only the subject of, not the shaper or interlocutor of, law, law understood as naturally, and oppositionally, secular.[18]

A live issue today for activists around the world is whether human rights, as expressed in national, regional, and international legal instruments or constitutions, are peculiarly "Western" or "Christian." Globalization adds urgency to the subject. To protect what are sometimes termed "religious human rights" through international legal instruments and institutions is to imply necessarily that there is something universal or natural about religion. Many proponents of religious human rights argue that religion is foundational to all other human rights because a religious understanding of the human person is necessary to support respect for human dignity, and thus religion deserves special political and legal recognition. Many philosophers, humanists, secularists, and scientists, in contrast, believe that religion narrows the range of human rights. They contend, instead, that respect for human dignity is implicit in the natural world and is best founded there with philosophies that can expand respect for human rights into a wider sense of common survival for the whole planet. Both are true, in my view. Religious ideas, institutions, and identities have led to division and have limited our understanding of human nature, but the persistence of religion also locates a universal aspect of human life, one that extends across phenomena that are now legally divided between the religious and the secular.

Universalizing and particularizing discourses about religion were used by all the participants during the trial. IFI used three discursive frames. At times, as we have seen, IFI spoke in an insider code that understands the Protestant Bible to be the only source of truth, salvation to be limited to those who are "born again," and all other religious practices as false. Using various identity markers, IFI signals to its constituency that it promotes "true" Christianity, that is, "Bible-believing" Christianity, as opposed to the enemy, secularism, and its evil twin, liberal Christianity. At other times, an intermediate position was evident in IFI's testimony: the claim that the basic Christianity it promotes is a generic, inclusive form of Christianity, one that is the foundation of American values and is so American as to be unremarkable and certainly constitutional as a basis for government action. The most embracing frame, however, was that IFI teaches what is truly universal, cutting across all specific religious and nonreligious cultures. At times, IFI seemed to assert that the religious is necessarily universal, whereas the secular is limited and historically bounded. These three frames are not exclusive to IFI. Most Americans make use of them.

How the history and phenomenology of American religion intersects with the jurisprudence of the First Amendment is complex. Evangelical Protestant Christianity, broadly understood, is both so naturalized as to be invisible in many U.S. contexts, but at the same time some Christians understand themselves to be an embattled subculture.[19] The simplest rhetorical strategy for IFI to avoid constitutional difficulties without denying its religious identity was to claim the middle route, that is, to claim that it is teaching a common denominator form of Christianity. The assumption underlying this IFI strategy is that from a constitutional and political viewpoint the advancement of cultural Christianity is recognized as a valid federal purpose, given the long history of Christian cultural dominance and much judicial rhetoric approving the celebration of Christmas as a national holiday, the posting of the Ten Commandments, the reciting of the Pledge of Allegiance at school, and the appointment of chaplains in legislatures. Not to mention a more pervasive naturalization of Christian cultural values throughout U.S. legal institutions. This strategy is a weak version of the Christian America position, where America is asserted to be Christian, but that fact should not be understood to exclude anyone, as it is meant in a weak, noncoercive sense.[20] It is a position that is widely accepted in the United States , as any presidential campaign makes evident.

The boldest claim that IFI makes, however, is that it is not promoting Christian values at all but instead is promoting universal values. IFI's purpose, it contends, is not proselytization, or even Christianization in a weak American sense, but rather the reduction of recidivism through a program that attempts to "civilize" the prisoners and teach them "universal" values. The evangelical Christian idiom is simply the language that IFI speaks. Individual IFI employees might wish prisoners to become Christians, IFI maintains, but the program is not about religious conversion. People need something like religion in order to change, IFI asserts, something that serves as a paradigm, a carrier, they say, for universal values. But any religion will do for this purpose because, they say, for this purpose all religions are the same. All are biblical. Religious particularism is subordinated to a universal human goal, one that is fundamentally religious, not secular.

Fully informed in advance of the biblical content of the program, prisoners who do not convert were apparently expected to internalize the values of the program through a process of recognition and translation—from the evangelical Christian idiom into their own, whether religious or secular. The assumption was that Americans should have no difficulty perceiving the universality in the particular language of evangelical Christianity. In other words, IFI's intention should be easily legible to its hearers. Any exclusivity others see in the IFI program is not something inherent in the project but something others bring to the reading. Let me illustrate with evidence from the trial testimony.

The IFI program is described throughout as being built on six values—integrity, restoration, responsibility, fellowship, affirmation, and productivity. They are defined as follows in the Field Guide given to prospective IFI participants during the introductory session:

> *Integrity, Truth*. By the use of the Bible verses, the inmate is encouraged to reflect and discuss their meaning. Members are taught to reflect on the consistency of their actions, words, and beliefs and match how they relate to the Bible. The *integrity* of members is central to the success of this prison community. For instance *"Who may dwell in*

your holy hill? He who walks uprightly, and works righteousness, who speaks the truth in his tent" (Ps. 15:102). *"Do not lie to each other, since you have taken off your old self with its practices and have put on the new self, which is being renewed in knowledge in the image of its Creator"* (Col. 3:9–10)

Fellowship is another Biblical value the program focuses on. It is rooted in Jesus' example of unconditional love for His friends and enemies as evidenced in His actions. This enables them to create similar relationships within the church when they leave prison. The Bible is permeated with references to the importance of unconditional love and community. For instance: *"Let us consider one another in order to stir up love and good works"* (Heb. 10:24). *"Exhort one another daily while it is called 'today' lest any of you be hardened through the deceitfulness of sin"* (Heb. 3:13). *"[T]herefore if there is any consolation in Christ, in any comfort of love, if any fellowship of the Spirit, if any affection and mercy, fulfill my joy by being like-minded, having the same love, being of one accord, of one mind"* (Philippians 2:1–2). *"But if we walk in the light as He is in the light, we have fellowship with one another, and the blood of Jesus Christ His Son cleanses us from all sin"* (1 John 1:7).

Affirmation is a value in both InnerChange and therapeutic models. However, affirmation within the IFI model is defined as God's affirmation of us rather than man's affirmation. Prisoners learn that it is important to affirm and encourage each other consistent with God's principles. Some inmates have never experienced affirmation given by another person and do not know what it means to be valued. Others have been affirmed for the wrong attitudes or behaviors. In other words, when affirming another it must be consistent with Biblical standards. For instance: *"Not he who commends himself is approved, but whom the Lord commends"* (2 Cor. 10:18). *"Let each examine his own work, and then he will have rejoicing in himself alone, and not in another"* (Gal. 6:4). *"It is a very small thing that I be judged by you. . . . He who judges me is the Lord"* (1 Cor. 4:3–4). *"My soul waits silently for God above. My expectation is from Him"* (Ps. 62:5).

Responsibility and Restoration are critical values of the IFI program. In IFI there is heavy emphasis on taking responsibility for our choices, both past and present. In IFI, members are taught to be accountable for their actions and take responsibility for initiating acts of healing and reconciliation with those they have alienated and hurt. In this way they are restored to their Creator, families, and communities. These verses illustrate the point: *"We must all appear before the judgment seat of Christ that each one may receive the things done in*

> *the body, according to what he has done whether good or bad"* (2 Cor. 5:10). *"Let the wicked forsake his way; and the unrighteous man his thoughts; and let him return to the Lord; and He will have compassion on him and to our God, but not according to knowledge. For they being ignorant of God's righteousness, and seeking to establish their own righteousness, have not submitted to the righteousness of God"* (Romans 10:2–3). *"[A]nd be found in Him, not having my own righteousness, which is from the law, but that which is through faith in Christ, the righteousness which is from God by faith; that I may know Him and the power of His resurrection, and the fellowship of His sufferings, being conformed to His death"* (Philippians 3:9–10).
>
> *Productivity* is an important value anchored in Biblical principles, and one that most inmates lack. In IFI, productivity is defined as the effective use of one's time in line with God's principles. Ephesians 5:16 states, *"redeeming the time, because the days are evil."* In this context, prisoners are taught to be good stewards of their time, investing in priorities that are in line with God's will. IFI trains prisoners to engage in productive work, so that they may become productive contributing members of their community after their release. The Bible instructs us: *"[B]ecause of laziness the building decays and through idleness of hands the house leaks"* (Ecc. 10:18), and *"whatever you do in word or deed, do all in the name of the Lord Jesus"* (Col. 3:17). *"And whatever you do, do it heartily, as to the Lord and not to men"* (Col. 3:23). Also, see these other references: Eph. 6:5–7; Mk 10:45; 1 Thess. 3:10.[21] (emphasis in original)

Each "universal" value is defined in the IFI Field Guide by reference to God and to the biblical text where authority for the universal and for epistemological certainty are located. The implication is that reliance on men, and on their own desires, has gotten the prisoners where they are. They need values and IFI values are universal because they are biblical. Judge Pratt was not entirely convinced. He quoted these definitions in full in his opinion, commenting that, "while these universal, civic values can logically be separated from the biblical context in which they are presented, the intensive, indoctrinating Christian language and practice that makes up the InnerChange program effectively precludes non-Evangelical Christian inmates from participating."[22]

The PFM and IFI staff and their lawyers did not simply assert the universality of IFI values at trial. To prove that the values are universal, they asked the prisoners themselves, and other witnesses, to confirm that IFI values are "universal." The IFI lawyers appeared to think that the answer was self-evident. The following questions are taken from the cross-examination of John Hammers, an early graduate of IFI and the first prisoner to testify in the case. The IFI lawyer asked Hammers about each IFI value, one at a time, first carefully defining the values in entirely secular terms, and then securing the prisoner's assent that IFI taught these values:

> Q. Okay. Let me turn your attention back to your participation in the IFI program back in the 2000–2001 time frame. You understood that the IFI program was a values-based program; right?
>
> A. That is correct.
>
> Q. Okay. And you recall that IFI—the IFI program is built on six main values, *integrity, restoration, responsibility, fellowship, affirmation, and productivity.* Do you remember that?
>
> A. Yes, I do.
>
> Q. Okay. And *integrity* in the IFI program, the way they teach it, means being honest with yourself and others, doing the right thing whether or not people are watching; right?
>
> A. That is correct.
>
> Q. Okay. And *restoration* means repairing broken relationships; right?
>
> A. Right.
>
> Q. And IFI teaches that *responsibility,* it means doing what is expected, being accountable, accepting consequences of failure without blaming others; right?
>
> A. That's correct.
>
> Q. And *fellowship* means working together to build community, bearing each others' burdens; right?
>
> A. Right. . . .
>
> Q. *Affirmation* means giving honest encouragement to others, bringing out the best in others under the IFI program; right?
>
> A. Right.
>
> Q. *Productivity* means making important contributions, stewarding time and other resources well; right?
>
> A. Correct.
>
> Q. Okay. You'd agree, wouldn't you, that these six values are basically the overall purpose and guiding principles of the IFI program?
>
> A. That is correct.
>
> Q. Okay. And the program is built around teaching and fostering these values, isn't it?
>
> A. Yes. (emphasis added) (pp. 101–3)

No mention of God. IFI's lawyer then asked Hammers about IFI's "Christian perspective":

> Q. *And as you testified on direct, these values are taught from a Christian perspective; true?*

A. *True.*
Q. *Using lessons and references from the Bible; right?*
A. Right. (emphasis added) (p. 103)

Having secured Hammers's agreement to IFI's own description of its mission, the lawyer deftly pressed his advantage:

Q. *Okay. You'd agree, wouldn't you, that these values, these six values, are not uniquely Christian, are they?*
A. *No, they're not.*
Q. They're common to a civilized society, aren't they? . . . These values, integrity, restoration, responsibility, fellowship, affirmation, productivity, apply to everyday life, don't they?
A. That's true.
Q. *Wouldn't you agree that they're universal, regardless of your faith?* . . .
A. *Yes.*
Q. And regardless of your nonfaith, true? You can accept these values without having a faith; isn't that so?
A. Yes.
Q. Okay. So isn't it true that you can accept and hold the values taught by the IFI program regardless of whether you're religious or not religious?
A. True. (emphasis added) (pp. 103–4)

Hammers agreed that IFI is teaching you the values that you need to be a civilized human being. Continuing, the IFI lawyer then carefully universalized the Bible by placing it in relation to other possible cultural narratives:

Q. Okay. In IFI, the lessons that illustrate these six values are drawn from the Bible, though; right?
A. Correct.
Q. *But these basic values, which are so universal, can be illustrated from other aspects of life; don't you agree?*
A. Such as?
Q. Well, do you recall the story about Dr. Seuss, The Cat In The Hat?
A. Yup.
Q. That's the story of responsibility, right, the cat and the children clean up the mess they made while their mother was away?
A. Right.
Q. Okay. And Dr. Seuss' The Grinch Who Stole Christmas is a story of fellowship, right? The town of Whoville coming together despite the Grinch's efforts to steal Christmas; right?
A. Correct.

Q. *So these six basic values taught by the IFI program can be found almost anywhere. Isn't that so?*
A. Yes.
Q. Wherever these values are drawn from, be it the Bible or Dr. Seuss, the values are the same, aren't they?
A. Yes.
Q. That's because they're so universal; true?
A. True.
Q. You'd not be surprised if lessons illustrating the value of responsibility, for example, could be found in the Koran, would you?
A. Not at all. . . .
Q. Likewise, someone could probably find lessons illustrating fellowship in the Book of Mormon, don't you think?
A. I don't know personally, but I'm assuming so.
Q. Okay. And you'd agree—and you agree, don't you, that you, as a non-Muslim and as a non-Mormon, could understand the lessons, and accept the values of responsibility and fellowship even if the lessons were illustrated by stories from the Koran and the Book of Mormon?
A. Of course.
Q. You could understand the lessons, accept the values without being a Muslim or a Mormon, right?
A. *Yes. They're core human values.* (emphasis added) (pp. 104–6)

The IFI lawyer worked to personalize the prisoner's assent:

Q. *You* agree, *you* buy into the values taught by the IFI program, don't *you, you* personally?
A. Yes.
Q. *And you agree that these values can be separated from the religious context in which they're sought, don't you—in which they're taught? . . .*
A. *Yeah. I think they're just society standards to be productive and have integrity, and those values.* (emphasis added) (p. 107)

Hammers had even written a letter of endorsement of the program that was offered into evidence:

Q. Mr. Hammers, if you could take a look at that letter real quick, and let me know if that refreshes your recollection about the letter that you wrote back in September of 2000.
A. Yes, I remember writing this note.
Q. In that letter you said in the first sentence, "If I had to list what I have gotten out of the IFI program so far, you would be reading

this for a while," suggesting you had gotten a lot out of the program, right?

A. Correct.

Q. And one of the things which you got out of the program which you mention about four sentences down was a saying that you said really affected you, which was, "Go slow, stay quiet, learn something, be thankful, be wise." Do you remember that?

A. Yes, I do. (p. 108)

Then, summarizing Hammers's testimony in his own words, he turned the letter into a testimonial:

Q. As you indicated in this letter, you found the program to be personally beneficial, didn't you?

A. Yes, I did.

Q. *And you agree that the IFI program can be beneficial to other inmates, don't you?*

A. *Yes, it can.*

Q. *The values taught by IFI, the six values we've discussed, need to be embraced by more inmates, don't you think?*

A. *Yes.*

Q. *And it's beneficial for inmates to have access to a program that teaches such values, don't you agree?*

A. *Yes.* (emphasis added) (pp. 108–9)

These questions were asked of all the prisoner witnesses.

Hammers's testimony exemplifies what IFI proposed as dispositive evidence concerning the constitutionality of its contract with Iowa. By eliciting a seal of consumer satisfaction and by placing the biblical text next to other texts, the IFI lawyer skillfully implied that, in a diverse country, each is constitutionally entitled to his own text, his own perspective, on the common values—and that the test of the effectiveness of social services rests with the customer. Evangelical Christianity appears in his telling no longer a dominant majority tradition but one among many, all created equal. IFI's theory of religion, as represented by its lawyers in their style of questioning, and by its own witnesses, is that to be Christian is to be universal. As Terry Mapes (now warden at Newton) testified at the trial, "what [IFI is] is a values-based program that has Christ-centered biblical teaching. The teaching is a mechanism to the values-based instruction, just as if they had done the Dr. Seuss education program. That is another method of reaching and achieving the same goals" (p. 1457).[23] In other words, one can reach these goals through the Cat in the Hat or through Jesus.

The plaintiffs' lawyers challenged the universalizing move. On redirect, the lawyer for the plaintiffs returned to the questions that Hammers were asked on cross-examination, first concerning the universality of the values:

> Q. When you were in IFI, were you taught any values from the perspective of Dr. Seuss?
> A. No. Not at all.
> Q. And were you taught any values from any perspective other than IFI's Christian perspective?
> A. No.
> Q. And was those six values that Mr. Angle mentioned, was that all you were taught in the InnerChange program?
> A. You have to be more specific.
> Q. *Were there classes in the InnerChange program that just related specifically to the Bible, or Bible studies, and weren't tied to those six values?*
> A. I think every class was in some way tied to those values, but it was predominantly how to do—how to practice them values in a Christianly manner.
> Q. And when you were being taught those six values, were—*was the teaching of the values in any way separated from IFI's Christian teachings, or references to the Bible, or Christ?*
> A. *No.* (emphasis added) (p. 129)

And then, concerning the letter Hammers had written about his personal experience in the program:

> Q. Now, I believe Mr. Angle showed you a letter. . . . If you look on the first page of this letter, Mr. Angle quoted some statements from the letter about what you had learned. And I was wondering if you could read some other statements. If you go to the first page . . . after the sentence "Go slow, stay quiet, learn something, be thankful, become wise," can you read the sentence after that?
> A. *"I have also come to know"—"also come to know Christ, which has given me a chance"—"a sense of peace in my heart."*
> Q. And can you skip down . . . and read the sentence starting with "I have seen that"?
> A. *"I have seen that God is in control, and I wouldn't be"—"and I wouldn't be held accountable if he wouldn't have allowed people, COs, counselors, warden, program manager, et cetera, to be in authority over me."*
> Q. Can you read the next sentence, please.

A. "Last, *I feel that I have gotten a better attitude overall because I know that Christ is working in my life.*"

Q. And if you could flip to page 2, please, and . . . read the sentence starting with the words "I have a need."

A. *"I have a need, a thirst, if you will, to learn all I can about the Bible, Christ, and how to live a Christian life-style."* (emphasis added) (pp. 129–31)

Here, IFI's particularist other self appears. Successful IFI prisoners appear to understand that corrections officials speak for God and that it is only through Christ that prisoners will know peace.

IFI's equating of traditions and sources might appear to be classic cultural relativism. Surely these high-profile evangelicals who boast on their Web sites and in their publications that IFI increases the number of Christians ("souls won for the Kingdom of God") cannot agree with John Rawls that, "for the purposes of public life, Saul of Tarsus and Paul the Apostle are the same person."[24] And Jesus and the Grinch and Moroni and Mohammed and the Cat in the Hat? I think they do, in part. What they all have in common is that they all teach "personal responsibility," the goal expressed in the title of the first welfare reform act signed into law by President Clinton in 1996.[25] All of these texts teach values, rather than the moral relativism believed to be the only message of the secular.

This cultural move—the assimilation of texts, persons, and traditions to a single acceptable ideology—is ubiquitous in contemporary evangelical Christianity. It is not exactly the same move as that of John Rawls, however, because the specific is not understood to be subordinated to a secular universal. The evangelical Christian position is, instead, a rejection of the necessary secularism of universality. IFI's own Christian universalism is achieved through the use of classic evangelical Protestant allegory. In the portion of Mr. Hammers's testimony quoted above, the universality of IFI values was proved through allegorization of the Dr. Seuss books, the Qu'ran, and the Book of Mormon. Each is found to be teaching biblical values. That all worthwhile narratives are seen to teach biblical values confirms the truth of Christian claims and makes both universal.[26]

Evangelical allegorizing, not just of other religious texts but also of artifacts of contemporary culture, is a prominent feature of the Christian subculture. It is now common, for example, for the mainstream press to feature reports about the "Christian" take on new films. This Christian reading is not simply a judgment on the acceptability of the moral content of films as the Roman Catholic Legion of Decency did for many years in the United States.[27] It is a transmutation of the culture. Consider, for example, conservative Christian interest in two recent films, *The Chronicles of Narnia* and *March of the Penguins*. The advertising for the film version of the first in C. S. Lewis's children's book series, *The Chronicles of Narnia*, included a segmented marketing campaign separately targeting evangelical and nonevangelical audiences, presenting the film as Christian for the former and as secular for the latter. The advertising strategy provoked articles in the mainstream press about whether Lewis himself intended the books to serve as a Christian allegory—and about whether it is appropriate to regard them as such, no matter what he intended. The *New York Times* also reported that the hit documentary *March of the Penguins* was well received by many evangelical Christians as making a strong case for Christian values: sacrifice, monogamy, good parenting, and intelligent design. The articles about these films in the mainstream media, like the evangelical Web sites dedicated to interpreting media and culture for wary Christians,[28] assume that it is possible to discern definitively the allegorical presence of biblical values in apparently non-Christian material—and thereby separate and isolate the sacred from the secular.

Allegory has a long religious genealogy in Christian biblical exegesis. It is also, of course, a technical term in literary circles, where it is understood to be a form of extended metaphor.[29] But allegory has a particular salience in modern Protestantism. The finding of Christian structures of meaning in non-biblical contexts is said to be a peculiarly Protestant rhetorical form in the modern period.[30] Protestant Reformation–era critiques of the heterodox dangers of Catholic allegorical biblical hermeneutics rapidly gave way to a specifically Protestant form of allegory that inverts the Catholic form; whereas the Catholic finds the world in the Bible, the Protestant finds the Bible in the world. Protestant allegorizing, as opposed to Catholic allegorizing, is applied to non-biblical events and texts. Rather than finding the narrow literal truth of the biblical text to be expanded as in a medieval Catholic allegorical reading, non-biblical events and texts are narrowed through a Protestant allegorical reading.

A classic early example of Protestant allegorizing is John Bunyan's *Pilgrim's Progress* about a man whose life story exemplifies the Christian struggle, a story Bunyan himself famously described as "a fall into Allegory."[31] Protestant allegory is an attempt to breach the radical separation between this world and the next that is foundational to Protestant theology. It is a way of overcoming the unavailability of mediating sacramental ties to the divine and the anxiety of not knowing whether one is saved.[32] Even a cursory review of conservative Christian media will find an almost obsessive search for allegory, a displacement, some have said, from the narrow literalism of permissible readings of the Bible. Not being allowed to allegorize scripture, one turns instead to allegorizing the world. At its most extreme, everything outside of the Bible serves as an extended metaphor of biblical truth. Nothing exists in its own right. Everything is transformed by the allegorizing, which lays claim to its object, legitimizing both the object and its Christian interpreter.

Living inside such an extended metaphor has its appeal, as can be seen from the testimony of the prisoners who found IFI to be "utopian" and salvific. This kind of allegorizing can also be experienced as confining—even claustrophobic; while allegory appears to confer meaning, it can eliminate complexity and ambiguity. As many pointed out in letters to the editor and on Internet blogs after the appearance of the *New York Times* story about evangelical fans of *March of the Penguins*, the lives of penguins are hardly models of Christian monogamy and parenting. The meaning of the lives of Antarctican penguins might just as well be discovered through the use of an evolutionist allegory—as the survival of the fittest—or, as one writer did in comparing the Chinese dissidents of Tiananmen Square to the same penguins, as heroic but ultimately meaningless acts.[33] Theodor Geisel's (Dr. Seuss's) politics were far from that of many conservative Christians, and neither the Qu'ran nor the Book of Mormon are understood by most of their adherents as teaching the particular values listed by IFI. Indeed, it is doubtful whether the Bible is so understood by most Christians outside the modern Protestant West.

As allegory attempts to reinvent the world as a confirmation of revelation, the need for that work emphasizes the radical separation between this world and the next. The cause of crime, IFI teaches, is sin, or alienation from God. The cure is an acknowledgment of this cause, followed by a reorientation of one's person in line with this insight—through allegory.

How can one understand the simultaneous employment of seemingly contradictory positions on the nature of humans by contemporary evangelicals? An individual's problems are said to be the result of sin, and so a restored relationship with God and Jesus is said to be necessary to cure those problems. Yet cure is also said to be possible without conversion, because the cure is defined as the absorption and putting into practice of universal values that are found virtually everywhere, even in the Qu'ran and *The Cat in the Hat*. Is this a sinister, sophisticated, and hypocritical form of theological (and political) double-talk? How is this transformation model related to models implied in liberal political discourse about self-improvement and in liberal philosophies and social sciences that theorize about the modern self? The liberal-minded give entirely different reasons than IFI's evangelical Christian employees offer for the proliferation of crime, and they also employ very different approaches to changing human behavior. How can they share universal values?

Distinguishing the religious and the secular also came up at the trial in the very mundane context of accounting. The plaintiffs' lawyer asked the IFI office administrator at Newton about IFI's office records that separated "nonsectarian" expenses, which could be billed to the state under Iowa's contract with IFI, from "sectarian" expenses, which IFI had to pay. It became clear during the office administrator's testimony that when she started the job in 2000, no standards were in place to distinguish between the two types of expenses. Although she was charged with making that decision, she stated that she did not understand the difference between sectarian and nonsectarian expenses, and, moreover, had never been instructed on how to make that distinction. She further testified that her own time, all of which was billed to the state, mixed secretarial duties for every aspect of IFI's work in the prison, whether explicitly religious or not. Only after the suit was filed in 2004 did IFI begin to formally separate the expenses with any care, and to develop a language to articulate its double life.[34]

When the program began, IFI, in its daily workings, seems to have been either overconfident because of the political legitimacy the White House was then conferring on faith-based initiatives or simply oblivious to the potential risks it ran of violating the Constitution. The blurred lines between the sectarian and the nonsectarian are also evident in the testimony of IFI staffer Chris Geil, who testified as an adverse witness for the plaintiffs.[35] Geil, a graduate of Northwest Missouri State with a master's degree from Trevecca Nazarene University, has been the IFI program manager at Newton since 2000. In the course of authenticating IFI business records being offered into at trial, Geil was questioned about a number of behavior contracts, or IFI written agreements with prisoners, that were used to discipline program members. The contracts committed prisoners to perform certain assignments as compensation for failing to measure up to behavioral standards. In the following exchange, Geil was shown several such contracts:

Q. Let's go to Exhibit C-228.[36] Is this another behavior contract?

A. Yes.

Q. And if you look at section 2 . . . was the inmate who was the subject of this behavior contract required to complete assignments on "You need revival when you have suffered God's discipline for your sins. Do you understand God's covenant, and a love relationship with God"?

A. Yes.

Q. And if you flip to page C-230, does this reflect the inmate completing the part of the assignment called "Do you understand God's covenant"?

A. I would assume so.
Q. All right. And what about on page C-232, does this reflect the inmate completing the part of the assignment called "A love relationship with God"?
A. Again, I assume so. (p. 1157)

At one point Geil stopped to translate the explicitly Christian language into the psycho-social language he preferred. Asked by the plaintiffs' lawyer about a document's reference to "an admission of sin," Geil distinguished the two voices of IFI:

Q. And Exhibit C-236, . . . paragraph 2 of this document says . . . "Each week for the next 30 days write a one-page admission of sin as it relates to anger and to share this on Friday with your IFI counselor." . . . [C]an you explain what an admission of sin is?
A. From my perspective or from the perspective that they were written?
Q. What the term means. I don't know what it means. What's an admission of sin?
A. I . . . would say that the assignment—it says, "If you've had trouble with anger during the week, you need to write about the trouble that you've had with your anger this week and talk to me about it at the end of the week." If I were writing this, that's the way I would write this. (pp. 1158–59)

Although the documents about which Geil testified seem to portray IFI as preoccupied with this prisoner's religious progress, Geil's instinct, like that of the other IFI staff witnesses, is to translate explicitly religious language into secular language. This is not, I believe, solely for constitutional reasons, as I have said, although there was no question that IFI witnesses had been carefully coached. The practical, the behavioral, the measurable—that is what Geil is interested in. That is how he is professionally trained. How the process is explained depends on to whom he is talking.

IFI's lawyer asked Geil to explain why IFI uses the Bible and references to Christianity if it is not trying to convert people. Geil responded:

> Our goal, our purpose is to reduce recidivism. That is the end goal for our program. . . . What I try to do, and what we try to do, is find ways that are consistent with our values as a program, and consistent with who we are as a program, and what we know to be right and true that's worked. We try to look at that end goal and we try to facilitate men, give them the opportunity, so they can facilitate a way to transform their hearts. *We're all about transformation. We are about that end goal. We're not—I'm not interested in men making any kind of profession of faith and then going out and committing crime and coming back to prison.* I'm not interested in that because that's not my purpose. My

> purpose is to help facilitate the transformation of men's hearts to the point that they do not come back to prison. Our curriculum is focused and we are focused. We're nearly neurotic to the point of we're singularly focused on that goal, the transformation of men so they don't come back to prison. (emphasis added) (pp. 1219–20)

Geil carefully distinguished between their theology—a theology of transformation that focuses on the heart and is both universal and particular and will lead to reduced recidivism—and the theology they reject, which they view as superficial and hypocritical, and one that pays lip service to religious commitments but is content with "making any kind of profession of faith and then going out and committing crime." IFI's theology supports their constitutional theory, a theory that also distinguishes between faith (true religion) and works or outward professions (false religion).

Geil was also asked by the plaintiffs' lawyer about the definition of "transformation" published in the old Field Guide (a new, somewhat modified version had been produced since the lawsuit was filed):

> *Q.* The old Field Guide . . . says, "True transformation begins with salvation, also called conversion. Conversion is when you turn away from what is negative and turn to Christ. Then you try to live your life by his example and instructions from the Bible." Does that language appear in the new version of the Field Guide?
>
> *A.* I don't know if it does, or not.
>
> *Q.* I'm going to represent to you that it does not. When you changed from the old Field Guide to the new Field Guide, did the nature of what IFI understands to be transformation also change?
>
> *A.* No. (pp. 1290–91)

Transformation, apparently, is both Christian and secular, in Geil's view, so it matters little to him which language is used.

In insisting on the secular nature of IFI's purposes and associating outward professions of faith with hypocrisy, Geil appeared to frustrate the judge, who finally jumped in at several points to insist on a straight answer. For example, IFI's lawyer asked Geil about the prisoner's required role in community meetings, whether and why prisoners were required to lead public prayer, and whether those prayers had to be Christian:

> *Q.* Okay. We've heard testimony about inmates having to give a prayer of some sort at community. What is that all about?
>
> *A.* Every man is, at least one time, if not more, scheduled to either lead prayer for the group or to give a devotion, and they will either do one or the other at a time. Everyone will do one of those and one

devotional. We are—these are men that have been in an antisocial community as criminals. They've been in an antisocial community in prison. We're taking them out of that environment, putting them in a prosocial community setting. We want them—we get to—those community times are very valuable. They are with other people. They have to look at other people in the face and address them. Yeah, you have to get up and talk about a devotional thought or just your own testimony. You get up. There are needs and men get up and pray for their needs.

Q. *Are they required to give a Christian prayer?*

A. They do. I don't know if required is a—I guess I've never had anyone necessarily say I want to give another kind of prayer.

Q. Have any inmates given things other than Christian prayers?

A. Well, we've had—we've had Native American men come and pray in their Native American language and their Native American way. We've had some people do it in a liturgical way. We've had some people get up and pray off the list. It's just different ways. (emphasis added) (pp. 1240–41)

Geil emphasizes diversity and equality in prayer, as the lawyer did in his litany about religious texts. The "Native American way." The "liturgical way." "Off the list." "It's just different ways." For Geil, most important about the prayers is that "they are with other people. They have to look other people in the face and address them." He seems indifferent to the actual words.

At this point, the Judge intervened:

THE COURT: Mr. Geil, is the answer to his question no? He said, "Is a Christian prayer required?"
THE WITNESS: Is a Christian prior [*sic*] required?
THE COURT: Right. That was his question.
THE WITNESS: At community meeting?
THE COURT: I believe that was his question.
THE WITNESS: I would say yes. (p. 1241)

IFI's lawyer followed up, helping his witness to help the judge:

Q. I guess the reason the Judge is asking you that, you also said that inmates get up and you have had inmates give a Native American prayer in their own native tongue, you've had people give other devotionals. *Do you consider a Native American prayer to be a Christian prayer?*

A. *I think the content of whatever he said was a Christian content.*

> *Q. Okay. Your definition of Christian is very broad?*
> *A. Yes.* (emphasis added) (p. 1241)

Geil appeared not to be able to imagine a non-Christian prayer. Anything that is permitted is, by definition, Christian—and useful for the purpose of promoting a prosocial community.

Later in Geil's testimony, Judge Pratt returned to the issue of religious transformation:

> THE COURT: Mr. Geil, I wanted to ask you a question. This goes back to my notes and what I remember of your discussion with Mr. Angle . . . about grading IFI inmates on their, quote, religiosity.
>
> THE WITNESS: Yes.
>
> THE COURT: You answered by defining religiosity as merely conforming outwardly to expectations of what is considered religious growth and that you do not. Okay. But IFI members are apparently graded on their—are they graded on their authentic or religious growth?
>
> THE WITNESS: It's difficult. I mean, therein lies our issue. On the one hand you're looking at externals. You're looking at externals because that's all you can see. At the same time you have to predict, have they embraced these principles in their heart and they're coming out, or is it I need to act this way not to get in trouble. It's tricky.
>
> THE COURT: Are they graded on their—
>
> THE WITNESS: I wouldn't say they're graded. There's no grade to it. It could be a treatment issue. It could be a counseling issue.
>
> THE COURT: Okay. *Does this true transformation that you talked about as the major thrust of the program as the goal, does that require a spiritual change in a person?*
>
> THE WITNESS: *It can.*
>
> THE COURT: No. *No. Does it require a spiritual change?*
>
> THE WITNESS: *Transformation happens with the spiritual change, but it is not the only time it happens.*
>
> THE COURT: *All right.* Thank you. (emphasis added) (p. 1291–92)

Behavior is what matters. This conversation between Geil and the judge echoes a classic theological question facing Christians: How does one know when religious conversion is genuine, and what value does external behavior have as evidence of internal motivation? Or, of God's favor?[37]

The judge, reading from the stipulated facts in the case, also asked Geil about IFI's policy on homosexuality: "This is Defendants' response to Plaintiffs' undisputed material facts. I'm reading from the document, 'IFI teaches inmates that homosexuality is wrong and sinful and that one cannot become a Christian if one is homosexual.' 'Admitted.' Is that the teaching?" Geil equivocated: "That is in the documents that were turned in. That is not—that's not a practice that we—we don't have that practice." But the judge insisted:

> THE COURT: Is that a teaching of IFI?
>
> THE WITNESS: Say it again.
>
> THE COURT: Well, the quote is, "IFI teaches inmates that homosexuality is wrong and sinful and that one cannot be a Christian if one is homosexual."
>
> THE WITNESS: I don't think that's an official teaching. I don't think anyone teaches that. We do have folks that have come from homosexual lifestyles that have asked us to help them not be that way. We will work with men. If men choose to have that outlook, then, obviously, they're free to have that outlook.
>
> THE COURT: The next paragraph . . . says, "IFI's disapproval of homosexuality is based on Prison Fellowship Ministry's religious doctrine." The response is admitted.
>
> THE WITNESS: Yeah. It's all in the paperwork. That's right.
>
> THE COURT: So if a volunteer makes disparaging remarks they're thrown out, but that's still the doctrine of IFI?
>
> THE WITNESS: If someone came in and said, you know, homosexuals—
>
> THE COURT: Just answer my question. I don't want any more hypotheticals.
>
> THE WITNESS: Okay. If someone came to me and said—and complained and said that this individual is complaining about homosexuals, I would talk with them and tell them not to talk about that. If they continued, I would remove them.
>
> THE COURT: *Well, is this correct that IFI's teachings are that homosexuality is a sin?*
>
> THE WITNESS: *Our official position would be yes.* (emphasis added) (pp. 1279–80)

After much effort to evade the judge's question, Geil agreed that IFI teaches that homosexuality is a sin.

IFI staff's claim is that the program's values are universal and that one learns such values by immersion in the world of the evangelical Christian Bible—by learning to be Christ-like. IFI insists that its teachings are *not* the same as proselytization. One can, they seem to argue, be "born again" as a "civilized" responsible human being with universal values, *without* necessarily becoming an actual Christian, as they define it. Is this claim a legalistic insistence that conversion is only technically accomplished when one is "born again" and utters the confession that one has "accepted Jesus Christ as one's personal savior and lord"—or is this claim a theological deference to conversion as something produced only by God? Is this a claim to a two-layered personal transformation in which moral salvation in this world is unavoidably multicultural but salvation in the next world depends on a particular evangelical understanding of the exclusiveness of Christian salvation? Or are "universal" and "Christian" actually interchangeable? For many conservative evangelicals, arguing that the universal and Christian are the same is as cogent as arguing that the secular and universal are the same, because, as they see it, postmodern theory dethrones the necessary secularism of the universal.

Certainly evangelical Christians, for biblical reasons, deplore forced conversion and embrace disestablishment. But the non-proselytizing nature of IFI's method was not defended ideologically or historically at trial. It was proved first on the basis of intention and then empirically on the basis of individual cases. Proof that the program is not in the business of making Christians, IFI contends, can be deduced from the fact that it disclaims any such intention and the fact that one can complete the IFI program without becoming a Christian. IFI offered evidence of prisoners who did just that, evidence that was adduced from prisoner witnesses, as well as IFI witnesses, who testified to the presence of nonevangelicals in the program (pp. 95–96, 107, 182–83, 412–13, 613, 1232–34, 1281–83, 2248, 2261–65, 2298–2301, 2343–44, 2385, 2787–90, 2831–32, 2879–81, 2912–14). In a triumph of just the kind of positivistic, scientistic thinking that Noll describes, IFI answers the charge that its program is a state-financed program of Christian conversion by supplying examples of non-Christian prisoners who successfully graduated from the program. IFI staff members have seen it with their own eyes. The program clearly cannot be meant to convert people because, they insist, one can complete the program while remaining a Jew, Muslim, Catholic, or Native American practitioner. The skepticism of the liberal secular critic is trumped by the actions of the people. Perhaps, like their evangelical brethren, many of those individuals, too, understand and participate in the world of supernatural rationalism and can indeed translate IFI's version of religion into their own. It is the religious that is universal, not the secular, according to PFM and IFI. Furthermore, this kind of religious universalism is, arguably, demanded by laws that purport to guarantee *both* religious freedom *and* disestablishment.

The Modern Imaginary

I have described IFI's project here as specifically evangelical in nature, as I did during the trial. Implied here, however, and at some points noted, are the ways in which the contemporary U.S. evangelical imaginary forms a part of a larger modern imaginary or imaginaries. I use the term "imaginary" here as it is elaborated by the philosopher Charles Taylor in his *Modern Social Imaginaries*, borrowing from others, to refer to the assumptions and practices that form the basis for thought and action for a certain population. Whether and how modernity may be described as distinctive and unitary, how ideas of both the religious and the secular played a role in its formation, and when modernity can be said to begin are complicated questions. I leave history and genealogy to others. Instead, my interest here is on how the lives of prisoners at Newton and their evangelical instructors are like many other lives around the world today, lives that are being described by a group of political philosophers and ethnographers who appear to be speaking to our current situation and the nature of contemporary religion in new and helpful ways, ways that have important implications for the state regulation of religion.

Significantly, particularly for the U.S. context, the evangelical and other modern social imaginaries share, in important and overlapping ways, an understanding of the modern self and a desire for discipline that owes much to John Calvin and the Scottish Enlightenment. They also share a common inheritance in distinctive new forms of warfare, urbanization, industrialization, mass literacy, and capitalism—all of which created the modern world in which we live. In a series of publications, Charles Taylor has described the characteristics of what he calls the "modern moral order." Most recently, in *Modern Social Imaginaries*, Taylor briefly outlines the complex historical shifts contributing to this new way of life on earth. A new way of being gradually moved, he says, from elite political theory to everyday life in an apparently seamless way that, to us, now seems the natural order of things.

Beginning in the sixteenth century with Hugh Grotius and John Locke,[38] as Taylor describes it, a new understanding of the political order was progressively articulated and then realized, one in which instrumental rationality focused on ordinary life, a shared worldly focus on the discipline needed to reform life on earth. This new moral order is non-hierarchical and non-idealistic but not necessarily secular in the strong modern sense.[39] Christians were involved in creating it, and Christians saw it as compatible with, if not positively demanded by, their understanding of Christianity. Perhaps the most distinctive feature of the modern moral order is what Taylor calls the "Great Disembedding" or what Max Weber described as disenchantment. Slavoj Žižek, speaking of the same phenomenon from a psychoanalytic point of view, highlights the significance for modern man of the loss of a God he describes as the "big Other." This loss, among other effects, Žižek says, curtails symbolic efficiency or "the minimum of 'reification' on account of which it is not enough for us, all concerned individuals, to know some fact in order to be operative."[40] The idea is that modern persons may live from time to time in small embeddings, or barely minimum reifications, but they no longer live as if their roles in life, and everything around them, are determined by cosmological ordering. In a sense, each person is on his own. Alone, but dependent on others, each seeks to work out his salvation on this earth without the comfort of a comprehensive divine ordering of all society.[41]

But divine ordering continues to haunt us. Whether or not you understand yourself to be religious, Taylor explains, a new moral order, the "order of mutual benefit," has followed the disembedding and determines our lives. But this new moral order demands that we practice virtue as if there had been no loss—as if that new ordering did not exist. Taylor summarizes:

> We can say that (1) the order of mutual benefit holds between individuals (or at least moral agents who are independent of larger hierarchical orders); (2) the benefits crucially include life and the means to life, although securing these relates to the practice of virtue; and (3) the order is meant to secure freedom and easily finds expression in terms of rights. To these we can add a fourth point: (4) These rights, this mutual benefit is to be secured to all participants equally. Exactly what is meant by equality will vary, but that it must be affirmed in some form follows from the rejection of hierarchical order.[42]

Whether or not you count yourself religious, as a modern you are likely to regard the practice of virtue—in the egalitarian context of "the order of mutual benefit"—as indispensable to human life on earth. The confusion is that the need to be virtuous implies a normative order embedded in a cosmological whole and the capacity for personal responsibility, whereas disembedding implies social-scientific explanations for human action. Whether you are liberal or conservative, and however you might be schooled in the naturalist explanation, you are likely to continue to think it relevant whether or not criminal acts and social pathologies such as racial segregation, religious discrimination, and criminal activity were the product of deliberate individual choice. Uneasiness about the nature and continued relevance of religion is one location for public reflection on the tension between religious, social scientific, evolutionary, and cognitive explanations for human intentionality.

In the United States, the modern moral order continues to be deeply and specifically inflected by its Puritan inheritance. Michael Walzer, in *The Revolution of the Saints*, describes the discipline of work and piety promoted by English Puritans in response, in part, to the phenomenon of the "masterless men" who were created by the rapid changes in English society in the sixteenth and seventeenth centuries, and the importance of John Calvin as a political thinker in imagining a new political order to govern such men. Although church and state were to be separate, and the government was no longer to be the absolute preserve of the sovereign, Christian discipline was still expected of those who were not converted. Taylor quotes Walzer quoting puritan Richard Baxter: "The magistrate [that is, the representative of the state], as Baxter thought, must force all men 'to learn the word of God and to walk orderly and quietly . . . till they are brought to a voluntary, personal profession of Christianity.'"[43] The church itself as a visible institution was to be made up only of the saints—only the genuinely converted—but the modern moral order was still very much Christian and the secular state would depend on "disembedded," disestablished religion to provide virtue.

The Puritan theory remains the dominant theory of church-state relations in the United States. The First Amendment disestablishes the state and church and guarantees religious freedom, thereby licensing a choice of religious disciplines (religious disciplines often broadly understood to encompass nonreligious, Dr. Seussian disciplines as well)[44] rather than ridding the country of religious disciplines. Unlike France, disestablishment in the United States is not, for most people, accompanied by the establishment of a nationalist, secularist, and anticlerical ideology.[45] An argument has been made that some in the founding generation favored such a secular establishment, but any popular appropriation of such a secularist republic position was, among other factors, countered by the success of evangelical Christianities in the early republic.[46] Since the time of the early republic, the United States has always had a more or less Christian culture, although that has meant different things to different people at different times.

Taylor identifies three "important forms of social understanding" underlying the new order: the economy, the public sphere, and the practices of democratic self-rule; we live, he says, in a world that values productivity, a secular public space, and an egalitarian "direct access" society.[47] IFI is a recognizable product of this new order: it is trying to create civilized men who can flourish in that world because they will know how to deal with one another as equals working together to create a mutually beneficial society. To this end, they must learn to appropriate the biblical/universal values of "integrity, restoration, responsibility, fellowship, affirmation, and productivity." As Taylor says of the new modern moral order, "Civility required working on yourself, not just leaving things as they are but making them over. It involves a struggle to shape ourselves."[48]

Religion, significantly, was a partner in the modern moral order from the beginning. As Taylor noted, "reforming governments saw religions as a very good source of discipline and churches as handy instruments, and many religious reformers saw ordered social life as the essential expression of conversion."[49] Both still do. IFI, like its Puritan and evangelical forebears, also employs Christian language, but its goals and methods can be understood to be authorized by the "modern social imaginary," in Taylor's larger sense.

It is tempting for many, particularly those focused on secular individual rights and egalitarian politics, to see contemporary U.S. religious actors as not modern, partly because the split in the U.S. Protestant evangelical community at the end of the nineteenth century marked the beginning of a new "formation of the secular," in Talal Asad's words, one that is now projected back onto U.S. history. The new secularization was prepared by the rational Christianity of the seventeenth and eighteenth centuries and accomplished partly by liberal Protestantism's later embrace of—and, some would say, willing submission to—modern science and social science. The result has been a much stronger rhetorical separation of the sacred and the secular, and the assumption that public religious voices can be nothing but regressive. But a growing number of anthropologists, and other scholars who study conservative and revivalist religious communities, are listening more carefully to the voices in those communities and hearing an engagement with the modern that is both continuous with and distinctive from common liberal assumptions about what makes democratic life possible in conditions of religious pluralism. IFI's six universal values—integrity, restoration, responsibility, fellowship, affirmation, and productivity—are modern values that in many ways exemplify the disciplined citizen of the modern state. They are not the premodern values of honor, hierarchy, and social embeddedness, and they are shared by the moderate Left and the moderate Right. But, it is important to note, they are not necessarily fostered only through explicitly secular disciplines. Religious modes of participation also engage and embody these values, and not just in America.

In *Formations of the Secular*, Talal Asad extended and complicated our understanding of the modern by drawing attention to the various ways that space is organized in different modern contexts where the relationship between law and religion is differently configured. Saba Mahmood and Charles Hirschkind, among others, have further explored the different modern secular spaces as part of their research into the techniques of developing moral discipline that are used today by Muslim men and women in Cairo. In her *Politics and Piety*, Mahmood describes the Egyptian women in Cairo whom she came to know during her research in the late 1990s. As Mahmood portrays them, they have together invented new religious forums to serve their need for religious guidance. Female religious experts have emerged in mosques all over Cairo. Although without formal clerical credentials, these experts offer weekly teaching sessions to women on how to live a modern Muslim life. Contrary to the picture of Muslim women often offered by Western feminism, Mahmood sees these women, both the self-appointed interpreters of the *Shari'a* and their followers, as active agents creatively exploring and affirming their traditions to serve them in new times.[50] Rejecting Western-style feminism, they imagine new selves in the context of the discipline of a received tradition, experienced and named as freedom but not necessarily in traditional ways, notwithstanding the ubiquitous *hijab*. Mahmood warns Western feminists not to understand submission as a necessary sign of oppression.

Charles Hirschkind's new book, *The Ethical Soundscape*, explores the common use of cassette tapes of sermons by young Muslim men in Cairo and in other Muslim cities. Hirschkind found that these tapes provide listeners with the resources to hear God's word and reflect on their place in the world: "Sermon tapes enable their listeners to orient themselves within the modern city *as a space of moral action*, with its characteristic challenges, threats and daily problems."[51] The book is an account of Hirschkind's year and a half spent listening to cassette sermons with taxi drivers and others in Cairo. Countering the usual assumption that the Islamic revival should be dismissed as a reactive and "fundamentalist" movement, and therefore both uninteresting and threatening, Hirschkind argues that serious attention should be given to the conversations occurring within these places. His work challenges the idea that "the very attempt to harness politics to a religious tradition necessarily imperils the pluralist framework essential to a multireligious and multiethnic society."[52]

Hirschkind found, for example, that the different positions his informants had regarding the proper place of Coptic Christians in Egyptian public life contain far more nuance and promise for the future than skeptics allow. Hirschkind reports that one topic focused on the forms of interpersonal address that should be used. How should Christians be addressed by Muslims: "Peace be upon you" in Islamic fashion or "Good Morning" as in the West? Some of his informants felt that respect required no distinction in greeting. Others felt that respect demanded difference. Hirschkind concludes:

> These discussions are notable both for the plurality of viewpoints expressed as well as the public arena in which they are discussed. . . . [T]he reason liberal and leftist ears remain deaf to the cadences of these various positions is, I believe, because they do not abide by the liberal prescription that we moderns must remain indifferent to people's religious affiliations. This is itself a moral position and, for many participants in the Islamic revival, its truth has yet to be demonstrated.[53]

The refusal to remain indifferent to religious affiliation remains salient in the U.S. context as well. The desire to discuss and engage religious difference, rather than deny it, is likewise palpable in the testimony of the Iowa trial. Prisoners resented IFI's efforts to suppress such conversations.

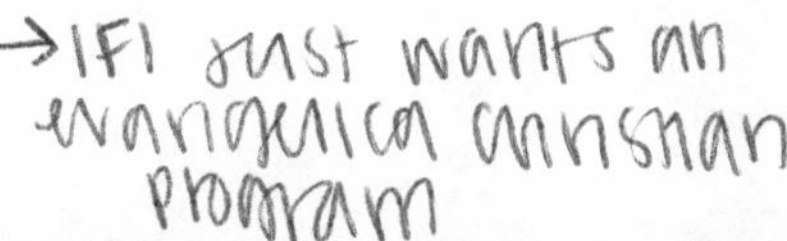
IFI just wants an
evangelical christian
program

The legal scholar David Engel, in an article analyzing his research in Thailand,[54] also describes a new religious subjectivity among some Buddhists today. His research reveals a recent shift in that country away from the use of the state courts toward a reliance on religious explanations and rituals to cope with the losses and injuries resulting from motor vehicle accidents. Engel returned to the site of earlier research, giving him the benefit of a twenty-five years' perspective, and shows us, based on extensive interviews with Thai Buddhists, new ways of understanding and coping with the role of victim. Whereas twenty-five years earlier his research had revealed a population availing themselves of the modern legal institutions of tort law, as well as customary forms of compensation rooted in village institutions, today Engel sees an increasingly displaced and urbanized Thai population employing the teaching of transnational Buddhist doctrine and various magical practices in place of modern law. Using religious ideas of *karma*, compassion, and non-duality, as well as local ghost traditions, these Thais seek multiple causal explanations and solutions for their predicaments; they strive to take responsibility for their own lives instead of finding wholeness either through the rule of law, as Western legal reformers would have them do, or through the village customary law that is not available to them in the city.

In my view, strong parallels exist between the injured Thai and the men and women of Cairo described by Mahmood and Hirschkind. All seem to be taking charge of their own lives through re-appropriations of traditional religions in ways that appear to reject both Enlightenment epistemologies *and* traditional hierarchical structures of religious authorities. Similar re-appropriations of tradition, deployed as resistance to secularism for the purposes of "cultivating virtue," can be seen in both Catholic and Protestant religious practices in Europe and the U.S. The French sociologist of religion Danielle Hervieu-Léger describes Catholic charismatic lay women's Bible groups in Paris reinventing Bible reading as a form of modern Catholic discipline.[55] In this country, too, Protestant evangelicals are rapidly changing church forms to adapt them to contemporary culture for the purpose of training Christians to live in a global world.

Religion is being used today, at least in part, for the very purpose that many Enlightenment political thinkers hoped, although probably in forms that would be unrecognizable to them. Seeking resources for the formations of modern selves, PFM and IFI are a part of the modern "universalism" of moral reforming projects across religions and cultures. Radically disestablished and deregulated religion, which is both practical and magical, is being used by individuals and groups to make the disciplined moral citizens who are necessary to the modern order and the modern state. Whether such projects of moral reform constitute religious freedom, or any kind of freedom, remains an open question. Legal disestablishment of such religion, however, does not seem possible without a degree of control that law cannot achieve.

In denying its own desire or capacity to establish religion, and inventing itself as the religion for all seasons, PFM, perhaps unconsciously, helps reorient the debate about religion in public life. If disestablished religion cannot be separated from public life because it is intrinsic to the nature of and dependent on the voluntary assent of the individual human, and efforts to do so are quixotic at best, then the appropriate way to address social issues must be debated in terms of the issues themselves, not on the grounds of whether their solutions can or cannot be denominated as religious. Focusing on whether a particular position is religious distracts from the question of whether a particular solution is a reasonable way to create a society that we want to live in. In the United States today, partly because of an ideology of separation, we find it difficult to have a conversation in which religious and nonreligious positions are compared and evaluated, or that acknowledges those often unmarked positions that resonate with the religion and history of the majority.[56]

CHAPTER 5

Beyond Church and State

THE PLAINTIFFS' LAWYERS in the Iowa trial argued that Iowa's contract with IFI was "a law respecting an establishment of religion" within the meaning of the First Amendment because prisoners of the State of Iowa were effectively coerced into participating in a pervasively religious rehabilitation program intended to transform the prisoners' relationship "to God, Christ and their fellow man" (p. 2297). The defendants' lawyers responded that the Iowa contract is not "a law respecting an establishment of religion," because prisoners freely chose to participate in the program, which was designed to reduce recidivism and instill universal, secular moral values. The plaintiffs saw discrimination in the exclusively evangelical Christian orientation of IFI and the unavailability of other comparable programs. The defendants saw discrimination in the plaintiffs' theory of the establishment clause, which the defendants believed "tends to disqualify people and groups from government funding streams"—and, it is implied, therefore, from participation in the formation of the secular and universal—"precisely because they are very religious."[1] The plaintiffs were concerned about coercion of, and discrimination against, prisoners; the defendants were concerned about discrimination against faith-based organizations and religious people generally. The defendants' argument, in a sense, is that it is wrong to consider IFI within the rubric of the establishment clause; they contend that they are tackling a difficult social problem, with courage and charity, in service to values shared by all Americans, and thus they are not engaged in "religious" activities.

How should the United States decide whether IFI is unconstitutionally religious? Indeed, is this question even the right one to ask? In this chapter I consider the prisoners' own complaints about the IFI program, their hopes for such programs in general, the possibilities of responding to the prisoners' desires within the framework of the First Amendment, and, more generally, how the relationship between religion and prison rehabilitation fits into current debates about the law and politics of religious pluralism.

The defendants in the Iowa trial, in their appeal briefs, arguments, and public statements, continued to argue that Judge Pratt's decision was wrong—that the plaintiffs and Judge Pratt misunderstood and misrepresented the defendants' arguments. While the defendants proved incorrect on the current state of the law, which Judge Pratt understood,[2] their position fits into a long-term trend in the jurisprudence of the First Amendment religion clauses. The individualization and naturalization of religion—the recognition by the courts, one might say, of religious discipline as a form of the modern secular—may make disestablishment anachronistic as a legal project. Legal tools for "separating" religion from government remain designed, in many ways, for premodern, hierarchical, and institutionalized religion. When religious authority resides in the individual, not in religious leaders and institutions, it is virtually unreachable by law. Legislation can outlaw certain activities and insist that government programs do not discriminate, but it cannot "disestablish" individual religion without violating personal integrity, an integrity acknowledged in the right to privacy and other individual freedoms, such as freedom of speech and of association.

But even if the defendants are right about the phenomenology of contemporary religion and the longer judicial trends, concerns remain about the ethical regulation of punishment and the permissible boundaries of coercive government support for one path to reintegration into the larger society. I begin with the voices of the prisoners themselves, who speak as modern individuals striving to find a way to live meaningful and disciplined lives of their own.

The Prisoners' Concerns

IFI staff members who testified at trial seemed to assume that, by characterizing IFI's ideology as generically biblical and Christian, they were avoiding any violation of the Constitution because they had apparently been told that the Constitution prohibits what can be characterized as "sectarian," that is, a particular form of Christianity. The paradoxes of this position were especially evident in the testimony concerning IFI's Statement of Faith as was mentioned in chapter 3. IFI Director Cox testified that, "what I understand of PFM's Statement of Faith, is that it's designed to be mainstream and reflect beliefs that the majority of Christians can comfortably agree to" (p. 2186). Other IFI staff members concurred.

PFM's Statement of Faith reads as follows:

> We believe in one God, Creator and Lord of the Universe; the co-eternal Trinity; Father, Son, and Holy Spirit.
>
> We believe that Jesus Christ, God's Son, was conceived by the Holy Spirit, born of the virgin Mary, lived a sinless life, died a substitutionary atoning death on the cross, rose bodily from the dead, and ascended to

> heaven where, as truly God and truly man, He is the only mediator between God and man.
>
> We believe that the Bible is God's authoritative and inspired Word. It is without error in all its teachings, including creation, history, and its own origins, and salvation. Christians must submit to its divine authority, both individually and corporately, in all matters of belief and conduct, which is demonstrated by true righteous living.
>
> We believe that all people are lost sinners and cannot see the Kingdom of Heaven except through the new birth. Justification is by grace through faith in Christ alone. We believe in one holy, universal and apostolic Church. Its calling is to worship God and witness concerning its Head, Jesus Christ, preaching the Gospel among all nations and demonstrating its commitment by compassionate service to the needs of human beings and promoting righteousness and justice.
>
> We believe in the necessity of the work of the Holy Spirit for the individual's new birth and growth to maturity and for the Church's constant renewal in truth, wisdom, faith, holiness, love, power, and mission.
>
> We believe that Jesus Christ will personally and visibly return in glory to raise the dead and bring salvation and judgment to completion. God will fully manifest His Kingdom when He establishes a new heaven and a new earth, in which He will be glorified forever and exclude all evil, suffering and death.[3]

Staff members and volunteers working for IFI are required to subscribe in writing to the Statement of Faith.

On cross-examination by the plaintiffs' lawyer, Cox explained why the Statement of Faith is important. Describing IFI as "a Christ-centered Bible-based Christian values program," he went on:

> The employees and volunteers that we use we recruit from and require them to be Christian for two reasons. If they're going to teach the Bible they should have some background. They should have some knowledge of it. We also feel that staff, particularly volunteers, need to be good role models and be living the values that we're teaching. It's important—social learning theory tells you that people often replicate behavior they observe if they see it to be positive. In a program that's based on Christian values and Christian principles we recruit Christians to serve as volunteers and employees . . . Because we use biblical examples to illustrate those particular values, they need to have an understanding of the Bible to even know where to go in the Bible. They need to understand how it relates—how the stories in the Bible illustrate and accent the values that we're teaching. If the question was could someone—could a non-Christian do that in a different program, the

answer is yes, they could find other examples from other sources for those same core values because those values themselves are not unique to Christians. (pp. 2198–99)

Subscription to the Statement of Faith is required both to insure the coherent identity of IFI's project and to insure that IFI staff model the biblical values that IFI seeks to instill in the prisoners.

Challenged by the plaintiffs' lawyer to consider the possibility that IFI's Statement of Faith excluded some Christians (as well as excluding non-Christians), Cox insisted on the uncontroversial nature of the Statement: "That statement of faith was drafted to represent mainstream Christian beliefs. . . . I grew up a Methodist, United Methodist Church. It was pretty mainstream. I found nothing in there that contradicted the creeds I grew up with, the Apostle's Creed, the Nicene Creed, and many others" (pp. 2184–85). Cox speaks out of his own experience. He is mainstream and the Statement is acceptable to him, so the Statement must be mainstream. The plaintiffs' lawyer persisted:

Q. If a person does not agree with the statement of faith, the PFM statement of faith, can they still be a Christian?

A. I'm sure they could, yes. I don't necessarily believe in speaking in tongues, but that—some Christians do. I consider myself a Christian.

Q. Now, when you use the term nondenominational to describe PFM, you understand that as not being affiliated with any particular Christian denomination; is that correct?

A. That's correct.

Q. And you are not claiming that what PFM teaches or adheres to in the statement of faith is inclusive of every Christian denomination, are you?

A. Repeat that, please.

Q. You're not claiming that what PFM teaches in its programs or what it professes in its statement of faith, you're not claiming that that is inclusive of all Christian denominations, are you?

A. What I'm saying, and I can speak primarily for IFI because I have the best knowledge of that, but *what I understand of PFM's statement of faith, is that it's designed to be mainstream and reflect beliefs that the majority of Christians can comfortably agree to.* (emphasis added) (pp. 2185–86)

The mainstream is defined by what he believes to be the majority. To be inclusive is to be mainstream.

Cox was pressed again to explain IFI's claim to inclusivity. The AU lawyer asked:

Q. I guess certainly the statement of faith and the IFI teachings certainly are not inclusive of all Christians, are they?

A. Well, there are some denominations that, perhaps, have beliefs like speaking directly to the devil or speaking in tongues, or using serpents in their worship, that would not be included in this statement of faith and who may object to it for some reason. The objective here is to be as broad and inclusive as possible without getting into the denominational doctrine that separates Christians. In other words, the purpose is to try to draw Christians together under a common purpose, and not to argue matters of doctrine, one with another. In IFI we make that very clear. When that becomes an issue, when volunteers begin to move into areas of doctrinal belief that tend to be some of the minority views, we try to bring them back to the mainstream issues. That's why we have the core values, because it helps us maintain focus, and then we can go to the Scripture and find healthy viable examples of how those values can apply in your life. (pp. 2186–87)

The lawyer was puzzled:

Q. And can you tell me why such a detailed statement of faith is needed if PFM and IFI's objective is to be mainstream and to avoid doctrinal disagreements?

A. Well, I was—I'm not a theologian. I can only give you so much—I can give you my opinion. *The—there are certain basic Christian values, very basic Christian beliefs. This statement of faith is designed to reflect those basic beliefs.* (emphasis added) (p. 2187)

The IFI Statement of Faith is understood by Cox to be that of the "healthy, viable" "mainstream," excluding only "minority views" such as "speaking directly to the devil," "speaking in tongues," or "using serpents in their worship." The practices he mentions, born out of Pentecostal readings of passages in the New Testament,[4] are representative, he suggests, of a small and marginal group of Christians. All others should be able to unite in IFI's uncontroversial "common purpose."

The IFI lawyer also questioned Chris Dye about the Statement of Faith. Dye, too, preferred a reading of the Statement as a marker of identity. He was asked to explained the purpose of the Statement:

A. The purpose of the statement of faith is basically to, since we are an organization, is for people to be on the same page. If you want to be an employee, if you want to be a volunteer, this will demonstrate that *we're on the same page.* That we believe in minimum things in common. Not that you can't believe other things, but these things we would agree to agree on.

Q. Do you have an understanding as to why IFI employees are required to sign it, the statement of faith?
A. My assumption is what I just said, *we're on the same page.*
Q. Okay. Does IFI employ people who are not Evangelical Christians?
A. Yes.
Q. Are . . . volunteers required to sign the statement of faith?
A. They are.
Q. Okay. For the same reasons?
A. Yes, so *we're on the same page.* (emphasis added) (p. 2269)

The Statement of Faith is a management tool, a collection of statements to which all employees are asked to assent in order to demonstrate that everyone is "on the same page."

Prisoners are not asked to sign the Statement. Something else is being asked of the prisoners, Dye explained, when asked why prisoners were not asked to sign the Statement: "Well, it isn't necessary because it isn't necessary for an inmate to declare a belief in any tenet in order to come to the program, graduate the program, and take on these values. . . . You can do that irregardless of what religious beliefs you have." (pp. 2269–70). For a staff member, the purpose of the Statement is to insure that everyone is "on the same page." The prisoner, on the other hand, apparently does not have to be "on the same page." The prisoners have a more complex task. They may come from various "pages." Apparently prisoners must translate their faith in order to understand and integrate what is being taught.

Many Christian creeds and statements of faith reflecting changing ideas about who Jesus was and the implications of his life and death for future generations have been generated over the last seventeen hundred years or so. Many volumes have been written dissecting their differences. The purpose of a creed is to set the bounds of orthodoxy, the grounds on which persons, ideas, and activities can be ruled in or out. Wars have been fought over the wording of these creeds. No one creed or statement of faith is authoritative for all who call themselves Christians or who would be called Christians by others—and, in the United States, unlike in countries with an established Church, there is arguably no constitutional method of legally preferring one version of what is Christian over another, no constitutional way of determining the Christian "mainstream."[5]

The nonevangelical prisoners who testified during the Iowa trial described themselves as Catholic, Mormon, Muslim, Native American, Jewish and Lutheran. They all admired certain aspects of the IFI program, but they all also felt actively discriminated against by IFI and by the State of Iowa—notwithstanding the claim that there was no religious test for admission to or graduation from IFI. The prisoners, too, operated out of a theory of the religion clauses of the First Amendment. For the most part, their theory was that it protected and honored the religious differences between them, rather than protecting the religious rights of those who would promulgate any commonalities.

The Catholic prisoners objected to several aspects of IFI's program: the exclusive use of a Protestant Bible—effacing different traditions of translation and editing as well as differences as to which books are considered canonical; persistent scheduling conflicts between mandatory IFI programming and the times at which Catholic Mass was offered; the exclusion of Marian devotional practices; and the occasional casual and ignorant anti-Catholic bigotry of some of the staff and volunteers. For example, Michael Bauer, one of the Catholic prisoners, mentioned certain conflicts concerning the differences between the Catholic and Protestant Bibles that had occurred during IFI events, and different ways of reading the Bible. He said in his deposition that: "[The instructors said that] *the* Catholic Bible wasn't a real Bible. Those books shouldn't be in there, you know. [The instructor] likened those books, the deuterocanonical books such as Wisdom and Maccabees, to the Koran, and I had a big problem with that."[6]

The Catholic prisoners and the IFI Protestant staffers and volunteers replayed time-honored exchanges and cultural misreadings marking the relationship of Catholics and Protestants in the United States. Bauer commented:

> Most of these volunteers being what I would say anti-Catholic, and you could really feel it in—if you'd make a statement on something, you know, because of your beliefs of Catholicism, and they would look at you and they would know where that thought—or not that thought, but that belief was coming from without you even saying it, they would try to skew you the other direction. I can remember one time one volunteer telling me that I needed to believe everything that was written in the Bible because that's the way it is. It's a literal truth, and I looked at her and I told her, I says, "Well, I don't have to believe like that." And her eyes got as big as silver dollars, you know. It was like, "Oh," you know, and it really bothered her, you know, and I remember that distinctly, and she really didn't have a lot to do with me from that time on.[7]

Bauer also mentioned Protestant/Catholic differences about the baptismal ritual that came up during the IFI program:

> There was a big baptism going on in the early goings of that program where they baptized, I suppose, 50, 60 people. I remember [one of the IFI staffers] asking me if I had been baptized at that time, and I told

> him, "Sure, I was baptized. I was baptized in the Catholic Church." And he said, "Did they just sprinkle it on you or full immersion?" I said, "Well, they poured it on me." He made the comment *that wasn't a real baptism because I wasn't fully immerged* [sic]. I told him he was wrong, and if he knew anything about baptism, he would know that baptism comes from your heart and not the actual water that's being poured on you.[8] (emphasis added)

There have been variations in modes of baptism since the early Church, as well as disagreements about which form is correct.

One complaint of the nonevangelical prisoners was that the State of Iowa paid for the water for the full immersion baptisms performed by IFI, whereas other minority religious groups raised money from their external religious communities to pay for religious equipment such as the rocks for sweat lodge rituals and extra food for keeping kosher. Several Catholic prisoners commented that derogatory remarks were made about the Pope. For example, Russell Milligan said that "[the IFI instructor] said that people are kind of scared of the Pope, kind of like people would be scared of Hitler. He went on to express that he wasn't comparing the Pope to Hitler, but he did say that they both yielded [*sic*] power that frightened people" (p. 241).

Some Catholic prisoners said that they were unaware before they entered the program that the Christianity taught by IFI might be different from the Christianity they were taught as Catholics. For example, Bauer commented:

> I knew there were some differences in some religions, but the scope of what the differences were were so vast that it really—it really shocked me. I mean you take Evangelical over Catholicism. I mean, Evangelicals are more literal in the sense of the word. . . . [M]y knowledge of Christianity was that most—almost all Christians were the same. I thought all of our beliefs were basically the same. I thought they were just teaching Christianity. I always thought that that's what Catholics were, were part of Christianity. . . . [A]t that time I was unaware of the vast differences. (pp. 435, 443)

Bauer's comments reflect the surprise of many Catholics that it is common in the U.S. evangelical community to distinguish rhetorically between "Christians" and "Catholics" as one would between different religions. Bauer concluded his testimony with the dramatic comment: "My No. 1 reason for leaving the program was that I personally felt spiritually crushed" (p. 429).

IFI lawyers also used the word "Christian" to distinguish IFI from Catholics. For example, during the cross-examination of Russell Milligan, the IFI lawyer, trying to make the point that IFI did not require conversion, asked him the following questions:

Q. You just testified you were able to take and complete the IFI program as a Catholic without accepting or converting to Christianity; right?
A. Well, again, I was a Christian—
Q. Right.
A. —to begin with.
Q. I guess I should say without changing your faith, you were able to take—
A. Yes, I was able to remain a Catholic. (pp. 256–57)

Although all the PFM and IFI staff that testified at trial said firmly that derogatory remarks about Roman Catholics, as well as about other religions, were both illegal and explicitly prohibited by IFI—and that staff and volunteers making such remarks were promptly disciplined—it was clear both that IFI theology had a limited capacity to address religious multiplicity and that most IFI staff and volunteers, like most Americans, have little knowledge of religious traditions other than their own.[9] (IFI is most sensitive to charges of anti-Catholic bias. IFI staff members are quick to point out that Charles Colson's wife is Roman Catholic, and that he attends mass with her on occasion. Colson himself frequently mentions his wife's Catholicism in his own writings and sometimes comments on her discomfort with certain aspects of evangelical religious practice.)[10]

Most of the prisoners who testified said they felt strongly that any program of the IFI type should be more broadly "interfaith," facilitating communication among all religious traditions, a kind of vernacular endorsement of the value of interreligious dialogue of a similar sort to that engaged in by the taxi drivers in Cairo of whom Hirschkind speaks. Michael Bauer expressed this point of view by commenting on the ethos in the IFI classroom:

> I believe [IFI] tries to proselytize men that come into there into the beliefs of those that are there. They don't have enough discussions on other religions and aspects of religion. . . . They need to make it an all-faith thing and divide the time up equally. . . . [T]hey still refuse to allow men to look at things and discuss things. . . . You know, a lot of times guys are cut off early, you know, when they're stating their points of view, and that's just not acceptable. I mean, if somebody is stating their point of view, that is his point of view. Whether you accept it, whether you like it, it is still his point of view. Now, with that said, that man there needs to also sit there and listen to somebody else's point of view. And if that's not happening, well, then maybe there should be

> some time taken out to discuss these things to let people know about diversity so everyone can have their time, so others can have the understanding and the knowledge of another group's religion. . . . [I]t's got to be done right or it shouldn't be done at all, you know, and—you know, that's how I see things today. It's got to be done right or it shouldn't be done.[11]

Non-Christians who participated in the IFI program felt particularly uncomfortable. One of the lawyers for the plaintiffs asked John Lyons, who described himself as Lutheran, about how non-Christian prisoners were described by IFI staff. He replied:

> Well, you know, many things, you know, the word *lost* comes to mind, you know. *Unsaved*. Some would even use a *pagan*, the word pagan. You know, I mean if you believe in certain things or worship certain things or, you know, it had a pagan worship nature, or you worshipped the sun-god or whatever it is, you know, if you come in from that druid group of people or the—I don't know the names of these outfits that were, you know, if you put—if you're serving mammon, is the word I think they use, I can't remember exactly what it is, but *when you're not serving God, you're serving the flesh; and when you're of the flesh, it's of Satan*, or of the devil or of deception or, you know, anything that, you know, distancing yourself from God is sinful behavior, and *if it wasn't all about God and all about the Bible and all about, you know, focused on Christ, then it was of Satan or it was of darkness.* If you weren't in the light, you were in the dark.[12] (emphasis added) (p. 580)

The attitudes reflected in Lyons' description of the comments of IFI staff mirror the dualism of a certain segment of the evangelical self-help literature used in the IFI curriculum, a dualism that sees the religious life as a struggle between light and dark.

Benjamin Burens, a Native American prisoner, in response to questions from the plaintiffs' lawyer about his experiences as a participant in the IFI program and how they had evolved, commented on the mixed message he received from IFI about the possibility of his continuing his Native American practices while in the program. At first, he said, IFI was welcoming and inclusive:

> *Q*. Did you express to Gene [the IFI instructor] your beliefs as a Native American at any time during that first quarter?
> *A*. Yes, I did.
> *Q*. And what did you tell him?
> *A*. I told him that obviously he knew I was Native American. I told him I didn't come down there to become a Christian. I came down there to hopefully learn something, learn something more about the

> Bible, take this like a college class. I was not trying to become a Christian. What I do out there on Wednesdays [in the sweat lodge] is what I do out there, I really don't want to discuss it with IFI. I basically left it at that.
>
> *Q.* What was your counselor, or teacher, Gene's response to that statement? . . .
>
> *A.* At first he was just glad I was there, hopefully I could learn something, learn something more, learn something more about what they had to offer, their beliefs. (pp. 757–58)

But, as Burens explained, attitudes in IFI shifted:

> At least once a month you had the one-on-one, and they evaluated your fruit of the spirit evaluation, just told you basically how you were doing in the program, how other people thought you were doing, how you were getting along with the work . . . He asked me was I saved, was I a Christian, did I believe in Jesus, and what was I doing going out to the sweat lodge ceremony. He said it was basically a form of witchcraft, it goes against what the Bible teaches, form of sorcery, I'm worshipping false idols out there, he doesn't see how I can go out there and come into the IFI and have the same beliefs. (p. 759)

The sweat lodge ritual, originating among Plains Indians, has become a pan-Indian spiritual practice, particularly in prisons.[13]

Three Muslim prisoners testified at trial. All felt uncomfortable with IFI, notwithstanding IFI's constant refrain that Muslims were welcome. Bobby Shelton (a.k.a. Bilal Shukr) was a prisoner at the Iowa State Penitentiary when he heard about the IFI program. He consulted with the chaplain there about whether he should apply. In response to questions from the IFI lawyer about why he decided not to volunteer, he answered, explaining Muslim views of the Bible:

> I learned that I would have to go to some Bible studies, and I didn't initially have a problem going to the Bible studies, because they were Bible studies. Being a Muslim we believe in the teachings of the Bible and we also follow the Bible. The problem that I would have had as a Muslim attending the Bible studies is when the prayer would begin, and the prayer would begin as to praying to Jesus Christ. As Sunni Muslims we don't view Jesus Christ as God or God's son, we just view him as a prophet, like Moses, Noah, and others. So to sit in congregation while that sort of prayer was taking place, I would essentially be blaspheming God. In Islam your [*sic*] taught that if a prayer like that is taking place, you're supposed to leave the room. If you stay in the room while it's taking place, you're essentially acquiescing to what is being said. So I had a problem with that. In Islam, it's taught if you can't change some-

> thing with your hand, you change it with your mouth. If you can't change it with your mouth, you change it with your heart. I would have not been in a place to change anything physically or verbally in those Bible studies. So the option I would have had was to change it in my heart by vacating. (pp. 161–62)

Regarding the curriculum generally, he further explained:

> I learned about the curriculum. And all the curriculum there was supposed to have been, from what I was told by the Chaplain, was strictly Christian based. There was no opportunity for any of the curriculum to be interfaith, as it's portrayed to the public as being an interfaith program, because there's no interfaith curriculum. It's all Christian curriculum. Again, if they're teaching Jesus Christ is God or God's son, I wouldn't be able to participate in that. (pp. 162–63)

Asked why he decided not to join IFI, Shelton said:

> From the information that was given to me about the IFI program, and its strict Christian-based curriculum, there was no possibility for me, as a Sunni Muslim, to partake in that program without desecrating my faith, without me blaspheming God. We believe there's only one God, and he doesn't have any sons or daughters or partners. He's the supreme ruler over all of mankind, and we are all brothers and sisters under one God. For me to embrace any type of curriculum contrary to that, I would be desecrating my faith. (p. 163)

He made this decision in spite of the real attractions of the program, as he explained:

> Part of the benefits of the InnerChange program that I think everyone in society knows is that it helps you to get out into society quicker than you would at a parole setting. That's part of what they advertise. They have a mentor program, in which a mentor helps you when you're out in society. They set you up with a church, help you get a job, those sorts of things. It's almost like—essentially a mentor program to help you, cut down the recidivism rate. Because of this mentor program, the interfaith program has only had—has about a 70 percent success rate, which is attractive to anybody who's trying to get out of prison and not be a recidivist. So that was one of the things that was attractive to me and others that have tried to get into the program who aren't necessarily Christian. (p. 164)

Like the Catholics, however, Shelton felt misunderstood and diminished by IFI:

> In light of 2001, and things of that nature, 9/11, it just seems to add to the perceived bias that some may perceive as a bias toward Islam. For me it's not a bias. I've experienced it in this Prison system at ISP [Iowa State Penitentiary], and I've experienced it out in society as I've been a Muslim since I was 16 years old. So it just added fuel to the fire, makes it appear as though the State of Iowa has a partiality toward Christian-based programs, and not faiths of different sorts. (pp. 165–66)

Shelton did not object to religious programming because it was religious; he objected to the program's failure to be interfaith, which many Americans view as the desirable mode of living with religious diversity.

Like other prisoners, Shelton wished for an IFI-type program based in his own religious community, Islam. The plaintiffs' lawyer asked him:

> *Q*. And to your knowledge does the Department of Corrections offer any intensive rehabilitation program to inmates that are taught from the perspective of any faith other than the InnerChange Christian faith?
> *A*. Not to my knowledge.
> *Q*. And do Muslims in the Department of Corrections' prison system receive, to your knowledge, do they receive any opportunities for intensive or concentrated teachings in their religion?
> *A*. No. In fact, most of the programs in the institutions, in ISP and Mount Pleasant, these other places in the State, they actually slight the Islamic religion.
> *Q*. And do Muslims—are Muslims given any opportunities in the Iowa Department of Corrections prison system to be housed together in one prison cell block or prison cell unit? . . .
> *A*. To my knowledge—to my knowledge, here at ISP and from talking to people that have come from Mount—not Mount Pleasant, but Anamosa and Clarinda, Fort Dodge, and even Mount Pleasant [other Iowa prisons], that you don't have any. If you said that you wanted to be housed with other Muslims—for instance, like, this month is the month of Ramadan. If we wanted to be able to all get together on a certain range to talk about Islamic things, as far as religion, as far as politics, we wouldn't be accommodated in that fashion. So the IFI program, they are accommodated in that fashion in that all the people that attend are Christians.
> *Q*. And if a program similar to IFI, but based on Muslim teachings, was available to inmates, would you be interested in such a program?
> *A*. Yes, I would. (pp. 166–67)

The inability of the corrections agencies in the United States to cope with the increased presence of Islam in the prisons is shown in part by the fact that in 2004 the Federal Bureau of Prisons imposed a moratorium on the hiring of Muslim chaplains because of fear of extremism.[14]

Prisoner Troy Redd also described himself as a Sunni Muslim. He had attended an introductory session given by IFI before the program started at Newton. When the plaintiffs' lawyer asked him what he was told about IFI's attitude toward Islam, he answered: "Mr. Paulus [an IFI staff member] advised me that it was a Christian-based program, that I could continue practicing my religious beliefs, but it would have to be done after—on my own time, basically . . . I could attend Jumah prayer as long as it didn't interfere with the curriculum of the IFI program" (p. 291). And then he was asked about his decision not to apply to join. He answered, rehearsing differences articulated over more than a millennium of Muslim-Christian interaction:

Q. Did you join IFI after that orientation program?
A. No.
Q. Why not?
A. Well, first of all, with my—it was totally different—Christian teachings is totally different from my Islamic teachings. And for me to be able to join a Christian-based program that did not lead to the same teachings as my Islamic teachings, it would cause me to become—what's the word I'm looking for?—denied my religion. It would commit blaspheme. *We are not idol worshipers, and Christians have a tendency of praying to idols,* and different things like that. . . .
Q. What other differences were there that you were aware of between the Christian teachings of IFI and your religion besides the idol issue?
A. They worship Jesus as being the Son of God. In fact, he went so as far as to saying in the Trinity that he was God himself.
Q. Mr. Paulus said in the training that Jesus was God?
A. The pamphlet they passed out was basically referring to the Trinity of teachings.
Q. And you disagree with those teachings; is that right?
A. Yes, I disagree with their teachings.
Q. And does the Bible play any role in your religion, the Christian Bible?
A. Yes, the Bible does. Yes, the Christian Bible does play. We are taught—Muslims study all religions. We study all books of God.
Q. . . . [W]hat happens to someone under your—what does your—under your belief system, what happens to someone who professes a belief in Jesus or prays in Jesus' name?
A. He would have committed sin against Allah, God. He was blasphemous. You were sparring partners with God at that time . . . It states

in the Koran that God would never—God would never forgive those as sparring with him.

Q. Mr. Redd, why couldn't you just join IFI, attend their prayer service, and then practice your religion on your own?

A. Because I fear God, that's why. Once I received the true teachings about God, I could not turn my back on God just for the possibility of me being released from prison, or anything else. *I know it's wrong to associate with that program.* (emphasis added) (pp. 290–92)

Idolatry. Polytheism. That is what characterizes Christian understandings of God. Muslims adhere to a more thorough monotheism. On cross-examination, the IFI lawyer pressed Mr. Redd about his decision not to participate in IFI, emphasizing the voluntary nature of IFI participation: "your decision not to participate was entirely voluntary, was it not?" He replied: "No. It was about a fear of God" (p. 300).

One sees here, writ small, what many are struggling with privately and publicly: How does one remain faithful to one's particular religious commitments while acknowledging common concerns, even common traditions? Both the prisoners and IFI moved back and forth between these two religious modes without finding an easy accommodation. All acknowledged common ground but if pressed too hard to define themselves as a part of the whole, both individual prisoners and IFI staff asserted a strong commitment to the particular, seeming to fear a loss of identity and belonging. A tension is also apparent between the languages the prisoners used to describe human behavior and obligation: on the one hand, a legal language—exemplified in the words, "your decision not to participate was entirely voluntary"—a language that understands the individual to act out of personal choice, and religious language, such as in the expression "fear of God," expressing the absence of free choice.

Kevin Watson, one of the prisoner plaintiffs, described himself as a member of the Nation of Islam. Responding to a question asked by the plaintiffs' lawyer about his religious practice, Watson answered: "I build on Islamic beliefs and I don't consume pork. I do prayer usually by myself because I have yet to get into the routine here. And from being at Newton Correctional Facility, I was so far out of the routine because the Nation of Islam wasn't really accommodated there, so I basically just do my own thing and remain steadfast in my own personal beliefs" (p. 909). Watson was also asked why he did not join, or attempt to join, IFI:

A. Well, because I would have to sacrifice or compromise my religious beliefs. Basically *I would have to pray to God in order to get through the program, and that was something that I wasn't willing to do.*

Q. Why would you think you would have to compromise or sacrifice your religious beliefs? Why did you think that?
A. Well, because the IFI program is a Christian-based program, and that's not my belief. They pray differently, they deal with religion differently than I do. So in order for me—it would have been either one or the other, and I would have to sacrifice myself in order to get through that program.
Q. Mr. Watson, under your beliefs as a member of the Nation of Islam, what happens to someone who prays to or in the name of Jesus Christ?
A. It would be damnation. *One would go to hell for such an act.* (emphasis added) (pp. 911–12)

At Kevin Watson's deposition the IFI lawyer had asked him about other Muslims who had decided to participate in the program. IFI lawyers often suggested that one or more Muslim prisoners had successfully graduated from the program, although the actual evidence was inconclusive. The lawyer seemed genuinely surprised by Watson's answers. In Watson's words:

> I would have to question the sincerity of the person that was the member of the Nation of Islam or Muslim that went through that program and graduated because one thing that I found you do not do is play with God, and if—*the teachings of Islam and what is written in the Bible, they are two different things.* We believe in one God. The Bible has the Father, the Son, the Holy Ghost. *There is no way as a member of the Muslim community or the Nation of Islam you can go through that program and not compromise your own faith. Either you aren't sincere with being a member of the Nation of Islam or you aren't sincere with being a Christian. You can't do both. Not and remain faithful to both sects.* You can't—you can't do it, so I would have to question whoever went through and graduated. Maybe they went through it and graduated. The term that's used around here is fake it till you make it. Maybe that's what they did.[15] (emphasis added)

Watson was also asked about IFI's openness to other faiths. He answered:

> That may be the politically correct statement which is broadcast from the program, but the reality of it is like I said previously, you don't play with God. I mean, being a member of the Nation of Islam, I can't faithfully go over there and pray the way that they pray. I can't go over there and acknowledge a lot of the teachings that they acknowledge and accept as being real. So being open is one thing, but *if I were to go over there, I would, in fact, compromise who I am, and that would be*

> *playing with God, and I'm not going to do that.* That's not the way to go.[16] (emphasis added)

These prisoners seemed to be instructing the lawyers questioning them as to what it means to be serious about one's religion.

Apparently the lawyer for IFI genuinely did not understand. He asked Mr. Watson directly why IFI's theory of learning, which is based on a civilized core of values common to all religions, cannot work for everyone: "If a member of the Nation of Islam participated in the IFI program, explain to me a little as to why they have to be converted into believing that there is more than just a single God? *Why can't they maintain their religious faith and learn that in Christianity one turns the other cheek or one does unto others and that that --how is that applied in a civilized society?* Why can't they learn that and adhere to their faith as taught by the Nation of Islam?[17] (emphasis added) Christianity and civilization, for him, are coterminous. Surely other worthwhile religions are as well? In good U.S. fashion, Kevin Watson tried a sports metaphor in explaining why he did not feel comfortable being taught values by IFI while remaining a Muslim:

> Well, most people already know those things. Whether or not people choose to display them in their lifestyle or the way they live, that's—most people here know right from wrong. They just chose to do wrong, but from a religious aspect --for instance, they say things like—when they pray, you know, they pray in Jesus' name. I firmly believe that if maybe a devout Muslim or simply a member of a Nation of Islam were to go over there, he would be ejected because he's not complying with the format that they've established over there. It's kind of like—what would be a good example? I don't know. *It would be kind of like going to a football field to play basketball.* I mean, you know, it's an athletic field, but the arena is designed for a particular sport, you know.[18] (emphasis added)

Watson seems to agree with IFI that religions have values in common but he also appears to suspect that the universality of religious practices was being too easily implied. Whether you pray to Jesus—or not—matters.

Watson, too, would have liked a Muslim IFI. He was asked by the plaintiffs' lawyer about that possibility:

> *Q.* Do you know of any other intensive rehabilitation programs offered by the DOC that are taught from the perspective of the Islamic or the Nation of Islam faith?
>
> *A.* No, I haven't heard of any.
>
> *Q.* And how do you feel about that, Mr. Watson?

A. Well, for all that that program offers the people that partake in it, as far as the groups, the computer learning, and the knowledge—the intense knowledge, the comprehension of one's religion, I think it's very unfair that people that are part of other religions can't get that same knowledge and understanding and the same benefits that the people in the IFI program have available for them.

Q. And if there were such a program offered by the DOC, an intensive rehabilitation program that taught from the perspective of the Islamic or Nation of Islam faith, would you be interested in joining such a program?

A. Yes. Definitely. (pp. 912–13)

The non-Christian prisoners all expressed a desire for what they understood could be an opportunity for intense engagement with their own religious culture—through an IFI-type program of their own.

Curiously, during the depositions, the IFI lawyer repeatedly used "turning the other cheek" as an example of a universal value. He seemed unconscious of his own Christian cultural bias. Or, perhaps, his language reflects a more general convergence in the U.S. consciousness of "Christianity" and what is termed "civilization." At my deposition, he asked a question similar to the one he asked Watson, trying to sort out the universal and the particular:

Q. Is turning the other cheek a religious or Christian—help me here. What's the word I'm looking for, doctor?

A. I don't know.

Q. Teaching?

A. Turning the other cheek refers to a specific event in the New Testament, in the words of Jesus, and in that sense they are a Christian teaching.

Q. But one can understand what that means and not have to agree that that teaching is—that one must become of that faith in order to understand that a civilized society doesn't strike back, it requires in instances, turning the other cheek; correct?

A. No.

Q. All right. Why is that not correct?

A. Could you define a civilized society for me?

Q. It's kind of hard to do in this day and age, I admit. You understand a society of laws?

A. I don't think there's a necessary connection between a society of laws and turning the other cheek.[19]

I believe that the IFI lawyer questioning me had never before considered the relationship between law, civilization, and Christianity.

One Jewish prisoner testified at the Iowa trial, Glendale More, who identified himself as Lubavitch Orthodox, that is, a member of a Jewish group that traces its descent from a Hasidic Jewish community that existed in Poland before World War II. More testified about his efforts to practice Judaism in prison and his concerns about IFI. The lawyer for the plaintiffs asked him about his religious practice:

> *Q*. And can you tell me what you do today to practice your religion, what types of things you do?
>
> *A*. Yes. One, I maintain the commandment to not shave my facial hair, *I maintain my beard*. Normally, if I was at Fort Madison [another Iowa prison in which More was formally resident], I would be wearing a yarmulke or ball cap, which was allowed down there. Another, *I perform my mitzvahs*. Another is *I stay kosher during the high holy days*, since I pay for all my own kosher food at this time. Other than that, *I say my prayers from time to time, and I stay in contact with my rabbis*. Other than that, there's not much else I can do while I'm incarcerated.
>
> *Q*. Can you explain what a mitzvah is for the Court?
>
> *A*. A mitzvah is doing good deeds that when you're done doing the good deed, most people will not know who did the good deed, so you're not going to get pats on the back or compensation for the good deed.
>
> *Q*. And why don't you wear a baseball cap or Yarmulke when you're at Newton?
>
> *A*. Well, one, they don't allow them, a baseball cap worn inside, or they don't allow a Yarmulke to be worn any place in here, it's not allowed in their policy yet. This is one of the many things—well, I guess partly because they don't have a Jewish program here, and *they don't know anything about Jews, apparently*. (emphasis added) (pp. 185–86)

He was also asked about what he had heard about IFI:

> I became aware of it while at Fort Madison. We were first made aware of it by not having any money for our library, our gym, our hobby shop. They told us the money was being diverted from those programs, from our telephone kickback, to a central location in Des Moines that was being diverted up to a program—a new program at Newton, and we pushed further and found out it was a new religious program. I became very upset about this. . . . I understood they had what would be called an honor house in most other camps, they had free phone calls, they had computer rooms, they had a music room, they had keys to their cells, they had cells with no toilets in it. They could go down a

> hall to a bathroom to relieve themselves so they wouldn't bother their cellmates. They had privileges that nobody else had, and that seemed to be a little bit above and beyond . . . *I understand it was a born-again Christian movement indoctrinating individuals who were willing to come to their program and a 24/7 Christian belief, trying to turn their lives around, teaching them to believe in Jesus Christ.* (emphasis added) (pp. 186–88)

When asked why he did not apply to join IFI, More replied, "because they worship Jesus Christ as the Lord, and I can't do that." Asked to explain further, he said, "*Jews are one on one with the Lord. Jesus Christ is just another Jew. He's a Rabbi. A Rabbi is a teacher. He's not the Lord*" (p. 189). As with the Muslims, praying to Jesus meant, in some sense, denying God. He explained this in answering the lawyer's questions:

> Q. I'm sorry to have interrupted you. How would you feel about having to worship or pray in Christ's name, in the name of Jesus Christ?
>
> A. I can't do that. That's worse than treason. I'm turning my back on the Lord, the creator, the one who gave me life. How can I turn my back on the one that gave us this entire planet, this entire solar system, the one who created everything we know? Just for his son? No, I can't do that.
>
> Q. What would it mean to you to do that, to turn your back on God? What does that mean to you in your life?
>
> A. That's worse than committing suicide. *You might as well commit suicide because you're taking the very essence of our lives as Jews away from us. One-on-one with the Lord is what we're about. We're born to be in his name. We cannot turn away from him.* (emphasis added) (pp. 189–90)

Having finished educating the lawyers about one's duty to the Lord, More said: "When people come to me wanting to know more about my religion, I tell them, 'You've come to the wrong person because I'm not a good Jew. I'm not the person you should be coming to. A good Jew would not be in prison. I'm not the best person to be coming to'" (p. 189). He said he would have liked a Jewish IFI: "If there was one for Jews, yes, I would go to it. I would probably have a rougher life, I'd be made to tow [*sic*] the line a lot more than I do now, but, yes, I would go" (pp. 190–91).

As with the other prisoner witnesses, More was asked about the six IFI values when he was cross-examined by IFI lawyers:

> Q. I do want to ask you some questions about your Jewish faith. Your Jewish faith I think values *integrity*; isn't that right?
>
> A. Yes, it does.

Q. And, indeed, the Bible talks about integrity. *Daniel in the lion's den, isn't that a story about integrity?*
A. Yes, sir, but I told you I'm the first person you shouldn't come to about—
Q. I think you know a lot about the Bible. I'm just going to see—do you know a lot about the Jewish faith? *Integrity* is part of your Jewish faith. How about *responsibility*, is that part of your Jewish faith?
A. Yes.
Q. How about promoting *restoration* among broken families, is that part of your Jewish faith, sir?
A. Yes.
Q. Sure. *Jacob and Esau, right, as an example?* Right?
A. Sir, I didn't come here to get into a discussion over Bible literature with you.
Q. I just need to understand what your position is in connection with IFI, that's why I'm asking these questions. But you agree that *restoration* is part of the Jewish faith?
A. Yes.
Q. The Jewish faith, as you understand it, values *affirmation*?
A. Is that a question?
Q. That is a question.
A. Okay. The way you phrased it, it didn't sound like a question.
Q. I apologize for—it may be the ICN [videofeed system], it may be my voice, I apologize. It's my burden to give you a clear question, so let me come back at you. The Jewish faith, as you understand it, endorses *affirmation* as a value?
A. I'll agree with you.
Q. And your Jewish faith, as you understand it, values *productivity*; right? I'm sorry. Your Jewish faith values *productivity* as a value; isn't that true?
A. All right.
Q. Okay. Did you know that those are the six values that IFI promotes in its program, *integrity, restoration, responsibility, fellowship*—I didn't ask you about *fellowship*. Surely the Jewish faith values *fellowship*. You'll agree with that, won't you?
A. Yes, sir.
Q. All these are the primary values that IFI seeks to teach. Are you aware of that?
A. Yes, sir. (emphasis added) (pp. 199–201)

Having bullied More into agreeing that each of the IFI values are also Jewish values that he could correlate with stories from the Hebrew Bible, the IFI lawyer continued: "So those values would be completely consistent with your Jewish faith, wouldn't they?" But More wasn't having it: "[Only] if they were being led down the line of worshipping the Lord instead of Jesus Christ" (p. 201). The way to get from where he is to an appropriation of those values was through the Lord, not through Jesus.[20]

Many of the prisoners who testified said that they felt pressured to become Christian. In response to questions from the plaintiffs' lawyer, John Lyons summed up IFI's objective as a spiritual awakening and a carrying of that experience to others:

> If and when you had that spiritual awakening that—recognizing that Christ died for you, for your sins, and he was the ultimate sacrifice, and he was your salvation, that Christ was the only avenue to God, that only by confessing Christ was the one and only salvation there ever is. There is no other possibility of salvation unless it is through the blood of Christ. Once you learn that, once you confess that, once you repent, you know, I mean you turn away from—Repentance means to turn away from your sin and start walking in that newness of God. You are to carry that to other people that were lost or anybody that was not saved. Anybody that has not confessed Christ is not saved. In other words, if you're not saved, you're not going to heaven. If you're not going to heaven, where you're going—from what they all say, you're going to hell. So anybody that's going to hell, we all want to get them going to heaven; right? So that's what we do as Christians. We go out and we witness to others, and we pull them into the flock, and we make the body of Christ or the body of believers or the group of people that believe that Christ is the salvation bigger and unified and grow. (pp. 580–81)

He concluded his explanation, saying "they thought it was really neat when you could witness to a correctional officer" (p. 581).

IFI's lawyer asked Bryan Chandler at his deposition whether he was ever required to convert. He responded, "Yes. The whole—Bruce's whole speech there in his orientations would be to convert to their—convert their way, to be able to walk the walk. He had told me time and time again about how that would—how the conversion would take effect on any—*any person that joined the program would be converted by the time they got out of the program* . . . Them are his words" (emphasis added).[21] One cannot help feeling that these prisoners, those who do not share IFI's specific religious understandings and practices, do, however, share PFM's insistence that it is through religion that one achieves values; the prisoners pushed back, though, insisting that one cannot get to those values through alien religious practices without losing something of oneself.

Joel McKeag testified concerning a conversation about his ideas about the Bible that he had had with the IFI recruiter Bruce Paulus. He then explained that he had realized after that conversation that he would not fit in, despite his wish to remain on Unit E. McKeag was asked by the plaintiffs' lawyer about this decision:

> *Q*. Were there some beliefs that you held from your own religious studies that, in your short time with IFI, you believed differed from the things you were being taught during your IFI initial orientation period?
> *A*. Yes, on numerous grounds. You have—I have trinity problems with Father, Son, and Holy Ghost. I believe God is more than that. That didn't come about until the fourth century, that way of thinking. Baptism, the sacraments that are given at the Lord's Supper. Even the word faith itself and belief itself I have problems with.
> *Q*. Ultimately, did you decide to enroll in the IFI program, or not?
> *A*. At the beginning . . . it was my full intentions to become involved in IFI. With my studies I kind of knew how Christianity in its totality views the Scriptures. . . .
> *Q*. So why did you decide not to be in the program?
> *A*. I knew that I would have a lot of problems there because it's in my nature to, if someone has a view on it, well, there are other views. I would like to share those views with them. I knew that this would be—would be counterproductive to what they're trying to teach. I knew that I would be rebuffed on every point. That it would be considered as nothing but disruptive conduct, and that I would be released from the program, quick, short and in a hurry. (pp. 1978–80)

McKeag wanted to discuss theology. IFI had different goals.

On cross-examination, IFI's lawyer pressed McKeag to acknowledge that IFI focused on values, rather than religion:

> *Q*. Mr. McKeag, during your time in the program, or in the introduction to the program, you were informed, weren't you, that the program was about teaching values, the values of integrity, restoration, responsibility, fellowship, affirmation and productivity. Do you remember that?
> *A*. Most religious things do teach values.
> *Q*. Okay. Do you remember that about the IFI program?
> *A*. Values was mentioned, yes.
> *Q*. Okay. And, in fact, that was the foundation of the IFI program, wasn't it, teaching the values of integrity, restoration, responsibility, fellowship, affirmation and productivity? (pp. 1987–88)

McKeag disagreed:

A. Not from my understanding. *It was basically the promoting of the religion.*

Q. Okay. You would agree, wouldn't you, that the values of integrity, restoration, responsibility, fellowship, affirmation and productivity, are consistent with your beliefs based on your studies of the Jerusalem School of Synoptic Research?

A. Under the Jerusalem School there's different interpretations to a lot of biblical Scriptures. It actually redefines and actually puts more on those values.[22] (emphasis added) (p. 1988)

McKeag had earlier explained his views on universal salvation, views he had learned from his correspondence course with the Jerusalem School, which had taught him about the Noahide laws, the Jewish laws that govern non-Jews. McKeag was full of information and sought a forum where he could argue about religion; IFI, in his view, was enforcing a religious orthodoxy rather than providing a place for religious self-realization.

The prisoners testified that they felt violated by IFI. Does that mean that the IFI contract violates the establishment clause of the First Amendment? Are the prisoners' concerns the result of "a law respecting an establishment of religion?"

The Law of the Case

After a three-week trial that took place in the fall of 2005, over several months, Judge Pratt heard closing arguments in February 2006. He issued his opinion in the case on June 6, 2006, declaring the Iowa contract with IFI to be a violation of the establishment clause. He also issued a virtually unprecedented order requiring complete restitution of all funds paid to IFI by the State of Iowa, an amount that exceeded $1.7 million. Pratt's careful and detailed consideration of the factual basis of his decision was immediately recognized by academic commentators as so thorough and comprehensive as almost to insure affirmation of the decision on appeal. (The restitution order was more controversial, as will be discussed later.)[23]

Where is establishment clause law today? Judicial interpretation of the establishment clause is particularly difficult to summarize briefly. Whether and to what extent government favoring of religion—and what exactly that means—is considered an unconstitutional establishment, and when such favor is permitted constitutionally, remains a particularly abstruse area of constitutional jurisprudence. The admonitions of the First Amendment are addressed to Congress. "*Congress* shall make no law respecting an establishment of religion." This wording reflects the concern of the writers of the Amendment that the reach of *federal* power be clearly delineated. Because the federal government had little power and interest in doing so for more than a century and a half (except with respect to federally governed populations such as Mormons and Indians), U.S. courts had little opportunity to consider the meaning of the words of the establishment clause. In its 1947 decision in *Everson v. Bd. of Education*,[24] however, the Supreme Court held that the Fourteenth Amendment made the prohibitions of the establishment clause applicable to the activities of *state* governments as well. Incorporation, as this legal act is called, has peculiar implications for the establishment clause, in contrast to the other rights that are understood to have been applied to the states by the Fourteenth Amendment.[25] The establishment clause does not give expression to a traditional "right" but, arguably, sets the legal and political conditions for the right to the free exercise of religion.

Legal scholars continue to disagree about whether the establishment clause should best be read as having been intended to be merely jurisdictional (intended simply to disable the *federal* government with respect to establishing a national church, leaving state governments to deal with the regulation of religion as they wish) or whether the clause also expresses a substantive commitment to "separation" or even secularism as an essential component of the guarantee of religious freedom. If the former is true, its application to the states arguably makes no sense, because the original intention is understood to have been solely applicable to the federal government and should have been unaffected by the Fourteenth Amendment. If the latter, debate continues as to whether states should be as limited as the federal government in deciding how to manage religious matters, both as a matter of constitutional interpretation and as a matter of public policy.[26] Ambiguity also remains about whether the establishment clause prohibits all government aid to religiously affiliated organizations or only requires that aid be provided in a nondiscriminatory manner among all religious organizations. Still unsettled is how courts should determine whether a particular organization is or is not religious within the meaning of the Constitution. Courts have consistently prohibited government financial support for core religious functions such as worship—but little clarity exists beyond that consensus as to the circumstances under which government funds and other favors can pass to religious organizations to support activities other than worship.

Establishment clause cases since the Supreme Court's 1971 decision in *Lemon v. Kurtzman*,[27] a suit challenging state subsidies for parochial schoolteachers, have primarily been evaluated by the so-called *Lemon* test.[28] The *Lemon* test provides a framework for distinguishing between those situations in which religion and government inevitably and benignly intersect, such as in the provision of police and fire protection for church buildings where any assistance to religion is understood to be incidental to more general government mandates to protect the public, and those cases that cross the line into an impermissible "establishment" of religion. The *Lemon* test has been supplemented in recent years with the Court's decisions in later cases finding that certain situations are better analyzed by considering whether particular government activity can be perceived as an "endorsement" of religion, in the case of the public display of religious symbols,[29] or as "coercive" in its effect with respect, for example, to public prayer.[30] The largest number of these cases have concerned schools, reflecting the importance they hold for American civic identity and the historic threat that Catholic schools were understood to pose to that identity.

The establishment clause cases are much criticized by members of the court as well as by legal academics. The critiques, along with recent changes in Court personnel, suggest to some Court watchers that further shifts in the jurisprudence of the establishment clause may be in the offing. Judge Pratt's description of the current state of establishment clause law in his opinion in the Iowa case reflects the often Byzantine complexity of current establishment clause jurisprudence. He writes:

> "Under the *Lemon* test, government practice is permissible for purposes of Establishment Clause analysis only if (1) it has a secular purpose; (2) its principal or primary effect neither advances nor inhibits religion; and (3) it does not foster an excessive entanglement with religion." . . . Nevertheless, the "Establishment Clause 'cannot easily be reduced to a single test. There are different categories of Establishment Clause cases, which may call for different approaches.' " . . .
>
> With respect to government aid, or funding cases, the Supreme Court refined *Lemon I* in *Agostini* by providing two other discrete factors to be used when determining whether government funding or involvement has the primary effect of advancing or inhibiting religion. First, the Court must evaluate whether the government program results in governmental indoctrination and, second, whether the government program defines its recipients by reference to religion. . . . *Lemon I* was further modified in *Agostini,* when the majority concluded that, because the entanglement inquiry consists of essentially the same factors to decide whether entanglement is excessive as does the inquiry to examine effect, "it is simplest to recognize why entanglement is significant and treat it [also] . . . as an aspect of the inquiry into a statute's [or program's] effect."[31] [citations omitted]

But the key query for lower federal courts in funding cases remains whether the law in question can be understood to have had a secular purpose and effect.

The plaintiffs in the Iowa trial did not challenge the assertion that the primary purpose of the contract was secular. The principle question, therefore, was whether the contract with IFI had the *effect* of establishing religion. Even the most revisionist positions on the establishment clause would regard the presence of state coercion or discrimination among religions as limits on state activities promoting or accommodating religion. The debate in the Iowa case came down to whether prisoners had a meaningful choice about engaging in specifically religious activities and whether prisoners were discriminated against based on their religious affiliation.

Prisons are a special case. Different law applies to prisons than to the "free world."[32] Prisoners' constitutional rights, including rights respecting religion, were virtually unknown before 1974.[33] As Melvin Gutterman wrote of the rights of prisoners in 1982, "The legal status of those persons convicted of committing a criminal act was long ignored by the courts. A century ago, the criminal offender was regarded as a 'slave of the State,' thereby providing prison administrators' acts with virtual immunity from judicial review. More recently, the courts took a 'hands-off' approach to the administration of prisons."[34] Courts have been reluctant to involve themselves in reforming prisons, notwithstanding a shocking history of abuse. Gutterman concludes that "the Supreme Court, although recognizing that prisoners are not wholly without protection of the Constitution, has continually failed to honor all but the most basic of human needs."[35] The standard today, as then, is deference to the judgment of prison administrators.[36]

Although religion is encouraged in most prisons because it is regarded as conducive to maintaining security, courts generally defer to the judgment of prison authorities with respect to the actual management of prison religion. Until 1987, the existence of a constitutionally protected right for prisoners to practice their religion was unclear.[37] In that year, a case came before the Supreme Court concerning Muslim inmates at a New Jersey prison who had been denied permission to attend Friday services because the time of the services conflicted with a work detail.[38] The Muslim prisoners ultimately lost their case, but the Court established criteria for determining when prisoners' rights to freely exercise their religion should trump prison regulations. Justice Brennan dissented from the decision, observing that "incarceration by its nature denies a prisoner participation in a larger human community. To deny the opportunity to affirm membership in a spiritual community, however, may extinguish an inmate's last source of hope for dignity and redemption."[39]

Enforcement of the establishment clause with respect to prisons also differs from that in free society. Courts recognize that in order for prisoners to practice their religion, as with anything else they do, they need active government cooperation. In other words, all prison religion is, in a sense, discriminatory, and all activities in prisons are, to some extent, coercive, as Judge Pratt noted in his opinion. Prisons are supposed to enable religious participation, within the bounds of their security obligations, but not prescriptively. The U.S. Court of Appeals for the Seventh Circuit has held, for example, that requiring a prisoner to attend a religiously based version of Narcotics Anonymous violates the establishment clause.[40]

Judge Pratt's opinion in *AU v. PFM* concluded, following *Lemon*, that the primary *effect* of the contract between Iowa and PFM was to promote religion. He found that separation of the religious and secular aspects of the program is impossible, that the prisoners had no real choice because of the numerous incentives to join the program, and that the state was excessively entangled with religion. Pratt wrote:

> The transformational model employed by InnerChange forecloses any possibility that secular and sectarian aspects of the program may be separated. The state, through its direct funding of InnerChange, hopes to cure recidivism through state-sponsored prayer and devotion. *While such spiritual and emotional "rewiring" may be possible in the life of an individual and lower the risk of committing other crimes, it cannot be permissible to force taxpayers to fund such an enterprise under the Establishment Clause.* "As the Supreme Court has repeatedly held, one of the few absolutes in Establishment Clause jurisprudence is the 'prohibit[ion against] government-financed or government-sponsored indoctrination into the beliefs of a particular religious faith.' "[41] (emphasis added)

The restitution order reflected Judge Pratt's judgment that a finding of the unconstitutionality of the contract was entirely foreseeable to both PFM and the State of Iowa, making its formation, in the face of such predictability, a matter of bad faith.

Pratt's decision was appealed to the U.S. Court of Appeals for the Eighth Circuit. Oral argument was heard in the case on February 13, 2007. In a surprising coincidence, considering the importance of her religion clause opinions during her tenure on the Supreme Court, Sandra Day O'Connor, by then retired from the Court, served as a member of the panel, by designation, as retired justices often do, with two judges from the Eighth Circuit, Judge Roger L. Wollman and Judge Duane Benton.

PFM and IFI were represented on appeal by the Becket Fund for Religious Liberty, a well-known, Washington-based nonprofit organization that describes itself as "dedicated to protecting the free expression of all religious traditions."[42] AU represented itself and the prisoner plaintiffs. In addition to the three appellate briefs filed on behalf of the parties, AU, the prisoners, PFM, and the State of Iowa, fourteen amicus briefs[43] were filed. Eight amicus briefs (some by coalitions of more than one organization) were filed in support of PFM and the State of Iowa, supporting its argument that the IFI contract was constitutional. Five amicus briefs were filed in support of the plaintiffs-appellees brief arguing that Judge Pratt's decision was correct.

The two sets of amicus briefs together convey a variety of perspectives on the meaning and purpose of the establishment clause and the IFI program, ranging from a whole-hearted endorsement of Pratt's decision to the broad claim that prisons are inherently a religious endeavor and therefore no business of the state. The briefs also showcase the current political rhetoric and landscape on these issues. The presence of multiple state governments, as well as the federal government, among the amici, highlights the hope that these governments place on the capacity of faith-based prison programs to solve the multiple social problems created by massive incarceration and high recidivism rates.

The eight amicus briefs supporting PFM and Iowa, were filed by the following organizations and governments, some collectively and some individually:

- Alliance Defense Fund,[44] National Association of Evangelicals,[45] Center for Neighborhood Enterprise,[46] Teen Challenge,[47] Time to Fly,[48] Center for Public Justice,[49] Evangelicals for Social Action,[50] The Coalition to Preserve Religious Freedom[51]
- American Center for Law and Justice,[52] and Travis Dagel, Sandro Navarro, Robert Wayne Robinson, and Rick Theeler (all IFI graduates)
- Catholic League for Civil and Religious Rights[53]
- The Commonwealth of Virginia and the States of Alabama, Arkansas, Colorado, Florida, Kansas, Missouri, South Carolina, and Texas
- Foundation for Moral Law[54]
- Iowa Family Policy Center[55]
- United States of America
- Wallbuilders, Inc.[56]

Many of the advocacy groups listed on these briefs actively support a greater public acknowledgment and support of the role of religion in public life. Many have experienced legal staffs that regularly file amicus briefs in religion cases.

Backing Judge Pratt's decision, five briefs were filed on behalf of the following organizations:

- American Civil Liberties Union[57]
- American Correctional Chaplains Association,[58] American Catholic Correctional Chaplains Association,[59] Jewish Prisoner Services International[60]
- American Jewish Congress,[61] Baptist Joint Committee for Religious Liberty[62]
- Anti-Defamation League,[63] American Jewish Committee[64]
- The Council for Secular Humanism,[65] Center for Inquiry[66]

These briefs also represent the views of familiar amici and regular litigants in religion cases.[67]

PFM and the State of Iowa argued in their briefs on appeal, as they had at trial, that the purpose of the IFI program was to reduce recidivism and teach universal values; that prisoners were entirely free not to participate, and those who participate were not required to convert—but, in any event, all participants had signed informed consent forms.[68] Both also argued that the judge had misunderstood evangelical Christianity and incorrectly relied on my testimony. The State of Iowa also argued that the Supreme Court's decision in *Turner v. Safley* requires judicial deference to correctional judgment.[69] PFM and IFI contended that Judge Pratt had incorrectly found that IFI staff were "state actors" whose religious actions could be attributed to the state,[70] and that state funding of IFI fell under the "indirect" funding exception to the establishment clause prohibitions, an exception worked out principally in the context of the school voucher cases and now being extended to the social services context.[71] As at the trial, the briefs of defendants/appellants and their supporters appeared caught between, on the one hand, assertions that IFI is uniquely successful because it is religious, and that PFM and IFI have equal rights as religious organizations to contract with the government; and, on the other, that IFI is essentially secular and provides a treatment program that is virtually identical with the secular classes available through the Iowa DOC.

Amici supporting the defendants argued a range of additional points. Challenging the statement by Judge Pratt that prisons are, by their very nature, a state function, the Alliance Defense Fund (ADF), and its co-amici, argued to the contrary, that the history of prisoner rehabilitation in the United States shows that it is inherently the province of the churches. The ADF offered an account of the history of the U.S. prison, one that legitimized, indeed demanded, the presence of religious reformers in the nation's prisons:

> The Quakers built the country's first prison. . . . The Philadelphians decided they would try to transform the criminal's character. . . . They sought to convert the offender—not to a particular church, but to a

> God-fearing life of decent behavior. . . . In the mid-1960's another sea change swept through the criminal justice system. Once again the idea was to make them better. . . . This triumph of the therapeutic largely supposed (however optimistically) that criminal behavior was not chosen but rather was caused by personal maladjustment and oppressive social conditions. . . . Reforming character is no longer part of the "corrections" skill set. . . . [T]he dramatic secularization of our constitutional law makes it impossible for the contemporary state to do what the Quakers did—deliberately foster religious renewal.[72]

The ADF entirely rejected the possibility of secular prisoner rehabilitation, implying that IFI is doing what the Quakers did, seeking "to convert the offender—not to a particular church, but to a God-fearing life of decent behavior." And that such "fostering of renewal" through the funding of religious organizations is a proper role of government.

The brief filed by the American Center for Law and Justice on behalf of itself and several prisoners claiming to be successful IFI graduates was written by Jay Sekulow, a well-known activist for a greater public role for religion. After quoting from prisoner accounts witnessing to the effectiveness of IFI in helping them change their lives, the brief focused on the order of restitution, arguing that the plaintiffs had no standing to seek such an order, and that such an order, if upheld, would have a chilling effect on the willingness of faith-based organizations to contribute to the solution of social problems.

Law professor Richard Garnett of Notre Dame Law School wrote the amicus brief for the Catholic League for Civil and Religious Rights, a group presenting itself as expert on the history and nature of U.S. anti-Catholicism. The brief states that IFI is not anti-Catholic, and offers a list of personal anecdotes about Charles Colson as proof, including that Charles Colson's wife is Catholic, and that, in 1994, Colson, together with the Reverend Richard John Neuhaus, a Catholic priest and former Lutheran pastor, instigated an evangelical/Catholic alliance articulated in a manifesto titled, "Evangelicals and Catholics Together."[73]

A letter of December 20, 1989, from the Jesuit priest Avery Dulles, addressed to Colson, is attached to the Catholic League brief. Garnett offers the letter in support of the proposition that Dulles did not find the PFM Statement of Faith "contrary to anything he believes." Strangely, Dulles's letter, written ten years before IFI was instituted in Iowa, has passages critical of IFI theology that resonate strongly with the Iowa Catholic prisoners' complaints of bias. Dulles, a prominent Roman Catholic theologian who was then a visiting professor at Boston College (and who since has been appointed to the faculty of Fordham University and created a cardinal by Pope John Paul II), had written to Colson, apparently in reply to an inquiry from Colson, about his views of Prison Fellowship:

> I have heard good things about your prison fellowship. . . . The only criticism I have heard is that some of your workers tend to raise the expectations of the prisoners too high in terms of future financial success, as though the latter were the criterion of their true worth. . . .
>
> I have several times read over *your statement of faith*. I do not find it contrary to anything I believe but at the same time it *strikes me as Calvinistic in tone. The language and emphasis are those of American conservative Evangelicalism. This is notably the case when redemption is described in terms of Christ's "substitutionary atoning death," terms that are rarely used in contemporary Catholicism. . . .*
>
> *In your letter you justify the emphasis on biblical inerrancy.* This was indeed insisted upon in some Catholic encyclicals of the 19th and early 20th centuries, but Vatican Council II in its Constitution on Revelation preferred to drop any mention of total inerrancy. *I do not think that the inerrancy of every proposition in the Bible can be defended. . . .*
>
> *To speak of all people as "lost sinners" is, again, quite defensible but foreign to the modern Catholic tradition.* I would prefer to say that all suffer for the effects of original sin and stand in need of redemption. The term "lost sinners" suggests personal guilt and liability to divine punishment from the very moment of conception or birth. . . .
>
> Finally *I would say that the statement of faith omits things that Catholics regard as essential, for example the sacraments. Thus the statement of faith must be regarded as incomplete from the Catholic point of view. . . .*
>
> I could sincerely make the statement, interpreting it in my own way. But *I would not as a Catholic feel comfortable with it.*[74] (emphasis added)

Dulles's reservations substantially confirm the reservations of Judge Pratt and the Iowa prisoners about IFI and undermine the argument in the Garnett brief to which it is attached.

The amicus brief filed by the nine states in support of IFI and Iowa, apparently written by the attorney general of Virginia who is listed first on the brief, sounds the alarm about the recidivism crisis and the "failure of the correctional systems," effectively claiming that because government has failed, "faith" should be allowed to step in. These states argue that IFI is constitutional under the *Lemon* test and that the Supreme Court's decision in *Turner* requires deference to correctional officials in considering the constitutionality of prison programs. The brief also cites what

Judge Pratt had found to be partisan and discredited research as to the efficacy of faith-based prison rehabilitation programs. The states concluded their brief as follows:

> The mere fact that faith-based programs have a religious component does not justify their exclusion while similar programs, which have no religious component but may be less effective in attaining the secular rehabilitation purposes, are allowed. A rehabilitation program based on the philosophy of Christ or Moses or Buddha or Muhammad should be treated the same as a rehabilitation program based on the philosophy of Marx or Rand or Nietzsche or a contemporary social scientist. The mere fact that the ideas being expressed have a religious component does not justify treating those ideas differently than other ideas.[75]

This rhetoric oddly and paradoxically echoes both the egalitarian ideology of the Dr. Seuss litany of the trial and Colson's dualistic worldview condemning soulless secularism. Like IFI, the states seem to argue at the same time that religion is the same and that it is different.[76] The brief also reads very much as if the states are at their wits' end with respect to recidivism and that this crisis alone should permit the introduction of faith-based solutions. There is little talk of how to help prisoners, only that religious organizations have as much right to try their hand at it as anyone else.

Judge Roy Moore, formally Chief Justice of the Alabama Supreme Court, filed a brief for his Foundation for Moral Law arguing for what he claims be an originalist reading of the religion clauses. (In 2003 Moore was removed from his post as Chief Justice because of his failure to obey a U.S. District Court order requiring removal of a monument of the Ten Commandments from the Alabama courthouse.) Moore argues in his brief that the originalist position would reject all "court-devised" interpretive tests, such as the *Lemon* test, for evaluating constitutional violations, preferring instead a reading of the religion clauses as simply constituting an explicit acknowledgment of the important and necessary role of religion in America. Judge Moore argues that "it is [a] reformation of the heart that InnerChange seeks to accomplish through its 'useful instruction' at the Newton facility in Iowa."[77] IFI is not, he insists, a religion. It is "religious" but it is not a religion: "No parties to the case dispute that InnerChange is 'religious,' even 'overtly' or 'pervasively' so. . . . Regardless, the InnerChange program still does not constitute an independent 'religion'"[78] "The district court may not like a voluntary 'Evangelical Christian congregation within the walls of one [of Iowa's] penal institutions,'" Moore concludes, quoting Pratt, "but its presence is not an establishment of religion."[79] Moore insists that, read literally, the establishment clause does not permit the establishment of a "religion," "an independent religion," but does permit government support of "religious" things.

The Iowa Family Policy Center states in the "interest of Amicus" section of its brief that "it is a religious organization which believes that biblical evils—gambling, sexual immorality, abortion, euthanasia, etc.—pose a threat to the stability of society and, as a result, to the rest of society."[80] The Center asserts that "the Religion Clause of the First Amendment" protects individuals from "government interference with their religion." To ban IFI, they say, would be to fail to protect the prisoners from government interference with their religion.

The brief of the United States supporting the defendants was addressed solely to the appropriateness of the restitution order. The argument was that the traditional remedy in an establishment clause case is an injunction against future activity. "A judicial order directing such recoupment," the Justice Department argued, on the other hand, "interferes with the discretion of the political branches over the public fisc, and the prospect of such retroactive relief threatens to deter private organizations (particularly those with limited resources) from participating in government funding programs."[81] The Department of Justice also argued that it is a violation of constitutional guarantees concerning the separation of powers for a court to order restitution of funds to the government when the government in question did not seek it. (The plaintiffs' lawyer addressed this issue in the oral argument, saying that the state cannot ask for restitution because to do so would be to admit the very bad faith that the state denies.)

The Wallbuilders, Inc., brief supporting IFI stated first that the district court had misunderstood the nature of evangelical Christianity. In an extended discussion the brief explains the diversity within contemporary evangelical Christianity, even on core commitments such as biblical inerrancy, and argues that Judge Pratt inappropriately used unwarranted generalizations about evangelical Christianity in characterizing PFM and IFI. But the brief went on to make the distinctive argument that the Iowa case should be decided under the decision of the Court in *Marsh v. Chambers*.[82] *Marsh* declared that the hiring of chaplains by state legislatures was not unconstitutional because legislative chaplains predated the passage of the First Amendment, and were therefore "grandfathered." Likewise, Wallbuilders argues, "the historic record demonstrates that state funding of religiously based programs has existed since the foundation of our Nation" and "religious rehabilitation, like InnerChange, is 'deeply rooted in our history and tradition,' just like legislative chaplaincies, and should therefore be understood to be constitutional."[83]

Most remarkable, the Wallbuilders brief concludes with a contention that even government funding of proselytization is constitutional, because such funding was built into federal Indian policy:

> During the eighteenth and nineteenth centuries, the government initiated a widespread policy to "civilize" the Indians. The policy included spreading the Gospel in order to convert the Indians to Christianity. . . . Early Americans (including prominent Founding Fathers) desired to assimilate the Indians into society by proselytizing and converting the Indians to the Christian faith. Similarly, early prison systems sought a conversion of inmates that would enable them to meld peacefully into lawful existence once freed. InnerChange should be upheld because the program is similar to other proselytizing programs from American history.[84]

Prisoners, like Indians, need to be civilized through Christian conversion. Civilization is, they say, an historic religious project of the United States government,[85] whether of Native Americans or of prisoners, and is therefore, apparently, constitutionalized by long practice.

In support of Judge Pratt's opinion, the ACLU brief focused on the narrow question of whether special constitutional considerations are relevant because this is a prison case. Replying to the state's demand that the court show special deference for correctional judgment, the ACLU brief argues that *Turner* is not applicable in establishment clause cases because the conflict in such cases is not between the rights of prisoners to practice their religion and the needs of prison administrators to maintain security. Instead, the ACLU maintains, PFM is using the *Turner* standard of deference to prison authorities to legitimize a prison's conclusion that it can only be run with the help of religious organizations, effectively abdicating its own responsibility.[86]

The brief filed by various correctional chaplains associations strongly seconded Pratt's conclusion about the unconstitutionality of IFI and offered an impassioned defense of traditional chaplaincy programs and of the professional and ethical standards to which those programs are held. Drawing a strong line between the religious and the secular, it declared first that "the primary purpose of chaplaincy programs is to address the religious needs of incarcerated inmates," and then lists other functions: "coordinating religious programs for all faith groups; providing both religious and secular counseling; advising prison authorities on issues concerning inmate faith practices and religious article and dietary needs; recruiting and training of volunteers; and serving as liaisons with the community and inmate families." All are subject to ethical "standards of practice requiring inclusion. Neutrality and nondiscrimination—and prohibiting indoctrination or compulsion—are at the core of every prison chaplaincy program."[87] These amici tell the early-nineteenth-century history of the prison as being a proud but long past chapter in the reforming spirit of the Enlightenment, not as an enduring endorsement of religiously based prisons:

> [A]s Defendants' amici note, many early prisons relied extensively on religious instruction and worship to provide comfort and encourage rehabilitation. . . . Undersigned amici, correctional chaplains and chaplaincy associations, acknowledge and honor this history . . . but defendants' amici overstate their case. The penitentiary system developed not only from religious influences but also from developing republican and Enlightenment notions of humane treatment that considered older punishments to be barbaric and misdirected.[88]

The lesson to be learned from the history of involvement of U.S. religious groups in the reform of prisons, today's chaplains say, is the spirit of reform, not the need for religion.

The brief filed on behalf of the American Jewish Congress and the Baptist Joint Committee for Religious Liberty argues vigorously for the proposition that the First Amendment requires the accommodation of the religious needs of all prisoners on a nondiscriminatory basis. They begin with a familiar yet nonetheless startlingly apt quotation from James Madison arguing against tax assessments to support religious education:

> Who does not see that the same authority which can establish Christianity, in exclusion of all other Religions, may establish with the same ease any particular sect of Christians, in exclusion of all other Sects? That the same authority which can force a citizen to contribute three pence only of his property for the support of any one establishment, may force him to conform to any other establishment in all other cases whatsoever?[89]

The brief then forcefully argues in support of Judge Pratt's decision.

The Anti-Defamation League (ADL) and the American Jewish Committee, as amici, make a strong claim that the establishment clause embodies the Jeffersonian commitment to the "separation of church and state." ADL holds that "a high wall of separation is essential to the continued flourishing of religious practice and belief in America, and to the protection of minority religions and their adherents."[90]

The Council for Secular Humanism and the Center for Inquiry, both avowedly atheist organizations, vociferously counter the implication of the defendants' and their amici arguments that violations of the Constitution are permitted if they save the state money:

> On defendants' logic, if religious organizations can run schools more cheaply, the state can simply fund sectarian schools and need not bother with supporting its own secular school system; if religious organiza-

> tions can assist the poor and unemployed more efficiently, there is no need for welfare; if religious organizations can regulate family relations inexpensively, then let state-funded churches, mosques and temples have exclusive control over marriage, divorce, birth and adoption. This Court needs to remind defendants that the Bill of Rights is not for sale.[91]

These observations were echoed in the oral argument.

At the oral argument in the Eighth Circuit, many of the same arguments were touched on by the judges and the lawyers, but the judges seemed most interested in the restitution order and the question of whether it was excessive. Toward the end of the argument, the lawyer for Americans United was asked by Judge Duane Benton of the Eighth Circuit Court of Appeals, who apparently was concerned that the restitution order would result in "unjust enrichment" to the State of Iowa, whether it was indeed the position of AU that PFM "gave no value to the state." Focusing on those prisoners who were happy with IFI, the judge queried: "Those who want to exercise their free exercise rights while they're in prison, which is protected by strict scrutiny, a recent federal law and a recent U.S. Supreme Court decision. That surely has some value, huh?" The lawyer arguing for Americans United responded:

> I would say it has value to those inmates. But, at the same time, this whole relationship—the benefits, the privileges—harms and discriminates against other inmates. And overall, I don't think that, when you take that into account, that value to the state or the public was provided. And I think it's wrong for the state to spend money on a program that is not appropriate for all faiths but creates discrimination and provides special benefits for those of one faith. And what would be correct under the Constitution, as well as correct as a matter of right and wrong, would be for the state to spend its money in a way that provides benefits and rehabilitation equally to all inmates, and that any private, any religious services or instruction be solely paid by private funds by whatever group wishes to pay for them.[92]

The lawyer for the plaintiffs was careful in the Court of Appeals, as he had been at the trial, not to condemn what he termed truly voluntary and nondiscriminatory religious prison programs. If a reasonably broad choice of programming were available, and if no state funding was provided and no special preference given to anyone, then religiously grounded prison rehabilitation was probably constitutionally permissible—and, from the point of view of his prisoner clients—desirable.

Anthony Piccarello for the Becket Fund, speaking for the defendants at the oral argument, said of Pratt's opinion that, "the rationale and remedy of the decision below are extreme and if they are allowed to stand they would nip in the bud the vital experimentation of states, like Iowa, working together in contractual relationships with faith-based groups, like IFI, to tackle intractable social problems like recidivism." Later in his argument, Piccarello argued that "the lower court's draconian remedy ... will deter faith-based providers from even bidding on contracts in the future."[93] Their brief made a similarly emotional appeal:

> The lower court struck down InnerChange, an innovative prison program that by all accounts has done enormous good. The program not only saved Iowa money that it could ill afford to spend on prisoners, but, more importantly, saved Iowans from the burglaries, robberies, rapes, and murders that went uncommitted because InnerChange reduced recidivism among former prisoners who completed its challenging curriculum.[94]

Piccarello speaks from a political position that regards private solutions as the most appropriate and economical approaches to solving "intractable" social problems, and private religious organizations as having a corresponding right to contract with the state.[95]

The Court of Appeals for the Eighth Circuit affirmed the finding of the trial court that the contract constituted "a law respecting an establishment of religion." For the contract years 2000–2004, during which payment was made through a cost-reimbursement arrangement, the appeals court found that "religious indoctrination can reasonably be attributed to Iowa's funding" and that "the InnerChange program was not allocated on neutral criteria and was not available on a nondiscriminatory basis" so that "the direct aid to InnerChange violated the Establishment clauses of the United States and Iowa Constitutions." For the years 2005–2006, when payment was made on a per diem basis, it found that, "in this case, there was no genuine and independent private choice. The inmate could direct the aid only to InnerChange. The legislative appropriation could not be directed to a secular program, or to general prison programs." However, regarding the restitution order, the Court of Appeals reversed and remanded, finding that the district court abused its discretion in granting the order because it found that there had been no bad faith on the part of IFI and Iowa.

Strangely, having substantially confirmed Judge Pratt's findings that IFI was coercive and discriminatory, the court of appeals, in a footnote, found that the district court had abused its discretion in receiving my testimony:

> Prison Fellowship and InnerChange assert the district court erred in admitting testimony from a law professor/Ph.D./author to describe "Evangelical Christianity." An inquiry into an organization's religious

views to determine if it is pervasively sectarian "is not only unnecessary but also offensive. It is well established, in numerous other contexts, that courts should refrain from trolling through a person's or institution's religious beliefs." The district court abused its discretion, as the professor's testimony is not relevant. However, in light of Prison Fellowship and InnerChange's sincere statements of their beliefs, this error is harmless.[96] (citations omitted)

Courts cannot inquire into an organization's religious views, according to the Eighth Circuit. Although Judge Pratt had said that he used my testimony only as background, examining religious beliefs at all is offensive by definition, they say. Religious beliefs are not constitutionally subject to "inquiry." "Sincere statements of their beliefs" are to be taken at face value—and, in this case, PFM's and IFI's own statements apparently prove the case against them without any need for expert interpretation.

Notwithstanding its losses in the courts, PFM has claimed victory in interviews and on its Web site. In announcing the Eighth Circuit decision, PFM proclaimed that, "Former Supreme Court Justice Leads Eighth Circuit in Overturning Federal Judge's Ruling to Shut Down Effective Faith-Based Prison Program," following with a story about the decision:

Appeals Court Reverses Ruling Requiring Closure of Effective Prisoner Rehabilitation Program and Repayment of $1.5 Million to Iowa

ST. LOUIS, Dec. 3, 2007—Today former United States Supreme Court Justice Sandra Day O'Connor and two appellate judges, Judges Roger L. Wollman and Duane Benton, reversed major parts of a federal district court judge's ruling against a voluntary faith-based pre-release program for prisoners launched by Prison Fellowship. Ruling for the Eighth Circuit Court of Appeals, they found that District Court Judge Robert Pratt over-reached in much of his 2006 decision in a lawsuit brought by Americans United for Separation of Church and State against the InnerChange Freedom Initiative (IFI), Prison Fellowship and the State of Iowa . . . "We are grateful to the Eighth Circuit for refusing to handcuff people of faith who are helping corrections officials turn inmates' lives around," said Prison Fellowship President Mark Earley. "What was at stake here, at its heart, is public safety. The keys to reducing recidivism and protecting the public from repeat offenses are the very kinds of effective rehabilitation and re-entry services provided by the InnerChange Freedom Initiative." . . . "This is a huge victory for faith-based programs," said Eric Rassbach, the Becket Fund's national litigation director. "A $1.5 million judgment against

> them would have crippled the most successful criminal rehabilitation program in the state. This court decided faith-based organizations aren't automatically suspect just because they are faith-based. States have to consider what the programs are actually doing."

While this story seems an absurd exaggeration on its face, IFI's confidence may reflect a larger trend.

Consider *Hein v. FFRF*, the only religion clause case decided by the U.S. Supreme Court in the October 2006 term.[97] FFRF (the fiercely atheist Freedom From Religion Foundation)[98] had alleged that expenditures by the director of the White House Office on Faith-Based and Community Initiatives on conferences that promote the participation of religious groups in government funding of private social services are an unlawful establishment of religion. *Hein* was an exceptional form of action known as a taxpayer suit, and the harm alleged was to the plaintiffs as taxpayers. A majority of the justices found that FFRF had no legal standing to bring the action. In other words, FFRF was not the proper plaintiff for such a suit. Although "standing" may appear to be the kind of legal issue that only a lawyer could love, the Court's opinions in this seemingly dry procedural ruling may signal a significant shift in the Court's understanding of its role with respect to religion, a shift contributing to the taste of victory expressed by PFM.

The vote in *Hein* was 5 to 4, with four different opinions. Justice Alito's opinion for three of the justices in the majority came close to overruling a key religion clause precedent, *Flast v. Cohen*,[99] but the three opinions by the justices in the majority are most distinctive in their common assertion that the danger of religious establishment no longer requires special constitutional vigilance. Indeed, they argue, such special treatment was a product of anti-Catholic animus in school funding cases, and therefore ought now to be abandoned. The president can promote religion, they say, just as he can promote any other social policy, limited only by electoral politics. And taxpayers *qua* taxpayers no longer have standing to complain.

Article III of the U.S. Constitution, which establishes the judicial branch of government, provides that the jurisdiction of the federal courts is limited to "cases and controversies." These words have long been interpreted to mean that federal courts cannot give advisory opinions, decide essentially political questions, or rule on moot issues, because to do so would violate the doctrine of separation of powers and invade the provinces of the other two branches of government. In developing the notion of justiciability, the Supreme Court has held that lawsuits initiated by federal taxpayers who are complaining of government spending and challenging the constitutionality of congressional statutes are not justiciable controversies because individual taxpayers lack a sufficient personal financial stake in such cases.[100]

Only one exception has been made to this rule against taxpayer suits. In 1968, in *Flast v. Cohen*, the Court allowed such taxpayer cases specifically to challenge the constitutionality of congressional acts alleged to be in violation of the establishment clause. Religion is special, the Court was saying in 1968, and established religion is especially dangerous. The *Flast* taxpayers challenged a federal grant of assistance to local schools, including religious schools, to purchase textbooks and other instructional materials for disadvantaged students. In an 8–1 decision, the Court held in *Flast* that the foundational importance of the principle of religious disestablishment demanded an exception to the non-justiciability of taxpayer suits. The implication was that all Americans are harmed by a violation of the establishment clause in a way quite different from other government acts. In his concurring opinion in *Flast*, Justice Douglas, in language characteristic of the time, cited "notorious" and "mounting federal aid to schools" as well as the risk that any money given to parents of parochial school children would be given directly to "the priest."

The 2007 *Hein* decision did not explicitly overrule *Flast* but formally only limited *Flast* to taxpayer establishment clause challenges to acts of *Congress*, distinguishing the White House Office as a part of the executive branch. But as Justice Scalia wrote in his concurring opinion, *Flast* had essentially been overruled. The strength and elegiac quality of Souter's dissent in *Hein* hearkens back to the *Flast* era, insisting that religion is special, that individual conscience must be protected by a high wall of separation, and that James Madison ought still to rule: "favoritism for religion," says Souter, "sends the . . . message to . . . nonadherents that they are outsiders, not full members of the political community." Souter's is increasingly a minority voice.

Faith-based initiatives have had broad support across the political spectrum at least since the Clinton administration. There is widespread acceptance of the idea that local, congregational, and community-based programs can address social problems in what is termed a more holistic way. There is much nostalgia for a supposedly simpler time when churches and communities are imagined to have done this work. Indeed, there is a sense shared by many in the middle that what is conceived as a hard-edged secularism purveyed by a vast professional social welfare bureaucracy does not accurately attend to the nature of the human or provide a workable basis for social intervention. Secularism is understood to have produced an arid and unlivable social space, the failure of government-run social programs of all kinds, and mindless globalization.

Religious ideas, people, and institutions enjoyed varying degrees of legal privilege in the various American colonies before the Revolution and many have enjoyed de facto legal privileges ever since. But the American colonies never witnessed anything like the particular union of religious and political power achieved in England after the Restoration, or the wealthy and politically powerful entrenchment of the Roman Catholic Church in France. Indeed, the sociologist José Casanova has argued that the lack of a previous establishment, in the strong sense, has created the conditions under which "public religion" continues to flourish in the United States.[101] While religion and government in the U.S. have formally gone their separate ways since independence, satisfactory consensus on the meaning and purpose of the establishment clause remains elusive. Contemporary interpreters of the establishment clause are divided roughly between two camps: those who argue that it prohibits all support of religion *qua* religion—however evenly distributed among different religions—versus those who believe it prohibits only a single national church and coercive proselytizing by the government but permits nondiscriminatory government support of religious institutions and activities as a public good. Both camps appeal to history; the first was in the ascendancy during most of the twentieth century, but the second is now gaining ground.

Beyond the Separation of Church and State

Judge Pratt's opinion described IFI as a form of "Protestant monasticism." Curiously, he apparently unwittingly identified a theme in contemporary evangelical post-fundamentalism, and in postmodernity more generally: a yearning for an imagined medieval piety and world of enchantment[102]—a piety embedded in a culture without skepticism or doubt, religious education in the context of a total social institution. The twenty-first century, of course, is not the Middle Ages, and so the prisoners and the IFI staff move in a legally constructed religious field where religious authority has increasingly come to center in the individual. Churches are no longer churches but temporary congregations of like-minded individuals.

The American Protestant rejection of explicit worldly power has, ironically, increased its dependence on secular institutions. Other institutions over the last five hundred years have gradually taken on certain traditional functions of the church. The structures of the military, the market, and government provide the institutional bones of the Protestant movement. Because all authority is understood to come from God, however, and because evangelical churches generally do not have institutional superstructures, obedience to civil authorities often stands in for obedience to God.[103]

Operating in a prison allows Prison Fellowship to rely on state structures of authority to enforce the discipline of their utopian Christian community. Post-church Christianity, a form of radical Protestantism, deftly avoids the challenges of disestablishment partly because it does not have its own visible religious establishment. As one prisoner commented, "I have seen that God is in control, and I . . . wouldn't be held accountable if he wouldn't have allowed people, COs, counselors, warden, program manager, et cetera, to be in authority over me" (p. 130). There is an uneasy slippage between religious and secular authority. He does not mention priests or rabbis or imams—or even ministers.

The importance of the state as the legitimizing authority for IFI was evident in the testimony of Chris Geil. When asked by the plaintiffs' lawyer whether non-Christian IFI inmates could substitute classes or studies in their own religious beliefs for IFI's Bible classes, Geil responded:

> *Our curriculum is treatment*, and our treatment classes and our treatment schedule is set. Anyone who wants to explore other things in their spare time, other chapel activities or other things they have to do it in their spare time, just like folks can't go to any other kind of religious practice and skip out on their GED, they can't go to some other kind of religious activity and skip out on their batterers' education. *It is a policy of the institutions that if you're scheduled for treatment, you have to be at treatment at that time.* (emphasis added) (pp. 1191–92)

IFI is state-sanctioned "treatment," and therefore adherence to the curriculum is mandated and enforced by state authorities. Asked about a document outlining IFI policy concerning internal governance, Geil answered: "Well, *we certainly want people to be submissive to all authority.* We certainly want people to display humility, which means to put others in front of them. Yeah, we look at submission and humility, yes, very much so" (emphasis added) (p. 1208).

Not surprisingly, staff for IFI seemed unsure about whether IFI is a part of the church or the state. Referring to InnerChange's recent modification of the prisoner accountability document to omit the reference to IFI being a "church," the plaintiffs' lawyer asked Geil about the adjustment: "Did InnerChange at that point stop being a church?" Geil responded:

> *A.* Well, you're asking me if I ever considered or if—what you're really asking me is, is InnerChange a church. That's what you're asking me. Is that correct?
>
> *Q.* You can—Well, the question was: Did InnerChange stop being a church? If you don't think it was a church in the first place, you can include that in your response. (p. 1212)

Geil fell back on the coaching he presumably received from IFI's lawyers urging him to ask for clarification if he was not sure how to answer a question: "Well, you'll have to define to me what you mean by a church." The lawyer for the plaintiffs asked back the question:

Q. What's your definition of a church?
A. What's my definition of a church?
Q. Yes.
A. You want me to go into the Greek, because I will.
Q. Go ahead.
A. Ekklesia in the New Testament is those that are called out. That's where you get the word church. People that have been called out. So really there is no religious connotation to it in the Greek at the time it was written. We've attached religious meaning to it throughout time, but at the time it was written, it's just the people that have been called out, the ekklesia. In one sense, are people called out into any kind? I mean, people are called out from different settings, if you want to have a broad definition. Now, are we defined as a church by the State of Iowa? Do we have all of the paperwork and all of the things that the State of Iowa says? Does the State of Iowa recognize InnerChange as a church in a legal status? I don't think they do. We are a program of men that have been called out, they've come to our program, they've been invited, they can come if they want to. So we're going to treat things in a community setting, in a program setting, in a treatment program setting. That's what we do. (pp. 1213–14)

The Greek New Testament reference is used to both authorize their practice and leave the relationship to the state ambiguous. InnerChange is a group of men who have been "called out."

But are they a church? The judge intervened:

THE COURT: Mr. Geil, called out by whom?

THE WITNESS: What now?

THE COURT: You answered here when you say called out, called out by whom?

THE WITNESS: In which part of that?

THE COURT: Well, you were asked by counsel, here's what your response was—you were asked by counsel the definition of the church. You said, "Do you want me to go into the Greek?" "Go ahead." "People that have been called out." That's a complete sentence.

THE WITNESS: Yeah. Yeah. In that setting—

THE COURT: Who calls the people out?

THE WITNESS: In, like, the Greek sense?

THE COURT: Well, in your definition here.

THE WITNESS: Well, in my definition, as far as InnerChange goes, we put posters out, people can contact us, they can come to the program. In that sense there's a call, and if you want this opportunity, you know, you can come. (p. 1214)

THE COURT: But, again, who is the caller? I know who the callee is. Who's the caller?

THE WITNESS: As far as—

THE COURT: Who is the one issuing the call?

THE WITNESS: As far as coming to InnerChange?

THE COURT: Yes.

THE WITNESS: Okay. The State has asked us to do this program, you know. We've put posters out and asked people if they are interested, if they want to come.

THE COURT: Okay. Thanks very much. (pp. 1214–15)

The state, as church—as God, perhaps—calls the prisoners to community. On cross-examination, IFI's lawyer confirmed this point:

Q. Mr. Geil, following up on that point, he was asking you about No. 79 of the summary judgment pleadings, and in there—in the summary judgment facts—and in there it says, "IFI uses the term church to mean community." Is that still true?

A. We use the term—I use the term community. We are very much like a therapeutic community. We are a prosocial bubble inside a very antisocial setting. (p. 1215)

What IFI achieved is close to what American Protestants attempted in the early nineteenth century in the public school: a locking-in of a particular understanding of the human expressed in the religious practices of American Protestants, while naming it as nondenominational, not specific to any church.

An important trend in current First Amendment jurisprudence is toward treating religion as not different.[104] For free-exercise purposes, the U.S. Supreme Court decision in *Employment Division v. Smith*[105] establishes the principle that there are no constitutionally mandated exceptions for religiously motivated persons from neutral laws of general applicability. For establishment clause purposes, equal access to government places and money, rather than exclusion, is the order of the day.[106] This trend reflects the collapse of religious authority outside the individual. If religion is not institutionally distinct, then the religion clauses cannot be made coherent. Whatever its future as a dominant principle of constitutional interpretation, careful attention to changes in religion in the modern period suggests that this jurisprudence has a certain historical logic. When evangelical petitioners before the courts demand equal treatment for their perspective, they both make use of the logic of post-modernism, as Fish notes, and they claim a common history of disestablished and deregulated religion, a modern history of disembeddedness—a post-church Christianity. They also claim the right, without discrimination, to help define the "rule of law" and its relation to morality.

What is the self that is imagined by the First Amendment religion clauses? Increasingly it is the individualist self of rational choice theory. Current First Amendment jurisprudence, like Evangelical Christianity and market economics, like all the elements of the modern imaginaries, places a high value on choice. Establishment clause jurisprudence has increasingly understood choice as *the* mechanism that determines state neutrality with respect to religion. Government can fund even "pervasively religious" organizations as long as the clients of those organizations are not coerced into participating in religious activities. This trend is particularly evident in the recent school vouchers cases. In *Mitchell v. Helms*[107] and *Zelman* the Court permitted direct payment to "pervasively religious" schools as long as the intervening choice by parents insulated government from choosing to favor religion.

As Ira Lupu and Richard Tuttle point out in their recent exhaustive review of the law relating to faith-based social services, constitutionally impermissible funding of religion is a diminishing field.[108] And as Judge Richard Posner said in *Freedom From Religion Foundation v. McCallum*,[109] which challenged the constitutionality of a parole officer's recommendation that a parolee choose a faith-based halfway house called Faith Works, "[The parole officer's] end is secular, the rehabilitation of a criminal, though the means include religion when the offender chooses Faith Works. . . . [T]he state may not require offenders to enroll in Faith Works. . . .The choice must be private, to provide insulating material between government and religion."[110] But Posner's implication is that if there is choice, a choice protected by "insulating material," then even inherently religious activity may be funded.

Evangelicals are demanding a share of government contracts, but they are also engaged in a critique of the human anthropology implied in the work of modern social service professionals. Their position is that the social problem of recidivism cannot be solved using behavioral methods based on environmental or biochemical theories of social pathology. Individual inmates, they argue, must take individual responsibility for their sin and choose discipline, the biblical discipline of the modern moral order. PFM says that it believes that individual prisoners can accomplish this transformation by way of any narrative—or what they call a "paradigm"—that at least momentarily roots that responsibility in a community and makes it possible for them to act. The Supreme Court seems to be saying that it is not the business of the courts, armed with the establishment clause, to prohibit religious entrepreneurs from contracting to do this work on a par with secular social service providers, as long as the clients—the prisoners—make such choices voluntarily.

CONCLUSION

IFI AND PFM ARE, in part, the distinctive products of a peculiarly American convergence of religious renewal and law-and-order politics. But they are also formations of the modern secular that exemplify a larger convergence, one that increasingly focuses on the rule of law and a distinctively modern form of religion as the twin solutions to our current global predicament. How these two might be related in such an imagined future is not obvious, but the example of IFI and of the U.S. faith-based movement generally suggests that responsibility for reconciling the two will often be passed on to the social service consumer.

Political actors across the ideological spectrum are now promoting the idea of extending the rule of law globally. Rhetorical evocations of the rule of law sometimes take on a transcendent utopian glow—as of an entire philosophy and practice sufficient for the peaceful coexistence of men on earth. Universal law as the successor to universal religion is a somewhat startling image for those of us who are lawyers, or who study law, and find law to be as violent, as historically messy, and as genealogically compromised as religion. And yet the rule of law as the quintessence of the secular, the acultural, the apolitical, and the necessary condition for morality continues to operate, at many different times and in many places, as the last best hope for mankind.

The rule of law. There is tremendous ambiguity in this small phrase. What do its promoters hope from it? In its strongest form, the rule of law has a powerful substantive quality making it akin to the foundational claims of natural law at their most expansive. In this version, law is singular, uniquely rational, self-evident, universal, and autonomous. When the rule of law is achieved, the implication goes, the lion will lie down with the lamb. Crime and violence and poverty will no longer exist. Other rule-of-law projects are more modest. In this weaker sense, the rule of law is more local, implying regularity, lack of corruption, transparency, equality before the law for all—including the sovereign—no secret or ex post facto laws, among other things. This more modest—but nonetheless difficult to achieve—version is about law reform and the training of judges and lawyers. In this sense, the rule of law is understood to provide some minimal conditions for a just society—and to make market capitalism possible—but not in itself to produce liberty or justice, or end the need for cultural and political imagination and negotiation and care for the "losers" in this ever more competitive environment. Commenting skeptically on the current confidence in freedom of contract, the French law professor Alain Supiot quotes Louis Dumont, quoting de Tocqueville: "I doubt whether man can support at the same time complete religious independence and entire public freedom."[1]

Coexistent with calls for global adoption of the rule of law, the "return of religion" is attested to across the world. This religious resurgence takes different forms and underwrites various legal and political projects. Universalist forms include the explicitly religious and ambitious ideologies and institutions of long-existing religious communities, the use of "spirituality" or "faith" to denote the acknowledgment of what is understood to be a universal human structure of experience, and the recent retrieval and elaboration of "political theologies" by political philosophers.[2] Local and particular religious approaches to life today include the apparent revival and remodeling of anti-modern or premodern religious forms, the growth of diasporic religion, and postmodern eclectic syncretisms—a complex and fissiparous field in which authority is increasingly located in the individual. Positivist modern law in all its guises, based as it is on the erasure or suppression of religion and idolatry,[3] seems to have few resources to cope with the return of religion in any form. Secular law needs a pliant religion.

Any theory of the rule of law must imply a theory of religion as well, particularly in the modern period. Because of the supremacy of the rule of law, and because of disestablishmentarian assumptions, as well as the increased acknowledgment of religious and legal pluralism, modern religion is practiced in places created by modern law. The reigning jurisprudential alternatives in the United States for affirmative legal regulation of this modern religion are found somewhere between those favoring affirmative government support for all "bona fide" religion and those favoring a "wall of separation" between church and state. Both reject overt management of religious life by the state and generally support exemptions of some kind from burdensome applications of the law for the sincerely religiously motivated, always understanding that what counts as bona fide religion is determined by the state, not the church. Reviewing the evidence in the Iowa case, and taking examples from recent U.S. lawsuits, I explore here the possibility that a third option is emerging in the United States.—and elsewhere—one that acknowledges the impossibility of both separation and accommodation in their traditional forms.

The distinctiveness of the U.S. religious landscape, in contrast to that of other industrialized countries, is a persistent topic for historians, literary theorists, and sociologists, who have generated a large literature on this subject.[4] As the evidence offered in the Iowa prison case shows, understanding the symbiotic relationship between evangelical Christianity and

U.S. law requires suspending the bright line that today is often assumed to separate religious and secular ways of being and acting in the world.

I will briefly outline three current U.S. legal models for administering religion in state institutions, and then correlate the understanding of religion in each model with a "church-state" model and a variety of secularism. I borrow for this purpose a typology of American secularism explored in a recent essay by the American religious historian Clark Gilpin.[5] Understanding the secular to be in some sense the defining mood of modernity, however problematic its definition and varied its appearances, Gilpin proposes three moments in the history of U.S. secularism—*religious* secularism, *irreligious* secularism, and *areligious* secularism—moments that he defines as spatial in nature. (I use Gilpin's terms, which, he says, were inspired by the work of Charles Taylor and Talal Asad, but in no way do I wish to suggest that he is responsible for my extensions of his suggestions into the realm of law.) They are not exclusively American but they take particular form in the U.S. context.

Rather than seeing a single secularism built on a continuing transfer of authority away from religion and the decline of individual religious consciousness, Gilpin sees in the United States various modes of secularism providing different spaces for a religion that is always understood to be plural in form: "the social spaces of the secular promote forms of secularism that are at once a philosophy of life and a way of life, both ideas and practices."[6] In other words, there are shifts in the location of religious authority, but these shifts are not consistently *away* from religion. The story of religion is not one of decline over time but one of a different use of space. The new religious resurgence is less a return of religion than its reorganization.[7]

As with all models, Gilpin's three types of secularism are not found in pure form and do not follow one another chronologically in neat order. Indeed, they are most useful, in my view, when thought of as overlapping and may all be present most of the time in much of the modern Christian West, with a different form ascendant at different times. However, they provide a suggestive framework for analyzing religion in the United States. Not surprisingly to students of American religious history, they are also, in some sense, enactments of Protestantism and find significant parallels in constitutional interpretation and in domestic models of the rule of law.

Gilpin uses *religious* secularism to denominate the new liberating American public space that resulted from urbanization and that became, in late-nineteenth, early-twentieth century America—the social gospel, a "pragmatic, this-worldly philosophy of social transformation."[8] That space was at once heir to the de facto nineteenth-century establishment in the United States of Protestant evangelical Christianity accomplished by the many pan-Protestant programs of social reform and founded in a frank, new de-mythologization of Christianity. Gilpin's *irreligious* secularism is quintessentially represented by the public school, where "critical thinking" explicitly supplanted the religious and which is mostly inhospitable to both the historic religions and to religious secularism. Irreligious secularism defines the place for enacting the politico-legal dogma of the "separation of church and state." *Areligious* secularism denominates a still emerging post-Christian space where religion is honored as a human universal and religious pluralism can be creatively negotiated in sites of cultural exchange. This form of secularism constitutes a new disestablishment, one that implies multiplicity rather than homogeneity or absence. Following Asad, these three secularisms are spaces for religious practice, not ideologies or institutions. In that sense, they are forms of the secular, rather than secularisms.

The most powerful form of the *religious* secular in the United States today is represented by conservative evangelical Protestantism and projects such as IFI, although analogous forms are found in other American religious communities. The Iowa prison program, and many other faith-based initiatives, are at once secular and Christian, or "nondenominational," as were their predecessors. The universal values promoted by IFI, when carefully examined, look less like those of the Bible, narrowly understood, and more like the values that multinational corporations look for in their employees; they seek people who will get up every morning, go to work, and support family values. This new promotion of "civilization" looks a lot like the nineteenth-century version that supported reform projects of various kinds, including eradication of the "twin evils of slavery and polygamy," the promotion of private property among Indians, prohibition, and the invention of the penitentiary. Notwithstanding its association with progressive causes, it is a formation of the secular deeply stained by anti-Catholic bigotry, racism, and colonialism.

The power of the religious secular lies partly in its denial of its religiousness. It takes its values, ideas, and practices from religion yet rejects the name. Relying on the state to provide the authority and the institutional bones of its project, this form of Christian universalism sees a seamless overlap between biblical law and the rule of law—a kind of Protestant natural law. IFI fits squarely in this lineage, but IFI's Christian secular shares space with other forms that are demanded by U.S. commitments to equality and neutrality. The increasing openness of PFM and other such para-church organizations to other religions, mandated by law, parallels the historical shifts documented by First Amendment historian Mark de-Wolfe Howe. Howe showed that early-nineteenth- and twentieth-century evangelical de facto establishments were modified, first in response to the increased power of the national government after the Civil War, and then with the advent of internationalism in the twentieth century.[9] Howe reads the Supreme Court as responding to each historical change by formally disestablishing, in turn, Protestant teaching in public schools, Protestant assumptions about church governance and the privileged constitutional place of religion. The overall result has been the opening of new types of secular spaces to religions no longer defined exclusively by Protestant orthodoxies. Yet the displaced early forms of the religious secular continue to reappear and challenge again the Constitution's mandate for disestablishment.

For Gilpin, the space created by irreligious secularism is, as noted, most characterized by the classic American public school, where religion—meaning Catholicism—was excluded by fearful Protestants who aligned themselves with new theories of education that emphasized critical thinking over the earlier Christian universalism represented in Bible reading and nondenominational prayer. The short version of that history is that Protestants changed the nature of the space because they did not wish to share it with Catholics. The First Amendment doctrine that emerged from this history is based in the privileging of a particular reading of Virginia church-state history, including the enshrining of Thomas Jefferson's famous phrase, "a wall of separation," as the metaphor of choice for describing American church-state relations.

Religion, in irreligious secularism, is entirely private, a matter of personal choice. Although the public school is paradigmatic of such a space, this version of secularism has also flourished in other state institutions—including the armed services and prisons—where, after the demise of the old, and before the advent of the new, evangelicalism, religion was managed and contained through traditional chaplaincies; these were designed to serve soldiers and prisoners by facilitating their individual practice of religion, leaving the professional work of each military or correctional institution to be defined by secular theories of the human. Thus the Iowa Statutes provide, in a section titled, "Time for Religion," that "any inmate, during the time of detention, shall be allowed for at least one hour on each Sunday or other holy day or in times of extreme sickness, and at other suitable and reasonable times consistent with proper discipline in the institution, to receive spiritual advice, instruction, and ministration from any recognized member of the clergy who represents the inmate's religious belief."[10]

For irreligious secularism, the rule of law in the guise of the doctrine of the separation of church and state has acted as gatekeeper to the public space, the irreligiously secular public space, the place of rationality, the rationality of modern science. It is exemplified in the judicial decisions prohibiting the teaching of alternatives to evolutionary biology.[11] But one of the reasons IFI exists is that the irreligious secular model is faltering as a result of its modernist assumptions about the nature of humans and of human language. It has failed because these spaces no longer make sense.

Areligious secularism is frankly emergent in Gilpin's description, although it has a longer genealogy. Gilpin offers, as an example of what he calls areligious secularism, the space revealed by the research of psychology professor Dan McAdams into what McAdams terms the "generative self," an American way of being characterized by the narration of redemptive stories. As Gilpin tells it, McAdams's informants "tell secular stories of their lives that incorporate elements derived from religious traditions into narratives that neither favor nor disfavor a religious reading of the self; theirs is an areligious secularism"—not an irreligious secularism. This research effort emphasizes the universality of "spiritual" practices for Americans. Although there are affinities here with other older readings of a religion of America, both the religions of nature and the nationalist versions, documented by Catherine Albanese and others,[12] Gilpin sees this form of the secular as structuring a new, more open pluralistic and negotiable space than that celebrated in the literature of Americanness.[13]

A similar areligious space might be found in the facts underlying a surprising, recent decision by a Wisconsin federal court, in which, the facts reveal the government's effort to create a legal place for religion that is not a comprehensive and integrating form of Protestant Christianity like IFI nor a private space of choice like traditional chaplaincies.[14] The complaint in *Freedom From Religion Foundation v. Nicholson*[15] challenged the constitutionality of a program of the National Chaplains Center of the Department of Veteran Affairs (VA). The VA operates 154 medical centers, 1,300 other "sites of care," 136 nursing homes, 43 residential rehabilitation treatment programs, and 88 comprehensive home care programs in the United States. In 2005, more than 5.3 million people received health care in VA facilities. According to the district court, the VA chaplaincy has evolved, since its founding in 1883, from a focus that was primarily what the court termed "sacramental"—the optional provision of various religious services to patients, such as last rites for Catholics—to a focus that is primarily "clinical," a service integrated into the care of *every* patient.

"To effectively implement its clinical chaplaincy program, the VA Chaplain Service was recently reorganized under the Medicine and Surgery Strategic Healthcare Group. The purpose of this reorganization was to recognize VA's chaplaincy as a clinical, direct patient care discipline."[16] To be sure, VA chaplains have an explicit duty to protect the patient's constitutional religious free-exercise rights, and protect patients "from having religion imposed on them." But, for the VA, the court insists, "spirituality is not necessarily religious because it concerns the meaning of life on a more general level."[17] As a part of its self-described "holistic health care model," and in response to a hospital accreditation requirement that all patients receive an initial spiritual assessment,[18] the VA chaplaincy has recently developed spiritual assessment tools, asking patients about their religious identity, beliefs, and practices. "Spirituality," to use the chaplaincy's term, is integrated into the treatment of patients in various ways.

The plaintiff in the *Nicholson* case, the Freedom From Religion Foundation, complained that "VA chaplains have crossed the constitutional line by incorporating religion into the delivery of VA health care services." In other words, they had slipped from the provision of an irreligious secular space to one characterized as the religious secular. Surprisingly, perhaps, the district court granted a motion for summary judgment in favor of the VA, deciding the case without a trial and concluding that no constitutional violation had occurred, because all religious activity by patients was entirely voluntary. This decision would formally be consistent with the focus on choice in decisions regarding school voucher programs, but there is more here. The Wisconsin court appears to endorse the VA's more thoroughly and ambiguously religious understanding of the human than is the case in the school voucher programs. The Wisconsin court seems to approve an understanding of the human as religious, or spiritual—a virtual naturalization of religion as a social and biological fact—in a way characteristic of the emergent third alternative to the classic religious and irreligious secularisms of U.S. history. In other words, what the court is saying to FFRF is that this is not the unconstitutional resurgence of the religious secular but is, rather, a form of the areligious secular.

There are real, old-fashioned, establishment-type problems with the VA program, particularly with the fact that the training and licensing of chaplains is controlled by mainstream religious organizations, thus increasing the likelihood that the program could be administered in ways that are blatantly discriminatory. There are also opportunities for the evangelization of a vulnerable population. But the court seems unconcerned with these risks. The opinion is replete with generalized approval of a broad effort to accommodate what is viewed as universal, "the spiritual"—what, in Gilpin's terms, might be viewed as government fostering of an areligious space for religion that acknowledges the eclectic and adaptive nature of contemporary religion where authority is vested in the individual. In legal terms, it is a way for law to deal with a religion that is no longer about churches but about persons who are less and less likely to be firmly embedded in, and subject to the authority of, religious communities.

The district court also explicitly states that the new VA program is a way to avoid the state's policing of orthodoxy that occurs with traditional chaplaincies. The court, in its opinion denying summary judgment, writes that,

> Interestingly, it is the relief requested by plaintiffs that would actually lead to excessive entanglement between government and religion. Plaintiffs request an order requiring defendants to establish rules, regulations, prohibitions, standards and oversight to ensure that future disbursements are not made and/or used to fund activities that include religion as a substantive integral component of the VA's medical treatment protocols. Such pervasive monitoring would excessively entangle the government with religion and would run afoul of the Establishment Clause.[19]

The courts are turning religion over to the people.

English prisons, recently surveyed by the sociologist James Beckford, have, arguably, been remarkably successful at using a somewhat creaky Church of England establishment to achieve something like the accommodation of diversity through generalizing or universalizing religion.[20] Beckford compares the modest English success in addressing the needs of Muslim prisoners in Her Majesty's prisons—where an established religion provides an umbrella of religious universalism, not unlike that in the VA program—with the utter failure of the French prisons to do the same.[21] The critical difference is the church-state model. French prisons do not officially know of the presence of Muslim prisoners, because French citizens are not identified by religious affiliation. They do not legally know their citizens as having religious lives. Theirs is, for the most part, an irreligious model of secularism.[22]

Current Iowa practice, too—apart from IFI—is not unlike the kind of "areligious" accommodation that is evident in England and may be evolving toward what is being attempted by the VA.[23] Asked to describe the various religious practices in the prison, the Iowa chaplain who testified at the trial that is the subject of this book, Perry Stevens, said at his deposition in the case:

> We have Native American sweat lodges. We have kind of an ecumenical Methodist Bible study every week. We have Catholic services every week. We have the facilities for, you know—materialwise for Jewish inmates. We currently do not have one now, but we did have. I've got Mormons that they're doing solitary practice right now, but I give them materials. I've got Wiccans, Satanists, Jehovah Witness. IFI does the church services, the protestant now. I do not. We just don't have the

> space to duplicate that. It wouldn't be right to do it anyway. I'm trying to think. I have a Hebrew Israelite who does solitary. I have four Buddhists, a Hindu, three Asatru.[24]

The Iowa chaplain, like his English counterpart, apparently sees himself as serving a universal human need by making a space for an ever-changing stew of religious practice. At the trial, Chaplain Stevens was asked about recording attendance at the sweat lodge ritual:

> *Q*. . . . [I]f five inmates signed up to go into the sweat lodge, can you tell me how many of them are Native American?
> *A*. They're all approved by the Native American consultant.
> *Q*. To go into the sweat lodge?
> *A*. That's correct.
> *Q*. Can you tell me how many of them believe in the Native American religion?
> *A*. I cannot. (pp. 666–67)

No effort is made to police the formal affiliation or orthodoxy of those who participate in religious services. Whereas in the past only those known to be of a certain religion could attend such rituals, now Stevens does not consider that his job is to keep track of religious adherence. His job is to provide spaces for religion, not to enforce orthodoxy.

All three forms of the secular remain potent possibilities in the United States as a response to religious pluralism. Each form responds to enduring ideological frameworks and enables sets of practices. Religious secularism, as exemplified by both right- and left-wing anti-liberalism, insists that, in the absence of moralizing religion, liberalism and the rule of law in the United States are fundamentally sterile, inhuman, and ahistorical. But the case presented by advocates of religious secularism denies the reality of the generative and subversive combination of pluralism and what American religious historians call the "voluntary principle." Irreligious secularism insists on the importance of rights analysis and makes a private place for the irreducible personality and integrity of different cultural identities, but it concedes little to the holistic ideology exemplified in new medical accrediting standards and the deep ambiguities that constitute the sacred-secular divide. Areligious secularism affirms the universality of religion but can have a flickering transient quality, one that may offer little resistance to the human person imagined by the rule of law and market capitalism.

A modest step in addressing the scandal and brutality of massive incarceration in the United States might begin by listening to the prisoners, rather than to the tired debate about the religion clauses. Without denying the many injustices of their situation, it is not an exaggeration, in my view, to see them as the fellows of the accident victims in Thailand and the men and women of Cairo discussed in chapter 4. The Iowa prisoners who brought the suit said that their initial attraction to IFI was the possibility of finding the resources to remake their lives. They wanted to learn how to be better persons. They wanted to learn about other religions as well as being affirmed in their own. They wanted the support of a community and mentors along the way. That does not seem too much to ask.

Notes

INTRODUCTION

1. *Americans United for Separation of Church and State v. Prison Fellowship Ministries*, Civil No. 4:03-cv-90074 (U.S. District Court for the Southern District of Iowa). The Memorandum Opinion and Order Following Trial, authored by Judge Robert W. Pratt of the U.S. District Court for the Southern District of Iowa, may be found at 432 F. Supp. 2d 832.

2. On appeal, the decision was affirmed in part and reversed in part. 509 F. 3d 406 (2007); a Petition for Rehearing *En Banc* of Defendants-Appellants State of Iowa, Prison Fellowship Ministries and InnerChange Freedom Initiative was denied by the Eighth Circuit Court of Appeals on January 16, 2008. No petition for certiorari was filed in the U.S. Supreme Court.

3. The convergence of these two aspects of American exceptionalism was first brought to my attention by the Rev. Santiago Piñón, whose concern with this conjunction arose out of his own ministry to ex-offenders. I have learned much from his effort to understand the troubling politics and theology underlying the often permanent disabilities facing ex-offenders in the U.S. in their return to the world.

Lew Daly, in *God and the Welfare State*, suggests that even more striking is the convergence of America's vaunted religiosity with its failures in the areas of poverty and equality. The precise significance of the convergence between social inequality and mass imprisonment is widely discussed among scholars of the sociology of crime and punishment. See, for example, Katherine Beckett and Bruce Western, "Governing Social Marginality." For the argument that American penal exceptionalism can be explained by market capitalism, see David Downes, "The *Macho* Penal Economy: Mass Incarceration in the United States—A European Perspective," in Garland, *Mass Imprisonment.*

4. For two different approaches to U.S./India parallels in this respect, see Peter van der Veer, *Religious Nationalism*; and Martha Nussbaum, *The Clash Within.*

5. See, with respect to the U.S., especially, Sidney E. Mead, *The Lively Experiment.* See also Grace Davie, *Europe: The Exceptional Case.*

6. Davie, *Europe: The Exceptional Case*, p. 44.

7. See Grace Davie, *Religion in Modern Europe*; Silvio Ferrari, "The New Wine and the Old Cask."

8. For a history of prisons in the U.S., see the classic two-volume study by David J. Rothman, *The Discovery of the Asylum* and *Conscience and Convenience*; and Norval Morris and David Rothman, *The Oxford History of the Prison.* In England, after the American Revolution, prisons replaced transporting criminals to the colonies, first by using ships anchored offshore as prisons and then through the construction of penitentiaries on the U.S. model. See Michael Ignatieff, *A Just Measure of Pain.*

9. David J. Rothman, "Perfecting the Prison."

10. See John Lardas Modern, "Ghosts of Sing Sing," for a fascinating account of the efforts of antebellum spiritualist reformers at Sing Sing Prison.

11. Morris and Rothman, *The Oxford History of the Prison*, p. 157. Tony Morrison's novel, *Beloved*, is set in the context of this history.

12. Rothman, *The Discovery of the Asylum*, p. xxxi.

13. For interpretive histories of nineteenth-century prisons and asylums in the U.S. and Europe, in addition to Rothman, *The Discovery of the Asylum*, and Ignatieff, *A Just Measure of Pain*, see Michel Foucault, *Discipline and Punish*, and Jan Goldstein, *Console and Classify.*

14. Morris and Rothman, *The Oxford History of the Prison*, p. xii.

15. For a journalistic account of the effect of privatization on U.S. prisons, see Joseph T. Hallinan, *Going Up the River.*

16. Melvin Gutterman, "Prison Objectives and Human Dignity," p. 906.

17. Ibid., p. 869.

18. For discussions of the interrelationship of theories of constitutional democracy and punishment, see Guyora Binder, "Democracy and Punishment"; and Marcus Dubber, "Toward a Constitutional Law of Crime and Punishment."

19. Much of political philosophy, especially on the Left, originates in thoughts about the millions of nameless victims of twentieth-century totalitarian regimes and about famous prisoners of the state. Antonio Gramsci, Franz Fanon, Malcolm X, Martin Luther King Jr., Nelson Mandela—these are men who have proclaimed freedom from within the "belly of the beast." For a discussion of the ambiguity of the sacred in relation to law and the state as read through *The Trial* by Franz Kafka, see the introduction to Austin Sarat, Lawrence Douglas, and Martha Merrill Umphrey, *Law and the Sacred.*

20. A longer history of the prisoner of conscience, predating the modern state, might include, among a great many, Socrates, St. Paul, and Joan of Arc. For a history of the medieval prison, see G. Geltner, *The Medieval Prison: A Social History.*

21. See discussion of the prison in literature in W. B. Carnochan, "The Literature of Confinement," pp. 381–406.

22. Much has been written about the modern origins of the linguistic convention of labeling certain aspects of human culture "religion." See, for example, Jonathan Z. Smith, "Religion, Religions, Religious"; Hans Kippenberg, *Discovering Religious History in the Modern Age*; Tomoko Masuzawa, *The Invention of World Religions*; Talal Asad, *Genealogies of Religion*; and idem, *Formations of the Secular.* "Religion" is also a product of the process of legal secularization. See, for example, Winnifred Fallers Sullivan and Robert A. Yelle, "Overview"; and Peter Goodrich, *Oedipus Lex.*

23. Recent scholarly attention to political theology explores the significance of the sacralization of the state. See, for example, the essays collected in Hent deVries and Lawrence E. Sullivan, eds., *Political Theologies*; and Matteo Taussig-Rubbo, "Outsourcing Sacrifice: The Labor of Private Military Contractors."

24. U.S. Department of Education, *Literacy Behind Bars.*

25. John Henry Schlegel, *American Legal Realism and Empirical Social Science.* See also Vincent Pecora, *Secularization and Cultural Criticism*, pp. 46–47.

26. Roberto Unger, *Law in Modern Society: Toward a Criticism of Social Theory*, 175, quoted in David Luban, *Legal Modernism*.

27. His concern with the effects of scientism on law is shared by the evangelical Christians who created the program with which this book is concerned, and also by many within the American law and theology movement.

28. Richard K. Sherwin, *When Law Goes Pop*.

29. Jeremy Bentham, for example, understood idolatry as a principal obstacle to legal rationalization. See Robert A. Yelle, "Bentham's Fictions," pp. 151–79.

30. See, for example, Harold Berman, *Faith and Order*. See also Robert Cover, "Nomos and Narrative"; and Elijah Anderson, "Going Straight."

31. Pecora, *Secularization and Cultural Criticism*, p. 20.

32. For a useful summary of these themes, see Gustavo Benevides, "Modernity." On the secularization of law, see Nomi Stolzenberg, "The Profanity of the Law." On antinomianism and the law, see Costas Douzinas and Ronnie Warrington, "Antigone's Law."

33. See Joan DelFattore, *The Fourth R*; and John T. McGreevy, *Catholicism and American Freedom*. In the United States, for example, disestablished religion has repeatedly offered itself as the repository of the moral conscience of the nation and as schoolmaster to its children.

34. Sullivan, *The Impossibility of Religious Freedom*. This book used another trial, *Warner v. Boca Raton,* 64 F. Supp. 2d 1272 (1999), on a charge that the City of Boca Raton had violated the plaintiffs' rights to the free exercise of religion, to critique the assumptions about religion underlying laws supporting exemptions for religiously motivated action.

35. Asad, *Formations of the Secular*; José Casanova, *Public Religions in the Modern World.*

36. Stanley Fish, *The Trouble with Principle*, pp. 309–12. Fish has also written explicitly about the religion clauses in ways not dissimilar from the points made in this book. See his "Mission Impossible."

37. Fish, *The Trouble with Principle*, p. 312.

38. For a comparative perspective on the mind/body problem and the philosophy of language, see Dan Arnold, "On Semantics and *Saṃketa*."

39. The German sociologist Ernst Troeltsch, in his *Social Teaching of the Christian Churches*, developed a typology to distinguish different kinds of Christian polities, depending on their relationship to the larger society. "Churches" he understood to be Christian polities that were larger coextensive with the dominant culture, whereas a "sect" was a minority religious group living in self-conscious tension with the larger society. These sociological types have been further developed by Rodney Stark and William Bainbridge, in *The Future of Religion*. The terms are further complicated today by the negative connotation sometimes associated with sects, cults, and various new religious movements. For the purposes of church-and-state law, it is helpful to distinguish a continuum of social types of religious organization even where, as in the U.S., all religious groups are, constitutionally speaking, equal with respect to the law (*Encyclopedia of Religion*, 2nd ed., s.v. "cults").

40. Other stories are also told about the complex motives and politics of those actors. See, for example, Luban's discussion of communitarianism without mysti-

cism in relation to the Montgomery school bus boycott (*Legal Modernism,* pp. 209–82). See also Glenda Gilmore, *Defying Dixie.*

41. And, of course, some among religious conservatives do. See Michael Lienesch, *Redeeming America.*

42. See n. 38 infra. For a market analysis of the church-sect dynamic in American religious history, see Roger Finke and Rodney Stark, *The Churching of America.*

43. See Mary Anne Case, "Marriage Licenses."

44. See Fish, "Mission Impossible."

45. The claim that fundamentalism is a modern phenomenon was elaborated at length in Martin E. Marty and R. Scott Appleby, *The Fundamentalism Project.*

46. This is a vast topic with an abundant literature. I use these terms rather loosely in this book to connote what is largely shared about the self-understanding of the nature of contemporary Americans, individually and in terms of their collective imagination, notwithstanding real differences. Particularly helpful to me in writing this book were Asad, *Formations of the Secular*; David Engel, "Globalization and the Decline of Legal Consciousness"; Mary Poovey, "The Liberal Civil Subject and the Social in Eighteenth Century Moral Philosophy" (I thank Cassie Adcock for calling my attention to this article); Eric Santner, *My Own Private Germany*; Charles Taylor, *Modern Social Imaginaries* and *Sources of the Self*; Pecora, *Secularization and Cultural Criticism*; and Slavoj Žižek, *The Ticklish Subject.*

47. In the words of Michael Emerson and Christian Smith: "The structure of American religion, and the values that both guide and grant influence to individuals, result in significant limits to religious authority. This is true regardless of the religion. . . . Personal choices in the context of one's social network, not official church teachings, are the primary shapers of beliefs and actions for the religious of the United States and many other places" Emerson and Smith, *Divided by Faith,* pp. 166–67.

48. See Charles Taylor, "A Different Kind of Courage," for a discussion of the death of cultures and the emergence of a new kind of human.

49. In the words of Sheila Suess Kennedy and Wolfgang Bielefield, in *Faith-Based Partnerships*:

> Today, discretion over the day-to-day operation of public programs routinely rests not with the responsible state or federal government agencies, but with a host of nongovernmental, "third-party" surrogates or "proxies" that provide programs under the aegis of loans, loan guarantees, grants, contracts, vouchers, and other new mechanisms for taking public action. This exercise of core governmental authority by non- and quasi-governmental entities is perhaps the most distinctive feature of America's "new governance."

A significant constitutional issue raised by this matter is whether privatization of government services narrows the scope of "state action" in such a way as to significantly lessen the reach of civil rights laws. Also troubling is whether social service providers are receiving adequate fiscal oversight and government monitoring to ensure that they adhere to professional standards. In his decision in *AU v.*

PFM, Judge Pratt found that IFI employees were state actors, a finding that was affirmed on appeal.

50. Section 104 of the 1996 Personal Responsibility and Work Opportunity Reconciliation Act (PRWORA) was the first statute to introduce the notion of "Charitable Choice." However, as Kennedy and Bielefeld wrote in *Faith-Based Partnerships*, it received a significant boost when,

> on January 29, 2001, President Bush announced the creation of the White House Office of Faith-Based and Community Initiatives, and the establishment of Faith-Based and Community Centers in five Cabinet agencies: Education, Health and Human Services, Housing and Urban Development, Justice and Labor. The Faith-Based Initiative was described as an effort to broaden the reforms effected by Charitable Choice legislation. The Administration vowed to help faith-based providers overcome unnecessary barriers to their participation, including government managers' reluctance to contract with providers whose programming was infused with religious doctrine.

Dismissal of a taxpayer lawsuit challenging the constitutionality of the White House Office was affirmed by the U.S. Supreme Court in *Hein v. Freedom From Religion Foundation, Inc.*, 127 S. Ct. 2553 (2007).

51. Daly, *God and the Welfare State*, p. 43.

52. See Smith, Steven Rathgeb, John P. Bartkowski, and Susan Grettenberger, *Comparative Views on the Role and Effect of Faith in Social Services*, for a discussion of differences between faith-based and secular social service providers. Findings included the general observation that there was more overlap between the two types than is usually acknowledged and that the claim that faith-based services are more "holistic" than secular is not well founded (p. 21).

53. See, for example, Donald S. Lopez Jr., "Belief."

54. For a discussion of these issues, see, for example, Robert Wuthnow, *Saving America?*; and Mark Chaves, "Religious Congregations and Welfare Reform."

55. Jeanette Hercik, Richard Lewis, and Bradley Myles, *Development of a Guide to Resources on Faith-based Organizations in Criminal Justice*.

56. See also Kent R. Kerley, Todd L. Matthews, and Troy C. Blanchard, "Religiosity, Religious Participation, and Negative Prison Behaviors," which suggests some positive correlation between religiosity and lower levels of argumentativeness in prison, but which also states that with respect to faith-based *in-prison* programs, "there has not been enough empirical research on this issue to reach any firm conclusions" (445); and Daniel P. Mears, "Faith-based Re-entry Programs." But see also Kennedy and Bielefeld, *Faith-Based Partnerships*, for a description of a Ford Foundation study comparing faith-based job training programs in various states.

57. Lisa M. Monteil and David J. Wright, "Getting a Piece of the Pie."

58. The Pew Charitable Trusts funds an excellent Web site, Roundtable on Religion and Social Welfare Policy (hereafter, The Roundtable, hosted by the Rockefeller Institute of Government, State University of New York, which monitors the legal vicissitudes of "faith-based" initiatives and produces an annual report on the state of the law. www.religionandsocialpolicy.org

59. There are also an increasing number of lawsuits challenging the constitutionality of these programs. The lead litigants in these cases are Americans United and the Freedom From Religion Foundation. See, e.g., *Freedom From Religion Foundation v. Richardson* (05-CV-1168, D. N.M. 2005) challenging a New Mexico contract with a private prison company, Corrections Corporation of America (CCA). CCA contracts with Chicago-based Institute in Basic Life Principles (www.iblp.org), an evangelical Christian biblical outreach ministry to provide "exclusively faith-based segregation pods" for their prisons. News release, November 8, 2005 (www.ffrf.org) (since dismissed on the grounds that the Supreme Court's decision in *Hein* disallows the action); *Freedom From Religion Foundation v. Gonzales* (06-C-0244-S W.D. Wisc. 2005) challenging the federal Bureau of Prisons invitation for bids for single-faith prison programs. The Roundtable monitors lawsuits challenging prison rehabilitation programs on its Web site.

60. The expression "technologies of the self" derives from an essay of that name by Michel Foucault; reprinted in Luther H. Martin, Huck Gutman, Patrick H. Hutton, *Technologies of the Self*, although the words have been glossed through use by many others.

61. Twelve-step programs have been found to be religious in nature and therefore unconstitutional if mandated in sentencing or correctional contexts. See, for example, *Kerr v. Farrey*, 95 F. 3d 472 (1996); *Warner v. Orange County*, 115 F. 3d 1068, reaffirmed, 173 F. 3d 120 (1997).

62. 432 F. Supp 2d. at 920. Among other projects of PFM is Operation Starting Line, described online as follows:

> Operation Starting Line (OSL) is a sweeping outreach that links the resources of Christian organizations, believers from local churches and other supporting organizations to evangelize and disciple prisoners, their families and the prison community. Since its launch on Easter Sunday 2000 the Operation Starting Line collaboration has grown to thirty-seven organizations working together to provide resources and network with each other to saturate America's prisons with the message of Christ's forgiveness and power. Since 2000, more than 717,000 inmates have participated in evangelistic events sponsored by Operation Starting Line. Through the evangelistic events of Operation Starting Line over 50,000 prisoners have either made first time decisions to accept Christ or made a re-commitment to Christ. Over 100,000 prisoners have signed up for continuing discipleship Bible based correspondence studies.
>
> (www.operationstartingline.net)

63. 432 F. Supp 2d at 869, 887. The amount of $199,823.42, paid to PFM after the district court order has since been repaid to the state. See Anthony Troy, letter to Judge Pratt, filed in the district court on April 24, 2008.

64. Americans United for Separation of Church and State was founded in 1947 as Protestants and Other Americans United for Separation of Church and State in response to proposals pending in the U.S. Congress to extend government aid to private religious schools. Its house organ, *Church & State Magazine,* was virulently anti-Catholic for many years. The organization has since renounced its anti-Catholicism; its name was changed, in 1972, to Americans United.

65. Judge Pratt is a Catholic who attended Creighton Law School, spent one year as a lawyer for legal aid, and then practiced law for twenty-two years in Des Moines, before being appointed to the bench by President Clinton in 1997. Pratt published an article on sentencing in the *Des Moines Register* in 1999, titled "Senseless Sentencing: A Federal Judge Speaks Out."

66. Dominick LaCapra, *"Madame Bovary" on Trial.* See also Gregory Matoesian, *Law and the Language of Identity: Discourse in the William Kennedy Smith Rape Trial.*

67. Robert P. Burns, *A Theory of the Trial*, pp. 4, 5, 171.

68. Ibid., p. 184.

69. Ibid., p. 132. David Luban, in *Legal Modernism*, argues that "trials and their stories are the embodiment of law's self-criticism" (p. 385).

70. Lawrence Rosen, *Anthropology of Justice*; Clifford Geertz, "Law and Fact in Comparative Perspective."

71. LaCapra, *"Madame Bovary" on Trial*, p. 70.

Chapter 1
The God Pod

1. "The First 20 Years," *Inside Iowa's DOC* 1, no. 1 (October 2003).

2. See Report to the Board of Corrections by the Iowa Department of Corrections, *Population Growth*, July 2006. See also Report of the Iowa Governor's Task Force on the Overrepresentation of African-Americans in Prison (December 2001).

3. The Durrant Group, *State of Iowa Systematic Study for the State Correctional System,* issued on April 13, 2007, is available on the Iowa DOC Web site: http://www.doc.state.ia.us/ (accessed April 30, 2007).

4. John J. Gibbons and Nicholas de B. Katzenbach, co-chairs, *Confronting Confinement* (2006).

5. Durrant Group, *State of Iowa Systematic Study for the State Correctional System*, p. xx.

6. *Americans United v. Prison Fellowship Ministries,* Trial Transcript, pp. 1991–92; hereafter, page numbers to the Trial Transcript are cited parenthetically in the text. Objections by lawyers and conversations between the judge and the lawyers are omitted without ellipses. The appellation "God Pod" is not unique to Newton. Other faith-based prison units around the country are also known by that name. See, e.g., David Miles, "Group Sues over Prison's 'God Pod' "; and Jane Lampham, "A Captive Audience for Salvation."

7. Tony Lamberti, the son of Don Lamberti, co-founder of Casey General Stores and a well-known Iowa businessman. was arrested on a drug charge in 1996. He credits his religious conversion in prison as helping him to recover and reenter society. His brother, Jeff Lamberti, is president of the Iowa Senate. See Angela Daunis and Angela Paneck, *Re-enter: The Social Cost of Incarceration.*

8. Kautzky deposition, p. 19.

9. Ibid., pp. 19–20.

10. Ibid., p. 21.

11. This unit is described on the Texas Department of Justice Web site: http://www.tdcj.state.tx.us/pgm&svcs/pgms&svcs-innerchnge.htm (accessed May 20, 2007).

12. For a short biography of Charles Colson, see the PFM Web site: www.prisonfellowship.org, accessed September 27, 2006. See also Colson's own autobiographical accounts of his conversion and the founding of Prison Fellowship Ministries in *Born Again* and *Life Sentence.*

13. See the Evangelical Council for Financial Accountability Web site at http://www.ecfa.org/ (accessed May 21, 2008).

14. A para-church organization is a venerable U.S. institution, a form of religious organization that flourished first in the ante-bellum period as a way for Protestant churches to work together, trans-denominationally, in service of various causes, from the distribution of Bibles and Sunday School materials to abolition and prohibition. As the denominations have declined in importance among Protestants in the U.S. over the past half-century, para-church organizations have gained in importance as a way for American Protestants to organize their ministries and charitable activities.

15. In response to the 2005 RFP, Emerald Correctional Management submitted a competing bid for the Newton facility that was unsuccessful. 432 F. Supp. 2d at 880–81.

16. Ibid., at 883–87. The Telephone Fund is controversial among the prisoners, as the profits made on the prisoners' phone calls is quite high. These funds, prisoners feel, should only be used to benefit all prisoners, such as funding recreational activities. See, for example, Trial Transcript, pp. 149, 186.

17. On May 23, 2007, Chet Culver, the then new governor of Iowa, signed a bill eliminating the annual appropriation for IFI. State funding expired on June 30, 2007. On June 29, 2007, IFI and the state reached an agreement permitting the program to continue with private funding, pending appeal. 432 F. Supp 2d at 886. Anne Farris, "Controversial Christian Prison Program Cites Recent Supreme Court Ruling in its Appeal."

18. 432 F. Supp. 2d at 880.

19. Plaintiffs' Appendix, p. 289.

20. The defendants' lawyers noted all such changes during the trial. They argued to the court that evaluation of the IFI contract's constitutionality should be based on evidence about the program as it existed at the time of the trial, that is, ignoring some of the more egregiously discriminatory aspects of the program in its inception. Over the course of the contract IFI had "secularized" the language in their documents and had become stricter regarding the use of exclusivist religious language by employees and volunteers. Among other changes, IFI staff members boasted at the trial that staff members or volunteers who expressed religious intolerance were immediately disciplined. The defendants unsuccessfully attempted to persuade the judge to exclude evidence of IFI practices from earlier years. 432 F. Supp. 2d at 870.

21. Plaintiffs' Exhibit 289.

22. Although federal rules permit videoconferencing in civil trials, and the reasons are obvious why such a practice would be convenient given the expense of transporting and housing many prisoner witnesses during a multi-week trial, questions remain concerning the many disadvantages to its use. ("The court may, for

good cause shown in compelling circumstances and upon appropriate safeguards, permit presentation of testimony in open court by contemporaneous transmission from a different location" [F. R. C. P. 43(a)]). It has been argued that, in criminal trials, videoconferencing may deny defendants their constitutional right to confront their accusers. See Anthony Garofano, "Avoiding Virtual Justice: Video-Teleconference Testimony In Federal Criminal Trials." See also Sherwin, *When Law Goes Pop,* on the pernicious effect of video culture on the administration of the law in general.

23. Bauer deposition, pp. 49–52.

24. Plaintiffs' Exhibit 48. The letter is dated April 30, 1999.

25. Ibid.

26. Plaintiffs' Exhibit 44.

27. See the argument of Anthony Piccarello during Oral Argument in the Eighth Circuit Court of Appeals.

28. Plaintiffs' Exhibit 70.

29. See, for example, Trial Transcript, p. 460.

30. 432 F. Supp. 2d at 901.

31. 532 F. Supp. 2d at 903.

32. Henry Cloud, *Changes That Heal*, p. 12.

33. Ramsey, *Total Money Makeover*, p. 221.

34. Eldridge, *Wild at Heart*, p. xi.

35. See Megan Sweeney, "*Beard v. Banks*: Deprivation as Rehabilitation." I also benefited from reading an unpublished draft excerpt from Sweeney's forthcoming *The Underground Book Railroad: Cultures of Reading in Women's Prisons*, still in manuscript and generously shared by the author. In September 2007 the Bureau of Prisons returned books removed under the chapel Library Project which had limited religious books in prison libraries to those appearing on an approved list. Bannerjee, "Prison to Return Purged Items to Chapels."

36. Blackaby and King, *Experiencing God*, p. 9.

37. Ibid., p. 9–10.

38. The use of these categories is being challenged in a number of lawsuits. See, e.g., preliminary decisions in an ongoing action brought against the navy charging discrimination against "evangelical" chaplains and in favor of "liturgical" Protestants and Catholics. *In re: Navy Chaplaincy*, 512 F. Supp. 2d 58, 516 F. Supp. 2d 119 (2007)

39. Plaintiffs' Exhibit 391.

40. See letter to IFI posted on the Web site of the Iowa Department of Public Health: www.idph.state.ia.us/.

41. Plaintiffs' Exhibit 391.

42. Anderson, *Freedom from Addiction*, p. 304.

43. Plaintiffs' Exhibit 390; and Anderson, *Freedom from Addiction*, pp. 310–11.

44. For an academic study of the Alpha program, see Hunt, *The* Alpha *Enterprise.*

45. Hunt, *The* Alpha *Enterprise*, p. 11.

46. Plaintiffs' Exhibits 350 and 390.

47. For a classic description of this community, see Nancy Tatom Ammerman, *Bible Believers: Fundamentalists in the Modern World* (New Brunswick, N.J.: Rutgers University Press, 1987).

48. Richard R. W. Fields, "Punishment and Crime: Perks for Prisoners Who Pray," p. 544.

49. For a description of what the Recovery Version claims, see www.recoveryversion.org/translation.html (accessed May 21, 2008).

50. 432 F. Supp. 2d at 908.

51. 432 F. Supp. 2d at 909.

52. Bauer deposition, p. 73.

Chapter 2
A Prison Like No Other

1. See, for example, Brief of Defendants-Appellants Prison Fellowship Ministries and InnerChange Freedom Initiative (filed in the U.S. Court of Appeals for the Eighth Circuit on September 13, 2006). The Eighth Circuit Court of Appeals, while substantially affirming Judge Pratt's finding of unconstitutionality, agreed, finding that he had indeed abused his discretion in admitting my testimony, as discussed below in chapter 4.

2. See, e.g., D. G. Hart, "When Is a Fundamentalist a Modernist?" See also Lienesch, *Redeeming America.*

3. Asad, *Formations of the Secular.*

4. The following description of the history of Prison Fellowship is based on Charles Colson's published writings about PFM; PFM's Web sites; testimony at the Iowa trial; and the summaries available on the Wheaton College Web site of the Records of Prison Fellowship Ministries—Collection 274—and of the papers of Charles Wendell Colson—Collection 275; and the Billy Graham Center Archives, which include PFM materials up to 1990, as of January 2007, though some materials are sealed for a time (www.wheatoncollege.edu [accessed May 21, 2007]).

5. "Historical Background," Records of Prison Fellowship Ministries—Collections 274. Billy Graham Center Archives, Wheaton College.

6. Colson, *Life Sentence*, pp. 40–41.

7. Ibid., p. 41. The cultural practice of hearing God speak, and the secularization that results when that no longer happens, is discussed in Leigh Eric Schmidt, *Hearing Things*; and T. M. Luhrmann, "Learning Religion at the Vineyard."

8. Hughes briefly considered running for president. See Harold E. Hughes (with Dick Schneider), *The Man from Ida Grove.*

9. Colson, *Life Sentence*, p. 46.

10. Ibid., pp. 46–47.

11. Michael O. Emerson and Christian Smith, *Divided by Faith*, p. 117.

12. They do note other differences between the two. For another discussion of the range of approaches to social issues among black churches, see also Omar McRoberts, *Streets of Glory.*

13. Colson, *Life Sentence*, pp. 209–10.

14. Prison Fellowship International (PFI), whose vision and mission are proclaimed on its Web site, operates in more than a hundred countries:

> Our Vision is: To be a reconciling community of restoration for all those involved in and affected by crime, thereby proclaiming and demonstrating the redemptive power and transforming love of Jesus Christ for all people.
>
> Our Mission is: To exhort and serve the Body of Christ in prisons and in the community in its ministry to prisoners, ex-prisoners, victims and their families; and in its advancement of Biblical standards of justice in the criminal justice system. (www.pfi.org)

15. Humaita in Sao Jose dos Campos, Brazil, had been described as the first contemporary prison "to adopt a completely faith-based approach to all aspects of prison administration." That program, which IFI names as its prototype, was the brainchild of a Brazilian lawyer, Mario Ottoboni. Innovations included "(1) turning over completely the day-to-day operations of the prison to religious volunteers rather than paid correctional staff, (2) saturating the prison environment with religious programming and instruction, and (3) promoting family visits, spiritual mentoring, and work-release." See Byron R. Johnson, "Assessing the Impact of Religious Programs and Prison Industry on Recidivism." Johnson, professor of sociology and co-director of the Institute for Studies of Religion at Baylor University, conducted a study comparing Humaita with another, secular, innovative Brazilian program that focuses on vocational training. According to Johnson, both programs witnessed a significant reduction in recidivism, with Humaita seeing a lower rate of reduction. Colson tells about his trip in 1987 to visit Humaita with a group of corrections officials in *Being the Body* (Charles Colson and Ellen Vaughn, *Being the Body*, p. 125).

16. Charles Colson, with Harold Fickett, *The Good Life*, p. 361.

17. Minnesota, Kansas, Missouri, and Arkansas, in addition to Texas and Iowa.

18. Mark Earley was a Virginia state senator (1988–1998) and attorney general of Virginia (1998–2001) before becoming president of PFM in 2002. He has also been active in The Navigators, an international evangelical Christian ministry to college students.

19. PFM 2006–2007 *Annual Report*, p. 5.

20. Norman Grubb, *Modern Viking*.

21. Ibid., p. 52. For a history of the Faith at Work movement, see David Miller, *God at Work: The History and Promise of the Faith at Work Movement*.

22. "Pentagon officials secretly met at the group's Washington Fellowship House in 1955 to plan a worldwide anticommunism propaganda campaign endorsed by the CIA, as documents from the Fellowship archives and the Eisenhower Presidential Library show. Then known as International Christian Leadership, the group financed a film called 'Militant Liberty' that was used by the Pentagon abroad" (Lisa Getter, "Showing Faith in Discretion").

23. Grubb, *Modern Viking*, pp. 106–7.

24. See Jeffrey Sharlet, "Jesus Plus Nothing"; Getter, "Showing Faith in Discretion"; Lance Tapley, "Does John Baldacci Belong to a Secretive, Conservative Christian Group?"; Max Blumenthal, "Born Again, Again"; and Anthony Lapp,

"Meet 'The Family.' " Academic treatments include D. Michael Lindsay, "Is the National Prayer Breakfast Surrounded by a 'Christian Mafia'?" an unpublished paper provided by Lindsay whose book on the subject is *Faith in the Halls of Power*; and Hugh Urban, "Religion and Secrecy in the Bush Administration."

25. For a description of The Fellowship, see Colson, *Born Again*, chap. 11. In 1978 a full-length movie was subsequently made of the book by AVCO Embassy Pictures.

26. *Born Again* begins with a first-person account of Colson as a world-class sinner, following the classic genre of the Christian conversion account, exemplified by Augustine's *Confessions*.

27. C. S. Lewis, *Mere Christianity*.

28. Colson, *Born Again*, pp. 112–17.

29. Colson focuses in his personal writings, following Lewis, on pride as the paradigmatic Christian sin. Such a focus is deeply problematic in the context of prisons, as it is for all those who are not powerful white male Christians. This point has been made repeatedly by feminist theologians, some of whom see women's sin to reside in submission. The extension by analogy of the sins of white male executives and politicians to those of men in U.S. prisons is particularly problematic, given the racialized, often racist, character of U.S. prisons and of the administration of criminal justice more generally in the U.S. For a profound theological reflection on the challenge of black "non-triumphalist" evangelical Christianity, see J. Kameron Carter, "Race and the Experience of Death." Carter indicts evangelicalism for, among other things, its "rush to resurrection."

30. See www.templetonprize.org (accessed May 21, 2008).

31. The sociologist Christian Smith lists as the most common error in understanding American evangelicalism what he calls "the representative elite fallacy," that is, believing that evangelical leaders "represent" the rank and file. Smith's extensive survey data on the beliefs of self-described evangelical Christians reveal a more complex picture. See his *Christian America? What Evangelicals Really Want*, p. 7.

32. Colson, *Born Again*, pp. 132–35.

33. The IFI prisoners, too, referred to one another as brothers (Trial Transcript, pp. 1070, 2016, 2915).

34. Colson, *Born Again*, p. 135. The Fellowship seems to be mostly, although not exclusively, male.

35. As well as Richard Lovelace, Jim Houston, and R. C. Sproul, names that are sprinkled throughout Colson's writings.

36. The best-known liberal evangelical leader is Jim Wallis, founder of *Sojourners' Magazine* and author of *God's Politics: Why the Right Gets It Wrong and the Left Doesn't Get It*.

37. Joshua Green, "Take Two: How Hillary Clinton Turned Herself into the Consummate Washington Player."

38. Hughes was governor of Iowa from 1963 to 1968 and senator from 1969 to 1975); he died in 1996.

39. Hughes (with Schneider), *The Man from Ida Grove*.

40. Ibid., p. 270.

41. Ibid., p. 276.

42. Ibid., pp. 322–23.

43. Ibid., p. 323.
44. See, for example, Colson, *Born Again*, pp. 146–58.
45. Hughes (with Schneider), *The Man from Ida Grove*, pp. 333–34.
46. Ibid., p. 335.
47. Ibid., pp. 335–36.
48. Bart Barnes, "Harold Hughes Dies at 74," p. D4.
49. Colson, *Born Again*, p. 10.
50. Ibid., pp. 11–12.
51. Ibid., p. 135.
52. Ibid., p. 319.
53. Ibid., p. 340.
54. Islam has, since 2001, increasingly been seen as another explicit enemy. See Saba Mahmood, "Secularism, Hermeneutics, and Empire." Mahmood describes the billions of dollars being spent to foster the development of an Islamic theology that historicizes the Qu'ran and the life of Mohammed in explicit parallel to the historicization of the Bible and of the life of Jesus carried out primarily by German theologians in nineteenth-century Europe. Mahmood notes the deep irony of a U.S. government made up largely of Bible-believing Christians who reject such a historicization for their own religion but advocate it for Islam. Or perhaps it is not ironic at all. Having seen the apparent demise of liberal Protestantism because of its willingness to embrace modernity, support for a modern Islam might be read as a deliberate effort to eliminate the competition.
55. Charles Colson, *Loving God*, p. 166. Page numbers to subsequent references to this work are given parenthetically within the quotation.
56. www.pfm.org (accessed May 23, 2008). PFM's Web site is sophisticated and is constantly updated.
57. Charles W. Colson and Nancy Pearcey, *How Now Shall We Live?*
58. Schaeffer's Swiss home, L'Abri, has become, since his death and the death of his wife, a center for the exploration of his legacy. Information about the foundation may be accessed at www.labri.org (accessed May 21, 2008).
59. Francis Schaeffer, *How Should We Then Live?* His last book, *The Great Evangelical Disaster*, warns against evangelical accommodation with secular humanism and calls for a recommitment to biblical truth.
60. The video was produced by Schaeffer's son, Frank Schaeffer, who joined the Eastern Orthodox Church in 1990 and has written a book criticizing evangelical Christianity, titled *Dancing Alone: The Quest for Orthodox Faith in the Age of False Religion.*
61. Schaeffer focuses particularly on Western art and the evidence he sees there for the decline of the culture. An art museum at Bob Jones University was partly inspired by Schaeffer's art history. See www.bjumg.org/ (accessed May 21, 2008). For this information I thank the art historian and philosopher David Carrier, who has visited the Bob Jones art museum and told me that he was impressed with its collection.
62. For one account of the radical challenge that Christian witness makes to humanism, see the 2001 Gifford Lectures, published as Stanley Hauerwas, *With the Grain of the Universe: The Church's Witness and Natural Theology.* See also Lienesch, *Redeeming America*, pp. 158–62, for a description of Schaeffer's "causes of corruption." .

63. For Colson's most recent apologetic restatement of Christian theology, see Charles Colson and Harold Fitchett, *The Faith: What Christians Believe, Why They Believe It, and Why It Matters.*

64. Plaintiffs' Exhibit 42.

65. http://www.pfm.org/section_hmpg.asp?id=30 (accessed March 31, 2007). The Web site has since been reorganized to list Worldview under the general rubric of BreakPoint (accessed May 21, 2008).

66. http://www.breakpoint.org/contentindex.asp?ID=145 (accessed March 31, 2007).

67. Lienesch, *Redeeming America*, p. 21.

68. See Tomoko Masuzawa, "Culture."

69. Ninian Smart, *Worldviews.*

70. Sigmund Freud, *Civilization & Die Weltanschauung* (1918).

71. For an evangelical account of this genealogy, see David K. Naugle, *Worldview.*

72. Colson himself has a complicated relationship with Roman Catholicism; notwithstanding the neo-Calvinism of his public theological positions, he also frequently speaks of the common cause shared by evangelicals and Catholics. He refers often to his wife's Catholicism and, together with Richard John Neuhaus, he co-founded a self-described Catholic-evangelical U.S. political alliance in 1994 called Evangelicals and Catholics Together.

73. Christian Smith, *Christian America?* p. 29.

74. Ibid., p. 222.

75. The most sophisticated analysis of the relationship between the jurisprudence of the First Amendment religion clauses and the changing nature of American religion continues to be that of Mark deWolfe Howe in *The Garden and the Wilderness.*

76. See also Lienesch, *Redeeming America*, for a discussion of evangelical church-state theories. pp. xxx.

77. 410 U.S. 113 (1973).

78. Sarah Barringer Gordon, *The Spirit of the Law.*

79. 494 U.S. 872 (1990).

80. Gerald N. Rosenberg, in *The Hollow Hope*, seriously questions the assumption that judicial decisions have the social effect often attributed to them, particularly such celebrated decisions as *Roe v. Wade* and *Brown v. Board of Education* (see p. 151). José Casanova, in *Public Religions in the Modern World*, offers a comparative sociological explanation for the continuing power of "public religion."

81. Noll, *American Evangelical Christianity*, pp. 22–23.

82. Lienesch, *Redeeming America*, p. 5.

83. Joel Carpenter, *Revive Us Again*, pp. 234–35.

84. Although Billy Graham's legacy is increasingly contested. See, for example, Neela Bannerjee, "Accolades, Some Tearful, in Pastor's Twilight Years," p. 16. For a summary description of the history and present-day configuration of evangelical Christianity in the U.S., see Mark A. Noll, *American Evangelical Christianity*; and Roger E. Olson, *The Westminster Handbook to Evangelical Theology.*

85. Lienesch, *Redeeming America*, p. 258.

86. Balmer, *Thy Kingdom Come*, pp. 200–201. See also Lienesch, *Redeeming America*, p. 171.

87. Smith, *Christian America?* p. 70. He also notes, however, that most of his informants also agreed that they themselves had experienced very little personal hostility.

88. See Mead, *The Lively Experiment.*

89. For a brief summary, see Mark A. Noll, *The Scandal of the Evangelical Mind*, pp. 84–85. See also idem, *American Evangelical Christianity: An Introduction.* Noll has elaborated these ideas in other publications, including his new history of the legacy of the great American religious thinker Jonathan Edwards, *America's God: From Jonathan Edwards to Abraham Lincoln.* See also Sidney Mead, "The Story of Evangelical Theology." But see David D. Hall, Review of *America's God*, *William and Mary Quarterly* 61 (2004): 539–43.

90. The Scottish Enlightenment was, of course, highly influential generally on U.S. political and social thought. See May, *The Enlightenment in America.*

91. Noll, *The Scandal*, pp. 87, 90.

92. Ibid., p. 127

93. Ibid.

94. See also Lienesch, *Redeeming America*, pp. 192–3.

95. Noll, *The Scandal*, pp. xx.

96. Ibid., pp. 109–145.

97. Nathan O. Hatch, *The Democratization of American Christianity.*

98. Donald E. Miller, *Reinventing American Protestantism*, p. 133.

99. Ibid., p. 132.

100. Noll, *The Scandal*, pp. xx

101. Ibid., p. 98.

102. Mary Poovey notes that the term "objective" to eighteenth-century moral philosophers meant "nonsectarian," not "secular." The idea was to avoid sectarian strife, not to deny the value of revelation. "The Liberal Civil Subject and the Social in Eighteenth Century Moral Philosophy," p. 140.

103. Noll, *The Scandal*, pp. 59–81.

104. Ibid., pp. 212–13.

105. Noll, *American Evangelical Christianity.* Lew Daly discusses the importance of this quotation from Kuyper for the supporters of faith-based policies in his *God and the Welfare State*, pp. 64–65.

106. See PFM 2006–2007 *Annual Report,* p. 32.

107. Interestingly, as Lew Daly notes, those countries in Europe where Kuyper's ideas have been most influential, The Netherlands and Germany, are much more secular than the U.S. and have far more generous social welfare programs. (Further complicating Kuyper's political legacy is that Kuyper's Calvinist politics has been understood by many to have legitimized apartheid politics in South Africa. See Daly, *God and the Welfare State*, p. 5.)

108. Colson, *Life Sentence*, p. 133.

109. Ibid.

110. Ibid., p. 284.

111. Although I speak here of this non-marked quality in a merely descriptive way, the non-marked quality of this language has also been read with suspicion

as a kind of code, or deliberate effort at concealment, by those who feel victimized by it. Moreover, evidence in the PFM archives suggests a strategic decision to use such language (Collection 274 and 275, Billy Graham Archives). For a discussion of evangelical linguistic conventions as a deliberate coding, see, for example, "Appendix: Decoding the Rhetoric of the Religious Right" in Randall Balmer, *Thy Kingdom Come*, pp. 193–201. Balmer, a professor of religious history at Barnard College, Columbia University, and self-professed evangelical Christian, writes as an insider about a culture he both criticizes and defends. He is also the author of *Mine Eyes Have Seen the Glory: A Journey into the Evangelical Subculture in America*.

112. John P. Bartkowski, *The Promise Keepers*, pp. 144, 145.

113. Promise Keepers is also active in prisons, sometimes in partnership with PFM. See www.promisekeepers.org (accessed June 18, 2007).

114. John Lardas Modern, "Ghosts of Sing Sing," p. 620.

Chapter 3
Biblical Justice

1. The Bible, New Century Version (NCV), Ps. 51:3, 4. The NCV describes itself as follows:

> This translation of God's Word was made from the original Hebrew and Greek languages. . . . Several guidelines were used to make the language clear for any reader. *The Living Word Vocabulary*, the standard used by *World Book Encyclopedia*, was the basis for vocabulary. Concepts were put into natural terms—modern measurements and geographical locations. Ancient customs were clarified in the text or footnotes. Rhetorical questions were stated according to the implied answers. Figures of speech and idiomatic expressions were translated according to their meanings. Obscure terms were clarified. An attempt was made to choose gender language that would convey the intent of the writers. The Tetragrammaton was indicated by putting LORD and GOD in capital letters. Hebrew parallelism in poetry and word plays were retained. Images of ancient languages were translated into equivalent English images, where possible. (www.tyndale.cam.ac.uk/scriptures/NCV.htm [accessed May 21, 2008])

In the Revised Standard Version, verses 3 and 4 of Psalm 51 read: "3: For I know my transgressions, and my sin is ever before me. 4: Against thee, thee only, have I sinned, and done that which is evil in thy sight, so that thou art justified in thy sentence and blameless in thy judgment."

2. Lk.19:1–10.

3. *The Sycamore Tree Project*. Plaintiffs' Exhibit no. 391.

4. Marc Mauer, "Comparative International Rates of Incarceration: An Examination of Causes and Trends," presented to the U.S. Civil Rights Commission by the Sentencing Project, June 20, 2003. Steep increases in the 1980s and 1990s were followed by a slower but steady growth in the prison population. See also U.S. Department of Justice, Bureau of Justice Statistics, "The Nation's Prison Population Continues Its Slow Growth"; and a recent report of The Pew Center on the States, *One in One Hundred: Behind Bars in 2008*.

5. The figures are 737 per 100,000 for the U.S., 624 per 100,000 for the Russian Federation. See International Centre for Prison Studies, King's College London, http://www.prisonstudies.org (accessed May 21, 2007).

6. David Garland, *Mass Imprisonment*, p. 1.

7. See U.S. Department of Justice, Bureau of Justice Statistics, available at http://www.ojp.usdoj.gov/bjs/reentry/recidivism.htm (accessed May 21, 2007).

8. David Garland, *The Culture of Control*, p. 1. See also Michael Tonry, "Theories and Policies Underlying Guidelines Systems"; and idem, *Thinking about Crime*. See also Jonathan Simon, *Governing Through Crime*.

9. John J. Gibbons and Nicholas de B. Katzenbach, *Confronting Confinement*, preface p. 8. An interesting note is that the report does not mention faith-based prison programs. A copy of the report is available at www.prisoncommission.org (accessed January 7, 2008).

10. Ibid.

11. In terms of the punitiveness of its penal system, the U.K. falls somewhere between the U.S. and the rest of Europe. See International Centre for Prison Studies, King's College London, http://www.prisonstudies.org. On crime and politics in the U.K. today, see Richard Garside and Will McMahon, "Does Criminal Justice Work?"

12. Like most criminologists, Garland seems mostly uninterested in religion. I could find very little academic treatment of the religious phenomenology or sociology of faith-based prison programs in the U.S. (I am not including law review articles considering their constitutionality or the University of Pennsylvania study of the effectiveness of IFI in Texas.) An interesting exception is an unpublished article titled "Faith-based Corrections as Symbolic Crusade" by Michael A. Hallett, professor of criminal justice at the University of North Florida, in which Hallett uses sociological categories such as status and power redistribution to analyze "faith-based corrections."

13. See Jonathan Simon, *Governing Through Crime*.

14. Garland, *The Culture of Control*, pp. 8–20.

15. Key publishing moments, among many others, in the penal history of the last thirty-five years include American Friends Service Committee, *Struggle for Justice*; Jessica Mitford, *Kind and Usual Punishment*; James Q. Wilson, *Thinking about Crime*; Francis A. Allen, *The Decline of the Rehabilitative Ideal*; John DiIulio, *Governing Prisons*; and Franklin E. Zimring, Gordon Hawkins, and Sam Kamin, *Three Strikes and You're Out in California*.

John DiIulio, professor of political science at the University of Pennsylvania, forms a bridge figure between the world of criminology and the world of faith-based politics. A prominent Roman Catholic layman, he is a scholar of inner-city crime who has been both a critic of getting tough on crime and a strong advocate for the improvement of prison administration. In 1996 DiIulio called crime the result of "moral poverty" in a book he jointly authored with William J. Bennett and John P. Walters, *Body Count: Moral Poverty . . . and How to Win America's War on Crime and Drugs*. DiIulio was also the first director of the White House Office on Faith-based Initiatives. After six months on the job he resigned, reportedly, in part, because he was skeptical that proselytization was the key to the crime problem. After resigning, he gave an interview to *Esquire* magazine criticizing the politicization of policy by the Bush White House and famously calling it "the reign of the Mayberry Machiavellis." See Ron Suskind, "Why Are These Men Laughing?" DiIulio continues to speak publicly about the importance of religion in public life. See, e.g., E. J. Dionne Jr. and John J. DiIuliio Jr., *What's God Got to Do with the American Experiment?*. His newest work, *Godly Republic: A Centrist Blueprint for America's Faith-Based Future*, criticizes the outcome in the *AU v. PFM* case, pending on appeal at the time of the book's publication.

16. See Mauer, "The Causes and Consequences of Prison Growth in the United States," p. 7.

17. Consider Ohio. A recent report to the Ohio General Assembly by the Ohio Task Force on Faith-Based Initiatives reveals that more than four hundred laws disable the Ohio prisoner as he makes his reentry into society. For example, programs in Ohio prisons train prisoners to be barbers yet Ohio law does not permit ex-felons to be licensed as barbers. The Ohio study recommends a complete review and revision of these laws while also advocating to the Ohio legislature that it find ways to encourage the participation of faith-based providers in serving prisoners' needs. The Ohio study emphasizes the need for "evidence-based" programming, nondiscriminatory treatment of prisoners, and access to prison service contracts for all religious and nonreligious providers. Published on the Ohio Department of Rehabilitation and Corrections Web site on December 20, 2006: http://www.drc.state.oh.us/web/fb.htm (accessed May 21, 2007). The report is discussed in an article on The Roundtable Web site (www.religionandsocialpolicy.org): Claire Hughes, "Ohio Group Details Ways to Expand Faith-Based Prison Programs," Roundtable on Religion and Social Welfare Policy (first published, November 28, 2006).

18. Marie Gottschalk, *The Prison and the Gallows*, p. 36. See also Susan Bandes, "When Victims Seek Closure." Concerning the peculiarities of the U.S. criminal justice system and the abuses and dangers to which it is subject, see also Francis A. Allen, *The Habits of Legality.*

19. James Q. Whitman, *Harsh Justice,* p. 55.

20. Ibid., pp. 64–65.

21. Ibid., p. 65.

22. Ibid., pp. 178, 197.

23. Ibid., p. 6.

24. Ibid., p. 271 n. 30. See also Erik C. Owens, John D. Carlson, and Eric C. Elshtain, eds., *Religion and the Death Penalty.*

25. Ibid., pp. 57,

26. See Loïc Wacquant, "Deadly Symbiosis"; and Elijah Anderson, "Going Straight."

27. Whitman, *Harsh Justice*, p. 201.

28. PFM 2006–2007 *Annual Report,* p. 7.

29. For a discussion of the Nation's early litigation and imprisonment, see Sarah Barringer Gordon, *The Spirit of the Law.*

30. Malcolm X, *The Autobiography of Malcolm X.*

31. For a recent study of Muslims in Ohio prisons, see Nawal H. Amman, Robert R. Weaver, and Sam Saxon, "Muslims in Prison."

32. Carolyn Nichols, "Nation's First Faith-based Prison Opens in Florida." For a study of the Lawtey prison, see Tanya Erzen, "Bodies and Souls: Imprisonment, Evangelicalism, and Faith-based Politics," book manuscript in progress.

33. Website of Florida Department of Corrections: http://www.dc.state.fl.us/oth/faith/index.html (accessed May 23, 2007).

34. C. S. Lewis, *God in the Dock*, pp 287–88.

35. Ibid., p. 288.

36. Ibid.

37. Ibid., p. 290.

38. See, for example, Charles W. Colson, "The Question is: What is Just?" under "Issues and Research," www.pfm.org (accessed July 1, 2007).

39. Charles W. Colson, "Capital Punishment: A Personal Statement."

40. Ibid.

41. Ibid.

42. Ibid.

43. Lewis's best-known academic work is *The Allegory of Love: A Study of Medieval Tradition*. His apologetic works include *Mere Christianity*, *The Screwtape Letters*, and *The Problem of Pain*. He also wrote fantasy fiction for adults, for example, *Out of the Silent Planet, Perelandra*, and *That Hideous Strength*. His books for children include *The Horse and His Boy*; *The Last Battle: A Story for Children*; *The Lion, the Witch, and the Wardrobe: A Story for Children*; *The Magician's Nephew*; *Prince Caspian: The Return to Narnia*; *The Silver Chair* ; and *The Voyage of the "Dawn Treader"*.

44. *The Westminster Handbook to Evangelical Theology*, s.v. "C. S. Lewis," pp. 119–121; Evangelical Christianity, in the British context, is configured in a different way. Structured historically, as Christianity has been in the U.K., by its formal, and informal, relationship to the established church, evangelically inclined Protestants exist both within the Church of England, which includes a wide spectrum of Christian liturgical expression from Anglo-Catholics to evangelicals, and without, among the "dissenting" churches, including Methodists and Baptists. Newer non-denominational fundamentalists, pentacostalists, and evangelicals, American-style, are also present in the U.K.

45. Scott R. Burson and Jerry L. Walls, *C. S. Lewis & Francis Schaeffer*, p. 229.

46. Justifying punishment is an enormously complex subject with a long philosophical pedigree. Although a notion of punishment seems to dominate populist politics today, some political philosophers and constitutional scholars are returning to first principles. We live in a time when punishment is being rethought in fundamental ways. Why punish? On what grounds can a free democratic society punish? What limits does the U.S. Constitution place on punishment? Guyora Binder, in his article "Democracy and Punishment," argues that it is more a political question than a moral one. Deirdre Golash takes this further, arguing against punishment in her *Case Against Punishment: Retribution, Crime Prevention, and the Law*.

47. Rothman, "Perfecting the Prison," p. 106.

48. Ibid.

49. Ibid., p. 111–12.

50. Elizabeth Mensch has surveyed the options for Protestant understandings of law and politics after Luther's destruction of the medieval synthesis, as well as the new understanding of the self resulting from the ensuing fragmentation of epistemology and political authority. She also explains the ways in which various theories find continuing authority in the biblical text. Mensch writes:

> At the clear risk of oversimplifying, it might be said that three basic models of the polity emerged from the changed Reformation conception of the self. In the first, the Hobbesian model of the atomized, materialistic self was paralleled by a sovereignty which was simultaneously artificial and absolute, with no coherent moral limits. In the second, associated with Harringtonian republicanism, the self as redeemed by the spirit of God was matched by a quasi-democratic polity also so infused by the spirit of God as to redeem the City on Earth, bringing unity out of Augustinian duality. Finally, in the earlier but arguably more influential work of Richard Hooker, the complex Protestant notion of the dual identity of the self, redeemed but still sinner, found its political reflection in dualities within the polity, chiefly in the distinction between law and politics. (See Elizabeth B. Mensch, "Images of Self and Polity in the Aftermath of the Reformation," p. 249.)

Contrasting the theories of Thomas Hobbes, James Harrington, and Richard Hooker, Mensch concludes that Hooker's Augustinian solution most approximates what she understands to be the dominant strain of the U.S. dualist understanding of law and politics: law retains a connection to natural law and morality, whereas politics is understood as a this-worldly and pragmatic affair. This dualist view of law and politics is reflected in a divided self, part redeemed and part sinner. These three basic models remain options for theorizing the relationship between self and polity in the U.S. Parts of the current evangelical revival seem to be reaching for a Harringtonian unity, abridging the productive dynamism of Hooker's plan.

51. The contemporary biblical counseling movement was launched with the publication of Jay E. Adams's *Competent to Counsel*. For a comparison of various religious and secular psychotherapies, see Don S. Browning and Terry D. Cooper, *Religious Thought and the Modern Psychologies*.

52. The White Paper is available at http://www.ifiprison.org/generic.asp?ID=2180 (accessed May 21, 2008).

53. "The Christian doctrine of sin is not unitary. There have been multiple theological understandings of sin in the last two millennia. Most evangelicals, though, adhere to an Augustinian understanding of sin as fundamental to the human condition. Augustine's interpretation of Romans 5 was that children inherit genealogically the sin of Adam and all humans are permanently and irreversibly affected by Adam's fall. While Reformed theologies can tend toward an entirely unregenerate view of mankind, Wesleyan-derived theologies tend to be more optimistic that, through grace, Christians can live lives pleasing to God" (*The Westminster Handbook to Evangelical Theology*, s.v. "Sin/Original Sin," pp. 267–69). For a comparative religions approach to the history of sin, see also *Encyclopedia of Religion*, 2nd ed., s.v. "sin."

54. Henry Brandt and Kerry L. Skinner, *Heart of the Problem*, p. 6.

55. Ibid.

56. *Christianson v. Leavitt*, 482 F. Supp. 2d 1232 (2007).

57. Ira C. Lupu and Robert W. Tuttle, *The State of the Law 2007*, p. 65.

58. Plaintiffs' Exhibit 84.

59. Plaintiffs' Exhibit 85.

60. The words from Matthew 18 are a critical text for all Christians. Their significance for the actual governance of Christian communities is much contested, and whether Jesus intended to found a formal community remains much debated by Christian biblical scholars. For most scholars today, the text attributed to Matthew reflects the immediate concerns of the second-century Matthean community rather than any original purpose to be attributed directly to Jesus. IFI's rhetorical move in its required "covenant" denies the contested nature of the text and effaces the distance between the second-century Matthean community and contemporary evangelical culture.

61. Rick Warren, *The Purpose Driven Life: What on Earth Am I Here For?* The many products of Rick Warren's ministry can be purchased through his Web site: www.purposedrivenlife.com (accessed July 20, 2007). Warren is reportedly working with the private prison company, Corrections Corporation of America, to develop faith-based, in-prison programs for their facilities. See Jane Lampham, "A Captive Audience for Salvation."

62. Mk. 1:13.

63. Warren, *The Purpose Driven Life*, p. 297.

64. Mk. 16:15.

65. Warren, *The Purpose Driven Life*, p. 298.

66. See Perez Zagorin, *How the Idea of Religious Toleration Came to the West*; and Benjamin Kaplan, *Divided by Faith*. For a discussion of the theology of the religion clauses, see also Howe, *The Garden and the Wilderness*; and Peter L. Berger, "Pluralism, Protestantism, and the Voluntary Principle."

67. Sam Dye was the Iowa director of IFI from 2000 to 2004.

68. Dye deposition, p. 26.

69. For a discussion of the status of heterodox religious opinions in U.S. courts, see Sullivan, *Impossibility*.

70. 432 F. Supp. 2d at 910.

71. Ibid., at 909.

72. Kautzky deposition, p. 93.

73. Charles Colson, "Evangelizing for Evil in Our Prisons."

74. Ann Chih Lin, *Reform in the Making*. On the need for dignity and decency in prisons in the U.K., see Alison Liebling, assisted by Helen Arnold, *Prisons and Their Moral Performance*.

75. 2006–2007 *Annual Report*, p. 7.

Chapter 4
The Way We Live Now

1. The practical and constitutional difficulties of authoritatively proving up religion in a U.S. court in a free exercise case were the subject of this author's previous book. See Sullivan, *The Impossibility of Religious Freedom*.

2. In its opinion partly affirming and partly reversing Judge Pratt's decision, the U.S. Court of Appeals for the Eighth Circuit held, in an unusual and almost certainly legally incorrect footnote that in receiving my testimony Judge Pratt abused his discretion. (See the next chapter for discussion of this point).

3. *Everson v. Bd. of Education,* 330 U.S. 1 (1947).

4. For a summary of this law, see Kent Greenawalt, *Religion and the Constitution*, vol. 2, *Establishment and Fairness.*

5. *Mitchell v. Helms*, 530 U.S. 793 (2000).

6. *Zelman v. Simmons-Harris*, 536 U.S. 639 (2002).

7. 432 F. Supp. 2d at 917.

8. Ibid.

9. Ibid., at 920.

10. Ibid., at 921.

11. Ibid., at 932. See *Williams v. Lara*, 52 S.W. 3d 171 (2001), in which the Texas Supreme Court declared a Christian religious educational program in a county jail unconstitutional, because the standard for what counts as Christian was explicitly acknowledged to be based in the Sheriff's personal religious views.

12. Scientific experts are classified by evidence scholars into three categories: the teaching witness, the reporting witness, and the interpreting witness. See Ronald L. Carlson et al., *Evidence: Teaching Materials for an Age of Science and Statutes.*

13. The defendants' moves to discredit my testimony provoked a strong response from Judge Pratt: "Defendants maintain that the Court should not rely on Dr. Sullivan's testimony. . . . The Court disagrees. . . . Dr. Sullivan's academic credentials as an expert in the fields of comparative religion and the history of Christianity are impeccable and, second, her testimony is considered by the Court only to situate, objectively, InnerChange and Prison Fellowship within the well-accepted context of religious tradition and practice as they exist now" (432 F. Supp. 2d at 873, fn. 9). Without a jury, as in this case, a federal judge usually has considerable discretion as to what testimony will be heard and how that evidence will be used.

14. Evangelical resistance to the social sciences, particularly interpretive or qualitative methods, including the academic study of religion, can be understood as a rejection of what the intellectual historian Mary Poovey terms "the long history of reification that we call modernity." In a 2002 article titled "The Liberal Civil Subject and the Social in Eighteenth Century Moral Philosophy," Poovey describes the gradual invention of secular abstractions as a way to talk about human nature and society. The initiation of this process depended on abandoning early modern understandings of providential order as authorizing generalized discussion of the social; these understandings were replaced with "classificatory categories" and "transindividual structures and processes" that "lie beyond consciousness and individual human beings." It is a shift Poovey describes as leading to "the view from nowhere," a phrase she borrows from Thomas Nagel's *The View from Nowhere.*

15. Is it an unconstitutional establishment of religion, for example, for the government to teach that "life is sacred" as President George Bush represented to Pope Benedict XV as the American belief? The answer is almost certainly not.

Presidents have a great deal of leeway in the language they use to describe their political positions. Yet, clearly, the implication was that he spoke for an American electorate in making that representation. See Laurie Goodstein and Sheryl Gay Stolberg, "Pope Praises Americans' Faith and Warns of Perils of Secularism."

16. *Brown v. Bd. of Education*, 349 U.S. 294 (1955). But see, too, *Parents Involved in Community Schools v. Seattle School District No. 1,* 127 S. Ct. 2738 (2007).

17. Gerald Rosenberg, *The Hollow Hope: Can Courts Bring about Social Change?* pp. 342–43. Resistance, in Rosenberg's view, is one of the risks social reformers take by litigating.

18. For an overview of the relationship of religion and law, see Winnifred Fallers Sullivan and Robert A. Yelle, "Overview."

19. See Smith, *Embattled and Thriving*; and Bartkowski, *Promise Keepers.*

20. A strong version of the Christian America position is exemplified in various efforts to legislate the Christian identity of America, as first delineated in Robert Handy's classic account *A Christian America: Protestant Hopes and Historical Realities.* A weak version of the Christian America position is exemplified by Chief Justice Burger's opinion for the majority in *Lynch v. Donnelly,* discussed in Winnifred Fallers Sullivan, *Paying the Words Extra.* Strong and weak versions of the Christian nature of Europe are also apparent in the recent debate over the new European Constitution. See Grace Davie, *Europe: The Exceptional Case*; and idem, *Religion in Modern Europe.*

21. Plaintiffs' Exhibit 74.

22. 432 F. Supp. 2d at 898.

23. See also Pratt opinion, 432 F. Supp. 2d at 881.

24. Rawls quoted in Fish, *The Trouble with Principle*, p. 11.

25. See chapter 1 n. 49, above.

26. Versions of this section of the book were published in the online column *Sightings* (http://divinity.uchicago.edu/news/sightings_archive/index.shtml#what) on January 16, 2006, and in the fall 2006 issue of the *Harvard Divinity School Bulletin.*

27. See Frank Walsh, *Sin and Censorship*

28. See, for example, www.christiananswers.net (accessed July 20, 2007). These sites are surprisingly catholic in their tastes. Few films are condemned outright. Many classic, apparently secular films are considered to teach valuable Christian lessons.

29. The *Oxford English Dictionary* defines "allegory" as follows:

> 1. Description of a subject under the guise of some other subject of aptly suggestive resemblance. 2. An instance of such description; a figurative sentence, discourse, or narrative, in which properties and circumstances attributed to the apparent subject really refer to the subject they are meant to suggest; an extended or continued metaphor.

30. For discussions of the distinctiveness of Protestant and Catholic cultural rhetoric, see Paul Giles, *American Catholic Arts and Fictions.* See also David Tracy, *The Analogical Imagination.*

31. John Bunyan, *The pilgrim's progress from this world to that which is to come: delivered under the similitude of a dream, wherein is discovered the manner of his setting out, his dangerous journey, and safe arrival at the desired countrey.* For a discussion of *Pilgrim's Progress* and other forms of Protestant allegory, see Thomas H. Luxon, *Literal Figures.*

32. This in contrast to Catholic interpretive strategies, sometimes termed "analogical". See Giles, *American Catholic Arts and Fictions*; and Tracy, *The Analogical Imagination.*

33. Jonathan Miller, "March of the Conservatives: Penguin Film as Political Fodder." An article in the *New Yorker* about one of the convicted activists from the Tiananmen Square protest, written by the activist's sister, tells of a friend who dismissively compared Chinese dissidents to the penguins in the film *March of the Penguins.* Jianying Zha, "Letter from Beijing: Enemy of the State: The Complicated Life of an Idealist."

34. Patricia Shade Deposition, pp. 19–20.

35. An adverse witness is one who is hostile to the party introducing him and may therefore be questioned on cross-examination. A party usually chooses to introduce an adverse witness when that party has access to evidence that is otherwise unavailable or when proof of elements of one's party's case can be more powerfully introduced out of the mouth of its adversaries.

36. Certain exhibits at the trial pertaining to individual prisoners were deemed confidential and marked as such. The plaintiffs presented large compendia of various notes, tests, contracts, and evaluations made by IFI counselors about individual prisoners. I quote only from those discussed in the transcript.

37. In the U.S. context, the difficulty of ascertaining the genuineness of a conversion was particularly acute in the New England colonies in the seventeenth and early eighteenth century when proof of conversion was necessary to be eligible to vote. For a discussion of the patterned nature of conversion narratives in colonies, see Patricia Caldwell, *The Puritan Conversion Narrative.*

38. Taylor, *Modern Social Imaginaries*, pp. 3ff.

39. Ibid., pp. 185ff.

40. Slavoj Žižek, *The Ticklish Subject*, p. 326.

41. Marcel Gauchet, in *The Disenchantment of the World*, argues that this shift began much earlier, in the axial age (ca. 500 B.C.E.) when the universalist religions were invented and religion ceased to be exclusively tribal.

42. Taylor, *Modern Social Imaginaries*, pp. 21–22.

43. Richard Baxter, *Holy Commonwealth*, p. 274; Michael Walzer, *The Revolution of the Saints*, p. 224; Taylor, *Modern Social Imaginaries*, p. 40.

44. See, for example, the Supreme Court opinions concerning the scope of the conscientious objector exemption to mandatory military service. See also Sullivan, " 'The Conscience of Contemporary Man.' "

45. For a comparison of French and English versions of church-state relations during the nineteenth century, see Jean Baubérot and Séverine Mathieu. *Religion, Modernité et Culture au Royaume-Uni et en France.*

46. Kathleen M. Sullivan, "Religion and Liberal Democracy."

47. Noll speaks of the important influence of the didactic enlightenment, as appropriated by American evangelicals in three spheres: politics, society, and economy. See Noll, *The Scandal of the Evangelical Mind*, pp. 69–76.

48. Taylor, *Modern Social Imaginaries*, p. 38.

49. Ibid., p. 39.

50. For a discussion of modern Jewish orthodoxy and forms of religious education, see Haym Soloveitchik, "Rupture and Reconstruction."

51. Charles Hirschkind, *The Ethical Soundscape*, p. 22.

52. Ibid., p. 210.

53. Ibid., p. 211.

54. David Engel, "Globalization and the Decline of Legal Consciousness."

55. Danielle Hervieu-Léger, " 'What Scripture Tells Me.' "

56. Such positions range over the entire landscape of public policy, including family law, tax and welfare law, zoning regulation, foreign policy, and policing. For a recent ethnography of moral life among AIDS volunteers, see Courtney Bender, *Heaven's Kitchen: Living Religion at God's Love We Deliver.*

Chapter 5
Beyond Church and State

1. Brief of Defendants-Appellants, p. 19.

2. For helpful summaries of the legal issues, see Ira C. Lupu and Robert W. Tuttle, "*Americans United for the Separation of Church and State (and others) v. Prison Fellowship Ministries (and others)* (United States District Court, Southern District of Iowa, decided June 2, 2006" and "Federalism and Faith"; Douglas Roy, "Doin' Time in God's House"; and Patrick B. Cates, "Faith-Based Prisons and the Establishment Clause."

3. Plaintiffs' Exhibit 79.

4. Acts 10:45–47, Mk 16:18; Lk 10:19.

5. If one compares the Apostles' Creed, the oldest and most widely used creed of the Western churches dating from the fourth century of the common era, to IFI's Statement of Faith, some distinctive IFI elements are apparent. The Apostles' Creed reads as follows:

> I believe in God, the Father almighty, creator of heaven and earth.
>
> I believe in Jesus Christ, God's only Son, our Lord, who was conceived by the Holy Spirit, born of the Virgin Mary, suffered under Pontius Pilate, was crucified, died, and was buried; he descended to the dead.
>
> On the third day he rose again; he ascended into heaven, he is seated at the right hand of the Father, and he will come again to judge the living and the dead.
>
> I believe in the Holy Spirit, the holy Catholic Church, the communion of saints, the forgiveness of sins, the resurrection of the body, and the life everlasting.

The Apostles' Creed developed over the first centuries of Christianity out of the statements required of newly baptized Christian converts. Most obvious, when compared to IFI's version, is the inclusion in the IFI Statement of Faith of a paragraph on the inerrancy of the Bible, although other details reveal doctrinal differences with other Christian communities, differences that evolved over the centuries.

6. Bauer deposition, pp. 66–67.

7. Ibid., pp. 150–51.

8. Ibid., p. 411.

9. Stephen Prothero attempts to encompass what Americans should know about other peoples' religions in his *Religious Literacy: What Every American Needs to Know—And Doesn't.*

10. See, for example, Colson, *Born Again*, p. 157.

11. Bauer deposition, pp. 72–94.

12. For a discussion of the use of a metaphor of lightness and darkness by evangelical Christians, see Ammerman, *Bible Believers*, pp. 72ff.

13. See Raymond A. Bucko, *The Lakota Ritual of the Sweat Lodge*; and Emily Brault, *Sweating in the Joint*. I am grateful to Harvey Markowitz, professor of religion at Washington and Lee University, for advising me about the use of sweat lodges in prisons.

14. See Stephen Seymour, "Note: The Silence of Prayer: an Examination of the Federal Bureau of Prisons Moratorium on the Hiring of Muslim Chaplains."

15. Watson deposition, pp. 65–6.

16. Ibid., p. 69.

17. Ibid., p. 68.

18. Ibid., p.70.

19. Sullivan deposition, p. 76.

20. One of the Muslim prisoners, Bobby Shelton, also refused to be led down the "universal path" by the IFI lawyer:

> *Q*. Would you say responsibility and fellowship and productivity are good values to seek?
>
> *A*. Are you asking me these question from an Islamic standpoint or American standpoint?" (p. 182)

For Shelton, too, the Islamic standpoint cannot necessarily be assimilated to the American, the Christian, the universal.

21. Chandler deposition, p. 40.

22. The Web site for the Jerusalem School explains their purpose:

> The Jerusalem School of Synoptic Research, a consortium of Jewish and Christian scholars, was chartered in 1985 as an Israeli non-profit scientific and educational organization dedicated to understanding better the Synoptic Gospels (Matthew, Mark and Luke), and to rethinking the Synoptic Problem. Examining the Synoptic Gospels within the context of the language, land and culture in which Jesus lived, this Jewish-Christian collaboration is unique and unprecedented historically. In 2003, the U.S. citizens of the Jerusalem School formed a sister-corporation in the United States which has been granted the IRS's 501c3 Charitable status for tax-deductible donations. (http://www.js.org/ [accessed May 21, 2007])

23. See, for example, Claire Hughes, "Potential for Widespread Fallout in Ruling against Iowa Faith-Based Prison Program."

24. 330 U.S. 1 (1947).

25. For a discussion of incorporation, see Lupu and Tuttle, "Federalism and Faith."

26. For a discussion of the possibilities for state independence on establishment clause issues, see ibid.

27. 403 U.S. 602 (1971).

28. The *Lemon* test has been widely criticized by academics and by the courts but has never been definitively displaced by the Supreme Court. For excellent summaries of the current state of establishment clause law as applied to prison cases, see Michael B. Mushlin, *Rights of Prisoners*; and Richard R. W. Fields, "Punishment and Crime."

29. *Allegheny v. ACLU*, 492 U.S. 573 (1989).

30. *Lee v. Weisman,* 505 U.S. 577 (1992).

31. 432 U.S. at 914–15.

32. Mushlin, *Rights of Prisoners*, p. 676.

33. For an impassioned history of the failures of court supervision of prison conditions, see Gutterman, "Prison Objectives and Human Dignity." For useful summaries of the special situation of prisoners with respect to constitutional rights today, see Mushlin, *Rights of Prisoners*; and *A Jailhouse Lawyer's Manual,* published online by the Columbia Human Rights Law Review, at www.columbia.edu/cu/hrlr/.

34. Gutterman, "Prison Objectives and Human Dignity," p. 858.

35. Ibid.

36. *Turner v. Safley,* 482 U.S. 78 (1987); *Beard v. Banks*, 547 U.S. 1001 (2006). But see also Religious Land Use and Institutionalized Persons Act (RLUIPA) 42 U.S. Code § 2000cc-1 et seq.

37. One notable exception is an 1879 California case awarding victory to a Chinese prisoner who claimed that the prison's regulation requiring him to cut off his queue violated the equal protection clause of the Fourteenth Amendment. See *Ho Ah Kow v. Nunan,* 12. Cas. 252, No. 6546 (C.C.D. Cal 1879).

38. *O'Lone v. Shabazz*, 482 U.S. 342 (1987). See also Edgardo Rotman, "The Failure of Reform," pp. 172–73.

39. 482 U.S. at 368.

40. *Kerr v. Farrey,* 95 F. 3d 472 (7th Cir. 1996). See also a similar decision with respect to Alcoholics Anonymous (AA): *Warner v. Orange County,* 115 F. 3d. 1068 (2d Cir 1997). For a discussion of the constitutionality of AA, see Michael G. Honeymar Jr., "Alcoholics Anonymous as a Condition of Drunk Driving Probation."

Prisoners' religious rights are also guaranteed by statute in the Religious Land Use and Institutionalized Persons Act (RLUIPA), passed by Congress in 2002. RLUIPA prohibits "substantial burdens on the religious exercise of a person residing in or confined to an institution" unless the burden is "in furtherance of a compelling governmental interest" and "is the least restrictive means of furthering that compelling governmental interest." The constitutionality of RLUIPA was upheld by the Supreme Court in *Cutter v. Wilkinson* in 2005. Justice Ginsburg, who wrote the opinion for the majority upholding its constitutionality, noted that the statute's reach extended only to what she termed "bona fide" religions. No RLUIPA claim was made in the Iowa case.

41. 432 F. Supp. 2d at 932.

42. "The Becket Fund for Religious Liberty is a nonprofit, nonpartisan, interfaith, legal, and educational institute dedicated to protecting the free expression of all religious traditions. We operate in three arenas: in the courts of law (litigation), in the court of public opinion (media), and in the academy (scholarship)." www.becketfund.org (accessed February 27, 2007).

43. An amicus curiae brief—literally, a "friend of the court" brief—is filed in the Court of Appeals by a non-party to the case who has an interest in the case. Nonprofit, lobbying, and trade organizations frequently have lawyers on the staff whose principal work is to file such briefs to advance the agenda of the organization. U.S. courts of appeal are fairly liberal in allowing such briefs to be filed, particularly when the parties to the case consent to such filings, as they usually do. In *AU v. PFM* the parties consented to the filings of all the amicus curiae briefs. Rule 29 of the rules of the United States Courts of Appeals provides that "the United States or its officer or agency, or a State, Territory, Commonwealth, or the District of Columbia may file an amicus-curiae brief without the consent of the parties or leave of court. Any other amicus curiae may file a brief only by leave of court or if the brief states that all parties have consented to its filing."

44. "The Alliance Defense Fund is a legal alliance defending the right to hear and speak the Truth through strategy, training, funding, and litigation. ADF was founded for a unique purpose: to aggressively defend religious liberty by empowering our allies, recognizing that, together, we can accomplish far more than we can alone. We work tirelessly to assist them in their efforts through strategy, training, funding, and, where necessary, direct litigation through our own ADF legal team." www.alliancedefensefund.org (accessed February 27, 2007). The Alliance Defense Fund also works abroad to promote and defend the rights of evangelical dissenters to European religious establishments.

45. "The mission of the National Association of Evangelicals is to extend the kingdom of God through a fellowship of member denominations, churches, organizations, and individuals, demonstrating the unity of the body of Christ by standing for biblical truth, speaking with a representative voice, and serving the evangelical community through united action, cooperative ministry, and strategic planning." www.nae.net (accessed February 27, 2007).

46. The National Center for Neighborhood Enterprise (NCNE), founded in 1981 by Robert L. Woodson Sr., "provides effective community and faith-based organizations with training and technical assistance, links them to sources of support, and evaluates their experience for public policy." www.sourcewatch.org (accessed February 27, 2007).

47. "Since 1958, Teen Challenge International USA centers have been recognized nationally as providers of recovery services for those who desire to transform their lifestyle and develop a new life free from the devastation of drug and alcohol abuse. Since its beginning, Teen Challenge centers have founded their programs on the teachings of Jesus Christ. These Biblical truths have physically, mentally, emotionally and spiritually unchained the lives of thousands of addicts. In-

stead of 'dope' pushers, Teen Challenge ministries are serving as 'hope' pushers. As their personal testimony, Teen Challenge students often claim the scripture, 'I have plans to give you a hope and a future' (Jeremiah 29:11, NIV). For the past thirty years, I personally have found nothing more satisfying than investing my time and resources into lives of hurting individuals. America needs to know there is a new life waiting for them through the life-changing power of Jesus. Teen Challenge is in the business of providing a hope and a future for families as well as individuals who desire a positive and optimistic transformation in their lives. There is no better time than the present for you to get involved in an exciting ministry. Take my challenge as you browse through this website. Please ask God how you can make a difference in your community, state and nation." Mike Hodges, President of Teen Challenge International USA, www.teenchallengeusa.com (accessed February 27, 2007).

48. "Time To Fly Foundation (TTF) is a grass roots faith based, public supported 501c3 non-profit organization. TTF is devoted to helping formerly abused women and their children regain their God given worth, break the generational cycle and strengthen the family unit with the unconditional love and transforming power of Jesus Christ!" www.timetofly.org (accessed February 27, 2007).

49. "The Center's mission is to Equip Citizens, Develop Leaders, and Shape Policy in fulfillment of its purpose to Serve God, Advance Justice, and Transform Public Life." www.cpjustice.org (accessed February 27, 2007). See Daly, *God and the Welfare State*, pp. 59ff.

50. "ESA's Mission: To challenge and equip the church to be agents of God's redemption and transformation in the world. ESA pursues this mission through:

- Reflection on church and society from a biblical perspective
- Training in holistic ministry
- Linking people together for mutual learning & action"
  (www.esa-online.org [accessed February 27, 2007])

51. "The Coalition to Preserve Religious Freedom is a multi-faith alliance of faith-based organizations devoted to preserving the freedom and autonomy of religious organizations that partner with government or are affected by government regulation. Key concerns include preserving and extending the freedom of faith-based organizations to use religious criteria in hiring staff members (whether or not the organizations accept government funds) and ensuring that federal laws and statutes respect both the religious character of faith-based organizations and the religious liberty of the people they serve. Members of the coalition represent diverse religious traditions and diverse organizations that serve the public good. Coalition organizations meet monthly on the third Thursday of each month in Washington, DC. The Coalition works with citizens, government leaders, and the media to advocate public policies that protect the religious freedom of all citizens and religious organizations. Instead of supporting the idea of a 'naked public square' or an incorrect interpretation of 'separation of church and state' in which an ideology of secularism is permitted to marginalize and privatize all religious ways of life that should legitimately flourish in the public square, the Coalition advocates true government neutrality to promote full religious freedom for people

of all faiths consistent with the First Amendment of the U.S. Constitution." www.cpjustice.org/cprf (accessed February 27, 2007).

52. "The American Center for Law and Justice (ACLJ) is committed to insuring the ongoing viability of constitutional freedoms. By specializing in constitutional law, the ACLJ is dedicated to the concept that freedom and democracy are God-given inalienable rights that must be protected. The ACLJ engages in litigation, provides legal services, renders advice, counsels clients, provides education, and supports attorneys who are involved in defending the religious and civil liberties of Americans. As a non-profit organization, the ACLJ does not charge for its services and is dependent upon God and the resources He provides through the time, talent, and gifts of people who share our concerns and desire to protect our religious and constitutional freedoms." www.aclj.org (accessed February 27, 2007).

53. "The Catholic League is the nation's largest Catholic civil rights organization. Founded in 1973 by the late Father Virgil C. Blum, S.J., the Catholic League defends the right of Catholics—lay and clergy alike—to participate in American public life without defamation or discrimination. Motivated by the letter and the spirit of the First Amendment, the Catholic League works to safeguard both the religious freedom rights and the free speech rights of Catholics whenever and wherever they are threatened." www.catholicleague.org (accessed on February 27, 2007).

54. The brief was authored by Judge Roy Moore, formerly the chief justice of Alabama, who was removed from office for refusing to remove a stone monument of the Ten Commandments from the courthouse. "The Foundation for Moral Law exists to restore the knowledge of God in law and government and to acknowledge and defend the truth that man is endowed with rights, not by our fellow man, but by God! Please partner with us to achieve this important mission." www.morallaw.org (accessed February 27, 2007).

55. "Iowa Family Policy Center is a non-profit organization dedicated to equipping, empowering and encouraging Iowans to build communities where families are valued and strengthened." www.iowaprofamily.org (accessed February 27, 2007).

56. The goal of WallBuilders is "to exert a direct and positive influence in government, education, and the family by (1) educating the nation concerning the Godly foundation of our country; (2) providing information to federal, state, and local officials as they develop public policies which reflect Biblical values; and (3) encouraging Christians to be involved in the civic arena." www.wallbuilders.com (accessed February 27, 2007).

57. "The mission of the ACLU is to preserve all of these protections and guarantees: Your First Amendment rights—freedom of speech, association and assembly. Freedom of the press, and freedom of religion supported by the strict separation of church and state. Your right to equal protection under the law—equal treatment regardless of race, sex, religion or national origin. Your right to due process—fair treatment by the government whenever the loss of your liberty or property is at stake. Your right to privacy—freedom from unwarranted government intrusion into your personal and private affairs. We work also to extend rights to segments of our population that have traditionally been denied their rights, including Native Americans and other people of color; lesbi-

ans, gay men, bisexuals and transgendered people; women; mental-health patients; prisoners; people with disabilities; and the poor." www.aclu.org (accessed February 22, 2007).

58. "The American Correctional Chaplains Association. Since its 1885 founding . . . the ACCA has served as a professional organization for pastoral care personnel in the corrections field . . . The current ACCA roster . . . covers the entire spectrum of religious entities. . . . ACCA is committed to insuring that the religious practices of all offenders are legally and properly provided for in all correctional settings." Brief Amicus Curiae, p. 7.

59. "The American Catholic Correctional Chaplains Association is the official Catholic organization which supports and certifies correctional chaplains and is committed to promoting and securing Restorative Justice for victims, offenders, and the community." www.catholiccorrectionalchaplains.org (accessed February 27, 2007).

60. The mission of Jewish Prisoner Services International is "to provide direct spiritual, outreach and advocacy services for Jewish prisoners and their lovedones while concurrently working in conjunction with several major Jewish organizations and social service agencies. Assistance is rendered throughout the United States, Canada, Israel and elsewhere around the globe." www.jewishprisonerservices.org (accessed February 22, 2007).

61. "The American Jewish Congress is an association of Jewish Americans organized to defend Jewish interests at home and abroad through public policy advocacy, using diplomacy, legislation, and the courts." www.ajc.org (accessed February 22, 2007).

62. "The mission of the Baptist Joint Committee for Religious Liberty is to defend and extend God-given religious liberty for all, furthering the Baptist heritage that champions the principle that religion must be freely exercised, neither advanced nor inhibited by government" (www.bjcrl.org [accessed February 27, 2007]).

63. "The immediate object of the League is to stop, by appeals to reason and conscience and, if necessary, by appeals to law, the defamation of the Jewish people. Its ultimate purpose is to secure justice and fair treatment to all citizens alike and to put an end forever to unjust and unfair discrimination against and ridicule of any sect or body of citizens" *ADL Charter* October 1913. www.adl.org (accessed February 27, 2007).

64. "AJC Mission: Safeguard the welfare and security of Jews in the United States, in Israel, and throughout the world. Strengthen the basic principles of pluralism around the world as the best defense against anti-Semitism and other forms of bigotry, enhance the quality of American Jewish life by helping to ensure Jewish continuity and deepen ties between American and Israeli Jews." www.ajc.org (accessed February 27, 2007).

65. "The Council for Secular Humanism cultivates rational inquiry, ethical values, and human development through the advancement of secular humanism." www.secularhumanism.org (accessed February 27, 2007).

66. "The purpose of the Center for Inquiry is to promote and defend reason, science, and freedom of inquiry in all areas of human endeavor." www.centerforinquiry.net (accessed February 27, 2007).

67. For a discussion of patterns in the amici filings of the National Conference of Catholic Bishops, see Sullivan, "Indifferentism Redux."

68. "Each potential InnerChange candidate is handed a consent form explaining the voluntary nature of the program. In order to enter InnerChange, an inmate must sign the consent form, called the Participation & Release of Information Form, that states, in relevant part:

> I, the above mentioned member of the InnerChange Freedom Initiative agree to voluntarily participate in the Values Bases Pre-Release Program (the "Program") conduct [*sic*] by Prison Fellowship Ministries at the Newton, Iowa [*sic*].
> I understand the following:
>
> - That my decision to participate in the Program is of my own free will;
> - That my decision to participate in the Program will not affect my consideration for parole;
> - That my good time will not be increased because I participated in the Program;
> - That the Program contains religious content and is based upon Christian values and principles;
> - That I do not have to be of the Christian faith to participate in the Program;
> - That I will be assigned inmate work as well as treatment;
> - That my activities and schedule will be different from those to which I have been accustomed . . .
> - That I can discontinue my participation in the Program. I also understand that Prison Fellowship Ministries has the right to dismiss me from the Program if it so chooses.
> - That I will not be penalized in any way if I withdraw from the Program.

The form then provides spaces for the signed and printed name of the inmate, his Dept. of Corrections number, a witness signature, and the date." 432 F. Supp. 2d at 893, n. 26

69. 482 U.S. 78 (1987); Brief of State of Iowa, pp. 4–14.

70. Brief of Prison Fellowship Ministries, pp. 21–26.

71. See, for example, *Teen Ranch v. Udow*, 479 F. 3d 403 (2007), rejecting the indirect aid exception in the case of the placement of delinquent children in faith-intensive programs.

72. Brief at pp. 9ff.

73. "Evangelicals & Catholics Together: The Christian Mission in the Third Millennium," in *First Things* (May 1994). Available online at http://www.firstthings.com/article.php3?id_article=4454 (accessed July 20, 2007).

74. Appendix A to Catholic League Brief.

75. Brief, p. 24.

76. See Sullivan, "Neutralizing Religion; or, What is the Opposite of 'Faith-based?' "

77. Brief, p. 19.

78. Brief, p. 27.

79. Brief, p. 32.

80. Brief, p. 1.

81. Brief, p. 3.
82. 463 U.S. 783 (1983).
83. Brief at 29.
84. Brief, pp. 30–31.
85. This project is related to a parallel project undertaken by British imperialists. Vincent Pecora, speaking of the Clapham evangelicals, including William Wilberforce, the abolitionist and great hero of today's U.S. evangelicals, stated that "the fellowship that gathered in Clapham was also committed to using the British empire for the purpose of promoting social reform and Christianity around the globe. As Sir James Stephen remarked of Claphamite missionary efforts, 'the religion of Christ was conquering and to conquer. . . . [I]f anything in futurity could be certain, it was the dominion, over the whole earth, of the faith professed by every nation which retained either wisdom to investigate, or energy to act, or wealth to negotiate, or power to interpose in the questions which most deeply affect the entire race of man.' " Pecora goes on to analyze the secularization of that vision by the great grandchildren of Clapham, including the author Virginia Woolf. Pecora, *Secularization and Cultural Criticism*, pp. 163–64.
86. A similar argument is made in Fields, "Punishment and Crime," pp. 550–553.
87. Brief, *passim.*
88. *Ibid.*
89. "Memorial and Remonstrance against Religious Assessments" (1785).
90. Brief, p. 1.
91. Brief, p. 14.
92. An MP3 audio file of the oral argument is available on the Web site of the U.S. Court of Appeals for the Eighth Circuit, www.ca8.uscourts.gov.
93. *Ibid.*
94. Brief, p. 1.
95. The recent National Commission Report on prisons argues, instead, that the fact that state and federal money has not been spent on developing professional solutions to the problems of prisons should be a source of national shame.
96. 509 F. 3d at n.2.
97. *Hein v. FFRF*, 127 S. Ct. 2553 (2007).
98. See www.ffrf.org (accessed January 17, 2008).
99. 392 U.S. 83 (1968).
100. *Frothingham v. Mellon,* 262 U.S. 447 (1923).
101. José Casanova, *Public Religion in the Modern World.*
102. See, for example, essays written by members of Protestant "intentional" communities, some of them evangelical, modeled on monastic establishments: The Rutba House, *School(s) for Conversion.*
103. Law professor Mary Anne Case has argued that conservative evangelical Protestants protest the erosion of traditional marriage laws in such doom-laden terms as the "Protection of Marriage" bills because they have no institutional mechanisms of their own for policing these matters, as, to a limited extent, Jews and Catholics still do. Without an internal law of their own, she argues, American Protestants depend on state law. Were the state to stop regulating marriage, many Protestants have no ready-made institution to fill the gap. In other words, most

Protestants, particularly evangelical Protestants, need the state. Mary Anne Case, "Marriage Licenses." (One might argue that Jews, Catholics, and others in the U.S. who are on the "Protestant" end of their respective traditions have the same dependence.)

104. This trend is particularly notable from the perspective of religious studies, given the deep ambivalence within at least the critical edge of religious studies about seeing religion as essentially different, cross-culturally, from other aspects of society. See, for example, Jonathan Z. Smith, "Religion, Religions, Religious."

105. *Employment Division v. Smith*, 494 U.S. 872 (1990).

106. *Zelman v. Simmons-Harris*, 536 U.S. 639 (2002); *Hein v. FFRF*, 127 S. Ct. 2553 (2007).

107. 530 U.S. 793 (2000).

108. Ira C. Lupu and Robert W. Tuttle, "The Faith-Based Initiative and the Constitution"; idem, *The State of the Law 2007.*

109. 324 F. 3d 880 (2003).

110. 324 F. 3d at 883.

Conclusion

1. Alain Supiot, *Homo Juridicus: On the Anthropological Function of the Law*, p. 95. Supiot is eloquent on the challenges facing those who would have confidence in the promise of law today.

2. For a range of current thinking on political theology, see Hent deVries and Lawrence E. Sullivan, *Political Theologies.*

3. For critiques of legal positivism from this perspective, see, among others, Robert A. Yelle, *The Disenchantment of Language*; Peter Goodrich, *Oedipus Lex*; and Costas Douzinas and Ronnie Warrington, "Antigone's Law."

4. See, among many others, *Sacred and Secular* by Pippa Norris and Ronald Inglehardt, for whom the explanation arises from anxiety produced by mobility; and *The Churching of America, 1776–2005* by Roger Finke and Rodney Stark, for whom the explanation rests in the vitality of the entrepreneurial competitiveness of the religious market in the U.S. produced by disestablishment. In my view, it is difficult to overstate the distinctiveness and extent of U.S. *legal* disestablishment.

5. W. Clark Gilpin, "Secularism: Religious, Irreligious, and Areligious."

6. Ibid.

7. This is not an entirely new idea. Historians and sociologists of U.S. religion have described this reorganization over the last fifty years. Two significant articulations of that reorganization are Mead, *The Lively Experiment*; Howe, *The Garden and the Wilderness*; and Robert Wuthnow, *The Restructuring of American Religion.*

8. Harvey Cox, *The Secular City.*

9. Mark deWolfe Howe, *The Garden and the Wilderness.*

10. Iowa Code §904.511 (2008).

11. *Kitzmiller v. Dover Area School District*, 400 F. Supp. 2d 707 (2005).

12. See, for example, Catherine Albanese, *Nature Religion in America.*

13. Areligious secularism might also usefully name many of the religious spaces observed in Nancy Ammerman, *Everyday Religion.*

14. A version of this section of the chapter was published as "The New Disestablishment," in *Religion and American Culture: A Journal of Interpretation* 18:1 (winter 2008).

15. *Freedom From Religion Foundation v. Nicholson,* 469 F. Supp. 2d 609 (W. D. of Wisc., 2007). See also *Bader v. Wren*, 2008 DNH 26 (District of New Hampshire), finding that requiring plaintiff prisoner to attend the Alternatives to Violence program provided by a private entity with Quaker roots and teaching that "the true source of nonviolence is spiritual power," what they call Transforming Power, did not constitute an establishment of religion because it is individualistic and has no reference to a higher power.

16. 469 F. Supp. 2d at 612.

17. 469 F. Supp. 2d at 613.

18. Accreditation for VA facilities is sought from the Joint Commission on Accreditation of Healthcare Organizations.

19. 469 F. Supp. 2d at 623.

20. James A. Beckford and Sophie Gilliat, *Religion in Prisons.*

21. James A. Beckford, Danièle Joly, and Farhad Khosrokhavar, *Muslims in Prison.* For a discussion of religious accommodation in prisons in the former East Germany, see Irene Becci, "Religion Through Prison."

22. However, the French government is involved in managing religion to a far greater degree than is permitted in the U.S. See a report on the status of the French political commitment to laïcité: *Le Rapport de la Commission Stasi sur la Laïcité,* issued on July 3, 2003, and published in *Le Monde* on December 12, 2003. See also John Bowen, *Why the French Don't Like Headscarves*, for a discussion of the current debate about Islam and French *laïcisme.*

23. This is so, at least as described by the court. Because the decision was on a motion for summary judgment, the full evidentiary record has not yet been developed. It is entirely possible, even likely, that such a record will reveal a much more uneven practice by the VA's many facilities reflecting instances of all three of Gilpin's types of secularism.

24. Stevens Deposition, p. 13.

Bibliography

Legal Cases

Agostini v. Felton, 521 U.S. 203 (1997).
Allegheny v. ACLU, 492 U.S. 573 (1989).
Americans United v. Prison Fellowship Ministries, 432 F. Supp. 2d 862 (S.D. Iowa 2006).
Americans United v. Prison Fellowship Ministries, 509 F. 3d 406 (2007).
Bader v. Wren, 2008 DNH 26 (District of New Hampshire),
Beard v. Banks, 547 U.S. 1001 (2006).
Brown v. Board of Education, 347 U.S. 483 (1954).
Christianson v. Leavitt, No. 482 F. Supp 2d 1237 (W. D. Washington 2007).
Cutter v. Wilkinson, 125 S. Ct. 2113 (2005).
Employment Division v. Smith, 494 U.S. 872 (1990).
Everson v. Board of Education, 330 U.S. 1 (1947).
Flast v. Cohen, 392 U.S. 83 (1968).
Freedom From Religion Foundation v. Gonzales, 2006 U.S. Dist. LEXIS 66745 (W.D. Wisc. 2006).
Freedom From Religion Foundation v. Nicholson, 469 F. Supp. 2d 609 (W.D. Wisc. 2007).
Freedom From Religion Foundation v. Richardson (05-CV-1168, D. N.M. 2005).
Freedom From Religion Foundation v. McCalllum, 324 F.3d 880 (2003).
Frothingham v. Mellon, 262 U.S. 447 (1923).
Hein v. Freedom From Religion Foundation, 127 S. Ct. 2553 (2007).
Ho Ah Kow v. Nunan, 12. Cas. 252, No. 6546 (C.C.D. Cal 1879).
Kerr v. Farrey, 95 F. 3d 472 (7th Cir. 1996).
Kitzmiller v. Dover Area School District, 400 F. Supp. 2d 707 (2005).
Lee v. Weisman 505 U.S. 577 (1992).
Lemon v. Kurtzman 403 U.S. 602 (1971).
Lynch v. Donnelly, 465 U.S. 668 (1983).
Marsh v. Chambers 463 U.S. 783 (1983).
Mitchell v. Helms, 530 U.S. 793 (2000).
In re: Navy Chaplaincy, 512 F. Supp. 2d 58 (2007).
O'Lone v. Shabazz, 482 U.S. 342 (1987).
Parents Involved in Community Schools v. Seattle School District No. 1, 127 S. Ct. 2738 (2007).
Roe v. Wade, 410 U.S. 113 (1973).
Teen Ranch v. Udow, 479 F. 3d 403 (2007).
Turner v. Safley, 482 U.S. 78 (1987).
Warner v. Boca Raton, 64 F. Supp. 2d 1272 (1999).
Warner v. Orange County, 115 F. 3d 1068 (2d Cir 1997).

Williams v. Lara, 52 S.W. 3d 171 (2001).
Zelman v. Harris, 536 U.S. 639 (2002).

Statutes

Internal Revenue Code 26 U.S. Code §501(c)(3).
Personal Responsibility and Work Opportunity Reconciliation Act of 1996 (PRWORA). Public Law 104-193. (1996).
Religious Land Use and Institutionalized Persons Act (RLUIPA) 42 U.S. Code § 2000cc-1 et seq.

Books and Articles

Adams, Jay E. *Competent to Counsel: Introduction to Nouthetic Counseling.* Grand Rapids: Ministry Resources Library, 1970.
Agamben, Giorgio. *Homo Sacer: Sovereign Power and Bare Life.* Translated by Daniel Heller-Roazen. Stanford: Stanford University Press, 1998.
Albanese, Catherine. *Nature Religion in America: From the Algonkian Indians to the New Age.* Chicago: University of Chicago Press, 1990.
Allen, Francis A. *The Decline of the Rehabilitative Ideal: Penal Policy and Social Purpose.* New Haven: Yale University Press, 1981.
———. *The Habits of Legality: Criminal Justice and the Rule of Law.* New York: Oxford University Press, 1996.
American Friends Service Committee. *Struggle for Justice: A Report on Crime and Punishment in America.* New York: Hill and Wang, 1971.
Amman, Nawal H., Robert R. Weaver, and Sam Saxon. "Muslims in Prison: A Case Study from Ohio State Prisons." *International Journal of Offender Therapy and Comparative Criminology* 48 (2004): 414–28.
Ammerman, Nancy. *Bible Believers: Fundamentalists in the Modern World.* New Brunswick, N.J.: Rutgers University Press, 1987.
———, ed. *Everyday Religion: Observing Modern Religious Lives.* Oxford: Oxford University Press, 2007.
Anderson, Elijah. "Going Straight: The Story of a Young Inner-City Ex-Convict." In *Mass Imprisonment: Social Causes and Consequences*, ed. David Garland. London: Sage, 2001.
Anderson, Neil T. *Victory over the Darkness: Realizing the Power of Your Identity in Christ.* 2nd ed. Ventura, Calif.: Regal Books, 2000.
———. *The Bondage Breaker.* Eugene, Ore.: Harvest House, 1990.
———. *Breaking Through to Spiritual Maturity: Overcoming the Personal and Spiritual Strongholds That Can Keep You from Experiencing True Freedom in Christ.* Gospel Light Living Word Curriculum, 1992.
Anderson, Neil T., Pete Vander Hook, and Sue Vander Hook. *Spiritual Protection for Your Children: Helping Your Children and Family Find Their Identity, Freedom, and Security in Christ.* Ventura, Calif.: Regal Books, 1996.

Anderson, Neil T., and Rich Miller. *Getting Anger under Control*. Eugene, Ore.: Harvest House, 2002.

Anderson, Neil T., Mike Quarles, and Julia Quarles. *Freedom from Addiction: Breaking the Bondage of Addiction and Finding Freedom in Christ*. Ventura, Calif.: Regal Books, 1996.

Appiah, Kwame Anthony. *Cosmopolitanism: Ethics in a World of Strangers*. New York: W. W. Norton, 2006.

Arnold, Dan. "On Semantics and *Saṃketa*: Thoughts on a Neglected Problem with Buddhist *Apoha* Doctrine." *Journal of Indian Philosophy* 34 (2006): 415–78.

Asad, Talal. *Formations of the Secular: Christianity, Islam, Modernity*. Palo Alto, Calif.: Stanford University Press, 2003.

———. *Genealogies of Religion: Disciplines and Reasons of Power in Christianity and Islam*. Baltimore, Md.: Johns Hopkins University Press, 1993.

Bailey, Waylon, and Todd Hudson. *Step by Step through the Old Testament*. Sunday School Board of the Southern Baptist Convention, 1991.

Balmer, Randall. *Mine Eyes Have Seen the Glory: A Journey into the Evangelical Subculture in America*. New York: Oxford University Press, 1989.

———. *Thy Kingdom Come: An Evangelical's Lament*. New York: Basic Books, 2006.

Banchoff, Thomas, ed. *Democracy and the New Religious Pluralism*. Oxford: Oxford University Press, 2007.

Bandes, Susan. "When Victims Seek Closure: Forgiveness, Vengeance, and the Role of Government." *Fordham Urban Law Journal* 27 (June 2000): 1599–1606.

Bannerjee, Neela. "Accolades, Some Tearful, in Pastor's Twilight Years." *New York Times*, June 1, 2007.

———. "Prisons to Return Purged Items to Chapels." *New York Times*, September 26, 2007.

Barker, Eileen, James A. Beckford, and Karel Dobbelaere, eds. *Secularization, Rationalism and Sectarianism: Essays in Honor of Bryan R. Wilson*. Oxford: Clarendon, 1993.

Barnes, Bart. "Harold Hughes Dies at 74; Iowa Governor; U.S. Senator." *Washington Post*, October 25, 1996, p. D4.

Bartkowski, John P. *The Promise Keepers: Servants, Soldiers, and Godly Men*. New Brunswick, N.J.: Rutgers University Press, 2004.

Barton, David. *Benjamin Rush: Signer of the Declaration of Independence*. Aledo, Tex.: Wallbuilder Press, 1999.

Baubérot, Jean, and Séverine Mathieu. *Religion, modernité et culture au Royaume-Uni et en France*. Paris: Gallimard, 2000.

Baxter, Richard. *Holy Commonwealth*. London: Thomas Underhill and Francis Tyton, 1659.

Becci, Irene. "Religion Through Prison: The Institutionalization of *Liminality* in the Secular Context of Eastern Germany" in *After Pluralism*, ed. Courtney Bender and Pamela Klassen. New York: Columbia University Press, 2009.

Beckett, Katherine, and Bruce Western. "Governing Social Marginality: Welfare, Incarceration, and the Transformation of State Policy." In *Mass Imprisonment: Social Causes and Consequences*, ed. David Garland. London: Sage, 2001.

Beckford, James A., and Sophie Gilliat. *Religion in Prisons: Equal Rites in a Multi-faith Society.* Cambridge: Cambridge University Press, 1998.

Beckford, James A., Danièle Joly, and Farhad Khosrokhavar. *Muslims in Prison: Challenge and Chance in Britain and France.* New York: Palgrave, 2005.

Bender, Courtney. *Heaven's Kitchen: Living Religion at God's Love We Deliver.* Chicago: University of Chicago Press, 2003.

Bender, Courtney, and Pamela Klassen, eds. *After Pluralism.* New York: Columbia University Press, 2009.

Benevides, Gustavo. "Modernity." In *Critical Terms for Religious Studies*, ed. Mark C. Taylor. Chicago: University of Chicago Press, 1998.

Bennett, William J., John J. DiIulio Jr., and John P. Walters. *Body Count: Moral Poverty . . . and How to Win America's War on Crime and Drugs.* New York: Simon and Schuster, 1996.

Berger, Peter L. "Pluralism, Protestantism, and the Voluntary Principle." In *Democracy and the New Religious Pluralism*, ed. Thomas Banchoff. Oxford: Oxford University Press, 2007.

———. *The Sacred Canopy: Elements of a Sociological Theory of Religion.* Garden City, N.Y.: Doubleday, 1967.

Berman, Harold. *Faith and Order: The Reconciliation of Law and Religion.* Atlanta, Ga.: Scholars Press, 1993.

Bevere, John. *Undercover: The Promise of Protection under His Authority.* Nashville, Tenn.: Nelson Books, 2001.

Binder, Guyora. "Democracy and Punishment: Punishment Theory: Moral or Political?" *Buffalo Criminal Law Review* 5 (2002): 321–71.

Blackaby, Henry T., and Claude V. King. *Experiencing God: How to Live the Full Adventure of Knowing and Doing the Will of God.* Nashville, Tenn.: Broadman and Holman, 1994.

———. *Experiencing God: Knowing and Doing the Will of God.* Nashville, Tenn.: Broadman and Holman, 2004.

———. *Hearing God's Voice.* Nashville, Tenn.: Broadman and Holman, 2002.

Blackaby, Henry T., and Melvin D. Blackaby. *Experiencing God Together: God's Plan to Touch Your World.* Nashville, Tenn.: Broadman and Holman, 2002.

Blackaby, Henry, and Tom Blackaby. *The Man God Uses.* Nashville, Tenn.: Broadman and Holman, 1999.

Blum, Edward J. *Reforging the White Republic: Race, Religion, and American Nationalism: 1865–1898.* Baton Rouge: Louisiana University Press, 2005.

Blumenthal, Max. "Born Again, Again: A New Biography of Charles Colson Is Yet Another Cover-up." *Washington Monthly*, July–August 2005.

Bowen, John. *Why the French Don't Like Headscarves.* Princeton, N.J.: Princeton University Press, 2006.

Bragonier, David, and Debbie Bragonier, with Kimn S. Gollnick. *Getting Your Financial House in Order: A Floorplan for Managing Your Money.* Nashville, Tenn.: Broadman and Holman, 2003.

Brandt, Henry, and Kerry L. Skinner. *Heart of the Problem.* Nashville, Tenn.: Broadman and Holman, 1997.

Brandt, Henry, and Kerry L. Skinner. "White Paper." Available on the IFI Web site at http://www.ifiprison.org/generic.asp?ID=2180 (accessed January 17, 2003).

Branham, Lynn S. " 'Go and Sin No More': The Constitutionality of Governmentally Funded Faith-based Prison Units." *U. Michigan Journal of Law Reform* 37 (2004): 291–352.

Brault, Emily. "Sweating in the Joint: Personal and Cultural Renewal and Healing through Sweat Lodge Practice by Native Americans in Prison." Ph.d. dissertation, Vanderbilt University, May 4, 2005. URN: etd-07012005–131713.

Brodsky, Alyn. *Benjamin Rush: Patriot and Physician.* New York: St. Martin's, 2004.

Brook, Daniel. "When God Goes to Prison." *Legal Affairs*, May–June 2003.

Browning, Don S., and Terry D. Cooper. *Religious Thought and the Modern Psychologies.* 2nd ed. Minneapolis: Fortress, 2004.

Bruce, Steve. *A House Divided: Protestantism, Schism, and Secularization.* London: Routledge, 1990.

Bucko, Raymond A. *The Lakota Ritual of the Sweat Lodge: History and Contemporary Practice.* Lincoln: University of Nebraska Press, 1998.

Bunyan, John. *The pilgrim's progress from this world to that which is to come: delivered under the similitude of a dream, wherein is discovered the manner of his setting out, his dangerous journey, and safe arrival at the desired countrey.* London: Nath Ponder, 1678.

Burns, Robert P. *A Theory of the Trial.* Princeton, N.J.: Princeton University Press, 1999.

Burnside, Jonathan. With Nancy Loucks, Joanna R. Adler, and Gerry Rose. *My Brother's Keeper: Faith-based Units in Prisons.* Devon, England: Willan, 2005.

Burson, Scott R., and Jerry L. Wallis. *C. S. Lewis and Francis Schaeffer: Lessons for a New Century from the Most Influential Apologists of Our Time.* Downers Grove, Ill.: Intervarsity, 1998.

Butler, Jon. *Awash in a Sea of Faith: Christianizing the American People.* Cambridge, Mass.: Harvard University Press, 1990.

Caldwell, Patricia. *The Puritan Conversion Narrative: The Beginnings of American Expression.* Cambridge: Cambridge University Press, 1983.

Carlson, Ronald L., Edward J. Imwinkelried, Edward J. Kionka, and Kristine Strachan. *Evidence: Teaching Materials for an Age of Science and Statutes.* Newark, N.J.: LexisNexis, 2007.

Carnochan, W. B. "The Literature of Confinement." In *The Oxford History of the Prison*, ed. Norval Morris and David Rothman. Oxford: Oxford University Press, 1995.

Carpenter, Joel. *Revive Us Again: The Reawakening of American Fundamentalism.* Oxford: Oxford University Press, 1997.

Carter, J. Kameron. "Race and the Experience of Death: Theologically Reappraising American Evangelicalism." In *The Cambridge Companion to Evangelical Theology*, ed. Timothy Larsen and Daniel J. Treier. Cambridge: Cambridge University Press, 2007.

Casanova, José. *Public Religions in the Modern World.* Chicago: University of Chicago Press, 1992.

Case, Mary Anne. "Marriage Licenses." *Minnesota Law Review* 89 (2005): 1758–97.

Cates, Patrick B. "Faith-Based Prisons and the Establishment Clause: The Constitutionality of Employing Religion as an Engine of Correctional Policy." *Willamette Law Review* 41 (2005): 777–826.

Caudill, David, and Lewis LaRue. *No Magic Wand: The Idealization of Science in Law.* New York: Rowman and Littlefield, 2006.

Chaves, Mark. "Religious Congregations and Welfare Reform: Who Will Take Advantage of 'Charitable Choice' ?" *American Sociological Review* 64 (1999): 836–46.

———. "Secularization as Declining Religious Authority." *Social Forces* 72 (March 1994): 749–74.

Cloud, Henry. *Changes That Heal: How to Understand Your Past to Ensure a Healthier Future.* Grand Rapids, Mich.: Zondervan, 1992.

———. *Boundaries: When to Say YES; When to Say NO; To Take Charge of Your Life.* Grand Rapids, Mich.: Zondervan, 1992.

Colson, Charles W. *Born Again.* Grand Rapids, Mich.: Chosen Books, 1976.

———. "Capital Punishment: A Personal Statement." *oldspeak: an online journal devoted to intellectual freedom.* Rutherford Institute, November 11, 2002.

———. "Evangelizing for Evil in Our Prisons: Radical Islamists Seek to Turn Criminals into Terrorists." *Wall Street Journal,* June 24, 2002.

———. *The Faith: What Christians Believe, Why They Believe It, and Why It Matters.* With Harold Fickett. Nashville, Tenn.: Zondervan, 2008.

———. *The Good Life.* With Harold Fickett. Wheaton, Ill.: Tyndale House, 2005.

———. "Kingdoms in Conflict." *First Things* 67 (1996): 34–38.

———. *Life Sentence.* Grand Rapids, Mich.: Barker Book House, 1979.

———. "The Question Is: What Is Just?" under "Issues and Research." www.pfm.org.

Colson, Charles W., and Nancy Pearcey. *How Now Shall We Live?* Wheaton, Ill.: Tyndale House, 1999.

Colson, Charles W., and Ellen Vaughn. *Being the Body.* Nashville, Tenn.: Thomas Nelson, 2003.

Columbia Human Rights Law Review. *A Jailhouse Lawyer's Manual.* www.columbia.edu/cu/hrlr/.

Cover, Robert. "*Nomos* and Narrative." *Harvard Law Review* 97 (1983):4–68.

Cox, Harvey. *The Secular City: Secularization and Urbanization in Theological Perspective.* New York: Macmillan, 1965.

Curry, Thomas J. *Farewell to Christendom: The Future of Church and State in America.* Oxford: Oxford University Press, 2001.

———. *The First Freedoms: Church and State in America to the Passage of the First Amendment.* Oxford: Oxford University Press, 1986.

Daly, Lew. *God and the Welfare State.* Somerville, Mass.: Boston Review, 2006.

———. "The Subversive Moral Essence of President Bush's Faith-Based Initiative." *Sightings,* November 5, 2006.

Daunis, Angela, and Angela Paneck, eds. *Re-enter: The Social Cost of Incarceration.* Published for the Annie E. Casey Foundation through the E. T. Meredith Center for Magazine studies. Available at www.reentrymediaoutreach.org/pdfs/reenter.pdf (accessed May 23, 2008).

Davie, Grace. *Europe: The Exceptional Case: Parameters of Faith in the Modern World.* London: Darton, Longman, and Todd, 2002.

———. *Religion in Modern Europe: A Memory Mutates.* Oxford: Oxford University Press, 2000.

DelFattore, Joan. *The Fourth R: Conflicts over Religion in America's Public Schools.* New Haven, Conn.: Yale University Press, 2004.

deVries, Hent, ed. *Religion: Beyond a Concept.* New York: Fordham University Press, 2007.

deVries, Hent, and Lawrence Sullivan. *Political Theologies.* New York: Fordham, 2006.

DiIulio, John. *Godly Republic: A Centrist Blueprint for America's Faith-Based Future.* Berkeley: University of California Press, 2007.

———. *Governing Prisons: A Comparative Study of Correctional Management.* New York: Free Press, 1987.

———. "Letter of Apology." *Esquire,* January 2003.

———. *No Escape: The Future of American Corrections.* New York: Basic Books, 1991.

DiIulio, John, and E. J. Dionne Jr. *What's God Got to Do with the American Experiment?: Essays on Religion and Politics.* Washington, D.C.: Brookings Institution, 2000.

Douzinas, Costas, Peter Goodrich, and Yifat Hachamovitch, eds. *Politics, Postmodernity and Critical Legal Studies: The Legality of the Contingent.* London: Routledge, 1994.

Douzinas, Costas, and Ronnie Warrington. "Antigone's Law: A Genealogy of Jurisprudence." In *Politics, Postmodernity, and Critical Legal Studies: The Legality of the Contingent*, ed. Costas Douzinas, Peter Goodrich, and Yifat Hachamovitch. London: Routledge, 1994.

Downes, David. "The *Macho* Penal Economy: Mass Incarceration in the United States—A European Perspective." In *Mass Imprisonment: Social Causes and Consequences*, ed. David Garland. London: Sage, 2001.

DuBois, W. E. B. *The Souls of Black Folk: Essays and Sketches.* Chicago: A.C. McClurg, 1903.

Dubber, Markus Dirk. "Toward a Constitutional Law of Crime and Punishment." *Hastings Law Journal* 55 (2004): 509–72.

Duff, Antony. "Legal Punishment." In *Stanford Encyclopedia of Philosophy,* ed. Edward N. Zalta. Online publication of the Metaphysics Research Lab. Available at http://plato.stanford.edu/.

Durrant Group. *State of Iowa Systematic Study for the State Correctional System* (2007). http://www.doc.state.ia.us/.

Eicher, Tim. "Scaling the Wall: Faith-based Prison Programs and the Establishment Clause." *Georgetown Journal of Law and Public Policy* 5 (2007): 221–40.

Eldridge, John. *Wild at Heart: Discovering the Secret of a Man's Soul.* Nashville, Tenn.: Nelson Books, 2001.

Emerson, Michael O., and Christian Smith. *Divided by Faith: Evangelical Religion and the Problem of Race in America.* Oxford: Oxford University Press, 2000.

Engel, David. "Globalization and the Decline of Legal Consciousness: Torts, Ghosts, and Karma in Thailand." *Law and Social Inquiry* 30 (Summer 2005): 469–514.

Farris, Anne. "Controversial Christian Prison Program Cites Recent Supreme Court Ruling in Its Appeal." Roundtable on Religion and Social Welfare Policy, July 2, 2007. www.religionandsocialpolicy.org (accessed May 23, 2008).

———. "Probe of Religious Discrimination in Prisons Includes Faith-Based Ministries." The Roundtable on Religion and Social Welfare Policy, February 12, 2008. Available at www.religionandsocialpolicy.org (accessed May 23, 2008).

Ferrari, Silvio. "The New Wine and the Old Cask. Tolerance, Religion, and Law in Contemporary Europe." *Ratio Juris* 10 (March 1997): 75–89.

Fields, Richard R. W. "Punishment and Crime: Perks for Prisoners Who Pray: Using the Coercion Test to Decide Establishment Clause Challenges to Faith-Based Prison Units." *University of Chicago Legal Forum* (2005): 541–67.

Finke, Roger, and Rodney Stark. *The Churching of America, 1776–2005: Winners and Losers in Our Religious Economy.* 2nd ed. New Brunswick, N.J.: Rutgers University Press, 2005.

Fish, Stanley. "Mission Impossible: Settling the Just Bounds between Church and State." *Columbia Law Review* 97 (1997): 2255–2333.

———. *The Trouble with Principle.* Cambridge, Mass.: Harvard University Press, 1999.

Fitzpatrick, Peter. " 'The Damned Word': Culture and Its (In)compatibility with Law." *Law, Culture, and the Humanities* 1 (2005): 2–13.

Foucault, Michel. *Discipline and Punish: The Birth of the Prison.* Translated by Alan Sheridan. New York: Vintage Books, 1977.

French, Rebecca. "Shopping for Religion: The Change in Everyday Religious Practice and Its Importance for Law." *Buffalo Law Review* 51 (2003): 127–98.

Freud, Sigmund. *Civilization & Die Weltanschauung* (1918).

Garland, David. *The Culture of Control: Crime and Social Order in Contemporary Society.* Chicago: University of Chicago Press, 2001.

Garland, David, ed. *Mass Imprisonment: Social Causes and Consequences.* London: Sage, 2001.

Garofano, Anthony. "Avoiding Virtual Justice: Video-Teleconference Testimony In Federal Criminal Trials." *Catholic University Law Review* 56 (2007): 683–714.

Garside, Richard, and Will McMahon, eds. "Does Criminal Justice Work? The 'Right for the Wrong Reasons' Debate." Crime and Society Foundation, Centre for Law and Justice Studies, King's College, London, October 2006.

Gauchet, Marcel. *The Disenchantment of the World: A Political History of Religion.* Translated by Oscar Burge. Princeton, N.J.: Princeton University Press, 1997.

Geertz, Clifford. "Law and Fact in Comparative Perspective." In *Local Knowledge: Further Essays in Interpretive Anthropology*. New York: Basic Books, 1983.

Geltner, Guy. *The Medieval Prison: A Social History*. Princeton: Princeton University Press, 2008.

Getter, Lisa. "Showing Faith in Discretion." *Los Angeles Times*, September 27, 2002.

Gibbons, John J., and Nicholas de B. Katzenbach, co-chairs. *Confronting Confinement: A Report of the Commission on Safety and Abuse in America's Prisons* (2006).

Giles, Paul. *American Catholic Arts and Fictions: Culture, Ideology, Aesthetics*. Cambridge: Cambridge University Press, 1992.

Gilmore, Glenda. *Defying Dixie: The Radical Roots of Civil Rights, 1919–1950*. New York: W.W. Norton, 2008.

Gilpin, W. Clark. "Secularism: Religious, Irreligious, and Areligious." *The Religion and Culture Web Forum*. http://marty-center.uchicago.edu/webforum (March 2007) (accessed May 23, 2008).

Golash, Deirdre. *The Case against Punishment: Retribution, Crime Prevention, and the Law*. New York: New York University Press, 2005.

Goldstein, Jan. *Console and Classify: The French Psychiatric Profession in the Nineteenth Century*. With a New Afterword. Chicago: University of Chicago Press, 2001. First published, 1987.

Goodrich, Peter. *Oedipus Lex: Psychoanalysis, History, Law*. Berkeley: University of California Press, 1995.

Goodstein, Laurie, and Sheryl Gay Stolberg. "Pope Praises Americans' Faith and Warns of Perils of Secularism." *New York Times*, April 17, 2008.

Gordon, Sarah Barringer. *The Mormon Question: Polygamy and Constitutional Conflict in Nineteenth-Century America*. Chapel Hill: University of North Carolina Press, 2002.

———. *The Spirit of the Law: Religion and Litigation in the Twentieth Century*. Cambridge, Mass.: Harvard University Press, forthcoming.

Gottschalk, Marie. "Black Flower: Prisons and the Future of Incarceration." *Annals of the American Academy of Political and Social Science* 582 (2002): 195–227.

———. *The Prison and the Gallows: The Politics of Mass Incarceration in America*. Cambridge: Cambridge University Press, 2006.

Gottschalk, Peter. *Beyond Hindu and Muslim: Multiple Identity in Narratives from Village India*. Oxford: Oxford University Press, 2000.

Green, Joshua. "Take Two: How Hillary Clinton Turned Herself into the Consummate Washington Player." *Atlantic Monthly*, November 2006.

Greenawalt, Kent. *Religion and the Constitution*. Vol. 2, *Establishment and Fairness*. Princeton, N.J.: Princeton University Press, 2008.

Grubb, Norman. *Modern Viking: The Story of Abraham Vereide, Pioneer in Christian Leadership*. Grand Rapids, Mich.: Zondervan, 1961.

Gutterman, Melvin. "Prison Objectives and Human Dignity: Reaching a Mutual Accommodation." *Brigham Young University Law Review* (1992): 857–915.

Hallett, Michael A. "Faith-based Corrections as Symbolic Crusade." Unpublished paper. Available at www.unf.edu (accessed May 23, 2008).

Hallinan, Joseph T. *Going up the River: Travels in a Prison Nation.* New York: Random House, 2001.

Hamburger, Philip. *Separation of Church and State.* Cambridge, Mass.: Harvard University Press, 2000.

Handy, Robert T. *A Christian America: Protestant Hopes and Historical Realities.* 2nd ed. Oxford: Oxford University Press, 1984.

Hart, D. G. "When Is a Fundamentalist a Modernist? J. Gresham Machen, Cultural Modernism, and Conservative Protestantism." *Journal of the American Academy of Religion* 65 (Fall 1997): 605–33.

Hatch, Nathan O. *The Democratization of American Christianity.* New Haven, Conn.: Yale University Press, 1989.

Hauerwas, Stanley. *With the Grain of the Universe: The Church's Witness and Natural Theology.* Grand Rapids, Mich.: Brazos, 2001.

Hercik, Jeanette, Richard Lewis, and Bradley Myles. *Development of a Guide to Resources on Faith-based Organizations in Criminal Justice.* National Institute of Corrections, 2004.

Hervieu-Léger, Danielle. " 'What Scripture Tells Me': Spontaneity and Regulation within the Catholic Charismatic Renewal." In *Lived Religion in America: Toward a History of Practice*, ed. David D. Hall. Princeton, N.J.: Princeton University Press, 1997.

Higgins, Andrew. "In Europe God Is (Not) Dead: Christian Groups Are Growing, Faith Is More Public. Is Supply-side Economics the Explanation?" *Wall Street Journal*, July 14–15, 2007.

Hirschkind, Charles. *The Ethical Soundscape: Cassette Sermons and Islamic Counterpublics.* New York: Columbia University Press, 2006.

Hollinger, David A. "The Knower and the Artificer." *American Quarterly* 39 (Spring 1987): 37–55.

Honeymar, Michael G., Jr. "Alcoholics Anonymous as a Condition of Drunk Driving Probation: When Does It Amount to Establishment of Religion." *Columbia Law Review* 97 (1997): 437–72.

Howe, Daniel Walker. "The Evangelical Movement and Political Culture in the North During the Second Party System." *Journal of American History* 77 (March 1991): 1216–39.

Howe, Mark deWolfe. *The Garden and the Wilderness: Religion and Government in American Constitutional History.* Chicago: University of Chicago Press, 1965.

Hughes, Claire. "Ohio Group Details Ways to Expand Faith-Based Prison Programs." Roundtable on Religion and Social Welfare Policy, November 28, 2006.

———. "Potential for Widespread Fallout in Ruling against Iowa Faith-Based Prison Program." Roundtable on Religion and Social Welfare Policy, June 6, 2006. Available at http://www.religionandsocialpolicy.org/news/article.cfm?id=4384 (accessed July 20, 2007).

Hughes, Harold E., with Dick Schneider. *The Man from Ida Grove: A Senator's Personal Story.* Lincoln, Va.: Chosen Books, 1979.

Hunt, Stephen. *The* Alpha *Enterprise: Evangelism in a Post-Christian Era*. Aldershot, U.K.: Ashgate, 2004.

Hunt, T. W., and Claude King. *In God's Presence: Your Daily Guide to a Meaningful Prayer Life*. Nashville, Tenn.: LifeWay, 1994.

Ignatieff, Michael. *A Just Measure of Pain: The Penitentiary in the Industrial Revolution, 1750–1850*. London: Penguin Books, 1970.

Iowa Department of Corrections. "The First 20 Years." *Inside Iowa's DOC* 1, no. 1 (October 2003).

———. "Population Growth: Report to the Board of Corrections," July 2006.

Iowa Governor's Task Force. "Report on the Overrepresentation of African-Americans in Prison," December 2001.

James, William. *The Variety of Religious Experience*. New York: Longmans, Green, 1902.

Johnson, Byron R. "Assessing the Impact of Religious Programs and Prison Industry on Recidivism: An Exploratory Study." *Texas Journal of Corrections* (February 2002).

Johnson, Greg. "Incarcerated Tradition: Native Hawaiian Identities and Religious Practice in Prison Contexts." In *Historicizing Tradition in the Study of Religion*, ed. Steven Engler and Gregory P. Grieve. Berlin: Walter de Gruyter, 2005.

Kaplan, Benjamin J. *Divided by Faith: Religious Conflict and the Practice of Toleration in Early Modern Europe*. Cambridge, Mass.: Harvard University Press, 2007.

Kemp, James W. *The Gospel according to Dr. Seuss*. Valley Forge, Pa.: Judson Press, 2004.

Kennedy, Sheila Suess, and Wolfgang Bielefield. *Faith-Based Partnerships: The View from the States*. Washington, D.C.: Georgetown University Press, 2006.

Kerley, Kent R., Todd L. Matthews, and Troy C. Blanchard. "Religiosity, Religious Participation, and Negative Prison Behaviors." *Journal for the Scientific Study of Religion* 44 (2005): 443–57.

Kippenberg, Hans. *Discovering Religious History in the Modern Age*. Princeton, N.J.: Princeton University Press, 2001.

Kripal, Jeffrey J. *Esalen: America and the Religion of No Religion*. Chicago: University of Chicago Press, 2007.

LaCapra, Dominic. *"Madame Bovary" on Trial*. Ithaca: Cornell University Press, 1982.

Ladd, Mason. "Expert Testimony." *Vanderbilt Law Review* 5 (1952): 414–31.

Lampham, Jane. "A Captive Audience for Salvation." *Christian Science Monitor*, April 19, 2006.

Lapp, Anthony. "Meet 'The Family.' " Available at http://www.theocracywatch.org/secret_theocrats.htm (accessed May 23, 2008).

Lawrence, Bruce. "Transformation." In *Critical Terms for Religious Studies*. Chicago: University of Chicago Press, 1998.

Lea, Thomas, and Thomas Hudson. *Step by Step through the New Testament*. Nashville, Tenn.: LifeWay, 1992.

Lewis, C. S. *The Allegory of Love: A Study of Medieval Tradition*. London: Oxford University Press, 1938.

———. "The Humanitarian Theory of Punishment." *20th Century: An Australian Quarterly Review* 3 (1949): 5–12. Reprinted in C. S. Lewis, *God in the Dock: Essays on Theology and Ethics.* Grand Rapids, Mich.: Eerdmans, 1970.
———. *Mere Christianity.* New York: Macmillan, 1953.
———. *Out of the Silent Planet.* New York: Macmillan, 1943.
———. *Perelandra.* New York: Macmillan, 1944.
———. *The Problem of Pain.* New York: Macmillan, 1962.
———. *The Screwtape Letters.* New York: Macmillan, 1961.
———. *That Hideous Strength.* New York: Macmillan, 1946.
———. *The Horse and His Boy.* New York: Macmillan, 1956.
———. *The Last Battle: A Story for Children* New York: Macmillan, 1956.
———. *The Lion, the Witch, and the Wardrobe: A Story for Children.* New York: Macmillan, 1953.
———. *The Magician's Nephew.* New York: Macmillan, 1955.
———. *Prince Caspian: The Return to Narnia.* New York: Macmillan, 1951.
———. *The Silver Chair.* New York: Macmillan, 1953.
———. *The Voyage of the "Dawn Treader."* New York: Macmillan, 1953.
Liebling, Alison, with Helen Arnold. *Prisons and Their Moral Performance: A Study of Values, Quality, and Prison Life.* Oxford: Oxford University Press, 2004.
Lienesch, Michael. *Redeeming America: Piety and Politics in the New Christian Right.* Chapel Hill: University of North Carolina Press, 1993.
Lin, Ann Chih. *Reform in the Making: The Implementation of Social Policy in Prison.* Princeton, N.J.: Princeton University Press, 2000.
Lindsay, D. Michael. "Is the National Prayer Breakfast Surrounded by a 'Christian Mafia' ? Religious Publicity and Secrecy within the Corridors of Power." Unpublished paper provided by author.
———. *Faith in the Halls of Power: How Evangelicals Joined the American Elite.* Oxford: Oxford University Press, 2007.
Long, Charles. *Significations: Signs, Symbols, and Images in the Interpretation of Religion.* New York: Fortress, 1986.
Lopez, Donald S., Jr. "Belief." In *Critical Terms for Religious Studies*, ed. Mark C. Taylor. Chicago: University of Chicago Press, 1998.
Luban, David. *Legal Modernism.* Ann Arbor: University of Michigan Press, 1997.
Luhmann, Niklas. *Law as a Social System.* Translated by Klaus A. Ziegert. Oxford: Oxford University Press, 2004.
Luhrmann, T. M. "Learning Religion at the Vineyard: Prayer, Discernment and Participation in the Divine." *Religion and Culture Web Forum,* September 2006.
Lupu, Ira C., and Robert W. Tuttle. "*Americans United for Separation of Church and State (and Others) v. Prison Fellowship Ministries (and Others)* (United States District Court, Southern District of Iowa, decided June 2, 2006)." Roundtable on Religion and Social Welfare Policy, June 13, 2006. Available at www.religionandsocialpolicy.org (accessed May 23, 2008).
———. "The Cross at College: Accommodation and Acknowledgment of Religion at Public Universities." *William & Mary Bill of Rights Journal,* forthcoming.

———. "The Faith-Based Initiative and the Constitution." *DePaul Law Review* 55 (2005): 1–118.

———. "Federalism and Faith." *Emory Law Journal* 56 (2006): 19–105.

———. *The State of the Law 2006: Legal Developments Affecting Government Partnerships with Faith-based Organizations.* Roundtable on Religion and Social Policy. www.religionandsocialpolicy.org (January 6, 2007) (accessed May 23, 2008).

———. *The State of the Law 2007: Legal Developments Affecting Government Partnerships with Faith-based Organizations.* The Roundtable on Religion and Social Policy. www.religionandsocialpolicy.org (January 6, 2007) (accessed May 23, 2008).

Luxon, Thomas H. *Literal Figures: Puritan Allegory and the Reformation Crisis in Representation.* Chicago: University of Chicago Press, 1995.

Madison, James. "Memorial and Remonstrance Against Religious Assessments" (1785).

Mahmood, Saba. *Politics of Piety: The Islamic Revival and the Feminist Subject.* Princeton, N.J.: Princeton University Press, 2005.

———. "Secularism, Hermeneutics, and Empire: The Politics of Islamic Reformation." *Public Culture* 18 (2006): 323–47.

Malcolm X. *The Autobiography of Malcolm X.* New York: Grove, 1966.

Martin, Luther H., Huck Gutman, and Patrick H. Hutton, eds. *Technologies of the Self: A Seminar with Michel Foucault.* Amherst: University of Massachusetts Press, 1988.

Marty, Martin E. *Religion and Republic: The American Circumstance.* Boston: Beacon, 1987.

Marty, Martin E., and R. Scott Appleby, eds. *The Fundamentalism Project.* 5 vols. Chicago: University of Chicago Press, 1991–95.

Masuzawa, Tomoko. "Culture." In *Critical Terms for Religious Studies*, ed. Mark Taylor. Chicago: University of Chicago Press, 1998.

———. *The Invention of World Religions.* Chicago: University of Chicago Press, 2005.

Matoesian, Gregory. *Law and the Language of Identity: Discourse in the William Kennedy Smith Rape Trial.* Oxford: Oxford University Press, 2001.

Mauer, Marc. "The Causes and Consequences of Prison Growth in the United States." In *Mass Imprisonment: Social Causes and Consequences*, ed. David Garland. London: Sage, 2001.

———. "Comparative International Rates of Incarceration: An Examination of Causes and Trends." Presented to the U.S. Civil Rights Commission by the Sentencing Project, June 20, 2003.

May, Henry. *The Enlightenment in America.* Oxford: Oxford University Press, 1976.

McClain, Linda C. "Unleashing or Harnessing 'Armies of Compassion': Reflections on the Faith-based Initiative." *Loyola University of Chicago Law Journal* 39 (2008): 361–426.

McCutcheon, Russell T. *Critics Not Caretakers: Redescribing the Public Study of Religion.* Albany: State University of New York Press, 2001.

McDaniel, Charles, Derek H. Davis, and Sabrina A. Neff. "Charitable Choice and Prison Ministries: Constitutional Challenges to Rehabilitating the American Penal System." *Criminal Justice Policy Review* 16 (2005): 164–89.

McGee, Robert. *The Search for Significance*. Houston: Rapha, 1990.

McGreevy, John T. *Catholicism and American Freedom: A History.* New York: W. W. Norton, 2003.

McRoberts, Omar. *Streets of Glory: Church and Community in a Black Urban Neighborhood*. Chicago: University of Chicago Press, 2005.

Mead, Sidney E. *The Lively Experiment: The Shaping of Christianity in America.* New York: Harper and Row, 1963.

Meares, Tracey, and Kelsi Brown Corkran. "When 2 or 3 Come Together." The Social Science Research Network Electronic Paper Collection: http://ssrn.com/abstract_id=835664 (accessed May 23, 2008).

Mears, Daniel P. "Faith-based Re-entry Programs: Cause for Concern or Showing Promise?" *Corrections Today*, April 2007, 30–33.

Mensch, Elizabeth B. "Images of Self and Polity in the Aftermath of the Reformation." *Graven Images* 3 (1996): 249–64.

Meyer, Joyce. *Battlefield of the Mind: Winning the Battle in Your Mind*. New York: Warner Books, 1995.

Miles, David. "Group Sues Over Prison's 'God Pod.' " *New Mexican*, November 9, 2005.

Miller, David W. *God at Work: The History and Promise of the Faith at Work Movement*. Oxford: Oxford University Press, 2007.

Miller, Donald E. *Reinventing American Protestantism: Christianity in the New Millennium*. Berkeley: University of California Press, 1997.

Miller, Jonathan. "March of the Conservatives: Penguin Film as Political Fodder." *New York Times*. September 13, 2005.

Mitford, Jessica. *Kind and Usual Punishment: The Prison Business*. New York: Knopf, 1973.

Modern, John Lardas. "Ghosts of Sing Sing or the Metaphysics of Secularism." *Journal of the American Academy of Religion* 75 (2007): 615–50.

Monteil, Lisa M., and David J. Wright. "Getting a Piece of the Pie: Federal Grants to Faith-based Social Service Organizations." Roundtable on Religion and Social Welfare Policy. www.religionandsocialpolicy.org (February 2006) (accessed May 23, 2008).

Morris, Norval, and David Rothman, eds. *The Oxford History of the Prison*. Oxford: Oxford University Press, 1995.

Morrison, Toni. *Beloved*. New York: Alfred A. Knopf, 1987.

Mushlin, Michael B. *Rights of Prisoners*. 3rd ed. New York: Thomson West, 2002.

Nagel, Thomas. *The View from Nowhere*. New York: Oxford University Press, 1986.

Naugle, David K. *Worldview: The History of a Concept*. Grand Rapids, Mich.: Eerdmans, 2002.

Neuhaus, Richard John. "Evangelicals & Catholics Together: The Christian Mission in the Third Millennium." *First Things*, May 1994.

Nichols, Carolyn. "Nation's First Faith-based Prison Opens in Florida." *Florida Baptist Witness*. www.floridabaptistwitness.com (January 22, 2004) (accessed July 22, 2008).

Noll, Mark A. *American Evangelical Christianity: An Introduction*. Oxford: Blackwell Publishers, 2001.

———. *America's God: From Jonathan Edwards to Abraham Lincoln*. Oxford: Oxford University Press, 2002.

———. *The Scandal of the Evangelical Mind*. Grand Rapids, Mich.: Eerdmans, 1994.

Norris, Pippa, and Ronald Inglehart. *Sacred and Secular: Religion and Politics Worldwide*. Cambridge: Cambridge University Press, 2004.

Nussbaum, Martha. *The Clash Within: Democracy, Religious Violence, and India's Future*. Cambridge, Mass.: Harvard University Press, 2007.

Olson, Roger E. *The Westminster Handbook to Evangelical Theology*. Louisville, Ky.: Westminster John Knox, 2004.

Owens, Erik C., John D. Carlson, and Eric C. Elshtain, eds. *Religion and the Death Penalty: A Call for Reckoning*. Grand Rapids, Mich.: Eerdmans, 2004.

Pecora, Vincent. *Secularization and Cultural Criticism: Religion, Nation, and Modernity*. Chicago: University of Chicago Press, 2006.

The Pew Center on the States. *One in One Hundred: Behind Bars in 2008*, January 2008.

Poovey, Mary. "The Liberal Civil Subject and the Social in Eighteenth Century Moral Philosophy." *Public Culture* 14 (2002): 125–45.

Povinelli, Elizabeth A. *The Empire of Love: Toward a Theory of Intimacy, Genealogy, and Carnality*. Durham, N.C.: Duke University Press, 2006.

Pratt, Robert W. "Senseless Sentencing: A Federal Judge Speaks Out." *Des Moines Register*, January 10, 1999.

Prothero, Stephen. *Religious Literacy: What Every American Needs to Know—And Doesn't*. San Francisco: Harper Books, 2007.

Ramsey, Dave. *Total Money Makeover*. Nashville, Tenn.: Nelson Books, 2003.

Root, Orrin. *Training for Service: A Survey of the Bible*. Rev. ed. Cincinnati: Standard Publishing, 1983.

Rosen, Lawrence. The *Anthropology of Justice: Law as Culture in Islamic Society*. New York: Cambridge University Press, 1989.

Rosenberg, Gerald N. *The Hollow Hope: Can Courts Bring about Social Change?* Chicago: University of Chicago Press, 1991.

Rosky, Clifford J. "Force, Inc.: The Privatization of Punishment, Policing, and Military Force in Liberal States." *Connecticut Law Review* 36 (2004): 879–1032.

Rothman, David J. *Conscience and Convenience: The Asylum and Its Alternatives in Progressive America*. Rev. ed. New York: Aldine de Gruyter, 2002.

———. *The Discovery of the Asylum: Social Order and Disorder in the New Republic*. Rev. ed. New York: Aldine de Gruyter, 2002.

———. "Perfecting the Prison: United States, 1789–1865." In *The Oxford History of the Prison*, ed. Norval Morris and David Rothman. Oxford: Oxford University Press, 1995.

Rotman, Edgardo. "The Failure of Reform," In *The Oxford History of the Prison*, ed. Norval Morris and David Rothman. Oxford: Oxford University Press, 1995.

Roy, Douglas. "Doin' Time in God's House: Why Faith-Based Rehabilitation Programs Violate the Establishment Clause." *Southern California Law Review* 78 (2005): 795–834.

Rutba House. *School(s) for Conversion: 12 Marks of a New Monasticism*. Eugene, Ore.: Cascade Books, 2005.

Santner, Eric. *My Own Private Germany: Daniel Paul Schreber's Secret History of Modernity*. Princeton, N.J.: Princeton University Press, 1996.

Sarat, Austin, Lawrence Douglas, and Martha Merrill Umphrey, eds. *Law and the Sacred*. Stanford: Stanford University Press, 2007.

Schaeffer, Francis. *How Should We Then Live? The Rise and Decline of Western Thought and Culture*. Old Tappan, N.J.: Fleming H. Revell, 1976.

———. *The Great Evangelical Disaster*. Westchester, Ill.: Crossways Books, 1984.

Schaeffer, Frank. *Dancing Alone: The Quest for Orthodox Faith in the Age of False Religion*. N.p.: Holy Cross Orthodox Press, 1994.

Schaff, Philip. *The Creeds of Christendom*. New York: Harper, 1877.

Schlegel, John Henry. *American Legal Realism and Empirical Social Science*. Chapel Hill: University of North Carolina Press, 1995.

Schmidt, Leigh Eric. *Hearing Things: Religion, Illusion, and the American Enlightenment*. Cambridge, Mass.: Harvard University Press, 2000.

Seymour, Stephen. "Note: The Silence of Prayer: An Examination of the Federal Bureau of Prisons Moratorium on the Hiring of Muslim Chaplains." *Columbia Human Rights Law Review* 37 (Winter 2006): 523–58.

Sharlet, Jeffrey. "Jesus Plus Nothing." *Harper's Magazine*, March 2003.

Sherwin, Richard K. *When Law Goes Pop: The Vanishing Line between Law and Popular Culture*. Chicago: University of Chicago Press, 2000.

Simon, Jonathan. "Fear and Loathing in Late Modernity: Reflections on the Cultural Sources of Mass Imprisonment in the United States." In *Mass Imprisonment: Social Causes and Consequences*, ed. David Garland. London: Sage, 2001.

———. *Governing Through Crime: How the War on Crime Transformed American Democracy and Created a Culture of Fear*. Oxford: Oxford University Press, 2007.

Smart, Ninian. *Worldviews: Crosscultural Explorations of Human Beliefs*. 2nd ed. Upper Saddle River, N.J.: Prentice Hall, 2000.

Smith, Christian. *Christian America? What Evangelicals Really Want*. Berkeley: University of California Press, 2000.

———. *American Evangelicalism: Embattled and Thriving*. Chicago: University of Chicago Press, 1998.

Smith, Jonathan Z. *Imagining Religion: From Babylon to Jonestown*. Chicago: University of Chicago Press, 1982.

———. "Religion, Religions, Religious." In *Critical Terms for Religious Studies*, ed. Mark C. Taylor. Chicago: University of Chicago Press, 1998.

Smith, Steven Rathgeb, John P. Bartkowski, and Susan Grettenberger. *Comparative Views on the Role and Effect of Faith in Social Services*. The Roundtable on Religion and Social Policy, December 2006. Available at www.religionand socialpolicy.org.

Soloveitchik, Hayim. "Rupture and Reconstruction: The Transformation of Contemporary Orthodoxy." *Tradition* 28 (1994): 64–130.

Stark, Rodney, and William Bainbridge. *The Future of Religion: Secularization, Revival, and Cult Formation*. Berkeley: University of California Press, 1985.

Stolzenberg, Nomi. "The Profanity of the Law." In *Law and the Sacred*, ed. Austin Sarat, Lawrence Douglas, and Martha Merrill Umphrey. Stanford: Stanford University Press, 2007.

Sullivan, Kathleen M. "Religion and Liberal Democracy." *University of Chicago Law Review* 59 (1992): 195–223.

Sullivan, Winnifred Fallers. "Allegorize This!" *Sightings*, February 16, 2006. http://marty-center.uchicago.edu/sightings/index.html (accessed May 23, 2008).

———. "Comparing Religion, Legally." *Washington & Lee Law Review* 63 (Fall 2006).

———. " 'The Conscience of Contemporary Man': Reflections on *U.S. v. Seeger* and *Dignitatis Humanae*" *U.S. Catholic Historian* 24 (Winter 2006): 107–23.

———. *The Impossibility of Religious Freedom*. Princeton, N.J.: Princeton University Press, 2005.

———. "Indifferentism Redux: Reflections on Catholic Lobbying in the Supreme Court." *Notre Dame Law Review* 76 (April 2001): 993–1018.

———. "Neutralizing Religion; or, What Is the Opposite of 'Faith-based?' " *History of Religions Journal* 41 (2002): 4. Reprinted in *Religion: Beyond a Concept*, ed. Hent deVries. New York: Fordham University Press, 2007.

———. "Rehabilitation or Forced Conversion?" *Harvard Divinity School Bulletin* (2006).

Sullivan, Winnifred Fallers, and Robert A. Yelle. "Overview" to Law and Religion articles. In *Encyclopedia of Religion*, 2nd ed, edited by Lindsay Jones. Detroit: Gale Group, 2005.

Supiot, Alain. *Homo Juridicus: On the Anthropological Function of the Law*. London: Verso, 2007.

Suskind, Ron. "Why Are These Men Laughing?" *Esquire*, January 2003.

Sweeney, Megan. "*Beard v. Banks*: Deprivation as Rehabilitation" *PMLA* 122, no. 3 (May 2007): 779–83.

Tapley, Lance. "Does John Baldacci Belong to a Secretive, Conservative Christian Group?" *Portland Phoenix*, May 9–15, 2003.

Taussig-Rubbo, Matteo. "Outsourcing Sacrifice: The Labor of Private Military Contractors." *Yale Journal of Law and Humanities* (forthcoming, 2009).

Taylor, Charles. *Modern Social Imaginaries*. Durham, N.C.: Duke University Press, 2005.

———. *Sources of the Self: The Making of the Modern Identity*. Cambridge, Mass.: Harvard University Press, 1989.

———. "A Different Kind of Courage." Review of Jonathan Lear, *Radical Hope: Ethics in the Face of Cultural Devastation*. Cambridge, Mass.: Harvard University Press, 2006. *New York Review of Books*, April 26, 2007.

Taylor, Mark C., ed. *Critical Terms for Religious Studies*. Chicago: University of Chicago Press, 1998.

Tonry, Michael. "Theories and Policies Underlying Guidelines Systems: Obsolescence and Immanence in Penal Theory and Policy." *Columbia Law Review* 105 (2005): 1233–75.

———. *Thinking about Crime: Sense and Sensibility in American Penal Culture*. Oxford: Oxford University Press, 2004.

Tracy, David. *The Analogical Imagination: Christian Theology and the Culture of Pluralism*. New York: Crossroad, 1981.

Troeltsch, Ernst. *The Social Teaching of the Christian Churches*. Translated by Olive Wyon. Chicago: University of Chicago Press, 1976.

Urban, Hugh. "Religion and Secrecy in the Bush Administration: The Gentleman, the Prince, and the Simulacrum." Available at http://www.esoteric.msu.edu/VolumeVII/Secrecy.htm (accessed January 25, 2008).

U.S. Department of Education. *Literacy Behind Bars: Results from the 2003 National Assessment of Adult Literacy Prison Survey* (May 2007).

U.S. Department of Justice, Bureau of Justice Statistics. "The Nation's Prison Population Continues Its Slow Growth: Up 1.9% Last Year." Press Release, October 23, 2005. Available at www.ojp.usdoj.gov/bjs (accessed May 21, 2007).

van der Veer, Peter. *Religious Nationalism: Hindus and Muslims in India*. Berkeley: University of California Press, 1994.

Viswanathan, Gauri. "Literacy in the Eye of the Conversion Storm." In *The Invention of Religion: Rethinking Belief in Politics and History*, ed. Derek Peterson and Darren Walhof. New Brunswick, N.J.: Rutgers University Press, 2002.

Wacquant, Loïc. "Deadly Symbiosis: When Ghetto and Prison Meet and Mesh." In *Mass Imprisonment: Social Causes and Consequences*, ed. David Garland. London: Sage, 2001.

Wald, Kenneth D. *Religion and Politics in the United States*. 4th ed. Lanham, Md.: Rowman and Littlefield, 2003.

Wallis, Jim. *God's Politics: Why the Right Gets It Wrong and the Left Doesn't Get It*. New York: Harper Collins, 2005.

Walsh, Frank. *Sin and Censorship: The Catholic Church and the Motion Picture Industry*. New Haven, Conn.: Yale University Press, 1996.

Walzer, Michael. *The Revolution of the Saints: A Study in the Origins of Radical Politics*. Cambridge, Mass.: Harvard University Press, 1965.

Warren, Rick. *The Purpose Driven Life: What on Earth Am I Here For?* Grand Rapids, Mich.: Zondervan, 2002.

Whitman, James Q. *Harsh Justice: Criminal Punishment and the Widening Divide between America and Europe*. Oxford: Oxford University Press, 2003.

Willow Creek Community Church, *Walking with God* series. Chicago, Ill. www.willowcreek.org (accessed January 15, 2008).

Wilson, James Q. *Thinking about Crime*. New York: Basic Books, 1975.

Wuthnow, Robert. *The Restructuring of American Religion: Society and Faith since World War II*. Princeton, N.J.: Princeton University Press, 1989.

———. *Saving America?: Faith-based Services and the Future of Civil Society*. Princeton, N.J.: Princeton University Press, 2004.

Yelle, Robert A. "Bentham's Fictions: Canon and Idolatry in the Genealogy of Law." *Yale Journal of Law & the Humanities* 17 (2005): 151–79.

———. *The Disenchantment of Language: Protestant Literalism and the Discourse of Modernity from England to India,* forthcoming.

Zagorin, Perez. *How the Idea of Religious Toleration Came to the West.* Princeton, N.J.: Princeton University Press 2007.

Zha, Jianying. "Letter from Beijing: Enemy of the State: The Complicated Life of an Idealist." *New Yorker,* April 23, 2007.

Zimring, Franklin E., Gordon Hawkins, and Sam Kamin. *Three Strikes and You're Out in California.* Oxford: Oxford University Press, 2001.

Žižek, Slavoj. *The Ticklish Subject: The Absent Centre of Political Ontology.* London: Verso, 1999.

Index

AA. *See* Alcoholics Anonymous
Abraham, 44–45
ACLJ. *See* American Center for Law and Justice
ACLU. *See* American Civil Liberties Union
Adams, Jay E., 256n51
ADF. *See* Alliance Defense Fund
ADL. *See* Anti-Defamation League
affirmation: as IFI value, 115, 156, 158, 159, 175, 176, 200, 202, 203; as practice, 122; therapeutic, 109, 110
Agostini v. Felton, 205
Alabama, 208, 212
Albanese, Catherine, 232, 270n12
Alcoholics Anonymous (AA), 62, 66, 263n40
Alito, Samuel, 219
allegory, 259n29; and the Bible, 164; and Catholics, 164, 259nn30 and 32; and Evangelicals, 163, 164–65, 259nn29 and 31; and Protestants, 164, 259n30
Allegory of Love, The, 255n43
Allen, Francis, 253n15, 254n18
Allen, Gordon, 16
Alliance Defense Fund (ADF), 208, 208n44, 209–10
Alpha Enterprise, The, 52
Alpha Series, 50–52
altar call, 45–47
America's God, 251n89
American Catholic Arts and Fictions, 259nn30 and 32
American Catholic Correctional Chaplains Association, 209, 267n59
American Center for Law and Justice (ACLJ), 208, 209–10, 266n52
American Civil Liberties Union (ACLU), 209, 214, 267n57
American Correctional Chaplains Association, 209, 266n58
American Evangelical Christianity, 250nn84 and 89
American Friends Service Committee, 253n15
American Jewish Committee, 209, 215, 266n64
American Jewish Congress, 209, 215, 266n61
Americans United for Separation of Church and State (AU), 1, 16, 144, 183, 208, 216, 218, 242nn59 and 64
Americans United for Separation of Church and State (and others) v. Prison Fellowship Ministries (and others). See *AU v. PFM*
Amman, Nawal H., 254n31
Ammerman, Nancy Tatom, 246n47, 262n12, 271n13
Analogical Imagination, The, 259nn30 and 32
Anderson, Elijah, 239n30, 254n26
Anderson, Neil T., 41, 42, 48
Anti-Defamation League (ADL), 209, 215, 267n63
apologetics, 75, 91; and Evangelicals, 85, 92; and C. S. Lewis, 71, 106, 147; and Francis Schaeffer, 77, 106, 147
Appleby, R. Scott, 240n45
Aquinas, Thomas, 77
Arkansas, 208
Arnold, Dan, 239n38
Asad, Talal, 9, 65, 176, 229, 230, 238n22, 240n46
AU. *See* Americans United for Separation of Church and State
AU v. PFM, 1–2, 15, 64–65, 218, 261n2; appeal of, 207–19, 208n43; defendants in, 16; plaintiffs in, 16; and prisoners, 244n22; trial strategy in, 140–41, 180–81, 244n20
Auburn Correctional Facility, 4, 107
authority, religious: and Evangelicals, 80, 84, 87, 136; and God, 10, 147, 182; and the individual, 2, 9, 82, 88, 90–91, 149, 178, 228, 233, 240n47; institutional, 3; and law, 85, 141, 181, 224; location of, 229; and the state, 6, 8, 221, 222, 28, 229, 233, 240n47
authority, state. *See* state

Bailey, Waylon, 42
Bainbridge, William, 239n39

Balmer, Randall, 85, 92, 251n111
Baltimore Catechism, 148
Bandes, Susan, 254n18
Bannerjee, Neela, 250n84
baptism, 148, 186–87, 202
Baptist Joint Committee for Religious Liberty, 209, 215, 267n62
Bartkowski, John, ix, 92–93, 241n52, 259n19
Battlefield of the Mind, 40, 41
Baubérot, Jean, 260n45
Bauer, Michael, 29–30, 40, 62, 129–30, 186–89
Baxter, Richard, 175
Beaumont, Gustave, 4, 107–8
Becci, Irene, 271n21
Becket Fund for Religious Liberty, 207–8, 216–18, 264n42
Beckett, Katherine, 237n3
Beckford, James, 234
behavior: and crime, 4, 5, 14, 105, 121, 137, 152, 165, 194, 210; and IFI, 24, 29, 38, 52, 108–39, 166–67, 170, 182, 225; pro-social, 54, 60, 115, 124–25, 131, 137
Being the Body, 42, 247n15
Beloved, 238n11
Benevides, Gustavo, 239n32
Bennett, William J., 253n15
Benton, Duane, 207, 216, 218
Berger, Peter L., 257n66
Berman, Harold, 239n30
Bevere, John, 42
Bible, the: and authority, 49, 70, 78, 87, 88; biblical inerrancy, 11, 77, 78, 86, 88, 93, 126–27, 182, 186, 211; biblical translation, x, 252n1; Catholic 34–35, 129, 178, 186; dispensationalism, 75, 76–77, 86, 87, 113; evangelical use of, 40–42, 44, 72–73, 80, 84, 86, 88, 93, 146; IFI use of, 34–35, 40–45, 48, 49–50, 52–54, 76, 94–95, 108–11, 112–16, 121, 124–30, 155–68, 182, 189–91, 222, 230; interpretation, 80, 88, 94–95, 164–65; and Islam, 190, 193, 195; and Jerusalem School, 202–3, 262n22; and Judaism, 200; New Testament, 58, 94, 184, 197, 223; and PFM, 68, 116, 129; Protestant, 146, 148, 154, 164, 186, 231; Recovery Version, 57
Bible-based programs and practices, 16, 68, 115, 121, 124, 130, 133, 147, 153, 182
Bible Believers, 246n47
Bible study: and Charles Colson, 66, 74; and Sam Dye, 119; and IFI, 23, 34, 50, 52–54, 68, 76, 81, 116; and Newton, 234; values of, 124, 138
biblical counseling, 42, 56, 61, 103, 108–11, 112, 256n51
biblical justice, 94, 101, 103–5
biblicism, 10
Bielefield, Wolfgang, 240nn49 and 50, 241n56
Binder, Guyora, 238n18
Blackaby, Henry T., 41, 42, 44–45
Blackaby, Melvin D., 42
Blackaby, Tom, 42
Blanchard, Troy C., 241n56
Body Count, 253n15
Bondage Breaker, The, 41
Book of Mormon, the, 160, 163, 165
Born Again, 70, 73, 244n12
born again experience, 46–47, 76, 80, 84, 171
Boundaries, 41
Bowen, John, 271n22
Bragonier, David, 41
Bragonier, Debbie, 41
Brandeis brief, 151
Brandt, Henry, 42, 108–10
Brault, Emily, 262n13
BreakPoint, 78
Breaking Through to Spiritual Maturity, 41
Brouwer, Rod, 59, 60
Brown v. Board of Education, 151, 250n80
Browning, Don S., 256n51
Bucko, Raymond A., 262n13
Buddhism, 48, 102, 178, 235
Bunyan, John, 164, 260n31
Burens, Benjamin, 189–90
Burger, Kenneth, 23, 24
Burns, Robert P., 16–17
Burson, Scott, 106
Bush, George W., 13, 68, 83, 89, 150, 241n50, 258n15

Caldwell, Patricia, 260n37
"called out," concept of, 223–24
Calvin, John, 144–45, 173

Calvinism, 65, 106, 211; neo-Calvinism, 64, 79, 89, 119, 148
capital punishment, 100, 104
Carlson, Frank, 71
Carlson, John D., 254n24
Carlson, Norman, 66, 67–68
Carlson, Ronald L., 258n12
Carnochan, W. B., 238n21
Carpenter, Joel, 83–84
Carter, J. Kameron, 248n29
Casanova, José, 9, 221, 250n80
Case Against Punishment, 255n46
Case, Mary Anne, 269n103
Cates, Patrick B., 261n2
Cat in the Hat, 159, 161
Catholic Charities, 13
Catholic League for Civil and Religious Rights, 208, 210, 266n53
Catholicism and American Freedom, 239n33
Catholics, 54, 82, 84, 102, 129, 148, 163, 178, 232, 234, 250n72; anti-Catholicism, 143, 188, 210, 230, 242n64; Baltimore Catechism of, 148; and IFI, 28, 34–36, 62, 90, 92, 128–30, 147–48, 172, 185, 186–88, 210; and Protestants, 130, 136, 148, 164, 186, 210, 211, 231, 259nn30 and 32
Chandler, Bryan, 27–28, 34–36, 201
Center for Inquiry, 209, 215–16, 267n66
Center for Public Justice, 208, 265n49
Changes That Heal, 41
chaplains/chaplaincies, 155, 232–33; prison, 14, 20, 23, 47, 67, 68, 102, 119, 155, 190–91, 193, 209, 214–15, 235, 245n38, 262n14
Chaves, Mark, 241n54
Chicken Soup for the Prisoner's Soul, 43
choice: and crime, 103; and faith-based initiatives, 13; and IFI, 32, 59, 93, 120, 137; and First Amendment, 80, 85, 144, 205–7; and morality, 174–75, 194, 216, 217, 225; and religion, 8, 231–33
Christ-centered programs and practices, 26, 32, 53, 147, 153, 182
Christendom, 33
Christian America, 248n31, 259n20
Christian Coalition, 83
Christianity: and civilization, 145, 196, 197, 214, 230, 269n85; and conversion, 22, 91, 114–15, 120–21, 144; evangelical (*see* evangelical Christianity); and moral order, 9, 65, 68, 106, 119, 129, 133, 173–76; naturalization of, 64, 65, 154–55, 196–97, 229–34; PFM and IFI, 51, 75, 79, 202; U.S., x, 3–4, 12, 71, 73, 80, 85–8, 144–45, 152, 175, 181, 187, 259n20
Christians, 92; conservative, 80, 82–85; evangelical (*see* evangelical Christianity); and non-Christians, 7, 48, 50, 64–66, 80, 102, 106, 113, 146, 164, 167–72, 189–97, 214, 222; as nondenominational, 15, 32, 54–58, 91–93, 112–18, 124–37, 141–42, 144–46; as subculture, 9, 11, 41–43, 47–48, 65–81, 85–88, 91–93, 154; theories of punishment of, 101–07; as universal, 11, 61–62, 64–66, 90, 128, 153–65, 167–72, 181–85, 197, 230
Chronicles of Narnia, The, 163–64
church and state, 11, 117, 175, 180–81, 221, 234, 239n39; and establishment, 116, 175, 180–81, 204, 215; Puritan theory of, 175; separation of, 7–8, 11, 86, 116–17, 175, 204, 215, 221, 228, 230, 231
Church of England, 86, 106, 234
churches, 18, 81–82, 85, 88, 153, 221; and faith-based initiatives, 13; and IFI, 23, 32–33, 45–48, 59, 77–78, 90, 112, 123–24, 156, 222–24, 255n44; para-church organizations, 43, 81, 142, 244n14; and state (*see* church and state); U.S., 3, 11, 45, 54, 56–57, 87, 141
Churching of America, The, 240n42, 270n4
civilization. *See* Christianity, and civilization
Clash Within, The, 237n4
Clinton, Hillary Rodham, 71
Clinton, William Jefferson, 163, 220, 243n65
Cloud, Henry, 41
Coalition to Preserve Religious Freedom, 208, 265n51
Coe, Douglas, 71, 72, 74
Cold War, 77
Colorado, 208
Colson, Charles, 250n63; awards received, 71; *Being the Body*, 42; *Born Again*, 70, 73; and capital punishment, 104–5, 255n38; and Catholics, 188, 210, 250n72; conversion, 70, 73; dualism, 74, 119, 212; as evangelist, 77–80, 90–91, 106, 138–39; and The Fellowship,

Colson, Charles (*cont'd*)
70–72, 74–75; *How Now Shall we Live?*, 77; and Harold Hughes, 66–67, 68, 72–73; and IFI, 32–33, 76–78, 101, 106; and C. S. Lewis, 70, 104–6; *Life Sentence*, 66–67, 91; and Prison Fellowship, 22–23, 33, 66–69, 78, 138–39; and Watergate, 22, 74
Communism, 70, 83
Comparative Views on the Role and Effect of Faith in Social Services, 241n52
Compassion Grant, 111
Competent to Counsel, 256n51
Confronting Confinement, 243n4, 253n9
Congress of the United States, 142, 203, 220
Conscience and Convenience, 237n8
Console and Classify, 238n13
Constitution of the United States, 151; Article III, 219; Bill of Rights, 216; and faith-based initiatives, 1, 20–21, 166, 216–17; First Amendment (*see* First Amendment); and IFI, 1,16, 63, 65, 117, 121, 142, 161, 166, 180–81, 207–219; and prisoners, 6, 15, 63, 206–7, 211, 214; and religion, 9, 20–21, 44, 80, 92, 110, 185, 232–33; and restitution, 203, 207, 210, 213, 216–17, 263n23; and standing, 219–220
Cooper, Terry D., 256n51
Cover, Robert, 239n30
conversion: and IFI, 1, 22, 67, 61–62, 76, 91, 114–117, 120–21, 132–34, 145–46; and PFM, 69, 101, 115, 116; to pro-social behavior, 115, 117, 131, 169; religious, 171–72
Corrections Corporation of America, 242n59
Council for Secular Humanism, 209, 215–16, 267n65
courts, role of, 151–52
Cox, Norman, 54, 111, 112, 113–19, 181, 182–84
creeds, Christian, 183, 185, 261n5
crime, 5–6, 14, 32, 67, 78, 96–98, 152; and sin, 94–95, 100, 101–11, 120, 136–37, 165, 167–68, 207, 248n29
Culture of Control, The, 96

Dagel, Travis, 208
Daly, Lew, 13, 89–90, 237n3, 251nn107 and 105, 265n49
Dancing Alone, 249n60
Daunis, Angela, 243n7
David (king of Israel), 94, 95
Davie, Grace, 3, 237nn5 and 7, 259n20
death penalty. *See* capital punishment
Decline of the Rehabilitative Ideal, The, 253n15
Defying Dixie, 239n40
DelFattore, Joan, 239n33
Department of Justice, U.S., 14, 213
Department of Veterans Affairs, U.S., 232–33, 234, 271n18, 271n23; National Chaplains Center program of, 232–33
Des Moines, Iowa, 198
deVries, Hent, 238n23, 270n2
Dickens, Charles, 107–8
DiIulio, John, 253n15
Dionne, E. J., Jr., 253n15
Discipline and Punish, 238n13
Discovering Religious History in the Modern Age, 238n22
Discovery of the Asylum, The, 237n8, 238n13
discrimination, 62–63, 128–29, 180, 185, 205, 216
disenchantment, 173, 260n41
Disenchantment of Language, The, 270n3
Disenchantment of the World, The, 260n41
disestablishment, 2, 8, 85, 150, 172, 175, 181, 270n4; and the modern state, 8, 178–79; and public space, 230–31; and taxpayer suits, 220
Divided by Faith, 257n66
Dobson, James, 71, 83
dominion theology, 85
Douglas, Lawrence, 238n19
Douglas, William O., 220
Downes, David, 237n3
Douzinas, Costas, 239n32, 270n3
Dr. Seuss. *See* Geisel, Theodor
Dubber, Marcus, 238n18
Dulles, Avery Cardinal, 210–11
Dumont, Louis, 228
Durrant Group, The, 19
Dye, Sam, 112, 119–28, 138, 184–85, 257n67

Earley, Mark, 69, 91, 218
Edwards, Jonathan, 251n89
Eisenhower, Dwight D., 70
ekklesia, 223

elder, 58–59
Eldridge, John, 42
Elshtain, Eric C., 254n24
Embattled and Thriving, 259n19
Emerson, Michael, 67–68, 240n47
Employment Division v. Smith, 83, 224
Engel, David, 178, 240n46
England. *See* United Kingdom
Enlightenment, 3, 86, 87, 93, 98, 153, 178, 215
Enlightenment in America, The, 251n90
Entanglement, 205, 207, 234
equality, 67, 68, 99, 106
Erzen, Tanya, 255n32
establishment of religion, 1, 65, 81, 142–43, 150, 180, 206, 212–13, 217
Ethical Soundscape, The, 177
Europe: prisons in, 95, 96, 98–100; religion in, 2–3, 85, 178
Europe, 237n5, 259n20
Evangelicals for Social Action, 208, 265n50
Evangelical Christianity: and allegory, 163–65; Church of England and, 255n44; and conversion, 172; and C. S. Lewis, 105–6; definition of, 12, 64–65, 84, 147–49; as disestablished, 141, 179; "The Evangelical Mind," 86; history of, 80–88, 14; human nature and, 80–93; IFI and, 64–65, 75–80, 88–93, 147–49, 154, 163; language of, 64–65, 92, 147, 189, 211, 262n12; and mainstream culture, 93, 163–64, 178, 259n28; and modernity, 86–88, 172–73; and PFM, 64–65, 75; and salvation, 106, 189; and science, 86–88, 172, 238n27; and Scottish Enlightenment, 86–8; and social problems, 67–68, 82–83; as subculture:, 71, 84–85, 88–93, 103
Evangelicals and Catholics Together, 210, 250n72
Everson v. Board of Education, 204
Everyday Religion, 271n13
Evidence, 258n12
evidence-based corrections theory, 22
Experiencing God, 41, 44–45
expert testimony, 140–42, 258n12;

Faith, The, 250n63
Faith Lesson Video Series, 42
Faith and Order, 239n30
Faith-Based Partnerships, 240nn49 and 40, 241n56
faith-based social services, 12–16, 108, 117, 152, 225–26, 240n49, 251n105; constitutionality of, 1, 117, 216–17, 225, 242n59; efficacy of, 13–14, 101, 212, 216–17, 241n56; and prisons, 20–23, 92, 102–3, 208, 253n12, 255n32
Falwell, Jerry, 83
Family, The. *See* Fellowship, The
Family Series. *See* Alpha Series
fellowship, 44, 49, 60, 115, 122, 124, 155–56, 158, 200–203
Fellowship, The: Charles Colson and, 70–71, 74; and Communism, 70, 238n22; Democrats in, 71; history of, 69–71; Harold Hughes and, 66, 71–73; and PFM, 66, 69–71, 75
Ferrari, Silvio, 237n7
FFRF. *See* Freedom from Religion Foundation
FFRF v. McCallum, 225
FFRF v. Nicholson, 232
Fields, Richard R., 263n28, 269n86
Finke, Roger, 240n42, 270n4
First Amendment to the U.S. Constitution, 1, 9, 142–43, 175, 185–86, 231, 258n4
—Christianity and, 81
—evangelical Christianity and, 65, 81, 113, 116, 141–42, 149
—establishment clause of, 1, 8, 9, 116, 142–45, 153, 203–21, 231–33; and choice, 145–47, 209; and coercion, 143, 180, 206, 233; and endorsement, 205; incorporation of, 143; indirect funding, 209, 268n71; and "pervasively sectarian", 143–44; primary effect of, 143–44, 205; primary purpose of, 205
—Fourteenth Amendment and, 142, 204, 263n25;
—free exercise clause of, 8, 141, 144, 204, 239n34
Fish, Stanley, 9–11, 150, 225
Fitchett, Harold, 240n63
Flast v. Cohen, 219, 220
Florida, 21, 102–3, 208
Florida Baptist Witness, 102
Formations of the Secular, 176, 238n22, 240n46
Foucault, Michel, 238n13, 242n60
Foundation for Moral Law, 208, 212, 266n54

Fourth R, The, 239n22
France: *laïcisme* in, 234, 271n22; prisons in, 99, 234; religion in, 175, 221, 260n45
Freedom from Addiction, 41, 48
Freedom from Religion Foundation (FFRF), 219, 233, 242n59. See also *FFRF v. McCallum*; *FFRF v. Nicholson*
Freud, Sigmund, 79
fruits of the spirit, 53, 54, 117, 190
fundamentalism, 65, 84, 87, 88, 106, 148, 240n45
Fundamentalism Project, The, 240n45
Future of Religion, The, 239n39

Garden and the Wilderness, The, 250n75, 257n66, 270n7
Garland, David, 95, 96–98, 101, 237n3
Garnett, Richard, 210
Garside, Richard, 253n11
Gauchet, Marcel, 260n41
Geil, Chris, 41, 50, 112, 123, 136–37, 166–67, 222–24
Geisel, Theodor (Dr. Seuss), 159, 161, 162, 163, 165
Genealogies of Religion, 238n22
Getter, Lisa, 247n24
Getting Anger under Control, 41
Getting Your Financial House in Order, 41
Gibbons, John J., 96
Gilbert, Allyn, 43, 90
Giles, Paul, 259nn30 and 32
Gilmore, Glenda, 239n40
Gilpin, Clark, 229–30, 231, 232
God: belief in, 45, 48, 56, 191; as judge, 45, 68, 72, 106, 156; obedience to, 41, 74, 76, 110, 193–94, 199, 201; and state authority, 94, 104–5, 162, 221–22, 269n103
God and the Welfare State, 237n3, 251nn105 and 107, 265n49
God Pod, 21, 243n6
God's Politics, 248n36
Godly Republic, 253n15
Goffman, Irvin, 99
Going up the River, 238n15
Golash, Deirdre, 255n46
Goldstein, Jan, 238n13
Goldstein, Laurie, 258n15
Gollnick, Kimn S., 41
Goodrich, Peter, 238n22, 270n3
Gordon, Sarah, 82, 254n29
Gottschalk, Marie, 98
Governing Prisons, 253n15
Governing Through Crime, 253n8
Graham, Billy, 71, 84, 250n84
Great Commission, 113
Great Evangelical Disaster, The, 249n59
Green, Timothy, 30
Greenawalt, Kent, 258n4
Grettenberger, Susan, 241n52
Grinch Who Stole Christmas, The, 159
Grotius, Hugh, 173
Grubb, Norman, 69
Gutterman, Melvin, 206, 263n33

Habits of Legality, The, 254,18
Hallett, Michael A., 253n12
Hallinan, Joseph T., 238n15
Hammers, John, 27, 38, 39, 50–51, 158–63
Handy, Robert, 259n20
Harsh Justice, 98–99
Hatch, Nathan, 87
Hatfield, Mark, 71
Hauerwas, Stanley, 249n62
Hawkins, Gordon, 253n15
Hearing Things, 246n7
Heart of the Problem, 42, 109–10
Hebrew Bible, 146, 200
Hein v. FFRF, 219, 220
Henry, Carl, 71
Hervieu-Léger, Danielle, 178
Hirschkind, Charles, 176, 177, 188
How Now Shall We Live?, 77
How Should We Then Live?, 77
Hodges, Charles, 88
Hollow Hope, The, 250n80
homosexuality, 83, 127–29, 170–71
Horse and His Boy, The, 255n43
How the Idea of Religious Tolerance Came to the West, 257n66
Howe, Mark deWolfe, 230–31, 250n75, 257n66, 270n7
Hudson, Thomas, 42
Hudson, Todd, 42
Hughes, Claire, 263n23
Hughes, Harold, 66–67, 68, 71, 72–74, 246n8
Humaita prison, 247n15
human nature, 93, 120, 154, 256n53
"Humanitarian Theory of Punishment, The." *See* Lewis, C. S.
human rights, 153–54
Hunt, T. W., 42
Hurley, Chuck, 23, 25

Ignatieff, Michael, 237n8, 238n13
Impossibility of Religious Freedom, The, 257n69, 257n1
In God's Presence, 42
"In God We Trust," 143
India, 2–3, 3n4
Inglehardt, Ronald, 270n4
InnerChange Freedom Initiative (IFI): Accountability Covenant of, 112; accounting of, 166; aftercare program of, 31, 59–60, 118, 125; and behavior (*see* behavior); and the Bible (*see* Bible, the); as church, 47, 112, 142, 222–24; classes, 40–45, 50, 109, 122, 123, 191; community meetings of, 40, 122–23, 168–69; as evangelical Christian, 12, 64–65, 141–42, 145–49, 163–65; and Iowa, 15–16, 24, 32, 39, 206, 207, 244nn17 and 20; description of, 15–16, 33–63; devotions of, 39–40, 121, 123, 134–36, 168; and discrimination, 62, 63, 128–29, 217; dismissal from program, 39, 40, 57, 138; effectiveness of, 20, 23, 59–63, 117–18, 139; family program, 50–52; *Field Guide,* 149–50, 155–57, 168; funding of, 1, 16, 24, 32–33, 78, 198, 244n17; and Newton Correctional Facility, 23–63; goals of, 26, 32, 89, 116, 119, 147, 149–50; and nonevangelicals, 28, 34–36, 92, 129–30, 145–47, 157, 172, 185–203, 35, 117, 188, 192, 195; Orientation, 33–39; and PFM, 15–16, 32, 68–69, 115–16, 119; and prayer, 34, 55, 129–30, 168–70; prisoner evaluation of, 53–58, 125, 170; and recidivism, 24, 33, 88–89, 137, 155, 167, 191; recruitment of inmates, 26–31, 33–34, 130, 131–32; religion, role of, 121–27, 128, 130–36, 137–39, 143–44, 212–13; revivals, 32–34, 45–47; and social psychology, 106–7, 111–13; substance abuse program of, 40, 47–50; *The Sycamore Tree Project,* 94–95; in Texas, 24; and transformation, 33, 94, 108–11, 114, 116–17, 137, 152, 167–68, 170, 207; as treatment, 27–28, 31, 39, 60, 61, 62, 64, 119, 222, 268n68; volunteers of, 26, 32, 33, 45, 47, 50–51, 59, 116, 123, 182–83; and worship, 43, 45–47, 123–24
Institute in Basic Life Principles, 242n59
integrity: and behavior, 125; and Christianity, 79; as IFI value, 44, 115, 121, 155–56; as universal value, 131, 146, 158, 199–200, 202–3
International Christian Leadership (ICL), 70, 247n22
Invention of World Religions, The, 238n22
Iowa, 139; Department of Corrections, 19–20, 21, 29–30, 62, 129, 192, 196–97; and IFI, 1, 15–16, 23–25, 68, 144, 180, 187, 244n17; penal history of, 19, 100–101
Iowa Family Policy Center, 208, 213, 266n55
Isaac, 44–45
Islam, 48, 102, 249n54; and the Bible,190–91, 193; and IFI, 138–39, 190–97; Mohammed, 212; Nation of Islam, 102, 194–97; prayer, 190–91, 194–95; Qu'ran, 249n54

Jailhouse Lawyer's Manual, A, 263n33
Jefferson, Thomas, 215, 231
Jerusalem School. *See* Bible, the
Jesus Christ: and Charles Colson, 67; and Harold Hughes, 72; and IFI, 150, 165, 181; and Jews, 199; and Muslims, 190, 193; relationship with, 46, 47, 54, 93, 171; and salvation, 49, 79, 58; as teacher, 89, 156
Jewish Prisoner Services International, 209, 267n60
Jews, 92, 146, 172, 198–201, 234
Jianying Zha, 260n33
Joan of Arc, 238n20
John, Gospel According to, 53
John Paul II, 187, 211
judges, role of, 97, 103–4, 140–41, 144, 151, 153
Just Measure of Pain, A, 237n8, 238n13

Kafka, Franz, 238n19
Kamin, Sam, 253n15
Kansas, 139, 208
Kaplan, Benjamin, 257n66
Katzenbach, Nicholas de B., 96
Kautzky, Walter, 21–22, 23–24, 25, 137–38
Kennedy, Sheila Seuss, 240nn49 and 50, 241n56
Kind and Usual Punishment, 253n15
King, Claude V., 41, 42, 44–45
King David. *See* David
Kingery, Dale, 54, 56, 57, 112, 130–36
Kippenberg, Hans, 238n22

Kirkpatrick, Clint, 128–29
Koran, the. *See* Qu'ran, the
Kuyper, Abraham, 89–90, 251n107

LaCapra, Dominic, 16–17
Lakota Ritual of the Sweat Lodge, The, 262n13
Lamberti, Tony, 243n7
Lampham, Jane, 257n61
language: ambiguous use of, 26, 65; of Evangelicals, 53–54, 91–93, 251n111; fusion of secular and religious, 26, 118–19, 194; IFI use of, 58, 65, 91, 106, 111–13, 136; and law, 9–12, 17–18
Last Battle, The, 255n43
law: and the modern state 7; and religion, 7, 10, 18, 114 , 141, 142–43, 153, 178, 203–4, 219, 228, 239n34, 257nn69 and 1, 259n18, 270n3; rule of, 7, 11, 225, 227–28, 231
law and order politics, 4, 19, 75, 96, 98
Law and the Language of Identity, 243n66
Law and the Sacred, 238n19
Lea, Thomas, 42
Left Behind series, 43
Legal Modernism, 7, 239n40
Lemon v. Kurtzman, 204, 207
Lemon test, 204–5, 211, 212, 263n28
Lewis, C. S., 105–6, 255n43; and Church of England, 106; and evangelicals, importance to, 105–6; "The Humanitarian Theory of Punishment," 103–4; *Mere Christianity,* 70; the *Narnia* series, 105, 164; Francis Schaeffer, compared with, 106; and theories of punishment, 103–4
Liebling, Alison, 257n74
Lienesch, Michael, 83, 84–85, 240n41, 246n2, 249n62
Life Sentence, 66, 67, 91, 244n12
Lin, Ann Chih, 139
Lipscomb, Larry, 26
Literal Figures, 260n31
Lively Experiment, The, 237n5, 270n7
Local Church Movement, 56–57
Locke, John, 173
Lopez, Donald S., Jr., 241n53
Luban, David, 7, 239n40
Luchenitser, Alex, 16
Luhrmann, T.M., 246n7
Luke, Gospel According to, 94, 95
Lupu, Ira, 225, 261n2, 262nn25 and 26
Luther, Martin, 90–91
Lutherans, 46, 65, 185, 188
Luxon, Thomas H., 260n31
Lyons, John, 28–29, 36–27, 38, 45–47, 48, 52–54, 62–63, 189, 201

"Madame Bovary" on Trial, 16–17
Madison, James, 215, 220
Mahmood, Saba, 176–77, 249n54
mala in se, 100
mala prohibita, 100
Malcom X, 102, 238n19
Malik, Yakov, 73
Man from Ida Grove, The, 72, 73
Man God Uses, The, 41, 42
Mapes, Terry, 161
March of the Penguins, The, 164, 165, 260n33
Marsh v. Chambers, 213
Marty, Martin, 83–84, 240n45
Mass Imprisonment, 237n3
Masuzawa, Tomoko, 238n22, 250n68
Mathes, John, 25
Mathieu, Séverine, 260n45
Matoesian, Gregory, 243n66
Matthew, Gospel According to, 112, 257n60
Matthews, Todd L., 241n56
May, Henry, 251n90
McAdams, Dan, 232
McKeag, Joel, 31, 202–3
McGee, Robert, 42
McGreevy, John T., 239n33
McMahon, Will, 253n11
McRoberts, Omar, 246n12
Mead, Sidney E., 237n5, 270n7
Mears, Daniel P., 241n56
Mensch, Elizabeth B., 256n50
mercy, 100, 104
Mere Christianity, 255n43
Methodists, 69, 72, 119, 234
Meyer, Joyce, 41, 43
Missouri, 166, 208
Miller, Don, 87
Miller, Rich, 41
Milligan, Russell, 29, 40, 51, 187–88
Mine Eyes Have Seen the Glory, 251n111
Minnesota, 72, 139
Mitchell v. Helms, 143, 225
Mitford, Jessica, 253n15
Modern, John Lardas, 93, 238n10
Modern Social Imaginaries, 173, 240n46

modern, premodern, and late-modern concepts of crime and punishment, 97–98, 101
Moody Bible Institute, 59
Moore, Roy, 212–13
moral majority, 83
moral order, 104, 105, 173; and Christianity, 65, 173; and IFI, 75, 175; and the individual, 9, 68; and Puritans, 174–75; and religion, 175–76; and virtue, 86, 174–75; as universal, 178
moralism, 84, 148
More, Glendale, 198–201
Mormons, 48, 147, 185, 204, 234
Morris, Norval, 5, 237n8
Morrison, Toni, 238n11
Mushlin, Michael B., 262nn28 and 33
Muslims, 102, 172, 176–77, 185, 190–97, 206, 254n31
Murdoch, Iris, 16
My Own Private Germany, 240n46

Nagel, Thomas, 258n14
Narcotics Anonymous, 207
National Association of Evangelicals, 208, 264n45
National Center for Neighborhood Enterprise, 208, 264n46
National Conference of Catholic Bishops, 268n67
National Prayer Breakfast, 70
Native Americans, 102, 146, 169, 172, 189–90, 204, 213–14, 234
Nature Religion in America, 270n12
Naugle, David K., 250n71
Navarro, Sandro, 208
Navigators, The, 71
neo-Calvinism. *See* Calvin
Neuhaus, Richard John, 210, 250n72
new paradigm church, 87–88
Newton Correctional Facility, 1, 19, 30, 31; bids for programming contracts at, 21–22, 24, 244n15; construction of, 21; Unit E in, 20, 21, 24, 26, 33, 36–39
Nixon, Richard, 22
Noll, Mark, 83, 86, 89, 93, 107, 118, 152, 172, 250nn84 and 89, 261n47
"nondenominational" term, 35, 56, 64, 183–84, 224, 230
Norris, Pippa, 270n4
Northwest Marriage Institute, 110–11
Novak, Michael, 89
Nussbaum, Martha, 237n4

O'Conner, Sandra Day, 207, 218
Oedipus Lex, 238n22, 270n3
Olson, Roger E., 250n84
Operation Starting Line, 242n62
Out of the Silent Planet, 255n43
Owens, Erik C., 254n24
Oxford History of the Prison, The, 5, 237n8

Paneck, Angela, 243n7
para-church organizations. *See* churches
Paul, 238n20
Paulus, Bruce, 28, 34–35, 201, 202
Paying the Words Extra, 259n20
Pearcey, Nancy, 77–78
Pecora, Ferdinand, 7, 11
Pecora, Vincent, 7, 11, 238n25, 240n46, 269n85
Pennsylvania, 4, 107
Pentecostal Christians, 65, 83, 84, 148; and fruits of the spirit, 54; practices of, 46, 130, 184
"pervasively sectarian" term, 143–44, 218
Philips, Tom, 70, 72
Piccarello, Anthony, 216–17
pietism, 64, 65, 84, 148
Pilgrim's Progress, 164, 260n31
pluralism, religious, 12, 80, 117, 176
Political Theologies, 238n23, 270n2
political theology, 228, 270n2
Politics and Piety, 176
Poovey, Mary, 240n46, 258n14
positivism, 87–88, 251n102
Posner, Richard, 225
Pratt, Robert W.: at trial, 25, 116, 134, 148, 169–171; biography of, 243n65; opinion of , 39–40, 57–58, 59, 65, 129, 136, 143–44, 157, 180–81, 203, 207, 218, 240n49
Pratt, Thomas, 25
prayer, 25, 34, 35, 39, 40, 46–47, 55, 124, 129–130, 131, 168–70
prayer breakfasts, 69, 71
Prison Fellowship Ministries (PFM), 1–2, 14, 64, 75; Angel Tree Ministries of, 81; *Annual Report,* 69, 89, 91, 101, 139; *AU v. PFM*, 218–19; and biblical justice, 101; *BreakPoint,* 78; and The Fellowship, 66, 69–72, 75; founding of, 22, 66–69; funding of, 22–23, 242n63; and

Prison Fellowship Ministries (*cont'd*)
IFI, 15–16, 32, 68–69, 92, 115–16; as ministry, 138–39; mission of, 68, 115–16; Prison Fellowship International of, 247n14; Statement of Faith of, 125–26, 144, 181–85, 210–11, 261n5; *The Sycamore Tree Project,* 81, 94–95
prisoners: of conscience, 6, 238n20; dignity of, 99, 105; and freedom of choice, 103, 144, 206, 207, 226; mental health of, 5, 7; reentry into society, 254n17; and religion, 6, 15, 102, 263n37; rights of, 103, 107–8, 206, 263n33, 263n40; and substance abuse, 7
prisoners, IFI: daily routine in IFI, 39, 53, 121–24; dismissal from IFI, 39, 40, 57; evaluation of progress of, 53, 54–58; preparations for release of, 59–61, 116; reasons for joining IFI, 27–31, 36–39; reasons for not joining IFI, 28, 36, 187, 191, 193–95, 199, 202
prisoners, Iowa, 19–20, 24–25, 236
prisons: criticism of, 4–6, 96, 98, 99, 107–8; European, 4, 95, 98–100, 253n11, 257n74; history of, 4–5, 93, 209–10, 214–15, 253n15; and massive incarceration, 19, 96, 101, 235, 237n3; and modern state, 4–6; National Commission on, 96, 253n9, 269n95; overcrowding of, 96; penal policy, 96–100; physical attributes of, 99; rates of incarceration, 3, 5, 91, 95, 96, 101, 252n4; reform of, 4–5, 96, 107, 215; religion in, 1, 6, 14n59, 14–15, 20, 43, 102, 206–7, 209–10, 247n15; in Russia, 95, 253n5; treatment programs in, 95; U.S., 95–101
Prisons and Their Moral Performance, 257n74
productivity, 115, 122, 146, 155, 157, 158, 159, 175, 176, 200
Promise Keepers, 92–93, 252n113
Promise Keepers, 259n19
proselytization, 102, 113, 121, 138–39, 213
"Protestant monasticism," 221, 269n102
Protestants, 58, 65, 130, 136, 244n14; and Catholics, 148, 259nn30 and 32; and public schools, 231; as standard, 130, 181, 183; in the United States, 11, 64, 86–88
Prothero, Stephen, 262n9
psychology: and biblical counseling, 110–11; IFI use of, 91, 106–7, 111–12; psychotherapy, 104, 107–8, 256n51; and punishment, 104
Public Religions in the Modern World, 250n80
punishment: corporal, 4; history of, 98–100; justifications for, 103, 104–5, 255n46; theories of, 4–6
Purcell, Graham, 72
Puritan Conversion Network, The, 260n37
Purpose Driven Life, The, 113–14

Quakers (Society of Friends), 1–2, 209–10
Quarles, Julia, 41, 48
Quarles, Mike, 41, 48
Quie, Albert, 71, 72
Qu'ran, the, 146, 160, 163, 165, 186, 194, 249n54

Ramsey, Dave, 41
Rapport de la Commission Stasi sur la Laïcité, Le, 271n22
Rassbach, Eric, 218–19
Rathgeb, Steven, 241n52
rational choice theory, 98, 225
Rawls, John, 163
Raytheon Industries, 70, 72
Re-enter, 243n7
Reagan, Ronald, 83
recidivism: and faith-based rehabilitation, 101, 225, 247n15; and IFI, 24, 33, 88–89, 92, 111; as secular goal, 113, 137; in the U.S., 95
reconciliation, 20, 60, 61, 62, 68, 95, 97, 139, 156, 210
Redd, Troy, 193–94
Redeeming America, 240n41, 246n2, 249n62
rehabilitation, 62, 95, 139; in Europe, 99; and faith-based programs, 20, 210; and IFI, 60, 61, 68, 120, 150; and Iowa, 100, 144
religion: "bona fide," 114, 144n11, 228, 263n40; and law, 7, 18, 141–44, 153, 178, 203–4, 220, 228, 39n34, 257n69, 257n1, 259n18; modern, 6, 7–8, 101, 176, 178–79; naturalized, 1–2, 233; and prisons, 14–15, 20, 101, 206–7, 242n59, 247n15; public, 83, 179, 221, 250n80, 261n56; return of, 228, 270n7; and the secular, 7, 230; as universal, 10, 44, 82, 137, 153–54, 172, 178–79, 196,

262n20; U.S., 2–3, 9–13, 80, 82, 228–236, 239n33
Religion and the Constitution, 258n4
Religion and the Death Penalty, 254n24
Religion in Modern Europe, 237n7, 259n20
Religion, Modernité et Culture au Royaume-Uni et en France, 260n45
Religious Land Use and Institutionalized Persons Act (RLUIPA), 263n40
Religious Literacy, 262n9
Religious Nationalism, 237n4
Religious Thought and the Modern Psychologies, 256n51
repentance, 32, 48, 64, 76
responsibility: as IFI value, 26, 121, 122, 124, 137; and prisons, 37–38; as universal value, 158, 163, 200
restitution. *See* Constitution
restoration, 26, 61, 115, 155, 156–57, 158, 200, 221
Restructuring of American Religion, The, 270n7
retribution, 98, 104–5
revival meeting. *See* IFI, revivals
Revolution of the Saints, The, 174
Rewired, 78
Rights of Prisoners, 262nn28 and 33
Robertson, Pat, 83
Robinson, Robert, 43–44, 59–62, 208
Roe v. Wade, 82, 151, 250n80
Root, Orrin, 41
Rosen, Lawrence, 17
Rosenberg, Gerald, 151, 250n80
Rothman, David, 4–5, 100, 107, 237n8, 238n13
Rotman, Edgardo, 263n38
Roy, Douglas, 261n2
Rutba House, 269n102

sacraments, 148, 164
sacred, the, 9, 176
Sacred and Secular, 270n4
salvation, 172; and Charles Colson, 77, 80; and Evangelicals, 85, 93, 110; IFI and, 32, 53, 44, 111, 116, 201; and C. S. Lewis, 106
Santner, Eric, 240n46
Sarat, Austin, 238n19
Saxon, Sam, 254n31
Scalia, Anthony, 220
Scandal of the Evangelical Mind, The, 152, 251n89, 261n47
Schaeffer, Francis A, 71, 77–78, 79–80, 106, 249nn58, 59, and 61
Schaeffer, Frank, 249n60
Schmidt, Leigh Eric, 246n7
school prayer, 82–83
School(s) for Conversion, 269n102
science, behavioral, 91, 11,
Scottish Enlightenment, 86, 251n90
Screwtape Letters, The, 255n43
scripture. *See* Bible, the; Book of Mormon, the; Qu'ran, the
Search for Significance, The, 42
sect, 81–82, 239n39
sectarian, 10, 56–57, 64, 65, 144–45, 147–48, 181
Section 501(c)(3), 13, 66
secular, the, 258n14; areligious secular, 229, 230, 232, 233, 234, 235, 271n13; and IFI, 33, 64, 65, 78, 113, 116, 120, 136, 138, 141, 153, 168, 206; irreligious secular, 229–30, 231–32, 233, 235; and religion, 7, 82, 229; religious secular, 229, 230–31, 233, 235; and the sacred, 9, 164, 176; secularization, 9, 17, 83, 176
secular humanism, 74, 75, 77, 90, 152, 249n62
secularism, 65, 75, 92, 117, 154, 163, 172, 178, 220
Secularization and Cultural Criticism, 238n25, 240n46, 269n85
Sekulow, Jay, 210
self: and *AU v. PFM*, 12; creation of, 15, 175, 177, 178; and discipline, 12; and faith-based social service programs, 12, 15; and First Amendment, 225; and prison, 99
Seymour, Stephen, 262n14
Sharlet, Jeffrey, 247n24
Shelton, Bobby, 190–92, 262n20
Sherwin, Richard, 7, 244n22
Shukr, Bilal. *See* Shelton, Bobby
Simon, Jonathan, 253n8
sin, 93, 109, 256n53; addiction as, 48; admission of, 46, 48, 136–37, 167; and crime, 94–95, 111, 136–37; and IFI, 138–211; and Islam, 193–95; of pride, 248n29
Skinner, Kerry L., 108, 109–10
Smart, Ninian, 79

Smith, Christian, 67–68, 80, 85, 240n47, 241n52, 248n31, 251n87, 259n19
Smith, Jonathan Z., 238n22, 269n19
social learning model, 118–20, 182
social sciences, 104, 105, 150–52, 176, 258n14
social services, 101, 139, 149, 211, 240n49
Social Teaching of the Christian Churches, 239n39
Socrates, 238n20
Sojourners' Magazine, 248n36
Soloveitchik, Haym, 261n50
Sources of the Self, 240n46
Souter, David, 220
South Carolina, 208
Southern Baptist Convention, 42
speaking in tongues, 46, 130
Spirit of the Law, The, 254n29
spirit theology, 54
Spiritual Protection for Your Children, 41, 42
spirituality: religion, as compared to, 228, 233; and treatment, 232–33; as universal, 228, 232, 233
standing. *See* Constitution
Stark, Rodney, 239nn39 and 42, 270n4
state, the: and punishment, 5–6, 99–100, 104; and religion, 6, 11, 94, 204, 217, 263n26; and sovereignty, 99–100
Step by Step through the New Testament, 42
Step by Step through the Old Testament, 42
Stevens, Perry, 47, 234–35
Stolberg, Sheryl Gay, 258n15
Stolzenberg, Nomi, 239n32
Stowers, Dean, 16
Streets of Glory, 246n12
Struggle for Justice, 253n15
substance abuse, 20, 25, 31, 40, 47–50, 118, 119, 242n61
Sullivan, Lawrence E., 238n23, 270n2
Sullivan, Winnifred Fallers, 141–42, 143, 145–47, 148–50, 197, 217–18, 238n22, 257n69, 257nn1 and 2, 258n13, 259n20, 260n44, 268nn67 and 76
"supernatural rationality," 87, 107, 152
Supiot, Alain, 228, 270n1
Supreme Court of the United States, 24, 81–83, 99, 142, 204, 206, 231
Suskind, Ron, 253n15
sweat lodge, 147, 190, 234, 235, 262n13
Sweating in the Joint, 262n13
Sweeney, Megan, 245n35
Sycamore Tree Project, The. See IFI

Taussig-Rubbo, Matteo, 238n23
taxpayer suits, 219–20
Taylor, Charles, 71, 173–74, 175–76, 229, 240nn46 and 48
"Technologies of the Self," 242n60
Teen Challenge, 208, 264n47
Telephone Fund, 24, 244n16
Templeton Prize, 71
Texas, 68, 139, 208; Carol S. Vance corrections unit in, 22, 23, 24
Thailand, 178, 235
Theeler, Rick, 208
theocracy, 11, 89, 90
Theory of the Trial, The, 16–17
"therapeutic model," 64, 108–9, 110, 111, 116–17, 156
Thinking About Crime, 253nn8 and 15
Thomas, Clarence, 143
Three Strikes and You're Out in California, 253n15
Thy Kingdom Come, 251n111
Ticklish Subject, The, 240n46
Time to Fly, 208, 208n48
Tocqueville, Alexis de, 4, 107–8, 228
Tonry, Michael, 253n8
Total Money Makeover, 41, 42
Tracy, David, 259nn30 and 32
Training for Service, 41, 43
Trial, The, 238n19
trials, theories of, 16–17, 141
Trinity Theological Seminary, 110–11
Troeltsch, Ernst, 81, 239n39
Troutman, Sanders, LLP, 16
Troy, Anthony, 16
Turner v. Safley, 209, 211, 214, 269n86
Tuttle, Richard, 225, 261n2, 262nn25 and 26

Umphrey, Martha Merrill, 238n19
Undercover, 42
Underground Book Railroad, The, 245n35
Unger, Roberto, 7
United Kingdom: and Muslims, 234, 271n21; prisons in, 3, 96, 98–100, 234, 237n8, 253n11, 257n74
United States of America: amicus brief of, 208, 264n43; and exceptionalism, 2–3,

87, 237n3; penal policy of, 2, 253n15, 254nn18 and 29; religious culture of, 2, 228, 229, 270n4; religious history of, 3–4, 81, 86–87
universal values. *See* values, universal
U.S. Court of Appeals for the Eighth Circuit, 207, 216, 217–18, 246n1, 258n2, 269n92

values: Christian, 65, 85; and IFI, 26, 32, 51, 111, 115, 119–20, 121–25, 131, 137, 146–47, 155–57, 199–201; and PFM, 139; and religion, 201; universal, 11, 89, 115, 133–34, 137, 152, 153, 159–60, 165, 176
values-based programs, 22, 24, 26, 116, 119–20
van der Veer, Peter, 237n4
Vander Hook, Pete, 41, 42
Vander Hook, Sue, 41, 42
Vander Laan, Ray, 42
Vatican Council II, 211
Vaughn, Ellen, 42
Vereide, Abraham, 69, 72
Victory Over the Darkness, 41
View from Nowhere, The, 258n14
Virginia, 208
voucher systems, 24, 209, 225, 233, 240n49
voluntarism, 10, 11, 68, 80, 83

Wacquant, Loïc, 254n26
walk, Christian, 55–56, 102
Walking with God, 42
Wallace, Lorraine, 16
Wallbuilders, Inc., 208, 213–14, 266n56
Wallis, Jim, 248n36
Walls, Jerry, 106
Walters, John P., 253n15
Walzer, Michael, 174–75
Warren, Rick, 113, 257n61
Warrington, Ronnie, 239n32, 270n3
Watergate, 22, 70, 74
Watson, Kevin, 194–97
Weaver, Heather, 16
Weber, Max, 81, 173
Weltanschauung, 79
Westminster Handbook to Evangelical Theology, The, 250n84
What's God Got to Do with the American Experiment?, 253n15
When Law Goes Pop, 244n22
Whiddon, Robert, 110–11
White House Office of Faith-based and Community Initiatives, 219, 240n49, 253n15
White Paper, 108–9, 110, 111
Whitman, James Q., 98–100
Why the French Don't Like Headscarves, 271n22
Wide Angle, 78
Wiese, Jesse, 44, 51–52, 54–59
Wild at Heart, 42
Wilger, Jerry, 25
Willow Creek Community Church, 42
Wilson, James Q., 253n15
With the Grain of the Universe, 249n62
witnessing, evangelical use of, 28, 40, 54, 73, 124, 201
Wollman, Roger L., 207, 218
World War II, 102, 105, 198
Worldview, 250n71
worldview, 40, 16, 77, 78–79, 91, 111, 152
worship, 39, 43, 46–47, 87, 123–24, 144, 147, 148
Wuthnow, Robert, 270n7

Yelle, Robert A., 238n22, 239n29, 270n7

Zacchaeus, 94–95
Zagorin, Perez, 257n66
Zelman v. Harri, 225
Zimring, Franklin, 253n15
Žižek, Slavoj, 173, 240n46

Printed in the USA
CPSIA information can be obtained
at www.ICGtesting.com
JSHW021808100124
55153JS00002B/76